PRESENCE OF THE PAST

Presence of the Past

A HISTORY OF THE PRESERVATION MOVEMENT IN THE UNITED STATES BEFORE WILLIAMSBURG

by

Charles B. Hosmer, Jr.

G. P. PUTNAM'S SONS

NEW YORK

Acknowledgments

In the preparation of this book, the author has had the unselfish aid of many busy people, including a number of professors at Columbia University who sponsored part of the book as a doctoral dissertation. Professor Frederick D. Kershner, Jr., spent countless hours as the main sponsor. Along with Professor Kershner, the original dissertation committee included Professors Erling M. Hunt, Laurance F. Shaffer, Everard Upjohn, and Dean Clifford Lord.

Several people interviewed by the author freely offered memories of preservation work before 1926. Among these was Theodore Fred Kuper, who contributed in many ways to the chapter on Monticello. Three architects, A. Lawrence Kocher, Walter M. Macomber and Richard Koch, gave significant glimpses of some of the problems involved in the delicate process of restoration.

Among the individuals who helped the author in his exploration of preservationist literature were: Mrs. Helen D. Bullock of the National Trust for Historic Preservation, Washington, D.C.; Bertram K. Little, Dr. Abbott Lowell Cummings and Miss E. Florence Addison of the Society for the Preservation of New England Antiquities, Boston; William Henry Harrison of the Fruitlands Museum, Harvard, Massachusetts; William G. Wendell, Portsmouth, New Hampshire; Mrs. Russ A. Miller, Deerfield, Massachusetts; the Trustees of the Longyear Foundation, Brookline, Massachusetts; Mrs. Herbert B. Hosmer, Concord, Massachusetts; Clarkson A. Collins of the Rhode Island Historical Society, Providence; Gunther E. Pohl and the staff of the local history sec-

5

tion of the New York Public Library; Adolph K. Placzek and the staff of Avery Memorial Library, Columbia University; Miss Adelaide A. Cahill of the Metropolitan Museum of Art; Rabbi Isidore S. Meyer of the American Jewish Historical Society, New York City; S. Sydney Bradford of Morristown National Historical Park, Morristown, New Jersey; M. O. Anderson and John D. R. Platt of Independence National Historical Park, Philadelphia; Frank Barnes of the Northeast Region, National Park Service, Philadelphia; Rogers Young and Dr. Charles Porter of the National Park Service, Washington, D.C.; Randle Truett of the National Capital Parks, Washington, D.C.; George Pettengill of the American Institute of Architects, Washington, D.C.; Mrs. Mary T. Walsh of the National Society of the Daughters of the American Revolution Library, Washington, D.C.; Charles C. Wall, Walter Densmore, Frank Morse, and Edward Barnwell of the Mount Vernon Ladies' Association; James A. Bear, Jr., of the Thomas Jefferson Memorial Foundation, Charlottesville, Virginia; Ernest L. Wright, Jr., Abraham Lincoln Birthplace National Historic Site, Hodgenville, Kentucky.

Walter Muir Whitehill of the Boston Athenaeum, Reverend Maynard Geiger, O.F.M. of Old Mission, Santa Barbara, California, and Edwin Small of Boston National Historic Site, all read portions of this manuscript and gave valuable suggestions on various aspects of the history of preservation in New England and the Far West.

The author can never fully repay the debt he owes to his wife, Jeralyn P. Hosmer, for her ability to calm and encourage, while editing, revising and typing the final copy of this book. She has been a constant companion through these years of travel and research.

C. B. H.

Foreword

When there were fewer people, and less money, in the world, a soundly constructed building normally remained in use until it collapsed of sheer old age or an invading enemy destroyed it in war. Thirty-odd years ago, when I was studying Romanesque architecture in Spain, there were many more eleventh-century churches surviving in Catalonia than there are seventeenth-century houses in New England. Though in capitals like León and Burgos, Romanesque cathedrals of the last third of the eleventh century had been replaced by far larger Gothic ones, in a great number of remote villages parish churches of the earlier period continued in active use as a matter of course. In various mountain villages of the Catalan Pyrenees there had been money enough in the 1070's to build a respectable stone church. At no time since had anyone seriously felt the need, or had the means, to change it. A gilded Renaissance retablo might have been introduced in the main apse, concealing Romanesque mural paintings; perhaps a baroque chapel might have been added, if required by press of devotion to a local saint, but as there had been no Reformation, no Oliver Cromwell, no French Revolution, early medieval churches often survived in recognizable condition and served their purpose quite as well as they had nearly a millennium earlier. By contrast, wherever there is industrialization, or great cities to sprawl over the adjacent countryside, buildings seldom reach great age by the simple process of inertia.

Americans are a restless and wasteful people by comparison with the rest of the world. We make a dirty mess in one place and

7

move on to despoil another. When there were fewer of us, it was easier to ignore this national bad habit. Today we have reached the point where, as the late President Kennedy observed in his introduction to Stewart L. Udall's *The Quiet Crisis,* a once beautiful nation is in danger of turning into an "ugly America." As I write, the *U. S. News & World Report* has just published an interview with Edward Durell Stone on the theme "Are most cities too ugly to save?" As President Kennedy pointed out, "the crisis may be quiet, but it is urgent." As its urgency grows apparent, thousands of people are suddenly becoming aware of the need for natural conservation and historic and architectural preservation unless many parts of this country are to become indistinguishable from a suburb of Hell.

Among the many merits of Dr. Hosmer's book, it should be observed that it is the first of its kind. Historic preservation in the United States is a little more than a century old, yet this is the first record of its history in broad terms, the first study of the varied aspirations of the people who began to save buildings of the American past for the present and future. As the author is at pains to make clear, the motives behind these multifarious efforts in preservation were as disparate as the buildings themselves. They range from disinterested devotion to history and architecture, through regional and individual pride, patriotism, education, to muddled thinking and downright commercialism. At a time when many emergency efforts in preservation are being undertaken, it is singularly useful to have conveniently available this record of earlier efforts, which sets forth clearly the strengths and weaknesses, the successes and failures of various approaches.

The author shows us that until the early years of this century historic preservation was chiefly concerned with buildings in which great men had lived or great events had taken place. In this phase, buildings were esteemed for their associative value, rather than for themselves or for their relation to their surroundings. The first success was the purchase by the State of New York in 1850 of the Hasbrouck house in Newburgh, which had served as Washington's headquarters during the last two years of the Revolution. In his message to the legislature for that year, Governor Hamilton Fish had submitted "that there are associations connected with this venerable edifice which rise above the consideration of dollars and cents" and pointed out that it was "perhaps the last relic within the boundaries of the State, under the control of the legislature, connected with the history of the illustrious" George Washington. The legislative committee appointed to study the matter pulled out all stops, including the tremolo, in support of the proposal. Its argument, somewhat abbreviated, was as follows:

> If our love of country is excited when we read the biography of our revolutionary heroes, or the history of revolutionary events, how much more will the flame of patriotism burn in our bosoms when we tread the ground where was shed the blood of our fathers, or when we move among the scenes where were conceived and consummated their noble achievements. . . . No traveler who touches upon the shores of Orange county will hesitate to make a pilgrimage to this beautiful spot . . . and if he have an American heart in his bosom, he will feel himself a better man; his patriotism will kindle with deeper emotion; his aspirations of his country's good will ascend from a more devout mind for having visited the "Headquarters of Washington."

The preservation of Hasbrouck house, involving only the legislative appropriation of $8,391.02, was simple and inexpensive compared with the effort begun in 1853 by Miss Ann Pamela Cunningham of South Carolina to purchase Mount Vernon from its unwilling owner, John A. Washington, who had set the high price of two hundred thousand dollars upon the house and the two hundred acres of land that surrounded it. Miss Cunningham's Mount Vernon Ladies' Association, chartered in 1856, eventually succeeded, where government had failed, in saving Washington's home for the future, and thus set a precedent for accomplishing the seemingly impossible.

The successful preservation of Mount Vernon led many other groups to attempt to save historic sites related to the American Revolution or to great figures in American history. But as Dr. Hosmer points out:

> Many preservation groups thought that they could imitate the work done by Miss Cunningham, but they all found that she had achieved something that was not likely to be repeated for years to come. Now, as then, far too few preservationists, overwhelmed by the importance of their particular projects, realize how many *other* buildings are supposed to be "second only to Mount Vernon."

With the rescue of the Old South Meeting House in 1876, which I characterized in my *Independent Historical Societies* as "the first instance in Boston—and, indeed, the first of such magnitude in the United States—where respect for the historical and architectural heritage of the city triumphed over considerations of profit, expediency, laziness, and vulgar convenience," historic preservation moved into its urban phase. The appeal, as with the sites connected with Washington, was still associative and inspirational. Early in the campaign President Charles W. Eliot of Harvard said of the building:

> It is chiefly because we love it, I think, that we want to save it, and love is unreasoning, cannot be accounted for, has no logical processes. We love it because it has always been speaking to us of courage, uprightness, independence; we love it because of the memories of famous men which are associated with it; we love it because it is one of the familiar objects of our youth; we love it because it has always spoken to us that one emphatic word, which Thoreau, I believe, said was the whole speech of Bunker Hill monument, "Here." Here, on this very spot, within these very walls, were words spoken which were heard round the world. Here, in this very place, our forefathers were wrought up to resist the fearful power of Great Britain; here they worshipped their stern God. . . . I think we Americans particularly need to cultivate our historical sense, lest we lose the lessons of the past in this incessant whirl of the trivial present. . . . We need to recall our own past, to remember our fathers, to remember our heritage. In this present moment of political difficulty let us bear in mind what we owe to those who have gone before us; to the generations that were brought up in this old building,—in the very Old South that we desire to preserve. We depend at this very moment upon the political sense and sober second-thought, the self-control and readiness in emergencies which in good measure we have inherited from the generations that have gone before us. Let us pay this debt by reverently preserving the shrines of those generations. If we have any faith in free speech, if we have any faith in freedom of public meeting, why, the Old South is the best shrine of that faith.

The problems facing the friends of the Old South were more acute than those that confronted Miss Cunningham. As the meeting house stood in the center of a growing city, the land already had a purchaser ready to pay four hundred thousand dollars. The wreckers were just beginning work when the alarm was raised, and the first move was to secure only a seven-day respite. Although the Boston Tea Party had been brewed there, and the building had been the scene of other meetings that fomented the American Revolution, it appealed to the national imagination far less vividly than did the home of George Washington. But Wendell Phillips instantly aroused the populace, as Edward Everett had earlier for Mount Vernon, with ringing words, and when time for organization had been bought, President Eliot, James Russell Lowell, Ralph Waldo Emerson, Oliver Wendell Holmes, and others bent to the task and achieved their purpose.

Since the earliest preservationists intended to have the sites they saved operated as historic museums for the inspiration of visitors, considerations of architecture or of beauty seldom entered into their calculations. At a meeting held in the new Memorial Hall at Harvard College early in the Old South campaign, James Russell Lowell confidently asserted of the 1729 meeting house:

> Now the building which we are asked to save is not, I think—I see the Professor of Fine Arts [Charles Eliot Norton] in front of me, and I will not appeal to him to say that it is,—a model of architecture. [Laughter] I do not think it is in any aesthetic sense. It is not in that sense; but in another it seems to me a model of architecture. It was the best thing that our fathers could do in their day, and they thought it beautiful. . . . It was a great deal harder for our fathers to build such a building as the Old South than it is for us to build a beautiful hall like the one we are in now, exceedingly creditable as it is to the generosity of the Alumni of Harvard College.

Here is a classic instance of the mutability of taste, for after eighty-eight years the architecture of the Old South Meeting House is widely admired, while only a few—of whom I am one—have a good word to say for Ware and Van Brunt's Gothic Memorial Hall, which J. R. Lowell regarded in 1877 as the acme of taste and elegance. Today I would guess that the *appearance* of the Old South Meeting House is every bit as highly valued as its historical associations. Such a change in approach is in no small part due to the work of the antiquaries, architects, and museum directors that Dr. Hosmer describes in Chapter IX. The new direction is most explicit in William Sumner Appleton's statement of the purpose of the Society for the Preservation of New England Antiquities, which he organized in 1910, as

> to save for future generations structures of the seventeenth and eighteenth centuries, and the early years of the nineteenth, *which are architecturally beautiful or unique,* or have special historical significance. Such buildings once destroyed can never be replaced.

I have supplied the italics to emphasize the way in which this society—which has accomplished more for preservation with fewer people and less money than any other that I know—placed architectural values first.

Dr. Hosmer's account of William Sumner Appleton is perhaps the most valuable and least known element in this book. I knew Mr. Appleton fairly well during the last dozen years of his life. In 1936 I very nearly went to work for him, and I have served several terms on the board of the S.P.N.E.A. Yet Dr. Hosmer, who never laid eyes on him, has, by meticulous study of his correspondence, produced a picture of him that adds to my knowledge. Similarly, I doubt whether many of my fellow directors of the Thomas Jefferson Memorial Foundation know all the complicated elements in the history of Monticello, prior to its purchase in 1923 by the Foundation, that Dr. Hosmer sets forth in Chapter VIII. Certainly, if any of them remember some of the corny antics that their predecessors had to indulge in to raise money for the purchase—senators disguised as railway conductors and popularity contests that sent pretty girls to Paris—they refrained from telling me when I joined the board.

Sumner Appleton's first venture in historic preservation occurred when he was twenty-nine, five years before he, singlehanded, founded the S.P.N.E.A. In 1905 he joined with the older Henry Lee Higginson and William D. Sohier to raise money for the preservation "as a permanent patriotic memorial" of the house in North Square, Boston, that was the home of Paul Revere during the Revolution. Although the primary motive of the Paul Revere Memorial Association that was founded in consequence was associative and commemorative, emphasizing occupancy by a Revolutionary patriot, the building thus preserved is the oldest in the city of Boston. Built about 1680 and already old when Paul Revere occupied it, it is, indeed, the only surviving example of the type of wooden house, with an overhanging second story of English medieval inspiration, that predominated in seventeenth-century Boston. As Joseph Everett Chandler, who restored the house for the association in 1907–08, removed most later additions and went back to its 1680 exterior appearance, it was treated as an architectural monument to such an extent that Paul Revere, were he to return to North Square, would not recognize it as the house in which he long lived.

By the time he founded the S.P.N.E.A. in 1910, Sumner Appleton's motives had become more architectural than associative, so that he was chiefly concerned with *preserving* buildings, by any means possible, rather than exhibiting them for inspirational purposes. He was, as Dr. Hosmer points out, "a pioneer in his ideas concerning adaptive uses for old houses," for "he did not believe that all worthwhile buildings should be museums." Here we see the beginning of a principle that is widely accepted today as the only possible means of maintaining the character of our surroundings. We cannot crystallize or pickle the past, nor can we, where there is vigorous life in a community, turn back the clock as it was possible to do, through a combination of hardly-to-be-repeated circumstances, in Williamsburg. But we can and should, through imaginative adaptation, preserve, in large segments, not only isolated historic sites but whatever architectural and natural features will give continued grace and variety to our cities, towns, and countryside. As rallying points in the quiet but urgent crisis we can be grateful for the buildings preserved by the pioneers whose efforts are set forth in this volume.

It should be noted that Dr. Hosmer attempts to deal only with the earlier phases of historic preservation in the United States. By concluding his narrative in 1926, he necessarily excludes any account of Colonial Williamsburg, of Henry Ford's collecting, of the National Park Service, of the National Trust for Historic Preservation, of historic districts, and of innumerable private and governmental efforts in historic preservation of the past four decades. As he is a historian rather than a reporter, I believe that the limit that he set for his book is a wise one. Past 1926 the picture becomes too extensive, too complicated, too immediate, for presentation in this manner. But although Dr. Hosmer confines himself to the period 1850–1926, many of the experiences that he reports still have validity for the present and future. As he points out in Chapter XIII, "the majority of people who saved old houses did not understand that the word 'preservation' really meant maintenance of these structures throughout the years that followed." It cannot be too often emphasized that acquiring title to a building is simply the first step in preservation. One has to have something to do with it, and some means of keeping it up. Only in exceptional cases, like Mount Vernon and Monticello, will admission fees alone maintain historic houses, and in those instances that equilibrium was only achieved after years of laborious fund raising for purchase, restoration, and furnishing. For anyone venturing into historic preservation, Dr. Hosmer's book provides a thoroughgoing account of the hazards and challenges to be reckoned with and counterbalanced. These are bound to raise their unwelcome heads as inevitably today as ever in the past.

Along our highways today we see too frequent instances of the commercial exploitation of history; historically veneered amusements, waxworks, and other dubious "attractions" are sprinkled among the nut stands, snake farms, and souvenir shops that prey on the traveling public. Yet the nineteenth century had its hucksters and showmen long before the American people took to riding on wheels instead of rockers. Dr. Hosmer reports how businessmen in 1853 were attempting to buy Mount Vernon for a hotel site, and in the nineties sought the Mary Washington cottage in Fredericksburg as an "attraction" for the Chicago Columbian Exposition. While these efforts were nipped in the bud, there was genuine *opéra bouffe* in others that went further. The engine house at Harpers Ferry in which John Brown was captured indeed went to the fair in Chicago in 1893, but under such tardy and incompetent auspices that it was only open to the public for a few days, during which there were eleven paid admissions of fifty cents each.

> This fiasco immediately ended the John Brown Fort Company, which went into receivership. The John Brown "fort" wandered for several years before it came to rest on the campus of a Negro college in Harpers Ferry.

Then there is the episode of the inventor of the "quick lunch" joining with an evangelist to exploit the site of Lincoln's birth in

Hodgenville, Kentucky, with a cabin of uncertain pedigree, in connection with an encampment of the G.A.R. in Louisville in 1895.

> The admission fee was so high that very few veterans made the pilgrimage to Hodgenville. Bigham [the evangelist] did not give up easily; he dismantled the cabin and had it exhibited in Nashville in 1897 at the Tennessee Centennial. Bigham also provided a cabin supposed to be the birthplace of Jefferson Davis. A young reporter interviewed Bigham in front of the Lincoln cabin in an effort to find out more about the history of the little building. Many years later the reporter remembered Bigham's reply, "Lincoln was born in a log cabin, weren't he? Well, one cabin is as good as another."

This is a diverting as well as an instructive book. As it is carefully documented, it will serve as a guide for further exploration. When Edward P. Alexander, Vice-President of Colonial Williamsburg, lent me a Xerox copy of Dr. Hosmer's Columbia dissertation several years ago, I was at once delighted with the material that it contained and with its presentation. Mrs. Helen Duprey Bullock, Director of the Department of Information of the National Trust for Historic Preservation, and one of the most valiant and knowledgeable workers in this cause, who shared Dr. Alexander's and my enthusiasm for the work, offered the author many valuable suggestions. I am happy that this study, in expanded form, is now being presented to a wide audience, and that I have this opportunity to express my appreciation of the work.

WALTER MUIR WHITEHILL

Boston Athenaeum

Contents

Illustrations follow page 162

Introduction

Anyone desiring to study America's historic buildings can find an immense quantity of books on the subject, but this literature includes very little material on the history of the people who have saved these buildings for posterity.[1] Since the old buildings that have been preserved have attracted the attention of so many authors, it seems logical that historians should study the evolution of the American preservation movement. Those who are directly involved in administration and restoration may not realize that historic preservation in this country has been going on for a long, long time. Although certain particular aspects of the early history of preservationism have been recorded, such as the work of the Mount Vernon Ladies' Association, the larger, more comprehensive story has been left almost untouched.

The American preservation movement appears to have been a truly grass-roots effort. It sprang up spontaneously all through the nation as an amateur activity, and therefore it did not possess a national organization or leadership of the kind usually encountered in comparable movements. Perhaps the fact that there was no central core accounts for the absence of detailed historical treatments. Nevertheless, the sources for a history of American preservationism are extensive. A large part of the necessary factual information can be found in magazines and proceedings published by various local and regional organizations. Equally essential are certain archives which contain letters and manuscripts left by preservationist pioneers.

Splintered though American preservationism was, it contained powerful latent forces that were able to unite many diverse groups of people (on occasion) for specific purposes. Even in the early period before the Civil War there is abundant evidence of an emergent national consciousness that caused some individuals to look upon the preservation of historic sites as a sign of cultural maturity. As the years went by, preservationists found that they had many common problems as well as common purposes. Correspondence in various archives shows the gradual appearance of a sense of a community; these people found that they belonged, however vaguely, to a "national" movement. Still, as late as 1926 preservationism was largely disorganized and lacked any professional guidance.

Within this developmental framework, this book treats almost every type of preservation group that appeared in the United States before 1926. It seeks to answer the vital questions that should be asked about such a movement: Why did so many people concern themselves with this seemingly profitless activity? What did they think they were accomplishing? How did they go about saving old buildings? What sort of people were these preservationists?

Of necessity, details have been limited in most cases. Every historic structure has its individual story, and a complete history of preservationism would have to cover more than 2,000 buildings. Such comprehensive scope being beyond the practical limits of a volume of this kind, only a few outstanding examples have been selected for extended treatment from the 400 buildings studied.

The words "preservation" and "restoration" have been used many times with reference to the treatment of old buildings. Both terms are used here in their broadest sense. "Preservation" means the act of retaining all or any part of a structure, even if it is moved from its original location. "Restoration" refers to any treatment given to a building after the decision has been made to preserve it. Under the general heading of "restoration" one can find a great variety of methods, ranging all the way from preserving a structure intact to reconstruction of some historic monument that has disappeared.

Because of the vastness and fascinating variety of the subject, it has been necessary to restrict coverage in several ways. No archaeological sites or Indian dwellings have been treated, for movements favoring their preservation appear to have been quite different from those involving old buildings from the English and Spanish settlements. Nineteen twenty-six has been chosen as the terminal year because the costly and sweeping restoration of Williamsburg and Henry Ford's work in Dearborn, Michigan, had a powerful influence on the movement as a whole after 1927.[2] Moreover, during the middle 1920's preservation activity grew with such speed that it seems difficult to do much more than touch the surface of the story thereafter. Although the geographic limitations are somewhat indefinite, the eastern half of the United States is the main field of interest simply because most preservations before 1926 were in the areas of the country that were settled first.

In order to determine the degree of originality in American preservationism, it should be helpful to review briefly what Europeans were doing at this same time. The traditions of preservationism start with the Romans, but only the last century and a half are of direct concern here. Three main streams of thought in regard to the treatment of historic buildings arose in Europe during the nineteenth century, one in France, one in England and one in Sweden.

The French government began to take an interest in the historic sites that dotted the landscape when King Louis Philippe appointed an Inspector of Historic Monuments in 1830. A commission set up in conjunction with this new office made an inventory of all the old buildings in France. This inventory became the basis for a system of protection of these structures, both private and public, with the government reserving for itself the right to prevent any alteration of privately owned historic buildings. In addition to this, the government hired architects to supervise the restoration of some of the oldest castles and churches. The most renowned of these men, Viollet-le-Duc, was active through the middle of the nineteenth century. Because of his official position and thorough architectural training he was able to put into practice his theories concerning restoration. Viollet-le-Duc said that proper restoration took a building back to "a condition of completeness which could never have existed at any given time." [3] By this he meant that newer parts of old buildings should be taken off because they were considered too "late." In the place of later work that he removed Viollet-le-Duc added his own studied copies of features that he found on other buildings representing the "correct" period.[4]

In Britain the preservation movement did not develop under the sheltering arm of the government, as had been the case in France. Instead, private organizations appeared that attempted to preserve rather than restore. British preservationists, led by John Ruskin and William Morris, believed that restoration of old work was an impossibility. In his book *Seven Lamps of Architecture,* which first appeared in 1849, John Ruskin said that restoration was a form of destruction. He declared flatly that it was as hard to restore as it was to raise the dead. According to Ruskin, one cannot hope to re-create the spirit of the workmen of the past, no matter how clever he may be at copying old forms.[5] In 1877 a group of Englishmen who agreed with the ideas of Ruskin founded the Society for the Protection of Ancient Buildings. Under the leadership of William Morris, this society did all that it could to see that whatever remained of ancient architecture in Britain was protected, but not restored. The followers of Ruskin and Morris said that the only legitimate action open to contemporary workmen was to arrest the process of decay. No matter how venerable a building might have been, all later changes in it were to remain because they were just as valid as the original portions.[6]

A third line of thought has probably had more effect on American thinking than either the French or English practices. In 1891 Dr. Artur Hazelius began to assemble the world's first outdoor museum in a park in Stockholm, Sweden, which he called "Skansen." Skansen was a living display of Swedish cultural history, featuring old buildings that had been moved there to represent different regions in the Scandinavian countries as well as various periods in European history. People in costume acted as guides for this large exhibition, many of them serving as craftsmen or farmers who depicted aspects of the daily life of people in areas far away from Stockholm. Hazelius' idea began to spread into Northern Europe by the end of the nineteenth century, and before long some Americans started to agitate for the creation of similar museums.[7]

Today a traveler who is aware of the development of European philosophies of preservation can locate examples of each here in the United States. This does not necessarily prove that our country was directly influenced from abroad; it could well be that our own preservationists, who were relatively insulated from foreign ideas, treated old buildings in whatever manner they thought best.

If we look upon preservationism as a type of cultural crusade that has colored our own attitudes toward the past and toward our domestic architecture, then we are certainly justified in wanting to find out what caused people in the United States to take an interest in old buildings. America is generally known as a nation that has not been occupied with mere speculative thought; we are reputed to be a practical, active people wanting quick results from any endeavor that we launch. The saving of historic structures, then, was an enterprise that must have offered some form of concrete return. While material gain did not figure noticeably, there were sound reasons of a different sort for eagerness to save relics of bygone days. The history of the preservation movement in this country is largely our own story, not a mere echo of notes struck earlier in Europe. The record will show that it was an American response to an American need.

CHARLES B. HOSMER, JR.

PRESENCE OF THE PAST

I

The Earliest Attempts:
The Pattern for the Future

THE AMERICAN PRESERVATION MOVEMENT is nearly as old as the
country itself, and the story of saving America's historic buildings
contains a number of important sidelights on the development of
our nation. In writing history it is always dangerous to label anything as the "first"; so it is with the beginnings of the preservation
movement. Possibly the first evidence of preservation sentiment
is a notation in the *Pocket Diary* of Benjamin H. Latrobe for
August 3, 1796, expressing his regret at the impending destruction
of "Green Spring" in James City County, Virginia. "The antiquity
of the old house . . . ought to plead in [behalf of] the project, but
its inconvenience and deformity are more powerful advocates of
its destruction. In it the oldest inhabited house in North America
will disappear. . . ." [1] Green Spring was already considered an ancient building by 1796—and it is especially noteworthy that the
architect charged with its demolition had a mild interest in its
preservation. There was a flurry of protest in Boston newspapers
when the "Old Brick" meetinghouse was about to be torn down
in 1808. One writer noted that "after the demolition of the Old
Brick, there is scarcely a vestige of antiquity in the town." The
forces of commercialism triumphed and "Old Brick" fell before
the wrecker. [2]

Another early example of preservationism came in 1813 when
the State of Pennsylvania proposed selling the Old State House in
Philadelphia, now known as Independence Hall. A group of Phila-

delphia citizens addressed a "Memorial" to the legislature, offering several arguments against the destruction of the building. The memorialists began by referring to the usefulness of the structure as an election headquarters; but they considered the functional aspect of Independence Hall only part of the story. "The spot which the Bill proposes to cover with private buildings, is hallowed to your memorialists, by many strong and impressive recollections." The petitioners reminded Pennsylvania's legislators that the hall had witnessed the birth of "the only free Republic the world has seen." In spite of the interest of these spirited citizens of Philadelphia, the Memorial only won a stay of execution.[3]

Three years later the state finally determined to get rid of the square along with the obsolete State House by putting it up for sale for building lots. The proceeds of the auction would go toward the building of a new capitol. Independence Hall now faced the most serious threat of destruction it ever would meet, and one provision in the authorization for the sale became the avenue for the forces of preservation. The City of Philadelphia could purchase the hall and the square for $70,000, which it proceeded to do. One can only guess what may have motivated the purchase, though it would seem logical that many people in the city government sincerely wanted to save the building itself.[4]

Ironically just at the time it was saved for posterity, Independence Hall lost two of its most important features. Between 1812 and 1813 the original wing buildings and the old Library and Committee Room were torn down to make room for new "fireproof" buildings designed by Robert Mills.[5] A more incomprehensible example of vandalism occurred just before the City of Philadelphia took over the building from the County Commissioners. While the citizens slept serene in the knowledge that Independence Hall would not be lost, some workman was authorized to remove the priceless woodwork from the room that had witnessed the signing of the Declaration of Independence and the writing of the Constitution. By the summer of 1816 Philadelphians could only mourn their loss. That fall John Thompson ran for County Commissioner claiming that he had "resisted and protested against" the conduct of the other commissioners in the case of the lost paneling.[6]

Independence Hall emerged from the period of neglect with

the visit of Lafayette in 1824. Not only did the whole building receive a new coat of paint, but also many people became interested in restoring some of the lost features of the hall. In 1828 William Strickland completed a copy of the original steeple, which had been removed at the end of the Revolution. His spire was a bit too tall, but the form was essentially correct.[7] Three years later John Haviland, who had already made alterations in the second floor of the building, began a restoration of the Assembly Room woodwork. A letter from Haviland written in 1831 leads one to believe that he had very little to go on as he put new paneling into the room. In spite of some problems he was sure that he could restore the hall "to its former state" as instructed by the Philadelphia Common Council.[8]

During the two decades following the Haviland restoration, the Assembly Room gradually took on the outward aspects of a hallowed place. Even the State Supreme Court encountered protests from irate citizens when the judges tried to use the room in the middle of the 1840's. When the city repainted the Assembly Room in 1854 it contained the Liberty Bell, a statue of Washington, and a number of other objects of antiquarian interest. By the middle of the nineteenth century Independence Hall had been preserved, though there were many divergent views on how it should be restored.[9]

In the early 1820's several private individuals had become interested in historic sites, but the whole idea of public exhibition was not a major factor at all. In 1816 William Ferris Pell, a New York businessman, leased some property on the edge of Lake Champlain directly in front of the ruins of Fort Ticonderoga. The romantic history of the fort cast a spell upon its new neighbor. Pell rented the fort itself in 1820 and took measures to halt the removal of building materials from the ruins. He fenced in the property and then built a home below the fort on the lake front. Although the property remained in the hands of Pell's descendants, Fort Ticonderoga was not restored until early in the twentieth century. He had conducted an important holding operation against the forces of destruction and that was all.[10]

One of the most unusual documents in the long history of the preservation movement was the will of Abraham Touro, who died in Boston on October 18, 1822. Touro was a son of Isaac Touro, the former rabbi of the synagogue in Newport, Rhode Island. Wishing to induce more Jews to come to Newport and reopen the synagogue (which had been closed since the 1790's), Touro left the huge sum of $10,000 to the City of Newport and the State of Rhode Island "for the purpose of supporting the Jewish synagogue in that State." The municipal authorities of Newport and the state had to find a suitable custodian and make repairs on the synagogue as soon as possible.[11] There is evidence that the "repairs" made in the 1820's were also skillful attempts at restoration and reconstruction of the interior of the building.[12] Abraham Touro's brother, Judah, was also deeply concerned about the fate of the synagogue and several other historic monuments in Newport. When the portico of the Redwood Library showed signs of decay in 1843 he sent a check for $1,000 to help with the restoration. When he died in 1854 Judah Touro matched his brother's gift by leaving $10,000 to be set aside as a fund to pay a reader or minister once the synagogue had a congregation again. He also left $10,000 to buy the famous Old Stone Tower for the City of Newport and another $3,000 for the Redwood Library.[13] By the middle of the nineteenth century the old synagogue was in good repair and stood ready to receive a congregation—thanks to the generosity of the Touro brothers. It must be remembered that the prime motive in these actions appears to have been religious, though an interest in historic Newport cannot be discounted in the case of Judah Touro.

Another early preservation on the part of a prominent Jewish gentleman was Uriah Levy's purchase of Monticello, the home of Thomas Jefferson. Levy bought the estate in 1836, only ten years after the death of Jefferson, and it is doubtful that he intended to make the house a museum, though there is evidence that he venerated the memory of Jefferson.[14]

At about the same time that Uriah Levy made Monticello his summer home, two historic New England houses became the objects of embryonic preservation efforts. In 1834 a committee of the Rhode Island Historical Society tried to interest the citizens of Newport in the old Governor Coddington house in that city. Defeated by popular apathy, the society had to be content with saving one casement window from the building.[15] A year later the Russell house in Branford, Connecticut, was torn down. This building had some real historic interest because it had witnessed a meeting of a group of New England ministers which eventually led to the founding of Yale College. Sentimental attachment led the family who owned the house to have a painting made of it, as well as a sketch of the floor plan. The descendants of the Reverend Russell also saved the original doors and stored them in the garret of the new house built on the same site. These doors finally found a home in the Yale University Library.[16]

The first clear-cut example of an organized preservation movement in New England came about twelve years later in the little Massachusetts town of Deerfield. The last home in Deerfield which had survived the famous massacre of 1704 was still standing in 1847. Although the house had not been taken by storm, the French and Indians had managed to cut a hole in the front door through which they killed some of the occupants by musket fire. Local residents referred to the building as the "Old Indian House." The *Gazette and Courier* of Greenfield, Massachusetts, observed on November 23, 1847, "The house has long attracted the attention of the antiquary, and at this time has become a relic of public interest, which few travellers omit to visit, on their passage through the village." [17] That same year Henry Hoyt, the owner, decided that the building was inconvenient as a residence, so he offered it for sale. The Greenfield paper advanced an unprecedented suggestion, in appropriately courteous phrases:

> As the house has no intrinsic value, only as *a relic of olden time,* it is believed it may be purchased for a small sum, and another site procured for a reasonable price. Will the public feel such an interest in its preservation as to give their aid in the contemplated purchase and removal? or suffer the last memorial of Indian warfare in our part of the country, to be lost and forgotten.[18]

The appeal led to a town meeting on the subject. The townspeople passed a resolution favoring preservation of the landmark and then appointed a committee of five to address the public on the subject. The committee printed an emotional message in the Greenfield paper dated December 28, 1847. The petition, one of the first of its type published in the United States, reflected the interest in the past that was to develop with the preservation movement. One citizen of Deerfield, writing in the *Gazette,* hoped to ignite a sense of filial piety among his fellow townsmen:

> Can "worthy sons of noble sires," see the destruction of that soli-tary memento of departed days, so rich in reminiscences, and so varied in its pictures of past scenes, and not say to the fiat, "spare that house"? It cannot be, and we are glad to find a good spirit aroused in that elm-shaded, and favored town, to prevent the loss of this precious legacy of times when it really "tried men's souls" to live. But its citizens feel unable to accomplish the work them-selves. Did every man feel as *some do,* it would be done no doubt; but it is no disparagement to Deerfield, to say that her citizens in general, in antiquarian spirit, are much like those of other towns; and men who cherish not fondly the recollections of their prede-cessors, will not be ready to contribute liberally to the erection or preservation of monuments to perpetuate their remembrance.[19]

One older resident of Deerfield observed in later years accu-rately, if ungrammatically, that "a few worked hard, but scarcely no money was subscribed." That seems to summarize the net im-pact of the appeals. Within a year the house was torn down because the townspeople were unable to raise approximately $2,000 to buy the house and lot, or even $150 for removal of the building itself.[20] Like several other important homes which suffered a similar fate during the next decade, the fate of the Old Indian House was to become a source of regret for the preservationists of the future. On countless occasions George Sheldon and other antiquaries were to refer to this loss as a tragedy that must never be repeated.

Although the house was destroyed, the door with its grim hatchet marks was rescued. A few years after the actual demolition of the building a member of the Hoyt family sold the door to a Dr. D. D. Slade of Boston. For more than a decade Deerfield citi-zens organized groups and wrote Dr. Slade, requesting return of the relic. When Dr. Slade finally agreed to sell the door to some Deerfield citizens in 1868, he was asked to wait until Deerfield had completed paying for its monument to the men who had lost their lives in the late Civil War.[21] The door did return to its native town, and it now rests in the Memorial Hall of the Pocumtuck Valley Memorial Association.[22] When the house Henry Hoyt erected on the Indian House lot was torn down in 1960 it was found to contain a number of boards from the earlier house, along with 1,500 bricks of a very early type. Apparently much more of the Indian House survived than anyone had realized! [23]

The purchase of the Hasbrouck house in Newburgh, New York, can be considered the first success of the American preservation movement, though there was no real organized effort involved. The house had important historical associations, having been Washington's headquarters during the last two years of the Revolution. Nevertheless, as early as 1813 the Hasbroucks found it necessary to go to court to fight off an attempt to put a village street across their property. A change in the makeup of the village board permitted the house to remain unharmed.[24]

Sometime in the late 1830's Jonathan Hasbrouck, the last private owner, considered selling the house to a corporation formed for the purpose of purchasing and maintaining the property.[25] Apparently the effort failed, for by 1848 the corporation was no longer in existence.

Then fate itself took a hand in the situation. Jonathan Hasbrouck had borrowed $2,000 in 1837 from the Commissioners of the United States Deposit Fund. His loan was secured by a mortgage on the old house. Things went along smoothly for a decade, but in October, 1848, Hasbrouck was unable to raise the annual payment on his loan. He had made his contract with the United States Government—for the Deposit Fund represented the Treasury surplus of 1837. There were very clear provisions governing the disposition of the property that was mortgaged to the Deposit Fund. In spite of Hasbrouck's delaying tactics, the machinery of the government went into action.[26] As required by federal law, the commissioners for the Deposit Fund offered the house for sale for the price of the loan plus the fees and other costs. No one would pay this price, so the commissioners put the property up for auction. Under the provisions of the Deposit Fund, the house was again appraised, offered for sale, and bid in to the State of New York.

One of the commissioners, Andrew Caldwell, received low bids from certain private parties, but would have none of them. Instead, Caldwell and his friends attempted in vain to get the citizens of Newburgh to subscribe enough money to reimburse the Deposit Fund and make the house state property. Not yet defeated, Caldwell entered upon an extended correspondence with Governor

Hamilton Fish of New York.[27] Caldwell suggested to the governor
that the legislature request Congress to remit its claim to the $2,000
and the interest. Governor Fish replied that he was in sympathy
with the idea of keeping the headquarters as state property, but
he insisted that the legislature should pay the debt. In his annual
message for 1850, Fish expressed definite views on the issue of real
versus sentimental values. ". . . I respectfully submit that there
are associations connected with this venerable edifice which rise
above the consideration of dollars and cents. . . . It is perhaps the
last relic within the boundaries of the State, under the control of
the Legislature, connected with the history of the illustrious man
[Washington]. . . ." [28]

Even more important than the governor's appeal was the report of the legislative committee appointed to study the preservation of the headquarters.

> . . . If our love of country is excited when we read the biography
> of our revolutionary heroes, or the history of revolutionary events,
> how much more will the flame of patriotism burn in our bosoms
> when we tread the ground where was shed the blood of our fathers,
> or when we move among the scenes where were conceived and con-
> summated their noble achievements. . . . The Committee believes
> that the object which the petitioners have in view—"to preserve and
> perpetuate Washington's headquarters, in the village of Newburgh"
> —is worthy of their high character, and eminently deserving of legis-
> lative sanction. No traveler who touches upon the shores of Orange
> county will hesitate to make a pilgrimage to this beautiful spot,
> associated as it is with so many delightful reminiscences in our
> early history, and if he have an American heart in his bosom, he
> will feel himself a better man; his patriotism will kindle with
> deeper emotion; his aspirations of his country's good will ascend
> from a more devout mind for having visited the "Headquarters of
> Washington." [29]

The legislature reimbursed the Deposit Fund with $2,391.02
and appropriated an additional $6,000 for the purpose of buying
more land around the house in order to protect the site. On the
Fourth of July, 1850, General Winfield Scott came up the Hudson
from West Point to raise the flag over the first historic house museum in the United States.[30] In later years the state increased the

size of the lot and then in 1910 erected a museum building near the house.[31]

Not every building connected with Washington was so fortunate. The home that he had occupied on Cherry Street in New York City while he was President was dismantled in 1856 to make way for the newly widened Bowery. Benjamin Winthrop passed by while the work of destruction was in progress and managed to secure several old pieces of wood from the contractor. Using these, he fashioned an ornate American Victorian chair and presented it to the New-York Historical Society.[32]

1856 was a banner year for the forces of preservation in such widely scattered localities as Nashville, Tennessee, and Philadelphia. While Washington's Cherry Street home was being torn down, the Tennessee legislature passed an act which authorized the purchase of the Hermitage, the home of Andrew Jackson, for $48,000. The bill justified the acquisition on the following grounds: "It is good policy in a republican government to . . . inculcate sentiments of veneration for those departed heroes who have rendered important services to their country in times of danger. . . ." Also included was a provision that the property was to be offered to the federal government as a branch of the United States Military Academy at West Point. Should the government refuse this offer, the State of Tennessee proposed to sell all of the farm except fifty acres around the house.[33] Congress never showed interest in a southern branch of the U. S. Military Academy, and the State of Tennessee did not try to sell the remainder of the farm.

The Carpenters' Company of Philadelphia became important in the preservation movement the same year that Tennessee set aside Jackson's home. The Carpenters' Company was more than a century old in 1856, and it occupied Carpenters' Hall, which had witnessed the first meeting of the First Continental Congress in 1774. Conscious of their historic surroundings, the carpenters voted in April of 1856 to renovate their hall, taking care "to preserve, as much as possible, every feature in said Hall as it now exists indicative of its original finish." The work took about a year, and so on September 5, 1857, the company reoccupied its newly restored home with appropriate ceremony. Two years later the City of Philadelphia asked the carpenters to set a price on the building so that the city could care for both Independence Hall and Carpenters' Hall. The carpenters showed no sign of wanting to give up their home, and so respectfully answered the city fathers with a resolution:

> We in common with our fellow citizens venerate it [the hall] not only for its associations with the stirring events of the Revolution "But we also hold it as a sacred trust committed to us by our predecessors, which nothing shall ever induce us to part with" Also that having fitted up the Room Occupied by the first Congress as near as possible as it was originally finished we intend as heretofore to keep it open for the inspection of all who may wish to visit it. . . .[34]

Shortly before the Civil War some members of the Essex Institute in Salem, Massachusetts, began to take an interest in an old wooden building believed to be the first church built in the town (1634). For five years a committee appointed by the membership of the institute studied the situation, and finally concluded that the frame actually was from the first church. Acting on the recommendations of the institute, the committee took the structure apart and re-erected it on the grounds of the Salem Athenaeum. In 1865 the committee rendered its final report, proudly announcing that the authenticated first church had been rebuilt and was ready for inspection.[35] It now appears that this little building probably was the first Quaker Meetinghouse (1688) in Salem.[36]

The most significant failure in the early days of the preservation movement was probably the attempt to save the Governor John Hancock house in Boston, Massachusetts. One guidebook, written just before the Civil War, pictured it glowingly as a landmark sought by all tourists coming to Boston.[37] Years after it was torn down, Wendell Phillips described the effect of the Hancock Mansion on one Arkansas slave owner. Phillips found the southern traveler "standing with white lips and trembling knees on the door-step of that house." When Phillips approached, the gentleman asked, "Did the man who signed the Declaration really touch that door-latch?"[38]

In spite of the interest shown in the Hancock house by the visiting public, it was in great danger of destruction by 1859. The mansion occupied a valuable piece of property adjacent to the State House, facing Boston Common. That year the Hancock heirs offered the building and land to the Commonwealth for $100,000, though a newspaper estimated this to be about $25,000 below the commercial value of the land itself. A committee reported favorably on a bill to purchase the property, and the legislature passed a resolution to this effect. The governor expressed his approval of a proposal to use the house as a governor's residence. From the extant photographs of the structure, it appears to have been a truly dignified city mansion that would have lent itself nobly to the purpose of a town residence for the governors of Massachusetts. There was a delay in perfecting the title, and some state officials opposed the purchase, so the Hancock Mansion remained in the hands of the family.[39]

In the spring of 1863 Charles Hancock approached Thomas C. Amory, then a member of the Board of Aldermen of the City of Boston, with the sad news that two businessmen were offering the family $120,000 for the property. Hancock sincerely wanted to have the city buy the place if the family could be persuaded to hold off the would-be purchasers. While the City of Boston debated the wisdom of setting up a committee to offer the Hancocks a fair price for the mansion, the commercial developers succeeded in buying the land itself. When the city committee was ready to act, it was too late to save the house on its original site. The Hancock family eagerly offered to give the mansion and the furnishings to the city if the whole thing could be moved to a new location. Based on some offers from individuals the city committee proposed either placing the mansion on the common as a gardener's home or locating it on a site nearby at an expense of $17,500 ($6,000 of which were private funds already pledged for the purpose). When the order for removal of the building reached the City Council, one of the members reported that he had just consulted a competent builder who found the cement stronger than the stones, which could not be separated. The cost of moving the mansion would therefore exceed the estimate given, and so the council voted to give up the project.[40]

The Hancock Mansion fell before the wreckers' tools in the summer of 1863. One may still find portions of its woodwork in various parts of New England—evidence of a sale conducted while the house was being demolished. However, just prior to the destruction a young architect named John Sturgis made a set of measured drawings showing the floor plan. It was probably the first time in our history that an old house was recorded in this manner.[41] In "dying" the Hancock house contributed more to the preservation movement than it ever could have by remaining intact. Throughout the next five or six decades many preservationists used the Hancock Mansion as their rallying cry.

It is wise to pause here for a moment to show how these early attempts influenced the future of the preservation movement in several areas. The willingness of the City of Philadelphia to save Independence Hall and the purchase of the Hasbrouck house by New York State helped to lay a foundation for municipal and state preservation work in the whole Middle Atlantic area. In sharp contrast, the failure of the State of Massachusetts and the City of Boston in the case of the Hancock Mansion created a latent distrust of legislative machinery among New Englanders. In 1924 a well-known restoration architect lamented the loss of the Hancock house more than half a century before:

> The Hancock House is gone—destroyed after vain attempts to save it for four or five years by legislative acts; it was finally demolished in 1863; there being left only remnants of the architectural details here and there; which people have saved—as is very likely to be done with material things worth while; that is, by small and individual movements, not by legislative acts.[42]

While these scattered attempts at preservation were going on in the 1850's a great national movement was taking place that was to set the pattern for the next several decades in the history of preservationism. This was the successful effort of a group of women to purchase and care for Mount Vernon, the home of Washington.

II

The Shadow of Mount Vernon

TODAY IT IS HARD TO RECAPTURE the veneration that nineteenth-century Americans had for George Washington. A recently published study of a large number of early school textbooks tells us: "The heroic stature of Washington was unique; he appeared rather as divinity than as man. As a Christlike liberator the contrast between Washington and European heroes was sharp indeed. That this greatest of all men appeared in the United States is sufficient justification for American civilization. . . ." [1]

By 1822 Bushrod Washington, the President's nephew who had inherited Mount Vernon, had to post a sign warning steamboat parties that his farm was private property and that it would not be open for picnics on the lawns. Bushrod did welcome "respectable strangers and others." Mount Vernon was already well on its way to becoming a patriotic mecca. [2]

As the years went by, more and more people began to think of Mount Vernon as a shrine that ought to be the property of the nation. There is in existence a petition to Congress dated 1846 which warned that it would be unfortunate if Mount Vernon and the tomb of Washington were to continue to "be subject to the uncertainties and transfers of individual fortune." Included in the petition was a letter from John A. Washington telling the public that his mother, Jane Washington, was willing to sell the house and 150 acres to the federal government for $100,000. [3] In 1848 and 1850 there were more petitions calling upon Congress to purchase Mount Vernon, but apparently nothing much was done. [4]

An Army board wrote to John Washington in 1851 asking permission to visit Mount Vernon, with the object of making it an

41

asylum for the relief and support of invalid and disabled soldiers. The board also asked Washington to place a price on the farm.[5] Although Washington was not really out of sympathy with the idea of making Mount Vernon a military asylum, he said that his selling price would be $200,000, considerably more than his mother had asked five years before. He hastened to justify the change: ". . . The above-named price may appear to be extravagant, yet I have good reason to believe it is not more than could be readily obtained for the property were it in the Public Market." [6]

The damage was done. In the trying years that followed, John Washington never deviated from this price, and there is every reason to believe that he expected the government to pay him a sum equal to the amount he could get from businessmen. Unfortunately John Washington's determination forced him to face criticism from those who thought that he should have named a more "patriotic" price. The federal government was not ready to pay such an amount for a private home. Lieutenant Colonel Scott, representing the Army board, respectfully told Washington that $200,000 was far beyond the means of the board.[7] Washington answered that he had refused an offer of $100,000 in April of 1852 from W. W. Corcoran and some other gentlemen who wanted to give the farm to the United States Government.[8]

During 1853 there were persistent rumors that a group of businessmen were trying to negotiate with John Washington to purchase the whole plantation for a hotel site. Mount Vernon's riverside setting and its nearness to Washington, D. C., were potent arguments in favor of a park or a resort hotel. No doubt it was this report that finally set the forces of preservation into action.[9]

In December, 1853, within three days of each other, two important pleas for the preservation of Mount Vernon appeared. On the second day of that month, Miss Ann Pamela Cunningham broadcast an appeal to the women of the South. On the fifth of December, the governor of Virginia sent a message to the legislature asking that some method be devised for the rescue of Washington's home.

Governor Johnson told the Virginia lawmakers that it was opportune that the federal government had not listened to the appeals of the people who wanted to save Mount Vernon, for that gave Virginia the chance to do so. He suggested several possible uses for the estate, ranging from an agricultural school to a literary institution.[10] An obstacle had been thrown in the path of the State of Virginia—the same stumbling block that had defeated the federal government—John Washington's unwillingness to sell Mount Vernon for less than $200,000. Many people in 1853 did not believe that $200,000 was the commercial value of 200 acres and the house at Mount Vernon. The report of the special committee appointed by the Virginia legislature told the story eloquently. "The committee take occasion to say that they . . . have not been able to see the propriety, under the present condition of our finances, of recommending the acquisition of the property on the terms proposed." [11] This seemed likely to end the matter.

Governor Johnson was a persistent man, and his message for 1855 carried another rousing appeal to rescue Mount Vernon:

> The amount claimed by the proprietor may be considered exorbitant. In the ordinary transactions of business it might be true, but who shall undertake to calculate the value of the homestead and the grave of Washington, with its primeval simplicity, or to place an estimate upon the thousand sacred recollections which crowd the mind and cluster the heart in token of admiration for him whom all delight to honor. Dollars become as dust when compared with the inestimable patriotism inspired by a visit to the tomb. . . . However ready you may be to purchase and pay for this property, that honor has been partially wrested from you, and is reserved for the noble purpose of adorning the brow of female philanthropy.[12]

The governor went on to point out that some ladies had indeed collected a large sum of money for the purchase and desired that the title to the property should rest with the State of Virginia. Therefore the legislature on March 17, 1856, chartered the Mount Vernon Ladies' Association of the Union, carefully offering to accept the title without helping to raise the purchase money.[13]

Two years later the question of saving Mount Vernon was on the agenda of the Virginia legislature for a last time. The Mount Vernon Ladies' Association had requested a new charter permitting it to own the property. Virginia was to issue bonds to the amount of $200,000—providing that the association would repay that amount into the state treasury as the money was collected. An amended version of the bill did pass on March 19, 1858, with which Virginia left the work of saving Mount Vernon in the laps of the women of the nation.[14]

Back in December of 1853, just three days before Governor Johnson first broached the subject of Mount Vernon to the Virginia legislature, a remarkable woman wrote an article for the *Charleston Mercury,* of Charleston, South Carolina. Her appeal, directed to the "Ladies of the South," was a spirited account of the debt that all Americans owed to Washington, followed by an even more vigorous call to prevent the desecration of Mount Vernon by speculators. "Can you be still with closed souls and purses, while the world cries 'Shame upon America,' and suffer Mount Vernon, with all its sacred associations, to become, as is spoken of and probable, the seat of manufacturers and manufactories? . . . Never! Forbid it, shades of the dead . . . !"[15] The appeal was signed, with nineteenth-century modesty, "A Southern Matron."

Ann Pamela Cunningham was one of the two leading figures of the early period of the American preservation movement. She was a small, frail spinster who came from an upcountry South Carolina plantation called Rosemont. She was the daughter of a wealthy planter, Captain Robert Cuningham (Ann Pamela later added the extra "n" in her name). A visitor to the Cuningham home recalled that the captain lived in great luxury for his day and age; and the same friend remembered Ann Pamela as small, serious, intelligent and quite bewitching. Sometime around her seventeenth year, she had fallen from a horse, suffering spinal injuries of a type that often left her completely helpless.[16]

The exact circumstances surrounding the writing and publication of the first appeal are not clear, but there are some valuable clues. It appears definite that Miss Cunningham often visited Philadelphia with her mother in order to see Dr. Hugh L. Hodge, a well-known physician of that day. A friend of Miss Cunningham described what occurred during one of these visits:

> I was spending the winter in Philadelphia in the same house with Miss Ann Pamela Cunningham (whom I had known from childhood). . . . One evening I found her much excited over a letter she had just received from her mother, who had left her a week before to spend the winter South. She read it to me.

After telling of her safe arrival at home etc., she [her mother] said: "It was a lovely moonlight night that we went down the Potomac. I went on deck as the bell tolled and we passed Mount Vernon. I was painfully depressed at the ruin and desolation of the home of Washington, and the thought passed through my mind: Why was it that the women of his country did not try to keep it in repair, if the men could not do it? It does seem such a blot on our country!"

Miss Cunningham said: "I shall do it!" and she read me the letter which has since become famous, signed, "A Southern Matron." [17]

In later years, Ann Pamela admitted that the movement did not go the way she expected it would. She had hoped to remain behind the scenes and pull the strings in order to get the public fully aroused on the subject. She had been sure that the women of the South would rise as a group in order to keep Mount Vernon from commercial exploitation.[18] Things did not work out so easily.

At the age of thirty-seven, Miss Cunningham was actually embarking upon her lifework: the preservation and protection of Mount Vernon. First of all, she found that the most important people involved, the Washingtons who owned Mount Vernon, were not in sympathy with her project. In December of 1853, shortly after printing the first appeal, she penned a note to Mrs. Eleanor Washington, telling her of the patriotic work afoot and asking if her husband would consider selling the house to a group of southern ladies who would in turn transfer the title to the State of Virginia.[19] Evidently Miss Cunningham had believed that she would find Mrs. Washington a responsive correspondent through whom John Washington might be convinced of the altruistic spirit of the women. She found that she did not have an ally in Mrs. Washington, for a disappointing answer to the December letter came six months later. In her reply Eleanor Washington told Miss Cunningham that her husband thought there were too many practical difficulties facing the ladies to discuss seriously the program outlined in Miss Cunningham's letter. Through his wife John Washington added that it would be unethical for him to consider any plans while the legislature of Virginia was looking into the purchase of Mount Vernon.[20]

While this correspondence was dragging on, Miss Cunningham issued her second appeal to the women of the South, and it appeared in several newspapers throughout the region. The article contained an outline of her plans for an organization. There were to be central heads directing each state association. Soon Ann Pamela Cunningham was to show herself to be an able organizer, as well as publicizer of the Mount Vernon movement.[21]

Miss Cunningham later described the slow progress of the first year as merely a series of meetings in the Georgia and South Carolina area. Her sole ally was Mrs. Philoclea E. Eve of Georgia, who assisted her in every way possible. The first real effort to extend the influence of her ideas came in July, 1854, when she was able to arrange a meeting in Richmond, Virginia, under the supervision of Mrs. Ritchie of that city. Soon there was clamor among Miss Cunningham's northern friends for her to make the movement nationwide.

Probably no other organization in the preservation movement faced some of the problems encountered by Ann Pamela Cunningham and her small band of workers.[22] She faced jealousies among her southern followers that were overcome only after she took an active and determined role in setting up her association. Her first northern committee, located in Philadelphia, became cool to the Mount Vernon idea when it saw that the title to the property would rest with the State of Virginia. Here was one of the many times that Miss Cunningham's leadership was to be tested. She acted swiftly to meet the challenge. ". . . I wrote to my friend the Hon. John MacPherson Berrien [Mrs. Eve's uncle] . . . , explained our difficulties, and begged his advice. He advised me to apply to the Virginia Legislature for a charter to the Association—which, though the title had to be vested in Virginia, would satisfy all sectional feeling." [23] Although this particular charter, as passed in 1856, was not the final one, it was indeed the cohesive force that the movement needed at that time.

Just as the Virginia legislature was approving the charter, a new and important figure entered the battle for the preservation of Mount Vernon. Edward Everett, of Massachusetts, former Senator and well-known orator, was willing and ready to champion the new cause. One finds it difficult today to visualize the drawing power of such an orator in the middle of the nineteenth century. Before the Mount Vernon movement achieved final success, Everett delivered an address on the character of Washington 139 times

—averaging almost $500 for each appearance.[24] Everett first delivered his "Washington" before the Mercantile Library Association of Boston on February 22, 1856. Up to that time he had declined all invitations to give the address for other groups except one; in December of 1855 he had accepted the call of the Mount Vernon Ladies to speak in Richmond the following spring.[25] On his way south, Everett stopped in Philadelphia to meet the leader of the movement. He promised her that he would repeat the address in Philadelphia later.[26]

Everett's appearance in Richmond was a dramatic occasion. The lecture had been well advertised, and long before he arrived all the tickets had been sold. As Everett came onto the stage, Miss Cunningham, who had been too ill to be present, was wheeled in behind him on a couch, in order to hear the speech in person. Her courage had a magical effect on the workers.[27]

At times Everett's appeal with the masses created some feelings of jealousy. One man, who had been working for the Ladies' Association in Connecticut, found that Everett's name seemed "the rallying point of the undertaking in the popular mind." He was certain that Everett's address was far too long and repetitious, yet "how the sea of plumes before us nodded—how the jewels flashed as snowy hands clapped—how brighter eyes gazed with admiration!" Financially, and in many other ways, Everett was a success.[28]

Everett's oration always began with a long comparison between Mount Vernon and Blenheim Castle, England's gift to the hero Marlborough. He stressed the lack of ornamentation at Mount Vernon in order to show that Washington's greatness did not need the work of men's hands to embellish it.[29] More important than Everett's words was the fact that he was donating the proceeds of each of his performances to the ladies who wanted to save Mount Vernon. This was indeed a rare act of chivalry. So impressed were the people of South Carolina, who opposed Everett politically, that he was given free passage on her railroads.[30]

Perhaps the spirit behind South Carolina's action gives a clue to Everett's real interest in the Mount Vernon movement. His biographer believed that he was actually attempting to save the Union rather than just Mount Vernon, for it appeared to him that the Ladies' Association was a good vehicle for overcoming sectional differences.[31] In a letter to Ann Pamela Cunningham at the outbreak of the Civil War, Everett stated that he was unable to be neutral in the coming struggle, though he had sincerely fought over the years for national unity through his alliance with the Mount Vernon cause.[32]

The real work still had to be done by Miss Cunningham, for even the thousands of dollars that Edward Everett brought into the association's coffers were not enough. Although Virginia had granted a charter to the ladies, and prosperity seemed at last to be the association's destiny, in the spring of 1856 the one person who could wreck all that Ann Pamela had done, declared himself. John Washington announced that he was not satisfied with the terms of the charter because he did not want the ladies to give Virginia the money for Mount Vernon. It appeared that all was lost. In fact, Miss Cunningham and her group were eventually held up to public ridicule for collecting funds to no purpose.

Miss Cunningham saw that she herself would have to win John Washington's approval for the work of the association. In a letter written after the Civil War, she described in great detail the physical agony it cost her to visit him in June of 1856. She found him unyielding. In a state of discouragement, she was rowed out onto the Potomac to meet the boat going back to Washington, D. C. She just missed the boat and so had to return and spend the night at Mount Vernon. Even the next morning her most passionate arguments could not alter John Washington's resolution to sell the estate to Virginia, not to the association. As she waited for her carriage, Miss Cunningham told Washington that she had known that some of the terms of the 1856 charter were not to his liking, and consequently she had tried to change them.

> I assured him that I believed all the ladies concerned felt as I did—while we wished to succeed in our beautiful tribute we were grieved that his feelings were hurt, insulted so repeatedly because of it. I looked up to him as I said this. What a change in his face! Unawares I had at last touched the "sore spot," the obstacle no money could have removed. I now found that he believed the whole thing had been arranged between the Association and Virginia to put an indignity on him!! . . . I then told him if he would consent to overcome minor objections that I would prove to the country what were the feelings of the Association by going before the next legislature and asking it to make every change he re-

quired, but he must let the Association pay the money and not feel that his State or himself were lowered by the act! I held out my hand; he put his in mine.[33]

Whether she knew it or not, Miss Cunningham had probably performed her greatest single work for the Mount Vernon movement, for with the cooperation of John Washington, progress was assured. Edward Everett congratulated her for removing the "only insuperable obstacle to success." [34]

The Mount Vernon Ladies' Association finally was able to devote its energies to the vital task of creating the organization which was to raise $200,000. John Washington's attitude had so completely changed toward Miss Cunningham and the ladies that even when the Virginia legislature in 1858 did not give them the kind of charter he wanted, he still agreed to sell the farm to the association.[35]

At this point Miss Cunningham made her next great contribution—administrative skill and energy. It must be remembered that when she had worked out a charter there had been no precedents to go on; no organization of this type had ever existed before. Once the 1858 charter was approved, Miss Cunningham appeared more frequently in public, dropping the "Southern Matron" title in order to be "Regent" of the new association. She appointed a number of vice-regents, one for each state in which there was any hope of support for Mount Vernon. By 1860 she had appointed vice-regents for thirty states, all of whom she listed in each issue of her new official newspaper, *The Mount Vernon Record*.

In the archives at Mount Vernon there are numerous letters from Ann Pamela Cunningham to her vice-regents, giving them detailed instructions. In one such letter to a Maryland vice-regent, dated sometime during 1859 (Early Records XI, page 65), she began by stating the objective of the association: the "perpetual guardianship of Mount Vernon." Then she launched into a description of the duties of the vice-regent. She recommended that the system used by the Mount Vernon organizations in the southern states be adopted, namely that each vice-regent act as treasurer —to handle all funds as they were collected—and also choose a secretary. In order to expedite the collection of funds, the vice-regent was to appoint "lady managers" for every county, town, or

village in her state. Each of the lady managers in turn was to appoint subassistants to help her. In addition, the vice-regent was to
publish regularly in local papers the names of those who had contributed. Miss Cunningham recommended the methods used by
the businesslike and capable Miss Mary Hamilton, vice-regent for
New York, who had actually opened an office in downtown New
York City. Then she concluded that whether or not one followed
the northern or southern mode of organization, it was essential for
each vice-regent to enlist the aid of all zealous editors for the cause.
Miss Cunningham stated that the Ladies' Association had so much
difficulty in the North in getting newspapers to publish lists of
contributors that a group of gentlemen came to her aid by issuing
The Mount Vernon Record.

A feature of Ann Pamela Cunningham's work that was widely
imitated by other patriotic organizations in the years following
the Civil War was the selection of prominent women for vice-
regents. A most enlightening passage is to be found in a letter
which she wrote in 1873 to her successor, Mrs. Lily Berghmans. She
tried to warn Mrs. Berghmans of the pitfalls involved in choosing
vice-regents:

> . . . Get *only* the right kind of person—for—I *realized that* our
> *prosperity,* and hope of *perpetuating* anything *in a sex*—whose con-
> tentions are a "proverb"—depended upon—success!! Yet—there are
> some most unfortunate selections through *bad advisers,* too much
> value was put in their minds on *social* or *public* position—when the
> *individual character* is *paramount* to these—indispensable as they
> are. A Regent can rarely have it in her power to select from per-
> sonal acquaintance. . . .[36]

The two volumes of *The Mount Vernon Record* bear sufficient
witness to the organizational abilities of Ann Pamela Cunningham
and to the immense work of popularization carried on by Edward
Everett through his orations and newspaper articles. The *Record*
abounded with comments from other newspapers on the success
of the movement. It listed contributors to the Mount Vernon fund,
together with the names of the lady managers who collected this
money. There were citations of unusual donations—such as an
offer from the Adams Express Company to ship free of charge all
packages addressed to the association; [37] Laura Keene's contribution of the use of her theater, cast and one production of *Our*

American Cousin [38] (later seen by Lincoln on the night of his assassination); and the Missouri legislature's appropriation of $2,000 for the patriotic enterprise (voted unanimously).[39] There was the text of a letter from President Buchanan giving his approval to the project and enclosing a check for $50; [40] also, a facsimile of a letter from the late Washington Irving giving $500 to the association.[41] A detailed description of a Mount Vernon meeting in New York City included an account of the decorations in the room—a huge American flag with a scroll across it saying, *Woman Rescues His Home and Grave;* also a sketch of the audience which was supposed to be a mixture of "beauty, scholarship and worth, diplomacy and war, attracted thither purely, of course, from patriotic motives." [42] There was even a short article that loudly protested the notion that Washington had ever used profanity, citing some witnesses at the Battle of Monmouth who were certain that Washington had been very temperate in his language when speaking to General Lee.[43] There were varying ideas on just how Mount Vernon ought to be "preserved." Announcements of the financial condition of the association appeared periodically. In December, 1859, Miss Cunningham reported that Mount Vernon was clear of debt (except for a few thousand dollars) and that Edward Everett had raised almost $70,000 of the $200,000. Along with this happy news was a call for an endowment of $150,000 in order to insure the estate for the future.[44]

In spite of the success of the Mount Vernon movement, it was not without some criticism. Probably John Washington was attacked more for his high price than were the ladies who tried to raise the amount. When the Hancock family offered the John Hancock house in Boston to the state for $100,000, their proposal was described as "not so exacting as [that of] the owner of Mount Vernon." [45] A *Saturday Evening Post* editorial pointed out that not only were the American people being asked to give money for monuments to great Revolutionary heroes, but they were also being asked to help purchase Mount Vernon. ". . . Our sympathy is by no means increased when we reflect upon the exorbitant character of the demands of the present proprietor. Why should the American people be taxed to enrich Mr. John A. Washington?" The *Post* writer ended on a philosophical note by reasoning that George Washington really needed no monument.[46] In the same editorial the writer attacked the literary value of the "Mount Vernon Papers" that Everett was writing for Robert Bonner of the New York *Ledger*. The *Post* strongly suspected that Everett had volunteered for the Mount Vernon movement in order to satisfy his sense of self-importance. *Gleason's Weekly* showed more kindness when it implied that noble motives were behind Everett's efforts, even if his talents as a writer could be questioned.[47]

As though she had a clear vision of the impending storm, Ann Pamela Cunningham obtained John Washington's permission to have work done on the house even before the association took over the estate.[48] The timing of these repairs was fortunate, because a trying era was about to dawn on Mount Vernon and its new owners. For the duration of the Civil War Miss Cunningham, back in South Carolina, was cut off from all communications with those in charge at the farm. Mount Vernon was for many months in the no-man's-land between the Union and Confederate lines. Just before the war began, Miss Cunningham had hired two capable people who guarded Mount Vernon almost single-handedly throughout this harrowing experience: Upton Herbert as superintendent of the estate and Miss Sarah C. Tracy as secretary of the association.[49] The letters written by Miss Tracy from Mount Vernon during the war years have been edited and ably arranged in a book entitled *Presence of a Lady,* which covers in great detail the trials of the small colony at Mount Vernon.

Possibly the most important damage the war inflicted on the association was the loss of its steamboat, the only means tourists had for reaching the mansion. The federal government confiscated it shortly after the war began, thus depriving the association of its sole source of income. In addition, Miss Tracy often had great difficulty (though she obtained passes from high-ranking officers) getting back and forth from Alexandria with provisions for the people at the farm. An officer who was on the staff of Prince Napoleon when he visited this country in 1861 left a fascinating account of the loneliness and desolation that seemed to creep up on Mount Vernon. He also added several complimentary remarks on the efficient manner in which Miss Tracy managed the estate.[50]

The financial condition of the association became so grim that by 1864 a real split had developed on the question of the future of Mount Vernon. Everett and Miss Mary Hamilton, vice-regent for New York, favored asking the federal government to take charge of the property.[51] At the 1864 council meeting, George W. Riggs, the treasurer, offered to provide the money himself in order to get the association through the rest of the war.[52] Evidently Riggs and the group of vice-regents opposed to taking any precipitous action without the presence of Ann Pamela Cunningham succeeded in carrying the day.[53]

The decade following the end of the Civil War marked a period of consolidation and improvement at Mount Vernon. Miss Cunningham was able to attend the council of the association in 1866. At this meeting she gave her thanks to those members who had remained faithful to the concept of a national organization and had trusted her through the long years of the war.[54] This council meeting was far more than a mere reunion; it was a sign that Mount Vernon and its "national" association had both survived a time of trial.

There was much to be done in the way of repairs—yet the funds had apparently reached the vanishing point. Miss Cunningham had one more great service to perform for Mount Vernon, launching the association into the era of peace and prosperity. In order to retrench the finances of the organization, she volunteered to live at the house as regent and custodian. She would then be able to superintend the work on the mansion while she watched over the accounts.[55] As a start, it was essential that the association get a payment from the federal government for the loss of the boat and all tourist revenue during the war. Miss Cunningham made the painful trip up the Potomac several times in order to get a bill through Congress. This little South Carolinian was even forced to ask the aid of the militant Sumner of Massachusetts, a task she considered one of the most unpleasant of her career. Finally, in 1869 the bill did pass, awarding the Mount Vernon Ladies' Association $7,000 for repairs on the mansion and grounds.[56]

The 1869 appropriation virtually completed the great work of Ann Pamela Cunningham, for she found it necessary to retire in 1874. Before leaving, she began a highly useful labor—the compilation of some of the early records of the association for "our future history," which she hoped would be written someday.[57] Without these archives, it is certain that one would never know so much about the early days of this important organization. Many preservation groups founded long after the Mount Vernon Ladies' Association did not keep any significant records.

In her emotional farewell to the vice-regents of the association, read to the council of June 2, 1874, Miss Cunningham warned the ladies to keep Mount Vernon just as Washington had left it. In a declaration that still inspires the work at Mount Vernon she said, "Ladies, the home of Washington is in your charge—see to it that you keep it the home of Washington! Let no irreverent hand change it; let no vandal hands desecrate it with the fingers of 'progress'!" [58] She returned to her plantation in South Carolina and passed away within a year.

In looking back at her career a century later, it seems only fair to rate Ann Pamela Cunningham as one of the two most effective workers in the early years of the preservation movement. Here is the judgment of the second of these figures, William Sumner Appleton, written in 1918 in answer to an editorial attacking the Mount Vernon Ladies' Association:

> Of these ladies by far the most important was Ann Pamela Cunningham, Regent from December 2, 1853 to January 1, 1874. The record of her services in patriotic work on behalf of Mt. Vernon is an inspiring story in itself, and the writer of your editorial would do well to acquaint himself with it. If the services of the later Regents and Members has been less than Miss Cunningham's it has been not through unwillingness on their part but because Miss Cunningham left them less to do.[59]

Many things remained to be done in order to perfect the work of preservation, as well as improve the financial status of the association. In 1875 the ladies had to defend their monopoly over the boat traffic to Mount Vernon (the entrance fee to the mansion was then included in the boat passage). When another tour boat appeared on the river, the association had to lower the price for its own boat in order to force this competition off the river. The Board of Visitors (a supervisory men's group assigned by the charter to inspect the work at Mount Vernon) helped to protect the monopoly in the Virginia legislature by preventing enactment of a bill that would have permitted all shipping to stop at the Mount Vernon dock.[60]

The work of the association advanced gradually through the years, with assistance from a variety of sources. In 1876 Mrs. Halstead, the New Jersey vice-regent, managed to interest an architect in the idea of offering his services so that measured drawings might be made of the mansion.[61] She did not stop with this, for she secured free rail passage for him as a donation from the railroads.[62] In 1888 Jay Gould presented the association with thirty-three and a half acres adjacent to the farm for its protection.[63]

In a few cases Mount Vernon vice-regents led movements within their own states for the association. At the council of 1888 Mrs. Jenny M. Ward, vice-regent for Kansas, volunteered to create enthusiasm for Mount Vernon in her state if some object could be found for a donation of about $1,000.[64] The council decided that a suitable goal would be the reconstruction of the servants' quarters. During the remainder of the year Mrs. Ward conducted a campaign in Kansas. "It was considered no easy task to awaken interest in an object so remote in time and place among a people intensely occupied in building up and promoting the varied interests of our State. . . . Mount Vernon is nearly two thousand miles away and its history beyond the memory of all." Mrs. Ward plainly saw the obstacles to her work, but she wisely decided that she should try to collect small contributions from the school children of Kansas. A huge celebration of George Washington's birthday was held throughout the state school system on February 22, 1889. There were programs involving speeches, orations, essays and songs. By April the campaign was a complete success, and the school children of Kansas presented $1,000 for a faithful replica of the servants' quarters.[65] In 1892 the schools of St. Paul, Minnesota, raised $278.51 for the restoration of the interior of the spinning house. With this contribution the association purchased some spinning equipment from Mrs. Ben: Perley Poore, the widow of one of the pioneer collectors of Americana.[66]

Several of the vice-regents gave individual donations to the cause of preserving Mount Vernon. Mrs. Phoebe Hearst, mother of the journalist William Randolph Hearst, gave $6,000 for the draining and filling of a swamp near the mansion that had troubled every owner including General Washington.[67] Miss Alice Longfellow, daughter of the poet and vice-regent from Massachusetts, hired an architect to restore the library at her own expense. She also gave freely of her time and money in seeking old or original furnishings for the library.[68]

Just as the trying period of the Civil War was ending, Mrs. Abby Chace, the vice-regent for Rhode Island, wrote Miss Tracy about the challenges that the association would face in the years to come. "Criticism is always merciless on everything which women undertake to do and every failure in neatness or order will be soon chronicled." [69] It was not long before attacks began to come. They generally followed one or two familiar lines—either the ladies were not taking sufficient care of Mount Vernon, or they were entirely unfair in demanding a fee from the patriotic public to see the home of the Father of His Country. A booklet bearing the arresting title *Shall Mount Vernon Be Free?* appeared in 1878.[70] Evidently it had little effect since no group, including the federal government, was willing to take on the responsibility of Mount Vernon without some form of admission fee to support it. A Boston newspaper disclosed in 1883 that Mount Vernon was being neglected because the public was visiting other sights and therefore admissions were no longer paying for its upkeep. Mrs. Sweat, the vice-regent for Maine, immediately sent a letter of denial and a copy of the most recent annual report of the association. Unfortunately the paper did not retract its original statement.[71]

The Mount Vernon Ladies' Association did have champions as well as critics. A Baltimore paper summarized the attacks on the association in 1886 and then stoutly defended its work. The editor wrote to Mrs. Sweat at Mount Vernon that in the article he had tried to adhere to the facts set forth in the report of the association's work which she had previously furnished him.[72] Later an article entitled "Why Keep Mount Vernon as a Side Show?" appeared in the Boston *Herald* of May 12, 1918. It included the following protest: "It is an injustice to the country at large that a close corporation of women controls the home and tomb of the Father of His Country and establish rules under which visitors are permitted to pay their respects to that place." This was too much for that ardent New England preservationist, William Sumner Appleton, who replied, "Is it not rather a certainty that under public control all the positions connected with the management would be made the spoils of party politics and we would be treated to the unsavory sight of politicians scrambling for the salary attached to the care of Washington's grave?" [73] In 1921 the American Scenic and Historic Preservation Society passed a resolution approving the manner in which Mount Vernon was being managed. The resolution also expressed the opinion that a desire to change the ownership of the estate was really a desire to control more political patronage.[74]

Mount Vernon was the first successful nationwide effort at preservation. The leader of the movement, Ann Pamela Cunningham, had been a believer in publicity, for it should be remembered that she valued newsmen as allies in her work. In addition, the grand tour of Edward Everett had served to bring the Mount Vernon Association to the attention of thousands of Americans of all ages. Last, but by no means least, the Ladies' Association was not just a group of thirty vice-regents who assembled once a year to hear the orders of the regent; it also included hundreds of lady managers and their assistants. Combine these elements with the unquestioned national veneration for Washington, and one may foresee that the Mount Vernon movement would influence preservationism for years to come. This must have been what happened, for from the ranks of the younger lady managers of the Mount Vernon Ladies' Association were to come the leaders or parents of the leaders of the great wave of patriotic associations in the 1890's. The effect of Mount Vernon can hardly be overestimated, for almost every early preservation group had some contact with the Ladies' Association.

A clear case of the influence of the Mount Vernon effort can be seen in the work of Mrs. William H. Holstein at Valley Forge, Pennsylvania. In 1878 she wrote enthusiastically to Mrs. Sweat asking her to join a group that was trying to save the Washington Headquarters at Valley Forge:

> The plan [of her association] is designed to be similar to that of Mount Vernon, with Regent, Vice-Regents, and Lady-Managers. I wrote to Col. Hollingsworth . . . for a copy of [the] Charter and By-Laws—which is now in the hands of the Lawyers, as a guide in framing this for Valley Forge.
>
> My object in writing is to ask for all the information you can give me in reference to the present plans about Mt.V. If you have at your disposal a copy of [the] Constitution and By-Laws, I should be glad to have it, as the Lawyers desire to retain the one they have. Can you give me the names and P.O. address of the Ladies in the various States, who have been instrumental in furnishing rooms

at Mt.V. When the purchase money for Mt.V. was being collected I worked earnestly for it, as Lady-Manager of this County and have continued to feel the deepest interest in all pertaining to it.[75]

Mrs. Sweat politely replied that while she was in sympathy with the idea of glorifying the name of Washington, the safety of his home must come first. All of Mrs. Sweat's donations would thus go to Mount Vernon rather than to any other historic house.[76]

Mrs. Holstein was not satisfied with that answer. She wrote again and requested the names of "persons from the original 13 states, suitable for Vice-Regents in this organization." At that time she only had vice-regents in Massachusetts and Maryland, and she definitely wanted to find more. She invited Mrs. Sweat and any other Mount Vernon vice-regent who could attend, to come to the celebration at Valley Forge on June 19, 1878.[77] Shortly after this brief correspondence, Mrs. Sweat heard from a gentleman in Boston who hoped that she would be willing to serve as vice-regent in Maine for the Valley Forge Association. He enclosed a circular and some shares of stock that he was selling.[78]

There is clear evidence of three things in Mrs. Sweat's correspondence with Mrs. Holstein: (1) Mrs. Holstein had been a worker for the Mount Vernon cause before the Civil War; (2) she was founding an organization patterned closely on the Mount Vernon Association; and (3) she was turning to Mount Vernon for help and advice. When Mrs. Holstein was starting her group at Valley Forge, the Ladies' Association had been administering Mount Vernon for nearly twenty years.

It appeared that Mrs. Holstein had great difficulty in trying to form a national organization. She may well have been as capable a leader as Ann Pamela Cunningham and she hoped to profit by Miss Cunningham's example. Where was the difference? The answer to this question lay, to some extent, in the area of criteria for the selection of historic houses for preservation. The building at Valley Forge had been Washington's headquarters for a winter; and, according to Mrs. Holstein, it was remarkably unchanged.[79] It had some historic and architectural interest, but it was *not* the home of George Washington.

Unfortunately Mrs. Holstein and the ladies working for the Valley Forge headquarters were not the only ones to learn this hard lesson. A reading of preservationist literature shows that a host of earnest men and women throughout the country thought that old houses in their communities could be saved in the same manner in which Mount Vernon had been rescued. One more significant example illustrates the above point. In 1888 a searching letter arrived at Mount Vernon from a farm outside of Nashville, Tennessee. The writer inquired about the ownership of Mount Vernon and the methods by which it was governed. She asked how the admission fees were used and if they were sufficient. She explained, "Three years ago, I married Col. Andrew Jackson, the grandson (by adoption) of Andrew Jackson, and am still living in the 'Hermitage,' his old home." Mrs. Jackson went on to say that the State of Tennessee owned the place, and that a bill to sell it to the highest bidder had recently been defeated in the Tennessee legislature by a narrow margin. At last she got to the heart of the matter: "Please advise me how to proceed to have formed an Association similar to the Association controlling Mt. Vernon, whose purpose shall be to preserve and perpetuate the character of the Hermitage estate as the home and burial place of Andrew Jackson." Mrs. Jackson also added that her husband owned all of the original Jackson furniture.[80]

At about the same time, Colonel Jackson sent a letter of inquiry about the Mount Vernon Ladies' Association to Mrs. Philoclea E. Eve, one of the original vice-regents, who was then an elderly lady. In her answer, Mrs. Eve gave a short history of the Mount Vernon Association as she remembered it and then ended her letter with some good advice: "I rather think that our organization will not suit the case of the Hermitage, as the State of Tennessee stands ready to do honor to her noble son and perhaps needs no outside assistance." This was much more prophetic than the ladies in Nashville realized.[81]

At a meeting of the small group of workers interested in saving the Hermitage, Mrs. Eve's letter produced a mixed reaction. One gentleman rose and said that sixty million people knew of General Jackson, and soon more would join this throng. He pointed out that there were only four places where the "gaze of the world" rested—and two of them were Mount Vernon (naturally) and the Hermitage.[82] In spite of the optimism of some people, the effort to create an organization similar to the Mount Vernon Ladies' Association fared badly. Mrs. Mary C. Dorris, one of the founders of the Ladies' Hermitage Association, admitted in her book on the preservation of Jackson's home that the Mount Vernon precedent did not exactly fit the Hermitage situation. In the first place, since the State of Tennessee already owned the Hermitage, prospective contributors sometimes found it hard to believe that the state would allow people to help it take care of its own property.[83] Secondly, Mrs. Dorris said:

> To carry out the national idea the effort was made to appoint vice regents in every State of the Union, and the following ladies were appointed [a list of prominent women]. . . . They were notified by the Secretary, but none of them took up the work nor did anything, with the single exception of Mrs. Ellen Call Long, of Florida, whose father, General Call, was one of Jackson's aids [sic].[84]

In 1915 Mrs. Dorris described the membership of the Ladies' Hermitage Association as a group of 400 people, mostly in the Nashville area.[85]

Thus two attempts to imitate the national movement that had been so successful under Ann Pamela Cunningham failed to a certain degree, in spite of the historic importance of the houses involved. Both the Hermitage and the Valley Forge headquarters were saved, but the work of a national association was not a potent factor in either case. The correspondence cited above shows that each organization could not get people to volunteer to serve as chairmen in distant states. As with the Valley Forge Association, so with the Ladies' Hermitage Association, the preservers were not dealing with buildings that could obtain the same support that the home and burial place of George Washington had gained in the decade prior to the Civil War.

The influence of Ann Pamela Cunningham has extended into the twentieth century. Mrs. Mary Longyear, who had saved three houses associated with the life of Mary Baker Eddy (the founder of Christian Science), visited Mount Vernon in May of 1921. Mrs. Longyear noted in her diary that "Colonel Dodge took us through the rooms and told us of the organization of women who own and preserve it." [86] When Mrs. Longyear set up a foundation to care for her historic houses in 1926, she wrote into the *Declaration of Trust* that the trustees could form a voluntary organization "in general conformity with the plan of organization and administration of the 'Mount Vernon Ladies' Association of the Union.' . . ." [87]

These were not isolated cases, for other houses have been described as almost equal to Mount Vernon in interest to the historically minded. One of the highest compliments that one could pay to a building was to refer to it as "second only to Mount Vernon." A Georgia state regent of the Daughters of the American Revolution spoke of "Meadow Garden" in Augusta, the home of George Walton (a signer of the Declaration of Independence) as "the Mount Vernon of Georgia." [88] In 1906 the following statement was made about the farm where Lincoln was born: "Only a little more than fifty years ago Washington's home at Mount Vernon was going to decay. . . . The voluntary contributions of the American people saved that cherished historical spot. The same people will save the birthplace of the other great American, Abraham Lincoln." [89] A year later the same writer referred to the Lincoln farm as "a worthy companion of Mount Vernon in the affections of our countrymen." [90] In 1912 an advocate of Monticello's preservation said:

> We have two treasure houses—one, Mount Vernon, which, through the Mount Vernon Ladies' Association of the Union, has become a nation's shrine. . . . The other treasure house is Monticello, and I can think of no memorial to Thomas Jefferson more beautiful, more just, more dignified than that Monticello, which he loved so much, should, like Mount Vernon, belong to the Nation.[91]

The Site and Relic Society of Germantown, Pennsylvania, described a mansion it wanted to save in 1914: "Next to Mount Vernon, in Virginia, it is towards Stenton that the footsteps of those interested in colonial homes are turning." [92] In 1917 a member of the D.A.R. chapter in Vincennes, Indiana, spoke of the William Henry Harrison house in that city as a "Second Mount Vernon." [93] One writer in 1923 referred to "Kenmore" in Fredericksburg, Virginia, as a "lesser Mount Vernon." [94]

Some unselective writers and speechmakers included more than one building in the American pantheon along with Mount Vernon: "Gunston Hall, which after Mount Vernon and Monticello is probably the most interesting mansion in Virginia"; [95] and Theodore Roosevelt's birthplace in New York City, ". . . a third American shrine which will be visited in the years to come, as Mount

Vernon and the Lincoln log cabin are now visited by an ever-increasing host of patriotic pilgrims." [96] The examples were almost endless, but they all had one striking feature in common; no matter how extravagant or how conservative the claims for other houses were, no building surpassed Mount Vernon in importance. In fact, only a few were supposed to equal it!

Speaking from a more idealistic view, the Mount Vernon Ladies' Association represented something new and vital. It was one of the first successful women's organizations in the country. Descriptions of the early meetings of the Mount Vernon Association picture the ladies as amazed to find themselves "making speeches and passing resolutions like men!" [97] There is abundant evidence that the influence of Miss Cunningham's work was felt by women in many movements not directly connected with the saving of buildings. The success of the Mount Vernon enterprise began to affect the patriotic movement as a whole. More and more women and men began to realize that Ann Pamela Cunningham had been the pioneer. By 1900 the historian of the National Society of Colonial Dames of America could give Miss Cunningham full credit for leading American women to save Mount Vernon, saying, "The loyalty and good faith of manhood, the gentleness and purity of womanhood, will ever be inseparably associated with the name of Mount Vernon." [98] In 1908 an article about Miss Cunningham, written for the D.A.R., ended on a stirring note: "And while we bow our heads in veneration to our greatest American citizen and hero, let us breathe a word of gratitude and loyalty to the woman who has done this great deed for the nation—Ann Pamela Cunningham." [99]

In the period following the Civil War, the scope of the Mount Vernon movement, together with the influence of the centennials of various phases of the Revolution, combined to create a deeper appreciation of historic sites. Many preservation groups thought that they could imitate the work done by Miss Cunningham, but they all found that she had achieved something that was not likely to be repeated for years to come. Now, as then, far too few preservationists, overwhelmed by the importance of their particular projects, realize how many *other* buildings are supposed to be "second only to Mount Vernon."

III

The South and Its Great Men

FOLLOWING CLOSELY the model offered by the Mount Vernon movement, preservationists in the South attempted to make museums
out of buildings associated with famous men. Unlike the Mount
Vernon Ladies' Association, these southern groups looked to the
federal government or to their respective state governments for
help. The scattered rural population of the South, combined
with the economic distress of the Reconstruction, made locally
financed preservation work difficult except in a few heavy urban
concentrations such as Richmond and Nashville.

The first important post-Mount Vernon preservation in the
South was "Arlington," sometimes called the Lee Mansion. Instead
of being the focal point of a preservation drive, this building was
really a spoil of war. In May of 1861, shortly after the last private
owner, Robert E. Lee, had cast his lot with the South, federal
troops occupied the mansion and the grounds. An old friend of
the Lees used the house as his headquarters, apparently hoping to
protect some of the Lee furnishings that remained.[1] Within a year
the building became a residence for other Union officers and their
families.[2]

Murray Nelligan, historian of Arlington Mansion, believes that
Secretary of War Edwin M. Stanton determined that the Lee family should never occupy their home again. He placed a hospital on
the grounds, along with a freedmen's village for Negro refugees
from the South. Not stopping there, he had a tax levied on the
property which required payment by the owner in person. A relative of Mrs. Lee offered to pay the tax, but the authorities decided

that such a procedure did not fulfill the letter of the law, so the estate was put up for sale at public auction on January 11, 1864, in Alexandria, Virginia.³ Bidding was anything but spirited, because many people suspected that the confiscation and the sale of the mansion might be illegal. The direct tax that had been levied on the Lees might be declared unconstitutional, or the tax commission might later be found guilty of rejecting payment by a relative. Once the sale had ended, the title given to the government might have been considered invalid because the Lees had not been paid the balance of the purchase price. In spite of these uncertainties, the government was the highest bidder and paid itself $26,800 for the property.⁴ Even the sale did not satisfy Stanton's resolve that the property should never fall into the hands of the Lee family again. Through his urging, a national cemetery was established on the grounds in May of 1864. General Meigs, representing the War Department, made sure that some graves were located near the house itself.⁵

Mrs. Lee, now a widow, petitioned Congress in 1872 for some form of compensation for the loss of her estate.⁶ Her effort failed, but a few years later a new figure took up the battle for control of Arlington. General George Washington Custis Lee, son of Robert E. Lee, tried another line of attack. In April of 1874 he argued that his claim to Arlington was a just one, and then he offered to convey the estate to Congress in return for a fair settlement. Congress did not need to reply to his offer, for possession was indeed nine-tenths of the law.⁷ Lee's friends persuaded him to turn to the judiciary. The Arlington case moved up through the courts, reaching the Supreme Court in the 1880's. On December 4, 1882, the Supreme Court decided that George W. C. Lee was the rightful owner of Arlington and that the United States Government had been trespassing. Fortunately, Lee was still willing to settle for a fair price, rather than force the government to move Arlington National Cemetery! ⁸ Congress hastily appropriated $150,000 to pay General Lee for the property; and on the fourteenth of May, 1883, twenty-two years after the Union Army had seized it, the federal government acquired undisputed title to Arlington.⁹

Further proof that the federal "preservation" of Arlington had been an act of revenge was the fact that the first real attempt to furnish and restore the mansion did not come until 1921. At that time a Senator's wife proposed the formation of an association resembling the Mount Vernon Ladies' Association in order to treat the property as a historic site.[10] Not until 1924 did Congress pass a bill authorizing restoration of the house as it had been at the time of the Lee occupancy. The proponents of the bill claimed that it would prove that the bitterness of the Civil War era had been healed.[11] Thus, largely by accident, and for an unsavory purpose, the federal government came to own its first historic house.

The single example of preservation work in the South during the early 1880's scarcely fits the term "preservation," for it was only temporary. When the time came to celebrate the centennial of the British surrender at Yorktown, Virginia, in 1881, the Yorktown Centennial Association was made responsible for all arrangements. One logical part of the celebration was the purchase and rehabilitation of the Moore house, in which Cornwallis had signed the surrender document. The house had been reduced to a shell by bombardment during the Civil War. The association made no effort to restore the structure to its original state, but it did attempt to make the place habitable as a headquarters for visitors. This alteration included the addition of a porch and Victorian trim and the purchase of furniture and bric-a-brac for the interior. The important thing was that the house was structurally sound for the first time in twenty years. Some authorities feel that these repairs served to keep the house standing until it came into the hands of the National Park Service more than forty-five years later. Once the celebration ended in the fall of 1881, the property was resold back into private ownership. Consequently, one can hardly claim that the Moore house was preserved in 1881; it was merely strengthened fortuitously so that it was able to endure until the forces of preservation caught up with it again.[12]

The Association for the Preservation of Virginia Antiquities was the first large private preservation group to appear in the South after the Civil War. Founded in the spring of 1888, it was not limited particularly to men or women (although its membership lists show many more women than men), nor was it hereditary in its requirements for membership. The event which was supposedly the immediate cause of the founding of the A.P.V.A. was the collapse of an old brick ruin known as "Powhatan's Chimney." Miss Mary J. Galt and her mother noticed a newspaper item about this incident, and they agreed that something should be done to save what remained of the antiquities of Virginia. They called informal meetings in Williamsburg; then, late in 1888, in conjunction with a friend in Norfolk, they adopted the title Association for the Preservation of Virginia Antiquities. The association's first acquisition—purchased by Miss Galt—was an old building in Williamsburg known as the Powder Magazine, dating from pre-Revolutionary times. A year later the Virginia legislature gave the society a charter permitting it to own property in the state.[13]

The major interest of the A.P.V.A. after the year 1893 was the preservation of Jamestown Island. In 1904 the acting president declared that "the persistent efforts of the Association for its protection" had prevented the James River from washing away what was left of the historic section of the island. It appears certain that the great emphasis placed upon building a retaining wall at Jamestown Island, combined with the tremendous cost of upkeep and relative inaccessibility of the many Virginia mansions, prevented the group from doing much preservation work in that state.[14]

Before the A.P.V.A. began to expend its energies on Jamestown, it managed to rescue one historic house—the home of Mary Washington, George Washington's mother, in Fredericksburg. Mrs. Vivian Minor Fleming, the lady most closely connected with the campaign, tells the story:

> It was in May, 1890, that an agent came from Chicago to buy this Mary Washington cottage, to take it down [and] erect it again to grace the Columbian Exposition. The owner was willing to sell but demanded a high price. The agent said he must write back to Chicago.
>
> In the meantime, Mrs. R. C. Beale, who occupied part of the house, had overheard the conversation. She thought quickly. The Association for the Preservation of Virginia Antiquities had recently been formed and Mrs. Joseph Bryan of Richmond was President. She had a sister-in-law, Mrs. Spottswood Carmichael, living in Fredericksburg.
>
> Mrs. Beale put on her bonnet (they wore bonnets in those days) and hurried to Mrs. Carmichael. "Tucker," she said, "there is a man here from Chicago trying to buy the Mary Washington house. Telegraph your sister-in-law and ask if she and her new society can't save it."
>
> The telegram was sent and the immediate reply said, "Will give

$4,500." The place was bought on that authorization. Immediately an Association branch was formed in Fredericksburg and the movement began to repay the money to Mrs. Bryan, who had advanced it without interest.[15]

By 1896 the nine members of the Fredericksburg branch had raised almost $600 through a combination of membership fees, a colonial ball, and rent from rooms in the house itself.[16] In the years that followed, the Fredericksburg ladies were anxious to exhibit some of the rooms in the Mary Washington cottage, but their project was delayed because the additional rent from the rooms helped to finance the Jamestown preservation and aided in the purchase of old furniture for the house.[17] Still, the members never lost sight of their goal—the wholly restored Mary Washington cottage. They found some furnishings and continued to keep the building in good repair. In addition, this small group also took on the care of the Rising Sun Tavern in Fredericksburg, first renting it to tenants, then exhibiting it.[18]

After the turn of the century the A.P.V.A. centered its activities more in the Richmond area, making the John Marshall house its headquarters. The city acquired the property as part of the site for a proposed high school. Not long after it learned of this action, the association adopted plans to preserve the house. After considerable effort and much testimony in hearings, the association gained custody of the house in 1911.[19] A John Marshall House Committee set to work on the dual task of furnishing and rehabilitating the house, whenever possible obtaining pieces that had belonged to the Marshall family. The leaders of the A.P.V.A. appealed to bar associations for funds to further the restoration of the home of the great Chief Justice. Soon donations began to pour in, and within two years lawyers all over the nation gave over $2,500.[20] Later on, when the upkeep of the house grew to be an annual expense of some magnitude, the A.P.V.A. made vain attempts to raise an endowment from legal organizations.[21]

In 1914 the association was presented with another building in Richmond called the "Old Stone House," supposed to be the oldest structure in town.[22] After operating it for a few years, the association turned it over to the Poe Shrine in 1924.[23]

Although the A.P.V.A. was not strictly a patriotic or hereditary women's organization, it had many of the strengths and weaknesses of such a group. For instance, in the early 1890's the association used dances called "colonial balls" as one of its most successful money-raising schemes. One article on the association's activities contained a description of Richmond socialites disguised as John Rolfe, Pocahontas, and John Smith, dancing for the benefit of Jamestown Island.[24] The A.P.V.A. suffered from a malady that plagued many similar societies for years: it had to establish clearly the identity of its founder. The question arose in 1900 and was settled by a study of the efforts of Miss Galt of Norfolk and Williamsburg.[25] By 1923 that answer was no longer satisfactory, so a committee set out to determine just who should receive credit for the founding. Again Miss Galt won first place, but Mrs. Cynthia Coleman of Williamsburg shared the honors.[26] These efforts to locate a founder seemed harmless, but they constituted a digression from the work of preserving antiquities. One of the association's New England members, William S. Appleton, chided the A.P.V.A. for ignoring some historic buildings in the Old Dominion. The A.P.V.A. president sadly admitted, "It is a little mortifying to receive letters from life members, natives of other states, calling to our attention the neglect of Virginia's old public buildings. . . ." [27] Appleton found other shortcomings in the operations of the association. He wrote to the director of the Baltimore Art Museum in 1923, "[The association] does good work in a quiet way but is, I believe, somewhat given to tablets and memorials and working, as I understand it does, through chapters its energies are somewhat widely dissipated." [28]

Many of the A.P.V.A. members in the Richmond area were interested in other historical causes, such as the proper veneration of Confederate heroes. Shortly after the Civil War, some Richmond ladies had formed the Hollywood Memorial Association in order to decorate the graves of those men who had given their lives for the Confederacy. Mrs. Joseph Bryan, one of the leaders of the A.P.V.A., was president of the Hollywood Memorial Association in 1890, at a time when an important historic property required attention. She heard that the White House of the Confederacy, which was then being used as a school, was in some danger. Mrs. Bryan urged the formation of a new group, the Confederate Memorial Literary Society, with the intention that this organization would petition the City of Richmond to move the school and give the building to them. Finally in 1894 the city did turn the building over to the ladies after they had conducted a most successful Memorial Bazaar which yielded $15,000 for furnishing the new museum. The Literary Society received another $15,000 in donations after widespread advertising in southern newspapers. After a year of work on the building, the society opened it in 1896 as a Confederate museum. Each room was assigned to a state in the Confederacy, and each state was represented by a regent and a vice-regent (the latter residing in Richmond). Apparently the building filled with Confederate relics faster than the ladies expected—for there was talk of an additional museum building before long. By the end of the century the house was functioning as a museum with a nominal admission fee which was waived on Saturdays in order to encourage Richmond school children to come learn the "lesson of Constitutional Liberty." [29]

One significant restoration effort in Virginia should be mentioned in passing, for it was to bear rich fruit in the future. The vestry of Bruton Parish Church in Williamsburg, under the leadership of the Reverend W. A. R. Goodwin, voted to begin a restoration of the church edifice in May of 1903. Although it was costly and inconvenient, the work consumed nearly four years. When the little church reopened in 1907, most people were satisfied that it had been returned to its eighteenth-century appearance.[30]

While Miss Galt and other Virginians were busy saving some of the antiquities on the seaboard, the Ladies' Hermitage Association appeared in Nashville, Tennessee. This group, organized not to serve a whole region but to help a state preserve only one building, attempted to follow the example of Ann Pamela Cunningham and failed. It did succeed in its primary objective, the creation of an Andrew Jackson museum at the Hermitage. The immediate threat which created the necessity for the association was a bill in the Tennessee legislature that would have set the Hermitage property aside for twenty-five years as a home for Confederate soldiers. (Here was one of the few times where the aspirations of veterans ran directly counter to those of preservationists.)[31] A small group of Nashville ladies came to the conclusion that the proposed use of the house would destroy its value as a shrine. At a meeting with the proponents of the veterans' home, just before the opening of the legislature, the women tried to find a middle ground, but to no avail. They were determined to keep the Hermitage property intact, with 300 acres to enable the farm to support itself.[32] At a second meeting the men who had introduced the bill offered to set aside the house and 25 acres for the ladies. Again the meeting ended with no agreement.[33]

With some determined leadership in the person of Mrs. Mary C. Dorris of Nashville, the ladies began a real campaign. Mrs. Dorris wrote a preamble for a charter establishing the Ladies' Hermitage Association and obtained signatures from five prominent Nashville women.[34] In February of 1889 Mrs. Dorris, whose husband was a newsman, began peppering the Nashville papers with letters and articles pleading the cause of the association. She did not mince words:

> If such an Association is not formed now, it will never be, for this seems to be a crisis in the fate of the Hermitage. It may seem a little thing now and even a noble one to pervert it to other uses; but when the twenty-five years have rolled away and it is too late, the generation of that day will say: "What a pity it was that Jackson's home was not preserved!" . . . That Jackson's home should have remained so nearly as it was at the time of his death, forty-four years ago, is something remarkable and owing to the fact that the State allowed Andrew Jackson, Jr., and his son subsequently to occupy the premises.[35]

State Senator Crews, who had proposed the idea of a Confederate soldiers' home, amended his own bill to convey conditionally the Hermitage and twenty-five acres around it to the association. The bill was signed by the governor on April 6, 1889. It created a group of nine male "trustees" to oversee the efforts of the ladies —strangely reminiscent of the Board of Visitors that had been set up in Virginia to supervise the Mount Vernon Association. Women were not yet trusted to run their affairs unassisted.[36]

The women had to care for the property without any state appropriation for several years, so Mrs. Dorris and her friends appealed to the public for support. They found a composer who was willing to stage an operetta entitled *Birds of Tennessee* which finally netted the association $125. This was just the first of a multitude of fund-raising activities that ranged from concerts to dances.[37] Male supporters of the enterprise advised Mrs. Dorris and the other women to print an appeal to the general public and circulate it widely. Mrs. Dorris was not one to do things halfway; she had 10,000 booklets published stating the association's two main objectives: preservation of the Hermitage and purchase of the Jackson relics still in the possession of the family. The booklet ended on this note: "We hope that this appeal will strike the key-note of patriotism and that in a very few years the home of Andrew Jackson, the beautiful Hermitage, will be the Mecca of all true patriots in the United States and of historic interest to the touring stranger." [38] Evidently 10,000 booklets were too many, for years later Mrs. Dorris was still dispensing copies from her original store.

Mrs. Dorris' wish for a "Mecca" was not soon to be realized, mainly because of the isolation of the Hermitage in the period just before the automobile. The problem was made painfully evident in July, 1889, when the ladies invited delegates to the National Education Association Convention in Nashville to see the newly opened house. The boat landing was three miles away, as was the railroad station. In planning the excursion, the association had to engage wagons of all types to transport the visitors to the farm.[39] The next year the association made strenuous efforts to have railroad service to the Hermitage, but it was not able to raise the required sum of money, so the project failed.[40]

The major task confronting the Ladies' Hermitage Association was the furnishing of the building, not its preservation. Ironically, the original Jackson relics were still in use inside the house, but they were owned by the family! Colonel and Mrs. Jackson set a price of $17,500 for the furnishings and gave the association a four-year option on them in 1889. At that time the Jacksons were having financial difficulties, for the creation of the Confederate home had reduced their farm from five hundred acres to twenty-five. The ladies agreed to pay 3 percent a year on the purchase price in order to support the Jacksons.[41] The only large donation came from the millionaire Henry M. Flagler who permitted the association to use the Ponce de Leon Hotel in St. Augustine, Florida, for a grand ball. This benefit netted $2,082, which the ladies put in the bank as a "nest egg" toward the purchase of the relics. When the option expired in July, 1893, the Jacksons moved out of the Hermitage with all of their furniture.[42] The loss was not permanent, however; at the time of the Tennessee Centennial celebration in 1896, Colonel Jackson wrote to the association from

Cincinnati offering Andrew Jackson's state coach for a reasonable price. The coach was purchased, and the relics began to flow back to the Hermitage, room by room.[43] By 1907 the ladies had raised $27,721, the greater part of which they spent on the furniture.[44]

The Ladies' Hermitage Association had a reasonably satisfactory relationship with the state government. After the lean years of the early 1890's, Mrs. Marks, first vice-regent of the association and wife of an ex-governor, went before the legislature and secured an appropriation of fifty dollars a month for the care and upkeep of the property. Just after the turn of the century the state voted $1,000 for improvements and repairs; and in 1911 Tennessee doubled its monthly payments to the association.[45]

The association was unique in one other way—it was the only private preservation organization to receive financial aid from the United States Government prior to 1926. In 1907 President Theodore Roosevelt came to see the Hermitage. He was so impressed with what he saw that he promised to ask the next Congress for an appropriation to help the ladies.[46] In his message to Congress on December 4, 1907, Roosevelt kept his word. The bill in the Senate called for a grant of $25,000, one-fifth of which would be paid immediately and the balance put into United States Bonds as a fund for the Hermitage Association.[47] In its report to the Senate the next February, the Library Committee decided that the memory of Jackson was worthy of such an appropriation. When the bill actually reached the Senate floor, there was considerable confusion. Many Senators had the impression that the government was buying the property and believed that there was no precedent for such action—until it was explained that the sum in question was merely a contribution to the association. Only the $5,000 cash payment passed; the $20,000 reserve fund never came into being.[48]

As the nineteenth century wore on, the figure of Abraham Lincoln became a focal point in preservationist thought throughout the Midwest and Middle Atlantic States. In areas where he had lived people began to look for some reminders of his career. The first to be saved was his homestead, in Springfield, Illinois. In 1883 Osborn H. Oldroyd, an avid collector of objects connected with the life of President Lincoln, rented the Lincoln house and opened it as a museum. Oldroyd tried to get Robert Lincoln, the President's only surviving son, to give the property to the State of Illinois, but Lincoln was afraid that some political purpose might be imputed to such an act. Finally some prominent members of the Illinois legislature did succeed in persuading Robert Lincoln to turn the house over to a board of trustees set up by the state in 1887.[49] The new trustees asked Oldroyd to remain as custodian, and he promised to leave his collection to the state in return for a reasonable salary.[50]

The worship of Lincoln extended to the District of Columbia in the next decade. A group of distinguished and influential men (among whom was the Chief Justice of the United States Supreme Court) chartered the Memorial Association of the District of Columbia in 1892. Its object was to save "the most noteworthy houses at the Capital that have been made historic by the residence of the nation's greatest men." The association intended to mark other houses with tablets for the instruction of visitors to Washington.[51] The organization was to consist of only twenty-seven men: nine appointed by the President of the United States, nine by the President of the Senate, and nine by the Speaker of the House of Representatives. An act of Congress outlined the manner in which the association was to function. It was to "preserve some of the historical places here by appropriations from Congress making these places national property." That is, whenever a piece of property was purchased, the title was to rest with the government, not with the association.[52]

The Memorial Association began its preservation career in July, 1892, by renting the House Where Lincoln Died (also known as the Peterson house) at 516 Tenth Street in Washington.[53] Shortly afterward, the association succeeded in getting Oldroyd to bring his collection of Lincoln relics to Washington. He had just been ousted as custodian of the Lincoln homestead by Governor Altgeld of Illinois.[54]

The maintenance of the Peterson house tested the patience and the pocketbooks of the members of the association. From 1892 until 1896 the distinguished gentlemen of the Memorial Association paid the rent on the house, hoping that Congress would assume the burden. Finally the association forced a $50,000 item for the purchase of the property onto the Sundry Civil Appropriation Bill for the next year (1897). The Congressmen at the hearing brought up a point that was to appear at many future hearings dealing with historic houses. Sentimental values are speculative, and the government cannot pay for them; Congress can only appropriate enough for the "commercial" value of land. In the case of the Peterson house, extended testimony resulted in an estimate of $30,000 as its real value. The reasoning must have been convincing, since the final purchase price was exactly that amount. Once the bill had been worded, the chairman of the House committee warned the members of the association that the proposed appropriation would be subject to a point of order by any member of the House. He really meant that any Representative could strike the item from the bill.[55] Representative Sayers of Texas, who had introduced the measure, was not an advocate of government spending. In spite of these formidable obstacles the amendment went unchallenged in the House and moved on to the Senate where there was little opposition.[56]

1896 appeared to be an auspicious time for any preservation effort connected with the name of Lincoln. Two things in particular favored such a project. First, Lincoln was never more popular than he had become by the 1890's, a time when people were trying to erase completely the scars of the Civil War. He was a figure that Southerners and Northerners could admire. Second, the number of buildings actually proven to have some important connection with Lincoln was small. At the hearing on the Peterson house, the members of the Memorial Association testified that this building was the only one in Washington, aside from the White House, that illustrated the career of Lincoln. They had tried in vain to locate the boardinghouse where he had lived as a member of the House of Representatives.[57]

In presenting their case to the Congressional committee, the association members used a technique that other groups were to employ in the years that followed. They printed a booklet entitled *Words from Many Sources,* which was a compilation of letters from notable Americans from all walks of life, telling their individual reasons for favoring the preservation of the House Where Lincoln Died. It is difficult to rate the effectiveness of the booklet, since the discussion in some later hearings leads one to believe that overdependence upon testimonial letters often antagonized members of Congress who preferred to make up their own minds concerning the advisability of purchasing a building.[58]

The federal government acquired one more historic house in 1900 when the Shirley house was added to Vicksburg National Military Park in Mississippi. Geographic position, not history, was the main consideration here. The Shirley house was right on the top of the ridge that marked the Confederate defenses of the city. Two years after the purchase of the battlefield, the Secretary of War authorized the restoration of the Shirley house to its Civil War appearance. Although the house itself had not figured prominently in the battle, it was the only structure in the park that had survived the siege.[59]

With the exception of the A.P.V.A., every example of preservation work in the South after the Civil War became involved with the federal, state or local government. At this stage Southerners apparently thought that their region lacked the private financial resources to purchase and maintain houses of purely local interest, in the fashion characteristic of New England. In seeking government aid, southern preservationists selected buildings that were directly connected with heroes whose names could call forth support from large areas. No economy-minded legislator, north or south, cared to place himself in the position of blocking a step that would consecrate the hallowed names of Washington, Jackson and Lincoln.

IV

The Middle Atlantic States:
Restoring Memorials of the Revolution

THE AREA BETWEEN THE HUDSON VALLEY AND PHILADELPHIA contained many of the battlefields of the Revolution and possessed the advantage of a large urban and suburban population. Here was an ideal setting for preservation activity. It is not surprising to find that more historic buildings were preserved in the Middle Atlantic States than in the South prior to 1926. Unlike the southern birthplaces and homesteads, most of the historic sites saved in the area north of the Potomac were either headquarters associated with the Revolution or buildings connected with important events in the early days of the nation. Preservationists in this region usually sought support from state governments, often copying their brethren to the south in this respect.

The first significant preservation in the Middle Atlantic States after the Civil War did not fit the pattern described above. It was the enclosure of a number of handsome eighteenth- and early nineteenth-century houses as a part of Fairmount Park in growing Philadelphia. The motive was anything but bona fide preservationism. The Fairmount Park idea began when the City of Philadelphia constructed some waterworks on the Schuylkill River shortly after the War of 1812. A second area, containing a house called Lemon Hill, became city property in 1844 because a group of citizens wanted the city to protect the water supply of the Schuylkill River from commercial pollution.[1] Gradually the Lemon Hill section became a place reserved for public use.[2] The enabling act of 1867 that actually created Fairmount Park states forthrightly that the underlying "idea in originating the scheme of a park of great extent and beauty was to provide a place in which the poorer classes of . . . fellow citizens and their families might find health and recreation." [3] These sentiments reflected the beginnings of a civic-mindedness that rebelled at the crowding in urban industrial slums. Nevertheless, the end result was that a score of notable houses were saved which otherwise certainly would have been destroyed with the onward march of the city.

The people of Philadelphia were in the process of putting together one of the largest city parks in the world, and so the historic houses in the area had to serve some public purpose. Here is what the first chief engineer of the park, John Cresson, had to say about some of the best formal eighteenth-century architecture that has come down to us:

> Another building on the Sweetbriar grounds, west of the Schuylkill, has also been partially fitted up for the use of the officer engaged on the improvements in this vicinity.
>
> There are many other old mansions upon various portions of the Park grounds, which may be usefully applied to similar purposes, and also as residences for persons employed, whose presence in the extensive domain will be of service in preventing dangers that might arise, if the whole of its large area should be left uninhabited. . . .[4]

Cresson soon put his utilitarian ideas into practice, for he had Sweetbriar opened as a children's playground, and Woodford, one of the most graceful houses in the park, remodeled as his family quarters.[5] The Commissioners of Fairmount Park marked certain houses for destruction unless a use could be found for them. One of the better homes, Strawberry, was supposed to be torn down so that its debris could fill an unattractive gully. Only a last-minute decision of the Park Commission, at the instigation of an interested member, saved the mansion.[6]

An 1871 guidebook lauded the commissioners for their alleged intent to "restore" one park house and thus give a picture of Revolutionary days; but absolutely nothing came of it for half a century.[7] The city briefly turned in the direction of historic preservation when it moved an eighteenth-century town house into the park in 1883. The building was known as William Penn's cottage, a claim that does not seem to have been substantiated by research.[8] For many years afterward, the houses in Fairmount Park remained forgotten; the City of Philadelphia subordinated thoughts of restoration to a desire for a large recreation area.

Most of the preservation work in the Middle Atlantic States in the late nineteenth century was carried on by patriotic groups who hoped to save sites associated with the grim years of the Revolution. Within a fifty-mile radius of Manhattan Island there were a number of houses that served for varying periods of time as headquarters for George Washington and his generals. Not all of them had equal historic or architectural interest, and the authenticity of a few is still in question. Yet the golden aura which Washington's touch conferred upon each of his headquarters has preserved for posterity several stately historic edifices. With unerring instinct the Commander in Chief had selected for his headquarters the largest and finest buildings in every town he visited. As soon as Washington left such a house, no matter how short his stay, nothing was ever the same again. Frequently the structure became known simply as "Washington's Headquarters" (regardless of how many others there might have been within twenty miles), and the owners often preserved the furniture and fittings that Washington had used.

The Ford Mansion in Morristown, New Jersey, was the second of the Washington headquarters to attract public attention—after the famous Hasbrouck house in Newburgh. The Ford home had been occupied by Washington for a long period of time, and it had some architectural appeal. The story of its rescue is significant not only because it preceded the increased interest in the Revolution caused by the Philadelphia Centennial celebrations, but also because the organization involved was a men's group at a time when the preservation movement seemed to be a woman's crusade.

In the spring of 1873 local newspapers in northern New Jersey began to warn the public that the historic Ford Mansion would be sold at auction by the heirs of Henry A. Ford of Morristown. There were many suggestions for utilizing the headquarters: a historical society, a Y.M.C.A., or at least the home of a wealthy citizen who would appreciate its importance.[9] These newspaper articles, combined with advertisements for the sale of the property, must have stimulated some patriotic enthusiasm.

The Sacred Relic of Revolutionary Times Should attract the attention of every lover of his country. The dwelling house, around which cluster the associations our memories delight to dwell upon, Is 99 years old, and it is good For 99 years more. The Mansion will be open during the day for the inspection of Visitors, and the sacred associations of our Revolutionary days ought to secure a large and appreciative attendance.[10]

The historical associations of the mansion did indeed draw a large crowd for the sale which was held on the twenty-fifth of June, 1873. Several building lots around the house were sold; then a Masonic sash worn by Washington brought a high price. Finally the Ford Mansion itself was put on the block. Bidding began at $10,000 and moved upward past $20,000. Ex-Governor Theodore Randolph, General N. N. Halstead (husband of the Mount Vernon vice-regent), and the Honorable George A. Halsey "were trying to find a fourth person to join with them and hold the property for the State." The governor went before the crowd and announced the intentions of his group. He declared that he was so unwilling that this house should pass into "strange hands" that he would take a second share himself if necessary. At that point a Mr. W. V. Lidgerwood came forward and explained that the last bid of $24,100 was his and that he had had the same object in view. The four made common cause and purchased the house for $25,000, promising to offer it to the state at cost.[11]

It is important to consider why these men saved the Ford Mansion with the intent of turning it over to the State of New Jersey. Such a purpose would have been unlikely in New England, but in the Middle Atlantic States it was not unusual. Again it must be remembered that New York already had one historic house museum, and Philadelphia had been exhibiting the Assembly Room of Independence Hall for at least two decades. Some may wonder why four men should band together and raise $25,000 in 1873 to save this old building when the commercial value of the property without the house was increasing steadily. At least part of the motivation may be found in a speech given July 5, 1875, by ex-Governor Randolph, one of the collaborators:

... This historic mansion will become a "Mecca," toward which all patriotic Jerseymen will from time to time turn their steps, finding in time of peace a grateful repose from life's turmoil, and in times of danger to the country's peace or welfare obtain, as from a pure fountain, inspiration to patriotic purpose.[12]

So much for purposes. More important was the fact that the state did not take title to the house. Instead, the four men managed to get from the legislature a charter, approved on March 20, 1874, which named a distinguished group of Morris County men as the incorporators of a new organization. The men owned shares of stock in this corporation, the Washington Association of New Jersey. These shares could not be disposed of by direct sale; they could only be passed down to male descendants or to the state. The charter also established that the headquarters must be open free of charge as a historic museum with certain portions set aside for the State Historical Society. In return, the property was to be exempt from taxation and was to receive each year two payments from the state, each amounting to $1,250, to be used for care and maintenance. This close tie with the state can be partially explained by the fact that the incorporators were gentlemen of wealth and political prominence.[13]

It was almost no time before a problem arose to mar the harmonious relationship between the Washington Association and the state. A constitutional amendment was passed prohibiting payments of public money to private organizations after the year 1875, so the allowance paid to the association was halted. Fortunately the State Supreme Court decided in 1877 that the association's charter was valid, and payments were resumed. Once the state funds began to come in, the association formally acquired title to the property from the four original buyers.[14]

The members of the association continued to look for new ways to reduce the debt on the house. In 1875 they experimented with the idea of having a ladies' auxiliary. Although the idea fell somewhat short of realization, the women of Morristown held teas and parties at the headquarters and raised money to help the association.[15] At this same time the association made repairs to the mansion that included a restoration of the hall to its original dimensions. Some of the changes made at that time have been a great puzzle to restorers who have worked on the house in more recent times.[16] In 1884 the members made the first of many un-successful attempts to obtain money from the United States Con-gress. In a resolution put before the House of Representatives, the men asked for $25,000 to be used for "enlarging and improving the grounds, collections, and buildings of Washington's Head-quarters," and for the purchase of a Revolutionary cemetery nearby.[17] No money was ever forthcoming from Congress; nor was the Washington Association the last preservation group to be de-nied federal assistance.

By the 1890's, with the patriotic movement in full swing, the Washington Association achieved a position of some importance in the preservation movement. The building in its charge brought more than 9,000 visitors a year to Morristown.[18] The story of the association serves to illustrate the great willingness to work with governmental agencies that characterized the Middle Atlantic States, while its charter and its all-male membership were unique. In other parts of the country twenty years went by before men were to become as important as women in preservation work.

In the decade that followed the Civil War a new influence spread throughout the field of preservation. It was the enthusiasm generated by the Centennial celebration in Philadelphia. While the Centennial probably aroused more interest in the American Revolution than in old buildings as such, the latter could not fail to attract some attention. Comments made after the Centennial year (1876) by people who had traveled to Philadelphia show that many discovered they had "a past worthy of study." [19] Some ob-servers were fascinated by the Revolutionary relics that they saw and went home with a deeper interest in the war itself; others said that they gained a desire to learn more of the heroic deeds of the Continental Army and would take steps "to preserve such deeds from oblivion." [20]

The only building that profited directly from the Centennial observance was that shrine of patriotism, Independence Hall. Al-though the Assembly Room had already been set aside for the exhibition of relics by the 1850's, much remained to be done. The principal mover in the second restoration of Independence Hall was Colonel Frank M. Etting of Philadelphia. In April of 1871 he addressed a letter to the Philadelphia Committee of Councils on the Centennial, pleading for the restoration of the Independence chamber to its original appearance. Etting claimed that he had located four of the chairs that had been in the room at the time of the signing of the Declaration. He recommended that these chairs, together with portraits of the men who had debated the question of independence, should replace the "depository for miscellaneous portraits and objects of various sorts" which then defaced the Assembly Room.[21] Two years later, in 1873, Etting published a booklet entitled *Memorials of 1776* in which he asked the City of Philadelphia to consider setting aside the rest of Independence Hall as a national museum. He argued, "Such a practical mode of object instruction will continue to teach to all coming generations of Americans the lesson learned in 1776, and about to be rehearsed in 1876—that in national unity lies our strength. . . ." He proposed that the courtroom across the hall from the Assembly Room be set up as the museum with portraits and relics illustrating "different epochs" in American history.[22]

On the strength of his interest and influence, Etting became chairman of the Committee on the Restoration of Independence Hall in 1873. For more than two years this group labored to fulfill each part of Etting's design. The committee had the Liberty Bell moved into the tower, and refurnished the Assembly Room with the chairs that Etting had located. The committee also added four pillars to support the ceiling in both of the downstairs rooms, using the word of an older citizen as the guideline. By 1876 the exterior of the building had been cleaned by means of acid which was used to remove the paint. When the time came for the actual Centennial celebration, Independence Hall resembled Etting's vision of a national museum—at least on the first floor. Although there are things that one can criticize about the taste and the scholarship of the Etting restoration, there is no question that the good colonel did much to put Independence Hall before the public as a place of patriotic pilgrimage.[23]

Immediately following the Philadelphia fair, a group of people in Valley Forge organized "The Centennial Association of Valley Forge," in order to commemorate the hundredth anniversary of the departure of Washington's army from that encampment. The following February (1878) a committee of the new association reported that it would be in keeping with the spirit of Philadelphia to purchase the old Washington headquarters building at Valley

Forge. The committee suggested that the work be put in the hands of a group of ladies, the leader of whom was to be called a lady regent. Mrs. Holstein, who had corresponded with Mrs. Sweat at Mount Vernon, was chosen.[24] At the celebration on June 19, 1878, Henry Armitt Brown gave a stirring patriotic address. He told of the events that had taken place in the headquarters and spoke of the lesson to be learned by having groups meet at historic spots to commemorate sacrifices which had been made there. The ardor engendered by his address presumably helped the women in their efforts to raise the money for the purchase of the building.[25]

The ladies attempted to form a Mount Vernon-type national organization.[26] Mrs. Holstein worked diligently at her job as lady regent and managed to get $3,000 (perhaps half the purchase price) for the opening of the house on June 19, 1879.[27] This was a creditable achievement, though hardly comparable with Ann Pamela Cunningham's success at Mount Vernon. Mrs. Holstein was a sufficiently devoted champion of her cause. Unfortunately the building she was trying to save was not the home of Washington. Although she had competent orators at Valley Forge, there was no Edward Everett to tour the country for her.

At the dedication ceremonies for the Valley Forge headquarters the audience was greeted with a torrent of oratory which reveals to us much of the spirit with which patriotic campaigns were conducted in the early days of the preservation movement. Here are two vibrant excerpts:

> Let us indulge the hope that it may long remain—a fountain to which the people of our beloved land may ever turn and drink inspiration from the memories with which it is associated, and which cluster around and about it.[28]

> How precious are the old memories in our own homes and households! The ring worn by a beloved mother now in her grave, how we cherish the holy thing! . . . As with home, so with country. Patriotism is not merely a sentiment; it is a principle born in our nature and part of our humanity. Therefore we rejoice in the present, and honor those who in other years labored and died to make our nation great. Home and country! alike in the heart's best affections; present enjoyment and happy memory increase our devotion to both and intensify our patriotism. We are here to-day to

illustrate history and perpetuate these memories. The ladies of this "Association" by and through its organization, desire to accomplish this. May they be successful; and by your generous help they will. When patriotism ceases to be a virtue, and liberty be known only as a name, then and not till then, will Valley Forge, with its romantic and heroic memories, be forgotten.[29]

Former Governor James Pollock predicted that Valley Forge was going to be the "American Mecca." Indeed, it was a stock article of preservationist faith that each particular historic house would become a "Mecca" for the faithful. But how many meccas would the American people be willing to visit in one lifetime, before the arrival of the automobile age?

Morristown and Valley Forge were only two of the best-known Washington headquarters to attract attention during the Centennial years. The *Magazine of American History* in 1879 actually prepared a list of the General's headquarters and welcomed additions from interested subscribers! The list included a detailed account of the condition of each building and the names of the owners.[30] This particular periodical was the first of several that began to publish articles on historic houses during the 1880's and 1890's. Most of the accounts were descriptive and included a picture or two. Often the authors did not intend to give active support to the preservation movement; they simply acquainted the public with interesting buildings that were extant. Usually the articles stressed the romantic elements in the history of each structure, as do guidebooks of today.

One of the most unusual preservation efforts in the United States was a fruit of the Centennial of the signing of the Declaration of Independence. Thomas Donaldson, a middle-class Philadelphian with a passionate desire for historical accuracy, found that in 1876 four houses were pointed out to visitors as the spot where Jefferson wrote the Declaration. Over a period of several years he went through every available bit of evidence then in print and satisfied himself that one of these houses—700 Market Street—was the right one. His research appears to have been thorough, for the site of the house still bears a historical marker. Donaldson learned in 1882 that the Penn National Bank had purchased Number 700 Market and the house next door with the intention of tearing them down to make way for a new bank building. There was little or no protest to the sale or the possible destruction of the house.[31]

Donaldson decided to oppose the forces of "progress" all by himself. He wrote to Professor Baird, secretary of the Smithsonian Institution in Washington, and found that there was some hope that the Jefferson house (as it was called) could be rebuilt on the grounds of the Smithsonian.[32] In order to further this plan Donaldson made an agreement with the bank whereby he would buy the materials from the building on Market Street whenever it might be torn down. The bank was to notify him when this would take place. Unfortunately Donaldson had assumed too much in his dealings with the bank president.

> Early on the morning of Wednesday, February 28, 1883 (there was snow on the ground), I was riding down Market street in a street-car. We halted on the opposite side of Seventh and Market and I happened to look up at a dormer window on the Jefferson house, No. 700 Market street, when I saw a man come out of the window with an iron bar in his hand. I dismounted from the car at once. Presently another one came out, and after a bit, a dozen or more men, similarly armed, were on the roof of the historic house. I saw a huge Celt, at the word of command, thrust his crowbar under the shingles of the roof, and the destruction of one of the most historic buildings on the globe was begun.[33]

Donaldson tore over to the bank and demanded an explanation. The bewildered president finally discovered that a mistake had been made, and he authorized the contractor to give the irate Donaldson all the interior woodwork, most of the exterior decorations and the bricks from the second floor (where Jefferson had lodged). The bill for this material came to seventy-five dollars.[34] After storing the relics for a while in the basement of a friend's home, Donaldson removed them to a lot next to his house where he put them under a shed.[35] Finally he tried to stir the conscience of his fellow Americans by publishing a book in 1898 under the title *The House in Which Thomas Jefferson Wrote the Declaration of Independence.* In it Donaldson described each of the houses that was supposed to contain Jefferson's rooms—and then he told in scathing terms the story of his effort to save the relics.[36] He even objected to the placement of the historical marker on the bank building, pointing out that the tablet was actually not on the site of Number 700 Market Street.[37] Apparently nothing remains of the fragments that Donaldson rescued from the Jefferson house.[38]

Early in the 1890's a number of new patriotic societies in the Philadelphia area began to look for a worthy object on which to expend their energies just as the City Councils of Philadelphia were preparing to vacate the second floor of Independence Hall. A host of people joined a movement in 1894 for a total restoration of the venerable building.[39] The first patriotic organization to take an interest in the opportunity provided by the vacant second floor was the Pennsylvania Society of the Colonial Dames of America. The Colonial Dames petitioned the city to give them custody of the whole building, but the Committee on City Property refused to grant such powers to one organization.[40] The *Philadelphia Inquirer* supported this decision editorially by pointing out that the Colonial Dames were too small a group of women to handle such a task, and many of the ancestors honored by the Dames had opposed the Revolution itself. The *Inquirer* printed a cartoon which depicted a Quaker (representing Philadelphia) jealously keeping Independence Hall out of the reach of an imploring Colonial Dame. The caption read, "Nay, Nay, Pauline." [41]

The Colonial Dames reacted wisely by scaling down their request. In late 1894 the city granted them the right to carry out a restoration of the old Senate Chamber in Congress Hall, another building on Independence Square. Throughout the winter of 1896 the Dames paid for the work and provided a knowledgeable member of the Philadelphia Chapter of the American Institute of Architects, George C. Mason, to serve as supervisor. The whole effort was a notable success.[42]

The Sons of the Revolution and the Philadelphia Chapter of the D.A.R. engaged in a battle over the custody of Independence Hall for nearly a year. The Sons won the use of the second-floor rooms by means of an ordinance passed in April of 1895.[43] That should have settled the issue, but it did not. The D.A.R. politely asked the Sons for the right to hold four meetings a year in the coveted rooms. The gentlemen replied that only the city could give that permission, so the Daughters marched down to City Hall and obtained an ordinance that placed them on an equal footing with the Sons of the Revolution. Soon the Daughters tried to get the Sons to join them in forming a restoration committee—with no result. The Sons reacted by threatening to leave unless the city gave them sole custody of the building, which the city refused to do. On March 17, 1896, the Sons of the Revolution withdrew, leaving the D.A.R. in control.[44]

Independence Hall, now securely in the public eye, underwent a far-reaching restoration over the next few years. The D.A.R. began the process by donating money for the restoration of the second floor of the building. T. Mellon Rogers, a young Philadelphia architect, offered his services as a gift. The D.A.R. chapter and Rogers, each equipped with more enthusiasm than knowledge, began to plan changes in Independence Hall with some help from local historians.[45] The only force powerful enough to contain the patriots of '96 was Director of Public Safety Frank Riter—who had to pass judgment on the plans submitted. Riter was grimly determined to be sure that "errors" should be avoided as much as possible.[46] In spite of Riter's best efforts, Rogers depended upon imagination for some of his designs for the woodwork and fireplaces on the second floor. One archway was a free copy of a set of columns in "Cliveden," a great pre-Revolutionary home in Germantown.[47] The newspapers were lavish in their praise of the correct restoration that Rogers had wrought.[48]

The work of the D.A.R. did not end with the opening of the second floor of the building. Rogers and the Daughters won some valuable allies on the City Council, and at the end of 1896 the city agreed to pay for a complete restoration of Independence Hall at an estimated cost of $50,000! [49] The city hired Rogers at a regular salary, and he set to work on plans for the wing buildings and the downstairs rooms in the hall.[50] The appropriation of a large sum of money and the hiring of an architect did not mean that the restoration would be an easy process. Many of the problems that arose during the work had to be solved by means of compromises that sacrificed historical accuracy to expediency.[51]

The deteriorating relationship between Director Riter and T. Mellon Rogers may have been the most serious problem of all. Rogers had many enemies in the architectural profession, for he was not a member of the American Institute of Architects.[52] One of the historians hired as a consultant opposed him on major decisions where accuracy was involved. By early 1898 a committee of architects from the Philadelphia Chapter of the A.I.A. was working with Rogers to insure a reasonable degree of peace among the restorers.[53] Shortly after Independence Hall was opened as a restored monument on July 4, 1898, Riter and Rogers had a bitter exchange. The root of their difficulties may be found in a letter from Rogers to Riter which is tucked into the back of Rogers' *Diary* for 1898.

> I think it would be advisable, to modify and change, the cornice and door heads, also the mantels in the Second floor of Independence Hall, since the old original work in the lower rooms has been Restored & the original cornice in Independence Chamber and Judicial Chamber reinstated. There is a lack of similarity between the first & second floor cornices. . . .[54]

The storm broke in March of 1899 when Riter sadly announced to the press that, after spending $57,000 to restore Independence Hall, the city would have to spend about $5,000 more to re-restore the woodwork that Rogers had installed on the second floor.[55] The members of the D.A.R. reacted in various ways, some denouncing the critics of Rogers, others maintaining a dignified silence.[56] Rogers told reporters that he had had nothing to do with the restoration since Riter's answer to his letter in the summer of 1898. The whole job has had to be redone several times in the twentieth century, but still one cannot withhold a certain amount of admiration for the City of Philadelphia in its sincere efforts to return Independence Hall to its former condition.

The experience of the American Flag House and Betsy Ross Memorial Association further illustrates the serious controversy that could arise out of extreme enthusiasm for the Revolutionary era. Wallace Evan Davies, a student of American patriotism, has described the cultural climate which surrounded the movement to save the Betsy Ross house. He says that patriotism became a kind of secular religion in urban American society where old standards were dissolving. "The most extensive patriotic ritualism centered about the cult of the flag. This emerged in the late eighties and gained strength through the nineties. The banner became worshipped as the symbol of everything that was worthy of reverence in the American tradition." [57]

The Betsy Ross legend originated in a speech delivered in 1870

by William J. Canby, her grandson. He told the Pennsylvania Historical Society that his grandmother had made the first Stars and
Stripes flag in June, 1776, for a Congressional committee headed
by General Washington. The most recent authoritative history of
the flag rejects the Canby story because there is no evidence in the
papers of Congress that any flag committee existed in 1776.[58]

Soon amateur historians and descendants of Betsy Ross decided
that she had been living in a small house on Arch Street in Philadelphia when she made the first flag. A news item in a Philadelphia
paper of September, 1887, pictured the Betsy Ross house as it was
at that time. The article also contained an interview with the
owner, Mrs. Charles Mund, who was operating the house as a
tavern. Mrs. Mund was not oblivious to the patriotic possibilities
of the house. She said that she and her husband had been fighting
off souvenir hunters, though in one case they had given some floor-
boards to a man who promptly made them into a table which he
draped with the flag. The writer of the newspaper article added
that the Ross house was then in a manufacturing district where
property values were rising sharply.[59]

The patriotic fervor of the 1890's was so great that the Ross
house could not go unnoticed. In 1892 Charles M. Smith heard
that the house was to be torn down in two weeks to make way for
a factory. He bought the property—thus staking his claim as one
of those who helped to save the little home for posterity.[60]

The formation of some kind of organization was the next natural step. Three men united to lead the new American Flag House
and Betsy Ross Memorial Association: Charles Weisgerber, Dr.
Edward Brooks, and John Quincy Adams. Weisgerber appears to
have been the leader in the movement—and he had good reason
to be.[61] Reproductions of his painting "Birth of Our Nation's
Flag," which showed Betsy Ross holding up the flag for Washington's approval, were selling widely at the time. Dr. Brooks was
superintendent of schools in Philadelphia, and he had been very
interested in seeing that school principals bought the Weisgerber
painting.[62] John Q. Adams was a New York banker who willingly
loaned his famous name to the new organization and vowed to
help get more "prominent" men into it.[63]

An emotional booklet by Mrs. Addie G. Weaver was printed
as an appeal to the American people. It was entitled *The Story of*

Our Flag, although it contained such diverse elements as pages of patriotic songs followed by a long description of the benefits of giving ten cents to the association. Mrs. Weaver was one of the most optimistic writers in the preservation movement:

> All loyal American hearts will welcome the glad tidings that active steps have been taken to purchase the birthplace of the Star-Spangled Banner. . . . This landmark should be the mecca and shrine of the whole nation. It was associated with one of the most memorable incidents of our early history, and it is most fitting that it should be preserved for future generations. . . . To follow our flag from its birth until to-day would be to write a history which stands absolutely alone, and from the day of its creation to the present time it has never trailed in the dust, being the only exception among the flags of the world. . . . With all these glorious deeds, and others that must necessarily follow, let us as a grateful, patriotic people see to it that the birthplace of our nation's flag be preserved as a holy shrine.[64]

The association offered a certificate to those who contributed ten cents. On it was a reproduction of the Weisgerber painting, together with a drawing of the house and the grave of Betsy Ross. Anyone who was able to organize a "club" of thirty members received a large ten-color print of "Birth of Our Nation's Flag." [65] The contract with Weisgerber created a Betsy Ross House Fund which actually turned over 25 percent of the receipts to the association.[66] Apparently the campaign met with considerable success, for several D.A.R. chapters came out in support of the association.[67] Dr. Brooks contacted school authorities in other states in an effort to get teachers and superintendents to help in the sale of the certificates.[68]

Even with wide public support the association's directors had to face several financial problems. The Annual Report for 1903 showed that the association was just about $3,000 short of its $25,000 goal (for purchase of the property).[69] Newsmen learned of the contract with Weisgerber, and so the association had to fight rumors that a few men were making a great profit from the campaign.[70] Actually there is good evidence that the Betsy Ross house did not pay its own way. Around 1905 the association offered the property to Congress; but the Congressional committee which investigated the situation demanded proof of the authenticity of the house, and still the government refused the Ross house.[71] Two years later the directors of the association offered the house to the City of Philadelphia, and again they found that public officials did not want to assume the responsibility for a property that was so controversial.[72] The sale of membership certificates ended in December, 1905; from that date onward the directors had to pay for the operation of the Betsy Ross house through the sale of souvenirs and postal cards. Weisgerber reported to Brooks in 1910 that the property was still not self-supporting, for $800 was due in back taxes which the directors themselves might have to pay.[73]

Even after the Betsy Ross house was opened to the public as a museum, there always lay in the background the haunting fear that it might not really be the right building. In the first place, the good lady's right to the title of the first flag maker was open to dispute. Some historians were not sure that she had ever lived in the little house which bore her name. Weisgerber was very anxious to give the public all the evidence available to prove that the association was telling the truth.[74] In 1909 Oliver Parry, trying to verify the association's claims, had to fall back on affidavits from older residents as proof that Betsy had even lived in the house. One of the incorporators of the association said that the men had formed the organization only after they had "concluded there was no question concerning the validity of the flag-making event at 239 Arch Street." [75]

The affidavits and letters quoted by Parry still have not satisfied everyone as to the authenticity of the Betsy Ross house. The Joint State Government Commission of Pennsylvania cautiously described the house in 1949 as the "traditional birthplace of the American flag. Although there is no proof that Betsy Ross lived here, the house is an interesting example of the homes of the period." [76] Whether it was the real thing or not, 239 Arch Street in Philadelphia was undoubtedly a center of patriotic enthusiasm after 1898.

The one really large private restoration in the Middle Atlantic States at the turn of the century was at Ticonderoga, New York. The ruins of Fort Ticonderoga had remained in the Pell family long after the passing of William Ferris Pell in 1840. For a while the Pell house, known as the "Pavilion," served as a hotel for tourists in the northern lakes area.[77] Two young descendants of William Pell came to the house in 1882 on a summer visit. They were Howland and Stephen Pell, aged ten and eight respectively. While playing in the ruins of the fort, the boys found a well-preserved bronze flint box under one of the stones. Stephen Pell's son described the long-term effects of this discovery on his father:

> One can see them standing there after the first raptures of finding it were over, eyes shining, picturing the Fort in all its past glory, with the proud walls standing, the flags flying and men in bright uniforms on the parade grounds. The lives of men are swayed by seemingly unimportant things and in Stephen Pell's life always there was the little flint box and the youthful dream. As he grew older the imagination became an obsession, and the obsession became reality as stone by stone, timber by timber, wall by wall, he repaired and restored the Fort until it stands the old Fort Ticonderoga, all built from a flint box, a little boy's vivid imagination and a man's hard work, research and intelligence.[78]

Stephen Pell clung tenaciously to his dream. He told his future wife in 1900 that he had every intention of restoring the fort. The actual execution of the project came through a fortuitous series of events in 1907 and 1908. In the summer of 1907, Pell went to a historical meeting in Ticonderoga where he met an English architect, Alfred C. Bossom, who showed him sketches of a projected restoration of the fort.[79] During the winter of 1907–08 Mrs. Pell and her wealthy father, Colonel Robert M. Thompson, agreed to back the whole operation, although it was probable it would cost over half a million dollars.[80] The Pells began buying back shares of the original property from other members of the family and from squatters. The Stephen Pells moved to the Pavilion in the summer of 1908 and began to remodel it to serve as their permanent summer home.[81]

Now that Pell had the property, the money and the architect, he only needed a terminal date for his project. He finally selected the visit of President Taft to the 1909 Lake Champlain Tercentenary. Bossom and Pell used evidence contained in old maps, papers and drawings provided by the English and French governments. Many famous libraries loaned works on fortifications and on the history of Fort Ticonderoga. The two men also studied excavated areas around the ruins in order to discover all they could about the dimensions of the fort and the materials used in it.[82] The west barracks was ready for inspection on the Fourth of July, 1909, when President Taft came to view the reconstructed fort.[83]

Public interest helped to transform Fort Ticonderoga from a private restoration into a museum. One article printed at the time of President Taft's visit hinted that Stephen Pell might use part of the restored fort as a summer home.[84] As the years passed, visitors were attracted by the buildings and by Pell's collection of papers and relics associated with the history of the fort. When Stephen Pell left to serve in World War I, he closed the fort. The number of visitors was so great during his absence that Mrs. Pell had to hire a caretaker to show the buildings to tourists, and so Fort Ticonderoga was well on its way to becoming a popular attraction.[85] Even after the war the fort continued to be a family project, and Stephen Pell devoted the rest of his life to research in order to complete the fort as a reconstruction of an important military monument.[86]

While young Stephen Pell was dreaming of reviving Fort Ticonderoga, a civic-minded organization with a much broader field of interest was emerging in New York City. In 1895 Andrew H. Green, president of the Commissioners of the State Reservation at Niagara Falls, addressed a memorial to the New York State legislature on the subject of preserving scenery and historic sites. Green had studied the activities of the National Trust in England, the *Monuments Historiques* in France and the Trustees of Public Reservations in Massachusetts. In spite of the fact that the Massachusetts group had concerned itself exclusively with scenery up to that time, Green saw in it a model for a nationwide preservation organization.[87]

In his memorial to the state legislature, Green outlined a plan for an organization of private citizens (much like the Memorial Association of the District of Columbia) which was to own real estate in its own right and also serve as custodian of some state properties. The members were to get no personal profit or salary from their work. Green stated the objectives of the new society:

> It cannot be but that the intelligent administration of these objects and areas will tend to quicken a spirit of patriotism to act as an example and stimulus to a higher standard of care of public

grounds in villages and towns throughout the State, and to cultivate attachment to localities—a most desirable influence to be fostered.[88]

In the resultant Act of Incorporation the "Trustees" were not permitted to charge admission to their lands or to sell or mortgage any of their own property.[89] The first name of the organization, Trustees of Scenic and Historic Places and Objects in the State of New York, was a clear indication of the course it was to follow in the years to come. In other words, this group intended to administer the properties for the state, not to own them. In the first *Annual Report* of the trustees, dated 1896 (p. 8), Green warned that the organization would have to concentrate on areas of the greatest historic and scenic importance in the whole state. Two years later the title was changed to "Society" instead of "Trustees," and in 1901 the charter was radically amended to give the society national coverage under the new name, The American Scenic and Historic Preservation Society.[90] This did not alter the fact that the active preservation work of the society continued to be restricted almost entirely to the State of New York. C. R. Ashbee, an Englishman who crossed the Atlantic in 1900 with the idea of starting an American National Trust, addressed a meeting of the American Scenic in New York. He later commented:

> This society does much valuable work, and with the exception of certain bodies in Massachusetts it is I believe the only organization working in any large way on similar lines to ours [referring to the British National Trust]. Its scope is however more limited, and the difficulties of interstate legislation and interstate rivalry, will tend to confine its sphere to the State of New York. . . . I have noticed that there are many very active organizations centered in New York which claim a national character, but outside the State of New York this claim is not allowed.[91]

Ashbee's prediction was correct, for the United States was not yet ready for a national organization.

The New York group made some vital contributions to the preservation movement in spite of its limited field of endeavor. It possessed an advantageous relationship with the state, probably gained initially through the political prominence of Andrew Green, who had fathered many of the state's important reforms, including the uniting of the five boroughs into New York City.[92] An important feature of this relationship was the requirement that each year the society had to report on its activities to the legislature. The state then printed several hundred copies of each report and circulated them widely. Even now one can find these early reports in libraries as far north as Boston and as far south as Washington, D.C. If the American Scenic had done nothing but publish these volumes (some of which exceed 600 pages!) it would still have remained a principal clearinghouse for information in the early days of the preservation movement. The reports continued for thirty years, the last being printed in 1925.

A progressive step came in 1898 when the society hired a newspaperman, Edward Hagaman Hall, as secretary. Hall wrote virtually all of the gigantic annual reports from that year onward. In addition to reading avidly about the preservation field outside of New York, he worked with specific projects within the state and gathered much information concerning these activities.[93] In 1902 the work of the society became so demanding that Dr. Hall was hired as a full-time secretary with an office in the Tribune Building in New York City.[94]

Another aspect of the work of the American Scenic and Historic Preservation Society was its early recognition of the need for contacts with and an understanding of European preservation organizations. As early as 1902 a Columbia professor, A. D. F. Hamlin, gave a comprehensive lecture to the society on the status of preservation activity in Europe at that time.[95]

Both Dr. Hall and Andrew Green wrote at some length about the close tie which existed between the preservation of historic objects and scenery. They claimed that increased attention to these two areas would teach patriotism and thus make preservation a civic obligation rather than a luxury. Hall said that many historic sites were so stimulating to the imagination that they took on the character of public property even though they were privately owned.[96]

Green was murdered in 1903, the unfortunate victim of mistaken identity.[97] His first successor was Walter Logan, a distinguished lawyer, and the next president was George F. Kunz, an official in Tiffany's jewelry store.[98] Kunz, too, was interested in the progress of preservation work all over the world, and he commented on this subject in the society's reports.[99]

Although its membership was not based on hereditary right, the society was limited to men. Yet, once again, one finds that some of the most effective labors for preservation were done by women. In April of 1900 a meeting of representatives of New York City D.A.R. chapters concluded that a "Women's Auxiliary" to the American Scenic and Historic Preservation Society should be formed and that it ought to cooperate with that organization in every way possible. The ladies immediately established three goals —"the purchase by the city of Fraunces Tavern, the Morris Mansion (Washington's Headquarters), and the Poe Cottage."[100] The exceptional success of the auxiliary in preservation efforts was due to its emphasis on historic buildings in the New York City area, rather than on widely scattered scenic features. The ladies always managed to bring many members to city hearings whenever an impressive show of numbers was necessary.

Secretary Hall of the American Scenic was plagued with appeals for financial aid from all parts of the country, and he had no funds to distribute. In 1905 he asked for a gift of $50,000 to create an endowment in order to help the society to do effective work in the field. Green had bequeathed $10,000, the income of which barely covered the operating expenses of Hall's office.[101] The call for an endowment was repeated in 1913 in an effort to "place . . . [the society] beyond the vicissitudes of support by a necessarily fluctuating membership."[102] This appeal also went unheeded by the influential and wealthy members. Evidently the willingness of the American Scenic to permit the state to buy properties had meant that the organization did not have any specific goal to arouse enthusiasm with the society. Looking toward New England and its adherence to nongovernmental preservation, Hall thought it was "singular" that Massachusetts, a state so rich in history, had left her historic sites to be cared for by groups such as the Society for the Preservation of New England Antiquities.[103] When Hall looked back over the career of the American Scenic in 1924 he did not mention any specific preservation efforts.

> During the past twenty-nine years, our Society, with the advantage of a special charter from the Legislature and by the wide circulation at home and abroad of its official reports, has stimulated

the whole movement for scenic and historic preservation, which now includes the creation and protection of city, state, and national parks.[104]

Perhaps the best path to understanding the contribution of the society is to consider its efforts in behalf of two different houses. These cases serve to illustrate the society's strength as a publicity agent for the preservation movement—and its weakness as a medium for obtaining funds for the actual purchase of buildings. The first of these, Philipse Manor Hall, in Yonkers, was already owned by the city, which had bought it in 1868 for use as a city hall.[105] Over the years the City of Yonkers had found the structure inadequate and was considering its demolition and the erection of new offices on the site. In 1895 the newly chartered Trustees of Scenic and Historic Places and Objects joined other groups in protesting any changes in the building. Five years later the Common Council of Yonkers reviewed the Manor Hall situation. President Green wrote the council a spirited letter stressing the historic importance of the Manor Hall as a well-preserved example of a rare feudal farmhouse. He also remarked on the picturesque nature of the house.[106]

The following year a local group, known as the Manor Hall Association, tried to save the structure. The members of this association raised $2,500 to stop construction on a new firehouse on the adjoining property. The American Scenic urged that the offices of the city government be taken from the Manor Hall.[107] In 1903, at a conference of the various local organizations that were trying to save the house, some people presented a bill that would have the state purchase the property for $50,000 with the custody awarded to the American Scenic and Historic Preservation Society. The Common Council of Yonkers decided to accept this settlement, even though the land was worth more than the price mentioned, but the state refused to pass such a bill that year.[108]

After a period of inactivity the Civic League of the Women's Institute held a meeting in Yonkers, with the secretary of the American Scenic as one of the speakers. The next day Mrs. William F. Cochran informed the president of the institute that she was willing to give $50,000 to the state to purchase the Manor Hall if the state would hold the title and the American Scenic would be custodian. On April 27, 1908, with the approval of the legislature and the Yonkers Common Council, the proposal went into effect. Mrs. Cochran promptly increased her gift by another $5,000 to be used for restoration.[109]

The American Scenic and Historic Preservation Society had ample time to plan what it was going to do with the building, since the city did not vacate until four years later. By that time the society had engaged Howard Chamberlain, an architect, to draw up plans for returning the mansion to its colonial appearance and for protecting it from fire and other dangers. The heating plant had been moved to a special building erected on the grounds for that purpose. The society asked for and received an appropriation of $2,750 from the legislature for operating expenses for the next year.

Mrs. Cochran passed away in the meantime, and her son, Alexander S. Cochran, promised to give the money necessary to complete the restoration.[110] In 1912 he provided $11,550 to cover the cost of the plans and the projected restoration. Cochran also gave some colonial furniture to grace the building, along with his collection of early American portraits, valued at nearly $100,000.[111]

It is no wonder that by 1913 Dr. Hall could report that the Philipse Manor Hall was attracting a large number of visitors—since it was on the main road and was close to the New York Central railroad station.[112] During the years that followed, the society always included in its reports some account of important or unusual visitors to the Manor Hall. Secretary Hall prepared a book on the history of the building, and Cochran paid for its publication.[113] The American Scenic had been important principally in arousing interest in the preservation of the Manor Hall; other groups had done the spadework. The society had depended upon Mrs. Cochran's gift for the actual purchase and afterward relied on her son and the state for support of much of the custodial work at the Manor Hall.

The second building which claimed the attention of the American Scenic and Historic Preservation Society was Hamilton Grange, once the home of Alexander Hamilton, the first Secretary of the Treasury. The Grange was a farmhouse located in an area of Manhattan that was in the process of rapid urbanization toward the end of the nineteenth century. In 1889 the owner presented the Grange to St. Luke's Episcopal Church, which was a block away.[114] The church spent $10,000 moving the house several hundred yards in order to place it next to the new church edifice, where the building became a parish house and rectory.[115]

The first real effort to turn the house into a museum came in 1901 when the Alexander Hamilton Post, Grand Army of the Republic, succeeded in having a bill introduced in the legislature to get the state to buy the building.[116] This bill did not pass, nor did a similar measure pass the next year.[117] The American Scenic joined other historic and patriotic groups in public exercises held at the original site of the Grange on the one-hundredth anniversary of Hamilton's death. This meeting served to focus public attention upon the importance of saving the house and returning it to its original location. Finally, four years later, the legislature did pass a compromise bill giving New York City the right to buy the place or to receive it as a gift, but again nothing happened.

Several organizations in 1912 urged the Commissioner of Parks for the Boroughs of Manhattan and Richmond to consider the advisability of buying the house. The commissioner asked the American Scenic for advice. The society recommended the purchase of the Grange and its removal to St. Nicholas Park nearby. Hall offered to act as intermediary between the Park Board and the church. In answer to the society's inquiries, the rector reported that the church would sell the building for $30,000.[118]

The next year the New York City Board of Estimate and Apportionment authorized the expenditure of $25,000 for the purchase, removal and restoration of the Grange. The park commissioner found himself powerless to act in this case, because the church had consented to reduce its price by $5,000 but would not go any lower. The commissioner not only had to buy the building, but he also had to pay for removal and restoration within the sum specified by the appropriation. The matter was at a standstill.[119] The American Scenic and Historic Preservation Society endeavored once more to reconcile the church to a reduction in price, but the rector answered that his congregation could not reproduce the building for less than $25,000, and unless something was done soon the church would alter the structure to suit its own purposes.[120]

More time passed until the early 1920's when St. Luke's announced that it would have to tear down the Grange or sell it to someone for removal. A group in Chicago, the Hamilton Society, attempted to purchase the house for re-erection in that city. The threat posed by this offer galvanized the American Scenic as never before. President Kunz went to his influential friends in New York, and in 1924 he secured $100,000 as a gift for the society. Half of the amount was for the purchase of the house and lot, and the other half was a trust fund for its maintenance. J. P. Morgan, Jr., whose father had been the honorary president of the American Scenic, and George F. Baker, Jr., were the donors. The house was purchased in November of 1924, and the trust fund was set up in September of 1925.[121]

Although it had influence upon the preservation of other houses in New York State, by 1926 the society administered only the two properties mentioned above. The preservation of these buildings illustrates two aspects of its work. In the first place, the organization had not bought either house with its own funds, although it could be argued that the purchase price of the Grange had been donated to the society. Second, the American Scenic certainly had not been the only group interested in saving these historic spots. One might conclude that in the case of the Manor Hall, meetings of local organizations had been more helpful in preserving the building than the efforts of the American Scenic. For instance, the $2,500 raised to repay the contractor who had begun to construct a firehouse near the Manor Hall came out of the pockets of the citizens of Yonkers.[122] It must be remembered that the society had some influence on legislators in Albany and on officials in New York City. By attempting to extend its range to the whole United States, the society had overestimated its capabilities in an era when communications were more limited than at present, and when local groups were the backbone of preservationism.

In working through the medium of state and local government the American Scenic was the heir, philosophically speaking, to the kind of thinking that had helped to save the Hasbrouck house in 1850. Preservationists in the Middle Atlantic States still favored public ownership of historic properties. By 1926 New York State had acquired a number of historic buildings far exceeding those saved by other state governments. The American Scenic and Historic Preservation Society helped to lay the foundation for New York's work with the publicity that Hall had given in the fine Annual Reports.

Private preservation groups were active in the Middle Atlantic

area, but most people in that region looked upon saving old buildings as an educational activity which local and state governments
should support. In the degree that they saved sites connected with
Revolutionary heroes for the purpose of inspiring patriotism (with
state help), preservationists in New York and Pennsylvania resembled their southern brethren more than they did the antiquaries of
New England.

V

New England, the Home of Militant Private Preservation Organizations

ACROSS THE BORDERS OF NEW YORK STATE, in New England, lay the seat of the strongest nongovernmental preservation groups. Of the four hundred old buildings sampled for this book, more than twenty-five were saved or cared for by New England historical societies. Only five examples of similar private work could be found in the Middle Atlantic area, and but one each in the South and Midwest. Although these figures present only a partial view, they do illustrate a trend far too noticeable to be ignored. In New England the local historical society was, and still is, one of the most important preservation agents.[1]

The fate of the Hancock Mansion colored the history of New England preservationism in the sixty years that followed the Civil War. Leaders of preservation groups grew more and more determined to prevent the destruction of any other historic monuments through governmental neglect and inaction. In several notable cases private organizations banded together to assist New England states and cities in preserving the few historic structures that were government-owned. In the period that followed the loss of the Hancock house, people rarely turned to governmental agencies in emergencies, and it was obvious that New Englanders distrusted politicians in preservation work.

The preservation movement in New England had a distinctly regional flavor. A few New England historic house museums were associated with the great men of the Revolution; most of the remaining buildings open to the public appealed to local pride or commemorated the services of early inhabitants. The main motivation in a few cases was clearly ancestor worship. The desire for patriotic inspiration, when it did appear in New England, always included a recognition of the hardships endured by sturdy ancestral pioneers.

The most important and expensive preservation effort in New England was the campaign to save the Old South Meeting House. It came at the same time as the Philadelphia Centennial, though there was no direct connection between the two events. As early as 1869, the Old South Society wished to build a new church in the Back Bay, where the majority of its congregation was living at that time, although a vocal minority wished to keep the old meeting house at all costs. While the great Boston fire of 1872 stopped just short of the Old South, the proponents of new construction seized this as an excuse to transfer services to the Freeman Place chapel, and to rent the meeting house to the Post Office Department for two years. Then the Old South Society tried in vain to sell the building in 1873 to the Massachusetts Historical Society. Having failed in this effort to transfer responsibility for its preservation, while still gaining a substantial sum of money, the Old South Society had no remaining alternative save destruction of the meeting house, for only through sale to commercial interests could it get the true value of the land. The seventeenth-century will of Madam Norton, which presented the land to the Old South Society for a religious purpose, became a major obstacle to the sale. Slowly the society gained permission from the Massachusetts courts and legislature to set aside Madam Norton's will. The meeting house seemed to be doomed in spite of all that could be done. Henry Washburne pronounced a eulogy in the Massachusetts Senate:

> We may treasure these relics of the past, never so sacredly; we may watch over them with all the solicitude of the mother for her babe; but pass away they must, and take their place among the traditional memories of men. Such is life; such are the inevitable laws which govern and control all human affairs. We ourselves, and the works of our hands, and those of our fathers, will form no exception to the inexorable fiat of the hand of Time.[2]

Something had changed in Boston since 1863; for the Old

South Meeting House had a greater number of determined parti-
sans than the departed Hancock house. The final blow appeared
to have come when the venerable edifice fell under the auction-
eer's hammer on June 8, 1876, for the pitiful sum of $1,350 (its
value as a source of building materials). Workmen began to remove the clock from the tower when suddenly the firm of George
W. Simmons and Son stepped in on June 11 and bought the
right to hold the building intact for seven days. Simmons and Son
aroused the latent fires of patriotism by hanging a banner from
the tower which asked, SHALL OLD SOUTH BE SAVED? Immediately
a group of citizens arranged for a mass meeting in Old South for
the night of June 14—halfway through the precious week that had
been purchased.[3]

The main speaker of the evening was Wendell Phillips, and
he was at his magnificent best. Critics in the audience later judged
Phillips' effort the finest of his whole career. Fortunately it has
been reprinted as Number 183 of the *Old South Leaflets;* and
only by reading it aloud can one grasp the effect it must have
had on the people of Boston that night. Phillips began with the
arresting question: "Why are we here to-day?" He then praised
the freedom America had won and proudly described Boston's
role in the Revolution. He went on to show how Old South could
serve as a "school" for future generations. One excerpt will help
to give some of the flavor of the whole speech:

> . . . What is a statue of Cicero compared to standing where your
> voice echoes from pillar and wall that actually heard his philippics!
> How much better than a picture of John Brown is the sight of that
> Blue Ridge which filled his eye, when, riding to the scaffold, he
> said calmly to his jailer, "This is a beautiful country: I never
> noticed it before." Destroy every portrait of Luther, if you must,
> but save that terrible chamber where he fought with the Devil,
> and translated the Bible. Scholars have grown old and blind
> striving to put their hands on the very spot where bold men spoke
> or brave men died: shall we tear in pieces the roof that actually
> trembled to the words which made us a nation? It is impossible
> not to believe, if the spirits above us are permitted to know what
> passes in this terrestrial sphere, that Adams and Warren and Otis
> are to-day bending over us, asking that the scene of their immortal
> labors shall not be desecrated or blotted from the sight of men.[4]

Other speakers that evening tried to warn the audience that Bostonians must not permit the destruction of the one thing that set their city apart from all other American cities: the last visible reminders of a proud past. Some thought that Old South was admirably suited to serve as an American version of Westminster Abbey. A committee was created to raise funds, and several thousand dollars were subscribed that night.[5]

The new committee for the preservation of the meeting house found the Old South Society very difficult to deal with because the contract for the sale of the land to developers had already been signed.[6] The situation remained at an impasse throughout the summer of 1876, partly because the people who could give large amounts of money were not in Boston during the warmer months. The first positive action came when the women of Boston (in the persons of twenty ladies) bought the structure itself for $3,500. From that point on, no matter what happened to the land, the meeting house could be moved to a new site.[7] Still, the Old South Society refused to come to any agreement that was workable. Finally in the fall of 1876 a contract was hammered out. It called for a payment of $400,000 in cash to the society, plus a restriction banning any religious service in the meeting house for thirty years.[8] New England Mutual Life Insurance Company took on a $225,000 mortgage; the Citizen's Committee paid $75,000; and Mrs. Mary Hemenway contributed the last $100,000. Her gift was so dramatic that it breathed new life into the whole project.[9]

New England, still basking in the glow of its Golden Age of Literature, had much talent to give the Old South movement. The Citizen's Committee, incorporated on May 11, 1877, as the Old South Association in Boston, sponsored various balls and entertainments in the meeting house and in other public halls in Boston. President Eliot of Harvard and James Russell Lowell spoke at a meeting at Harvard on January 1, 1877. Another notable meeting came on May 4, when Oliver Wendell Holmes, Ralph Waldo Emerson, Julia Ward Howe, and Dr. Samuel Smith read from their own works. John Greenleaf Whittier was unable to attend that evening, but his absence did not dim the luster of the occasion.[10] A fair held in the meeting house during December of 1877 netted $36,000 for the fund.[11]

In 1878 a committee from the Old South Association went before the Massachusetts legislature and asked for an appropriation of $50,000. At the hearing on the bill, President Eliot brilliantly defended the high cost of the land on which the meeting house stood. He also deftly turned the loss of the original pews into an advantage by pointing out that the vengeful British had torn them out to set up a riding school. Wendell Phillips and others spoke in favor of the appropriation, citing the loss of the Hancock Mansion —but to no avail. The State of Massachusetts still refused to aid historic preservation.[12]

The story of Old South Meeting House has remained to this day an important symbol in historical work. The purchase of the building in the face of impossible odds must have been a source of inspiration to preservationists and lovers of history all over the nation. The idealism which went into the Old South campaign carried over into what was called "The Old South Work." The meeting house became a museum and classroom for the study of history. The Old South Association in Boston has published over 200 *Old South Leaflets* which cover the range of human history by means of speeches and documents.[13] One essay contest run by Old South in the late 1870's was designed to interest high school graduates in the field of history. It called for cash prizes to be awarded to students who wrote on such diverse topics as the treatment of Quakers by the government of Massachusetts Bay Colony or the growth of separatism in the colonies in the years before the Revolution.[14] There can be no question that the association has rendered a great service to many students all over the United States.

The restoration of the Old State House (more correctly, the Town House) in Boston was the most immediate effect of the renewed interest in antiquities that came in the wake of the preservation of Old South.[15] Like any old public building that had housed both city and state governments, the Old State House had a checkered career. During the late 1820's the Washington Monument Association of Boston sought a spot to put up Chantrey's statue of George Washington. The leaders of the association suggested that the Old State House be removed as an "incumbrance" in order to clear some busy streets and provide room for the precious statue. There was enough public outcry at that time to prevent destruction of the State House; and the city soon reacted by turning the building into the new city hall.[16]

The oratory that brought Old South Meeting House into the public eye in 1876 caused some antiquarians to look toward the disfigured State House, which had been full of commercial tenants since the city government had moved out. William H. Whitmore, a member of the Common Council of Boston, began pushing for a restoration of the Old State House in 1879. He helped to form the Boston Antiquarian Club in that year, and in 1880 he urged his colleagues in the club to appear at hearings called to study the problems involved in repairing the Old State House. Evidently Whitmore was a determined fighter, because the City Council passed an ordinance that set aside $35,000 for a restoration of the building.[17] Whitmore then proceeded to resign as president of the Antiquarian Club in order to clear the way for the formation of a new organization, the Bostonian Society. He told the members of the new society that it could perform a very useful service for Boston by occupying the upper rooms in the newly restored Old State House. The city promptly gave the group a ten-year lease with the intention that the upper floor of the building would be devoted to historical exhibits.[18]

Not long after the restoration had been completed under Whitmore's direction another antiquary, Dr. George H. Moore of New York, criticized several features of the repaired State House. Moore pointed out that Whitmore had mistakenly followed an 1830 floor plan that had been found in Cincinnati. He tried to prove that the colonial State House had not had a spiral staircase, such as the one Whitmore had just finished installing.[19] The argument ran on through the 1880's, and still persists today. Modern authors usually condemn Whitmore's restoration while they compliment him for his efforts in behalf of a Revolutionary landmark.[20] In spite of the controversy, one more thing must be remembered: the taxpayers of Boston contributed $35,000 to this restoration in 1881, and in 1908 they gave an additional $15,000 to repair the first floor after the Boston Transit Commission had finished with it. The city also spent $103,000 in 1898 in an effort to repair and fireproof Faneuil Hall, another landmark near the Old State House.[21] Here we have two unusual examples of historical groups in New England working successfully with a city government.

The year 1877 marked the renewal of substantial preservation efforts all over New England following the Old South movement.

Amateur antiquaries, who had immersed themselves in the study of local history, led two campaigns, one at Deerfield and another at Woburn, both in Massachusetts. In Deerfield Esther Dickinson bequeathed to the trustees of Deerfield Academy the old Parson Williams house, which was believed to have been built for one of the survivors of the famous Deerfield massacre. The academy trustees were divided over the question of what to do with the structure, since some favored its destruction. George Sheldon, who had recently founded the Pocumtuck Valley Memorial Association, was determined to save the old home. He remembered the fate of the Old Indian House a little over twenty-five years before, and so he did all he could to inform the public about the Williams house. Sheldon wrote a series of three articles for the Greenfield *Gazette and Courier* telling the history and significance of the house. It appears that the interest created by these articles and Sheldon's other activities prompted the trustees of the academy to move the house a short distance and preserve it as a dormitory.[22] Sheldon's papers and an article in *Harper's Monthly* reveal that he suspected the Williams house was a later building, constructed on the site by the Reverend Williams' son in the middle of the eighteenth century. Sheldon certainly could not afford to weaken his arguments in favor of the Williams house by admitting that it had little to do with the redeemed captive of 1704.[23]

In Woburn, Massachusetts, a group organized in 1877 and called itself the Rumford Historical Association. Its main purpose was the preservation of the birthplace of Benjamin Thompson, the famous scientist who later became Count Rumford. The association bought the birthplace through gifts rather than by public subscription. As time went by, some sizable bequests helped in maintaining the house. In all probability, this was the first house preserved and maintained by a historical society in the country's history.[24]

The Newport (Rhode Island) Historical Society decided in the early 1880's that it had outgrown its room in the Redwood Library and needed a new home. A committee appointed to find a suitable building reported that a rare historical bargain was available. The dwindling Seventh Day Baptist Society in Newport was willing to sell its old meetinghouse (built in 1729) for a mere $800! The historical society thus had an opportunity to buy a building to house its collections and also add a new relic at the same time. The society had the necessary money in hand by the end of June, 1884, and immediately began to repair the little meetinghouse, which had been vacant for more than fifteen years.[25] It had been open to the public only three years when the historical society decided that the little building was too close to the neighboring structures. In order to avoid the great danger of fire, the Newporters had the meetinghouse moved to a new location about a block away, next to Touro Synagogue. The society's collections and library grew with the years, so two further changes had to be made. In 1902 a brick building was put on in front of the lot; and in 1915 the meetinghouse made its last trip to the back of the lot in order to make room for a new wing on the historical society building. At that time the wooden meetinghouse was encased in bricks for even greater fire protection.[26]

The next preservation attempt in New England was again the fruit of antiquarian devotion and local pride. By the middle 1880's, Cummings Davis, proprietor of a small stationery store in Concord, Massachusetts, had amassed a hoard of antiquities from the Concord area. Davis was a town "character" who had searched out and acquired items of great age from attics and private sales. Many of the articles that he had bought for low prices were of a style and period not in favor at the moment, but time is usually on the side of the collector. Residents of Concord gradually began to appreciate the fact that Davis had gathered furniture and household items stretching back to the earliest days of the town. Moreover, the collection was uniquely local because of the restricted range of Davis' travels. Some civic leaders saw that such an exhibit would be an attraction for Concord if it could be preserved intact. In 1886 Davis himself proposed to some influential citizens that he donate the collection to them if in turn they would appoint him as custodian. After considerable discussion of the idea, the Concord burghers decided to give their approval. In January of 1887 this group, which had incorporated itself the year before as the Concord Antiquarian Society, agreed to Davis' terms. His salary as custodian of the collection was to be the fees received from visitors. If at any time these fees should be insufficient to support him, the society would provide a small allowance. The society also promised to house the objects properly.

That same year the Antiquarian Society fulfilled its end of the agreement by purchasing the Reuben Brown house. This home had historical interest because it had been damaged by the British while they were searching for hidden military stores during the Revolution. Probably more significant was the fact that the house was accessible to tourists, since it was situated on the Lexington Road near the center of town. Thus the Reuben Brown house was preserved not so much for its own sake, but because it would be a fitting place in which to display a notable collection of Americana.[27]

Other historical societies made some efforts to save the few houses that had witnessed the Revolutionary engagements that took place in New England. The year after the Concord Antiquarian Society opened the Reuben Brown house a member of the neighboring Lexington Historical Society began agitating for the preservation of another Revolutionary landmark. The Reverend C. A. Staples urged the citizens of Lexington to save the Hancock-Clark house, the place where Samuel Adams and John Hancock were staying when the British marched to Lexington and Concord. Paul Revere had stopped there briefly during his famous ride.[28]

Four years after Staples' initial plea for the Hancock-Clark house, the Lexington Historical Society began searching for a permanent home for its collections. Two different committees from the society looked into the possibility of using the house for a headquarters as two more years slipped quietly by.[29] An alarming threat to the old structure finally brought action. One member of the society reported to the annual meeting in March of 1896 that the owner of the Hancock-Clark house had decided that it was not fit to live in, and therefore she would make no further repairs on it. A committee selected at the meeting was instructed to save the building "from demolition" primarily for the honor of Lexington. Staples, as a member of the group, went to see the owner. He found the situation reminiscent of the Old Indian House in Deerfield half a century before—the owner would not sell the land and would not permit the house to remain on its original site. Here the parallel with Deerfield ceases; the Reverend Mr. Staples personally paid the owner $150 for the house itself.[30] The historical society voted to keep the new acquisition on Hancock Street and then created a committee of fifteen ladies to canvass the town for funds which would permit relocation of the house upon a new site. At this point a gentleman who owned a lot across the street from the Hancock-Clark house offered his land to the society for $1,500. Staples found the proposition agreeable and put up the necessary money. All through the winter of 1897 Staples and his committee worked quietly. The whole project eventually cost $3,107.42, including repairs to the building (once it was on its new foundation). The fund-raising campaign was successful because it had been well planned and the house had appealing historical associations.[31]

The story did not end there, for the preservation of the Hancock-Clark house was only a part of the work of the ambitious Lexington Historical Society. It eventually became the first New England historical society to own buildings other than its own headquarters. In 1911 James S. Munroe, a member, bequeathed his home to the society as a museum. The house (formerly a tavern) had been associated with the British march into Lexington in 1775. The society accepted the "Munroe Tavern" and agreed to maintain it as specified in Munroe's will.[32] The society had a third opportunity to demonstrate its public spirit two years later when it learned of the impending destruction of the "Buckman Tavern," where the Minutemen had gathered before the Battle of Lexington. The society called for a town meeting and then made a bold proposal. The members offered to raise $12,000 if the Town of Lexington would vote $30,000 more to buy the tavern and lot. The property faced the famous Battle Green, so many people saw that it would be a natural addition to the Lexington park system. Once the proposal had passed, the town and the historical society each raised the money it had pledged. The town took over the tavern in July of 1913, and the historical society assumed custody of it.[33]

From the middle 1880's until his death in 1904, the Reverend Mr. Staples had been the spearhead of the movement to make Lexington more aware of its historic past. He was an amateur historian, not an antiquary who stressed the importance of architectural refinements. Staples loved the great drama of history, and he considered Lexington an ideal setting for memorializing the Revolution.[34]

In stark contrast with Lexington, the Ipswich (Massachusetts) Historical Society was located in a town where no important events had taken place. Ipswich had age and charm, qualities which were deeply appreciated by a dedicated antiquary, the Reverend Thomas Franklin Waters. Thanks to his efforts, Ipswich contains today probably more examples of late seventeenth-century dwellings than any other town in America.

A tasteful photographic essay entitled *Under New England Roofs* (1894) included the following description of the Whipple house in Ipswich: ". . . No one with any feeling for the antique could stand before the subject of this article, noting its evident great age and its picturesqueness, without a conviction that here is one of those houses in which the novelist delights. . . . On every side are evidences of decay and coming demolition." [35] Three years later Waters, as president of the Ipswich Historical Society, spoke bluntly of the value of the architectural heritage of Ipswich: "Many of the most interesting old houses have disappeared, and the death-knell of others may be sounded ere we are aware of any danger. Our town owes no small portion of its great and growing attractiveness to strangers to its venerable mansions." He appealed for the preservation of the much-neglected Whipple house, emphasizing that it could serve as a superb headquarters building for the society, as well as a home for its collections. As far as Waters was concerned, a fireproof headquarters was an impossibility and would probably remain so; whereas the Whipple house was standing and was badly in need of care. He argued that the antiquity and architectural features of the house were known far beyond Ipswich.[36]

The appeal made in 1897 did not fall on deaf ears, for the society immediately set up a committee to report on the advisability of purchasing the Whipple property. The committee reported favorably, so the historical society bought and restored the house during the summer of 1898. That fall the society incorporated itself in order to become a better agent for owning the property. The entire operation had cost $1,650.[37]

At the dedication ceremonies in October, President Waters described the painstaking work of restoration with a remarkably forward-looking speech. Most preservationists in the 1890's based their philosophy on historical criteria: How important was a building, historically speaking? Had someone famous been born there? Was it a witness to some significant event? Waters, on the other hand, did not plead for greater worship of country; he simply called for an increased appreciation of a way of life that had vanished. "[The Whipple house] is a link that binds us to the remote Past and to a solemn and earnest manner of living, quite in contrast with much in our modern life." [38]

Word of the Whipple house restoration spread among New England antiquaries, for here was a building saved primarily for its architectural value. In 1902 old George Sheldon, who had done so much to further preservationism in Deerfield, could not resist paying Waters a visit. Mrs. Sheldon accompanied him on this trip and recollected that:

> Those who have made the pilgrimage to the quaint old town on the beautiful bay know what a rare and precious heirloom the Whipple house is, and what a monument it is to Mr. Waters' ceaseless effort. . . . Mr. Waters had no sympathy whatever with the prevailing custom of giving the name of true history to what is really fiction.[39]

Sylvester Baxter found the Whipple house "the most faithful reproduction yet achieved of the home environment of the primitive Colonial life of New England." [40] In 1919 William Sumner Appleton, a true arbiter among antiquaries, pronounced the work in Ipswich, particularly the careful repair of the Whipple house, to be a "pioneer work in the cause of preservation." [41]

One more example illustrates the diversity of people and methods to be found among the historical societies working in New England. A strict chronology of any movement does not always reveal its real leaders, as can be seen by the career of Miss Celeste Bush of East Lyme, Connecticut. In the winter of 1914 Sumner Appleton of the Society for the Preservation of New England Antiquities received a letter from Miss Bush asking for help in preserving the Thomas Lee house in East Lyme. She included photographs and a detailed description of the building. This material excited Appleton so much that he hurried to East Lyme to investigate the situation. He found the project entirely worthy of support, and his recommendation caused the S.P.N.E.A. trustees to vote $200 toward saving the Lee house. At that time the price of the property was only $500.

The remarkable thing about the rescue of the Lee house was the role played by Miss Bush. Appleton gave her a rare tribute:

"It may be noted in passing that this is one of those cases where success is entirely dependent on the initiative and energy of one individual—in this instance Miss Celeste E. Bush." [42] She had come to East Lyme late in her life to enjoy the peaceful existence of a small New England town. She joined the local historical society which consisted of twelve members and had fifteen dollars in its treasury. The old Lee house had a fascination for her, and, as had been the case before in the preservation movement, one determined lady decided that the structure must remain undisturbed. Her conviction initiated a campaign.[43] Through Miss Bush's letters and through the cooperation of an S.P.N.E.A. vice-president, the Connecticut Society of Colonial Dames donated $200, and the Connecticut Society of the Colonial Wars gave an equal amount. These gifts, together with that of the S.P.N.E.A., paid for the property. Almost $500 more came in from Lee descendants, most of whom had been located and contacted by Miss Bush. Appleton estimated that she had written over 500 letters personally in order to establish the history of the house and to raise funds.[44] Miss Bush summarized the whole experience in a letter to Appleton:

> It seems to me that one valuable lesson from our Society is that there is not a town in New England so small or so poor that there is not ample scope for a historical society. If people really love the things of the past enough to be willing to work for them they can restore and preserve their historical treasures; and every town in New England has treasures that ought to be preserved.[45]

The story of each preservation by a historical society could be included here, and there would be subtle differences in almost every case. Most historical societies did not come into being for the purpose of preserving old buildings, though many of them took a sincere interest in at least one old house. Appleton complained that local historical groups usually saved only one structure, and that one was often chosen without any reference to other worthwhile buildings that might be more significant. He noted wistfully, "It is much to be regretted that the preservation of the best local architecture is not as yet considered the normal work of these local societies." [46]

The larger state historical societies took even less interest in preserving buildings than did the local groups. State societies tended to become repositories for valuable manuscript materials which had to be kept in fireproof headquarters relatively near centers of population where their treasures could be available to students. One exception to this trend was the case of the Wadsworth-Longfellow house in Portland, Maine.[47] The Maine Historical Society was not at all sure in 1901 that it could maintain the house, which had been presented by the Longfellow family. The society made the best of the situation by erecting a new building in the rear of the lot to serve as a fireproof headquarters.[48]

There were groups in New England that commemorated nearly every cause imaginable, and often they saved old houses in the process. One such organization saved what might be termed literary memorials. A clear example of this sort of preservation occurred in Portsmouth, New Hampshire, in 1907. The house in question possessed the dual advantage of being the boyhood home of Thomas Bailey Aldrich and also the setting for his well-known autobiographical work, *The Story of a Bad Boy*. When Aldrich died in 1907, a group of Portsmouth citizens formed the Thomas Bailey Aldrich Memorial, which had as its avowed purpose the preservation of his home. The members raised $10,000 by public subscription with individual donations ranging as high as $1,000. They purchased the property and secured the assistance of the author's son in furnishing the rooms to match the description given in Aldrich's book. The house became a social document—representing an upper-middle-class Portsmouth home of the 1840's.[49] In later years Appleton referred to the Aldrich Memorial as "about the most successful period house in America." [50]

Family associations blossomed in New England shortly after the turn of the century. The Fairbanks Family in America, which saved its homestead in Dedham, Massachusetts, was typical. The methods used by this organization should serve to tell us much about preservationism in New England. It is likely that if the family group had not been formed the Fairbanks house would have been rescued anyway, for it was a surprisingly ancient building, the earliest part dating from about 1636. A curious incident threatened the house with a long period of neglect. In the summer of 1892 Miss Rebecca Fairbanks, the last person of that name to occupy the building, was at home with her dog. Lightning struck the house while she was asleep one night; although the dog was killed, she was unharmed. The experience so unnerved her that she moved to Boston shortly after and did not return until the following year. The fate of the homestead was undecided. It appeared that rising property values would soon bring about the destruction or removal of the building.[51]

The force of family ties was slowly moving in the direction of . saving the old house. In 1901 J. Wilder Fairbank arranged by mail to summon a homecoming for his particular branch of the family at a place near his home. Over 200 persons were present, some of whom were from great distances. They were so pleased with the idea of a reunion that they voted to have another meeting a year later at the old homestead in Dedham, with an invitation extended to all Fairbanks descendants. J. Wilder Fairbank worked diligently during the winter and sent out 3,000 invitations to people that could claim descent from Jonathan Fairbanks of Dedham.[52]

On August 27, 1902, more than 700 descendants assembled for the first reunion of the family at the ancestral home.

> Over the scene, between two noble old elms, floated the national flag and the Fairbanks banner, 9 × 16 feet, containing in gold and black, silver and blue, the family emblem and coat of arms, with the motto, "Finem Respice," all on a field of gray. . . . The old house was in holiday attire and never looked more picturesque.[53]

At this meeting the group voted to explore the possibilities of creating an association for the purpose of owning the house. A committee sent out a circular to the whole family early in 1903 stating that it was essential to incorporate the family association in order to own the homestead as a nontaxable historic property. The same notice inaugurated the sale of certificates of membership in the new family association at the price of one dollar for every man, woman, and child eligible to join. Naturally, it was hoped that affluent members could give more than that amount. The circular made an earnest plea for the "perpetuation and preservation of this historic landmark, which already is looked to with pride by vast numbers outside our family." On April 2, 1903, the Fairbanks Family in America, Incorporated, adopted a constitution which made the acquisition of the Fairbanks house one of its main objectives.[54]

J. Wilder Fairbank had not been idle during that winter. He had stepped up his efforts to locate a greater number of eligible descendants for the association. Before the time came for mailing the invitations to the 1903 reunion, he had found 5,000 names. He claimed that if someone had offered to finance genealogical research, he could have added 25,000 more eligible families. Truly this would have turned the homestead into a "veritable Mecca." [55]

The Fairbanks house was indeed a Mecca for at least a portion of the Fairbanks descendants on the twenty-seventh of August, 1903. They were the guests of the Codmans, who owned the property at that time. Prominent members of the family gave speeches concerning the great importance of the house as an object worth preserving. Dr. Arthur Fairbanks wistfully described the manner in which family associations could renew a sense of "home" for their members. He suggested a use for the certificate of membership in the association, picturing it as a wall decoration in the rooms of children:

> . . . [The children's] eyes may look on the picture of this old place and they will think of how many little children that bent old roof has sheltered; how many little ones have played about these quaint old doors and windows; and how many nights, through the long years, those little children have dropped to sleep safe in the protecting arms of its old oaken beams. And when, in the later years, life's troubles begin to crowd upon the dreams of childhood, these older children shall go from their rooms with courage strengthened in the thought of how many of their forefathers have, in the mornings of the past, gone forth to meet successfully the duties of *their* day.[56]

In the fall of 1903 a new periodical, *Ye Fayerbanke Historial*, made its appearance. It contained detailed accounts of the previous reunions; it advertised the sale of some views of the old house and the different homecomings; and, naturally, it included a plea for funds to save the homestead. The next issue of the *Historial*, which came out in the spring of 1904, called for another reunion that summer, and held out the hope that the property would then belong to the whole family—if each member would do his part. In the second issue the number of money-making devices increased noticeably. One clever promotion scheme involved the sale of campaign buttons that had the Fairbanks house pictured in the center with Theodore Roosevelt and the Republican 1904 Vice-Presidential nominee, Charles W. Fairbanks, on the other side. J. Wilder

Fairbank offered these campaign-year specials at forty cents a dozen to the younger set, who could then sell them for a small profit.[57]

The November, 1904, issue of the *Historial* carried the happy news that the house had been purchased with a $1,000 down payment. Fairbank bluntly warned the members of the association that the "burden of responsibility" was falling on a very few people. He said that if all the members did their best, the 1905 homecoming would include a mortgage-burning ceremony.[58] The actual burning did not take place until the 1912 reunion, but it was a notable achievement even then.[59] The wording of J. Wilder Fairbank's articles leads one to believe that the purchase of the Fairbanks home depended upon the financial support of a relatively small group, in spite of excellent attendance at family homecomings.

There were several other active family groups that saved old homesteads, notably the Aldens and the Howlands, who both claimed Mayflower Pilgrims as their immigrant ancestors. The Pilgrim John Howland Society, organized in 1897, published a small newspaper in 1911 called the *Howland Homestead* which invited all descendants of John Howland to congregate in Plymouth, Massachusetts, to help save their ancestral home.[60] The Howland family finally purchased the house in 1912.[61] The Alden family was successful in saving its homestead in Duxbury, Massachusetts. In 1905, at a family reunion, ten people agreed to give twenty-five dollars a year for five years, and others pledged lesser sums for a similar period. The pledging system must have worked, for the Alden Kindred obtained the property two years later.[62]

It was rare during the years prior to 1900 for a historic house museum to be the work of one individual. In 1881 Tristram Coffin of New York bought the crumbling Jethro Coffin house on Nantucket Island. He found the house in a ruinous condition and repaired it, and then locked it up for sixteen years. Friends finally persuaded him to open the building for public inspection in 1897. Coffin maintained the house for more than forty years before he finally sold it to the Nantucket Historical Association.[63]

The best example of individual sponsorship of a historic restoration was the rescue of "Fruitlands," a farmhouse near Harvard, Massachusetts. The farm had been the scene of a short-lived Transcendentalist community under the leadership of Bronson Alcott just before the middle of the nineteenth century. Miss Clara Endicott Sears, a Boston lady with literary interests, built a summer house on an adjacent site which had an awe-inspiring view of a section of central Massachusetts. She described her feelings toward the old farmhouse next to her property: "At the outset I became interested because the place adjoins mine at Harvard. It was going to rack and ruin and there seemed no one to take care of it." Since both the local historical society and the Alcott Society of Concord were unable to acquire the farm, she decided to dedicate the better part of a year to obtaining a complete title to the place, repairing and restoring it to the period of the Transcendentalist experiment.[64]

Miss Sears invited friends and relatives of Alcott to see the fully restored farm in June of 1914. She gave them a gala welcome, complete with a band and a speaker, Frank Sanborn, who represented the Concord school of philosophers.[65] That fall she opened Fruitlands to the officers of the S.P.N.E.A., who all reacted favorably to her work.[66] Appleton later described Fruitlands as "one of the most successful and encouraging examples of recent preservation work." He considered it more than a restoration, for the place had become a "specialized museum." [67]

Because Fruitlands was the handiwork of one woman, it is essential to understand what Miss Sears hoped to accomplish by her restoration. She wrote in her 1915 catalog for Fruitlands:

> Taken as an example of an old farm house of colonial times the house is an interesting one, apart from the interest that is attached to it through having been the setting for a unique experience tried by men of culture and of literary reputation. If, as some think the quality of the thoughts issuing from the human brain stir tenacious vibrations for good or evil in a house, then surely here there should still be felt an atmosphere conducive to high aspirations, a searching for knowledge, a love of deep meditation. . . .[68]

By 1930 Miss Sears had become more definite on the subject of the mission of her museum:

> This must always be a place where thinkers can come and find an atmosphere that is appealing to them. . . . There are public parks given over to recreation. This place is not meant for recreation. It is meant for inspiration. The surrounding view lends

itself to it. The history of Fruitlands and the Shaker house and the Indian Museum [which she added later] with its historic lore and the whole breadth of the Nashaway Valley are both conducive to it. It must always remain more or less like a poem.[69]

Naturally, it is difficult to estimate the degree to which Miss Sears' poetic goal was achieved. Fruitlands stands almost alone in the history of the preservation movement as a house saved purely for the inspiration of contemplative thinkers.

The fate of the Hancock house in Boston had shown that whenever state or local governments in New England got into the preservation field, they needed help from private groups. One of the first cases to illustrate the weakness of state agencies was the restoration of the Henry Whitfield house in Guilford, Connecticut. The Whitfield house had long been referred to as the "Old Stone House" because of its great antiquity (some date it as early as 1639). Thanks to a fire and some sweeping renovations, little remained of the original structure by the 1890's. In spite of these changes, local enthusiasm was powerful enough to cause the Connecticut Society of Colonial Dames to take an interest in the building. There were several mortgages on the property, and persuasive lawyers representing the mortgagees succeeded in getting both the D.A.R. and the Colonial Dames to go to Hartford to urge the Connecticut legislature to buy the land and house. When the appropriation passed in 1900, the Colonial Dames won custody of the building, although the state owned it. The financial arrangements surrounding Connecticut's first purchase of a historic house show how important private preservation organizations could be. The state paid approximately 45 percent of the total; the Town of Guilford added 35 percent; and the residents of the town subscribed another 10 percent, as did the Connecticut Colonial Dames. In addition to their original donation, the Dames later gave about $2,000, along with $1,000 from the state, to turn the Whitfield house into a museum. In spite of the interest shown by the Connecticut legislature, the Whitfield home remained for many years the only example of a New England state-owned historic house.[70]

On the other hand, the case of the Parker Tavern in Reading, Massachusetts, shows the lack of governmental interest which was more the rule in New England. In 1916 a number of residents generated enough enthusiasm in a town meeting to get the Town of

Reading to purchase the old tavern. The building was then leased to the Antiquarian Society for use as a museum to house its collections.[71] A few years later, interest in the historic structure must have declined, for there was a movement to require the town to sell the tavern to any private citizen who would buy it. Soon a countermovement developed within the community, and the town revised its offer. The tavern was put up for sale for $100 to anyone who would preserve and restore it.[72] A year later this impasse was solved through a compromise by which the Reading Historical Society bought and restored the tavern.[73] This seemed to be the most orderly retreat for the municipal government from its unpopular position of running a historic museum that had not been kept up properly.

The last great preservation effort in New England before 1926 brings us right back to the beginning of the story, for it was a contest between governmental negligence and aroused civic leaders. The building in question was the Old State House in Hartford, Connecticut, designed by Charles Bulfinch at the end of the eighteenth century. One hundred years later the Hartford State House, like its counterpart in Boston, became a city hall. By 1906 it seemed that a new city hall would be built elsewhere in Hartford. The Municipal Art Society of Hartford issued a booklet that contained letters from angry citizens who could not bear to see a commercial building replace a valued reminder of Connecticut's early history.[74] The fate of the Old State House lay in the balance for more than a decade as the work on the new city buildings progressed. In 1911 the Colonial Dames of Connecticut offered to raise $10,000 for the proper restoration of the State House once the city government moved.[75] The Municipal Art Society issued another booklet filled with emotional appeals to local pride. One lady assigned a scarcity value to the building: "Oh, no, Hartford, don't! What do you want, an office building? Office buildings are common. Bulfinches are scarce and there are no more making. You have got one of the best bridges, one of the best graveyards and one of the best second-hand State Houses in the country, Hartford. Keep them all." [76]

Finally in the fall of 1913 the city had to reach a decision on the future of the Old State House. The Colonial Dames had succeeded in raising their $10,000 to restore it.[77] Fortunately the irate people of Hartford had their way, and the Common Council decided to keep the building—but made no decision on its future use.[78] For several years the city held hearings in an effort to solve the problem of an unoccupied state house, and the Municipal Art Society again took the initiative by raising enough money to clean the exterior of the building.[79] A total restoration became the main objective of the defenders of the State House, and they found an effective champion in ex-Governor Morgan G. Bulkeley, a millionaire. He announced that in the spring of 1917 he would start a campaign to raise $50,000 to restore the structure. He gave $5,000 himself to begin the fund and invited ten other prominent men in Hartford to contribute similar amounts.[80] He was so persuasive that within a year wealthy citizens of Hartford gave about $80,000! That amount, when added to the $10,000 the Colonial Dames had already amassed and some money local D.A.R. chapters had given, came to a grand total of $95,000. Most of the restoration work was complete by the early 1920's.[81] The preservation and restoration of the Old State House in Hartford could hardly have been called a governmental enterprise, in view of the work of Morgan Bulkeley and other civic leaders.

Considering its size and population, New England certainly had the largest concentration of old buildings open to the public as historic museums of any section of the country in 1926. The heavy emphasis on local history in New England towns, combined with the more or less urban character of much of the region's population, gave preservationism a bedrock of support that it did not get elsewhere. People in New England wanted their ancient monuments to be an educative force—in the hands of private organizations whose objectives coincided with the older New Englander's desire to glorify his forebears. It was a case of keeping alive an understanding of the sufferings of the hardy pioneers who had first settled the rocky coasts or the determined men who refused to bow to the British.

VI

Preservation Work in the Far West

THE MEN AND WOMEN who set out to preserve the memorials of
the West had some advantages over their eastern counterparts that
help to explain the surprisingly strong preservation efforts in New
Mexico and California. To begin with, there is evidence that
Westerners wanted very much to take on all of the trappings of
what was considered "culture"—including historical societies.[1] In
many instances western preservationists were able to save buildings
that represented periods in the recent past, and so more accurate
restorations were possible. The wide range of historical themes
that could be commemorated by existing buildings was almost beyond belief. One California preservationist cataloged the types of
sites available:

> These romantic California shrines mark the route of the early
> navigators and explorers, record events when other nations held
> sovereignty over the California territory, recall the establishment
> of the Franciscan Missions, tell the story of the American occupa-
> tion, the transition period, the attempt to establish stable govern-
> ment, the gold discovery, the struggle for law and order which
> brought into existence Vigilance Committees, and many other
> equally outstanding events intimately associated with the State's
> early history.[2]

State and municipal preservation work was more important in
the West, for private groups tended to publicize, raise funds and
then give most of the administrative duties to governmental agencies. In some parts of the West the obstacles facing would-be preservers were indeed ominous, even within state governments.
Sometimes the flimsy nature of buildings in frontier areas caused

preservationists to reconstruct rather than restore. At times nature was a major obstacle, in the form of earthquakes and rainstorms. The most serious problem the preservationists faced in the West was the lack of geographical unity which often cut off many landmarks from the visiting public and also prohibited cooperation between preservation groups in various states.

The story of the "Adobe Palace" in Santa Fe, New Mexico, includes some of the difficulties that faced the history-minded pioneer in the West. As early as 1881 William G. Ritch, then Secretary of the Territory of New Mexico, sent an appeal to the Secretary of the Interior on behalf of the Historical Society of New Mexico, asking for some rooms in the palace. Thus, three decades before she was to achieve statehood, New Mexico already had a historical society which wanted to use the old adobe Spanish Governor's Palace in the center of Santa Fe. In 1882 Ritch addressed a petition to Congress asking that the old building be given over completely to the historical society. Behind these requests lay a story that was typically "western." The Second National Bank of Santa Fe occupied rooms in the building, but it promised to vacate them when its lease ran out in 1882. Suddenly the bank requested the right to stay until its new building was completed. The bank officers pointed out that, should the request be denied, they could only be ejected by a court of law. When the bank finally chose to move early in the winter of 1883, Ritch and his friends found that the rooms they had been hoping to get were in the hands of a gun-toting "squatter," a clerk of the Texas, Santa Fe, and Northern Railway! [3]

L. Bradford Prince succeeded Ritch as president of the historical society, and he renewed the appeals to Washington. Prince was a member of the Republican Territorial Committee and therefore had some influential connections. He warned the Secretary of the Interior that the Democrats (who would take over the Presidency on March 4, 1885) would certainly award the coveted rooms in the palace to the historical society. He argued that it was not too late for the Republican Party to gain some advantage for its New Mexican followers by giving the rooms to the society before President Arthur left office. On March 2, 1885, just two days before Cleveland's inauguration as President, the Department of the Interior granted two rooms to the society.

In 1898 Congress passed a law which gave the title to the palace back to the Territory of New Mexico. The historical society could then have control of the whole building for its own educational purposes. Shortly after 1900 the society did become custodian of the entire building—after some private companies using it had been ousted by the courts. Thus one of the oldest structures in the United States (built about 1611) became a museum.[4]

The most active area in the West for preservationism prior to 1926 was certainly southern California, where a mixture of historical groups, church orders, and the state government saved a number of important sites and buildings. This whole movement made good sense geographically and culturally, since southern California had more buildings of historical interest than any other area of the West of comparable size, and the population was growing quickly enough to support strong private organizations.

The major project was the rehabilitation and restoration of the Spanish missions, which dated from the latter half of the eighteenth century. In 1876 the buildings at San Luis Obispo de Tolosa Mission were saved from complete ruin, but the restoration work was not an attempt to recapture the original appearance of the mission. For one thing, the priest in charge had the bells of the mission hung in a small wooden belfry and then had all the exterior surfaces boarded up in order to protect the adobe walls.[5] At Mission San Miguel (near Paso Robles) the results of restoration were happier because only broken tiles and rotted boards were replaced when the Catholic Church reopened the church for services in the 1880's.[6]

If one critical event could have brought the mission situation before the public, it was the ceremony that marked the opening of the grave of Father Serra at the ruined San Carlos Borromeo Mission in Carmel. On July 3, 1882, over 400 people watched as the tomb of the founder of the California mission chain was located. Those present must have been shocked at the condition of one of the greatest mission churches in the state. The roof had fallen in thirty years before, and only a small section of the whole building was still protected from the elements. Within two years Father Casanova raised nearly $20,000 for a partial restoration of the church. The building was rededicated, and by the end of the decade the entire structure was safe from the ravages of the weather.[7]

Soon a number of hereditary organizations took an interest in California's historic buildings. The Native Sons of the Golden West adopted a resolution calling for the preservation of Sutter's Fort in Sacramento at their 1888 Grand Parlor (convention). Within three years the Native Sons subscribed a total of $20,000 for the purpose of purchasing the one remaining building at the fort and presenting it to the State of California. One of California's first millionaires, C. F. Crocker, gave $15,000 for this fund. In 1891 the legislature matched the Native Sons' donation with $20,000 for the rest of the property. Within a year the fort was under the care of a state board of trustees charged with operating it as a historical museum.[8]

Another secular group interested in the fate of the missions was the Landmarks Club of Southern California, founded about 1896 by Charles F. Lummis, publisher of a magazine called *Out West* (formerly *Land of Sunshine*). The Landmarks Club was instrumental in preserving a number of mission buildings before the turn of the century. For example, it expended more than $4,000 on the missions of San Juan Capistrano and San Fernando Rey de España. In both cases the club tried to restrain the forces of man and nature. Lummis reported in 1902 that ". . . these two Missions are being protected and not spoiled. The work has been conducted by experts in Spanish-American architecture, with scrupulous care to preserve the original character of the buildings and the plan." [9]

The Landmarks Club took on another charge in 1901 when Lummis asked for a report on the condition of the Asistencia of San Antonio de Pala. Lummis found that the local Indians around Pala were eager to help reroof the structure and repair the walls. Unfortunately, as is the case in so many well-intentioned restorations, some old work was destroyed. The priest who came to take charge of the Asistencia had the original Indian frescoes whitewashed off the walls.[10]

As the years went by, the Landmarks Club did not lose interest in the missions it had saved. In 1916 the San Fernando Mission was in great need of repairs, so the club instituted a "Candle Day." Each pilgrim that visited the mission that particular day (August

4) bought a candle to carry through the building. One witness saw something poetic in the celebration:

> The sight of six thousand American citizens, each having left behind him the business of the day in order to celebrate an historic event and each bearing a flickering candle, the receipt for a dollar contributed to the restoration fund, trooping through the whitened arches of the old building was an impressive and long-to-be-remembered picture.[11]

By the turn of the century the Native Sons of the Golden West were following up their success at Sutter's Fort by helping to preserve two old buildings at Monterey: Colton Hall and the Customs House. A member of the Stanford Parlor of the Native Sons managed to get a lease from the federal government which gave the Sons custody of the Customs House. A year later, in 1901, the State of California took over the lease on the property and made some much-needed repairs. Soon the Customs House was put under a board of trustees as a vital part of California's state park system. Colton Hall, the meeting place of California's constitutional convention, belonged to the City of Monterey. In 1900 the Native Sons succeeded in getting the California legislature to pass a $1,500 appropriation to help Monterey take care of the hall.[12]

Joseph R. Knowland, a member of the State Assembly and publisher of the Oakland *Tribune,* was an active figure in the preservation field. He devoted much of his time to speaking tours throughout the state. He delivered his lectures with stereopticon slides which illustrated the need for preservation work all over California. At the 1902 Grand Parlor of the Native Sons, Knowland urged the creation of a historic landmarks committee for the purpose of "investigating and reporting upon the condition of the remaining historic buildings throughout the state, and to suggest practical methods for their preservation and restoration." He served as chairman of that committee for many years.[13]

The time seemed opportune for bringing about a loose union of all the California organizations interested in historic preservation. In 1902 Mrs. Eliza D. Keith of the Native Daughters of the Golden West attempted to set up a California Historic Landmarks League—together with the Native Sons and many other historical and educational groups in the state. The league came into being a year later, and Joseph Knowland agreed to act as president.[14]

The new league immediately took on a forbidding task—the preservation of the Mission San Antonio de Padua near Jolon. Here one may see some of the great obstacles that nature placed in the path of the preservationist in the Far West. In the case of San Antonio, isolation was a factor because the ruins of the adobe mission lay many miles from any large town. The interior of the chapel was filled with debris from the fallen ceilings, so a cleanup operation was necessary before the restoration. Local Indians made thousands of adobe bricks for the walls, but before the work was complete winter set in. It was a particularly severe one; twenty-two inches of rain helped to weaken the structure so that the arch in the vestibule collapsed and parts of the newly repaired walls gave way. During the fall of 1905 the Landmarks League did succeed in putting a temporary roof over the chapel to keep the rain from damaging the work that had already been done. The great earthquake of 1906 caused portions of the rebuilt walls to crumble, and it took another year to repair them. By 1907 the league had expended over $7,000 in a project which involved nearly two complete reconstructions of the chapel. When Rexford Newcomb, author of *The Old Mission Churches and Historic Houses of California,* visited the mission in the 1920's the picture was still discouraging:

> Through the oaks a glimpse of the curved fachada, low towers, and broken arches gives the only indication that man has ever been here before. Poor, sad San Antonio! The bells are stilled and gone; the few remaining remnants of the buildings are fast returning to the mother earth whence they came! [15]

California preservationists struggled on, always bringing in more allies to assist in the battle against apathy and nature. The Mission of San Francisco Solano (in Sonoma) was no longer church property in 1903, and it showed signs of serious neglect. The California Historic Landmarks League, the Native Sons and Native Daughters, and other groups banded together with William Randolph Hearst of the San Francisco *Examiner* to raise $5,000 in order to give the mission to the State of California. The campaign was a success, and the state began a long program of restoration and reconstruction at the old mission.[16] Three years later Hearst led another campaign for California preservation groups. This time the object was the old Russian bastion, Fort Ross, on the coast. Again the effort was a success and the state acquired another reminder of the international competition for possession of California in the nineteenth century.[17]

In a few places historical organizations in California tried to save houses that represented the Mexican or Spanish periods in the state's history. The Pio Pico home in Whittier became a museum early in the 1900's, and the City of Whittier shouldered the burden for a decade. By 1914 it became necessary to deed the building to the state, and the house has been state property ever since.[18]

No discussion of preservationism in California would be complete without some attempt to survey the accomplishments of the organization most concerned with the missions, the Roman Catholic Church. All of the missions except two have come back into the possession of the Church, so the primary responsibility for their maintenance has rested with the priests in charge. At times individual priests have taken the initiative by dedicating great portions of their lives to the restoration of one particular mission. The best example of such work was the restoration of Mission Santa Ynez in Solvang by Father Alexander Buckler, who stayed at the mission from 1904 until his death in 1930. When Newcomb visited Santa Ynez in 1924 he discovered that Father Buckler had already collected more than $23,000 for his mission buildings. Buckler had done much of the restoration with his own hands, and so the money had gone a long way. Another priest, Father St. John O'Sullivan, gave twenty-five years of his life toward repairing the mission at San Juan Capistrano.[19]

One of the largest restoration projects undertaken in California up through 1926 was the reconstruction of parts of Mission Santa Barbara in 1926 and 1927. The mission was damaged by an earthquake on June 29, 1925, and the task of rebuilding the towers and setting the wall straight proved to be an expensive one. The two-year restoration cost nearly $400,000, of which more than half came from public subscriptions and private donations, although the Franciscan Fathers contributed a large amount. The strength of the preservation movement in California in 1926 was evident in the speed and magnitude of the public response to a great need on the part of one of the state's most significant historic buildings.[20]

One curious preservation effort came at the close of the Panama-Pacific Exposition in San Francisco in the fall of 1915. The citizens of San Francisco developed an attachment to Bernard Maybeck's Palace of the Fine Arts, which stood partly on land that belonged to the city and partly on the Military Reservation of the Presidio of San Francisco. Since the Fine Arts Palace had been constructed as a temporary feature of the exposition, San Franciscans faced a real challenge. In late November of 1915 the mayor appointed a committee to look into the preservation of the palace as an art museum for the city. Some people thought that the whole structure should be moved to the Civic Center, but the head architect of the exposition quickly pointed out that this was impossible because of the size of the palace.[21]

Finally Representative Julius Kahn (Republican) and Senator James D. Phelan (Democrat) managed to get an amendment to the Army Appropriation Bill of 1916 which authorized the Secretary of War to give the State of California jurisdiction over the portion of the Presidio needed for the Palace of the Fine Arts. The debate on the floor of the Senate on July 24, 1916, made it clear that Senator Phelan did not expect the palace to last more than ten years. He did not believe that the City of San Francisco should expend any money in trying to repair the building, because it would be so costly. The amendment passed, and so the citizens of San Francisco were legally permitted to sit by and watch their beloved palace disintegrate slowly. It would be only fair to add that Maybeck's masterpiece is still there! [22]

It can be seen that prior to 1926 preservationism in the Far West was widely scattered except for the concentration on the missions and houses of southern California. In most cases people turned to the state as the final agent for the care of historic sites, although there were certainly some successful campaigns run by private individuals and organizations.[23] From the foregoing chapters one would conclude that the preservation movement did not exist at all on a national scale; for it appeared to be a succession of "pockets" of historical activity all across the country. Actually this was only partly true, since there were several organizations that attempted to appeal to the whole nation in order to save historic buildings.

VII

National Preservation Organizations
Working Locally

FOR MANY YEARS after the successful campaign to save Mount Vernon, other groups sought to imitate the national organization set up by Ann Pamela Cunningham. The ladies who had saved the Washington Headquarters at Valley Forge and those who refurnished the Hermitage in Nashville failed to generate nationwide interest in their projects. These failures did not prevent other people from conducting national preservation campaigns in the years that followed. In almost every case these hopes were doomed to disappointment, for each national organization found that most preservation work had to be done on the state and local level.

Two of these patriotic organizations that were of sufficient size to contribute to the field of historic preservation were the Daughters of the American Revolution and the National Society of the Colonial Dames of America. Both groups traced their origins back to the early 1890's, and both were open exclusively to women with specific genealogical qualifications. From that point on, differences between them become evident. A study of the preservation techniques employed by these societies reveals some of the differences.

Preservation work quickly became one of the principal aims of the D.A.R. In a letter dated July 21, 1890, inviting women to join the new Daughters of the American Revolution, William McDowell (founder of the Sons of the American Revolution) expressed hope that the new society would encourage historical research and preservation of relics and sites connected with the

Revolution.[1] Once the D.A.R. began to grow, its activities spread into many fields that had some bearing on patriotism, and preservation was only one of them. The following questionnaire, sent out to local chapters by the Committee on Preservation of Historic Spots of the Ohio D.A.R. in 1920, illustrates what the Ohio Daughters considered to be historic preservation:

1. What memorial have you placed during the year 1919?
2. What historic spots have you marked or preserved during the year 1919?
3. How many graves of Revolutionary soldiers have been marked by your chapter in the past?
4. Do you know of any graves of Revolutionary soldiers in your locality or county that are not marked?
5. Would you like information in regard to prices of marking and from where obtained?
6. Will your chapter use its influence with the cemetery authorities to see that the old cemeteries in your locality are kept in good condition?
7. What work has your chapter done in the past in regard to the care of old cemeteries? [2]

In spite of these diverse interests, the D.A.R. saved a considerable number of historic buildings, and it contributed funds to preserve many more.

Early in the development of the D.A.R. it became clear to the national headquarters that the eastern chapters of the society would have to do most of the preservation and restoration, simply because so few Revolutionary sites were in the West or the Middle West.[3] In 1900 a plaintive cry came from a midwestern Daughter, "There are so few landmarks in this part of the country that it is difficult to find anything interesting. I often envy the Chapters of Eastern cities. . . . I fear they do not always appreciate their privileges." [4]

One feature of the D.A.R. which has set it apart from other patriotic groups has been its powerful national organization—with a headquarters in Washington. In 1892 one of the founders of the D.A.R. described this centralization: "Thus one National Society pervades the whole union of States and Territories each member being responsible to the National Society. . . ." [5] The D.A.R. also differed from all other hereditary societies in the magnitude of its membership. By the turn of the century the Daughters were numerous enough to formulate plans for the building of a large headquarters and auditorium in Washington on land that the society already owned.

In spite of all its elaborate national organization, the D.A.R. learned through bitter experience that its preservation work would have to be done through local chapters. The difficulties encountered in the purchase and restoration of one house in Georgia settled forever the issue of National Society ownership of historic sites. The building in question, Meadow Garden in Augusta, had once been the home of George Walton, a signer of the Declaration of Independence. The first evidence of interest in the house came in 1897 in a routine report from the Augusta Chapter. The ladies were considering the purchase of the property, "it being the only spot of any historic interest in this vicinity. . . . If utilized would have to be removed from its present site, as its surroundings are very objectionable, . . . and the rather vague associations that cluster about it not sufficient to arouse any great enthusiasm." [6]

The Georgia delegation proposed the purchase of Meadow Garden to the 1898 Continental Congress (the annual national convention). A committee studied the proposal and reported to the congress that the National Society should buy Meadow Garden and let the Augusta Daughters use it as their chapter house. When this report reached the floor of the congress, an explosive debate began over the use of National Society funds for the purchase of historic properties. Opponents of the appropriation pointed out that a campaign was under way to raise money for Memorial Continental Hall—a building that was to provide both the auditorium and headquarters offices for the D.A.R.[7]

At this critical point in the discussion, Miss Mary Desha rose to speak. She commanded respect as one of the original founders of the D.A.R.

> . . . Continental Hall can wait; these historic spots are passing away. And I believe that this Society will take a stand in the right direction when it appropriates some money to buy the historic spots that are passing away every day. We cannot stop their passing into the hands of improper people unless we do make that appropriation; and it will be one of the greatest things for this Society to take up the thing it was organized to do. (Applause) [8]

A while later a compromise motion passed: the committee which had proposed giving money to the Augusta Chapter for Meadow Garden was instructed to send a letter to every D.A.R. chapter in the country and request ten cents from each member. In this manner perhaps $3,000 could be raised in a year.[9]

When the Continental Congress convened in 1899 Mrs. Porter King, regent of the Georgia D.A.R., announced that the committee had been unsuccessful in its attempt to collect the purchase money for Meadow Garden. In the first place, most chapters considered war work more important at the time. Second, the committee had been unable to obtain a listing of the names and addresses of all the chapters. Mrs. King reported that, since only $233 had come in over the year, there would have to be a better method for raising the needed money. The committee's recommendation was: (1) that a part of the surplus funds in the D.A.R. national treasury be set aside each year for the "purpose of preserving and acquiring historical spots," and (2) that the Continental Congress appropriate enough money to purchase Meadow Garden.[10] A slightly amended motion favoring the general idea of preservation passed easily. It was quite another matter when the second motion was proposed calling for the preservation of Meadow Garden. With each state society expecting a fair share of the national treasury for its own historic houses, the floor of the convention hall became a battleground.

In order to prevent serious trouble, a committee of three was appointed with instructions to leave the room for half an hour and return with a motion. It must be remembered that at this time women had had little experience with parliamentary procedure.[11] In thirty minutes the committee returned with a motion to set up a permanent committee to act on the question of spending money for places of historic interest. The committee also recommended that $1,000 be appropriated for Meadow Garden. This whole procedure did not solve anything, and so someone moved that a Committee on Ways and Means be created to report to the next congress on all items for expenditures. The congress closed the matter by passing a motion recommending a $2,000 payment for Meadow Garden. Everyone seemed to be satisfied.[12]

Shortly after the beginning of the Ninth Continental Congress in February, 1900, the sword of battle was again drawn over the issue of Meadow Garden. Mrs. Park announced in her Georgia state report that the Ways and Means Committee created by the last congress had withheld payment of the $2,000 voted by that congress because the money had been "recommended," not "appropriated." The committee had chosen to bring the question before the new Continental Congress rather than part with the $2,000. Mrs. Park bluntly warned that the Meadow Garden appropriation was "one of the important questions to come up before the Society," and she added that Georgia was profoundly interested in its fate.[13]

When the debate began on the floor, it was again painfully evident that many of the ladies had not had prior experience in handling matters of this kind. The president general proceeded to rule that the Ways and Means Committee was correct in treating the action of the previous congress as a recommendation rather than an appropriation. Immediately Mrs. Park rose to her feet and moved that the appropriation of $2,000 for the purchase of Meadow Garden be approved, a red warning signal for another tussle over the use of National Society funds for local purposes. One delegate said:

> The Congress of 1898 . . . decided on its merits that all local memorial work should be done by the locality wherein the historical spot was situated. (Applause) Now I do not speak here today to say one word against the acquisition of historic spots. . . . The Colonial States are filled with these historical spots, where the blood of the heroes of the American Revolution was shed, and if we should commence and establish a precedent for the purchase of real estate from our national treasury, of these farms, or of any other places, no matter how important these places were, if we should begin that, we should need millions in our treasury. (Applause) [14]

Another delegate spoke ably to rebut her arguments:

> I would like to say that while historical spots are confined to localities, there are historical spots that are the property of the Nation and cannot be confined to one locality. Moreover, the historical spots are confined to the Atlantic coast. The descendants of the people who made these spots historical are spread over forty-five states. Are they to have no voice in the purchase or preserva-

tion of historical spots? Much as I desire the Continental Hall, I do not wish the old spots to tumble to pieces, while the Continental Hall is being built. Let us build with one hand and preserve with the other.[15]

Immediately Meadow Garden's importance as a historic site became an issue. Some northern ladies inferred that the house had only minor significance.[16] During the course of this melee, the president general had difficulty keeping order in the meeting. Some of the ladies were not sure that the word "appropriation" had been used in regard to Meadow Garden the year before. Debate over the cost of the proposed purchase had been bitter enough up to that time, but with sectional strife now a paramount element, further consideration of Meadow Garden constituted a menace to the unity of the entire organization. One Daughter grimly observed that it was hard to find southern ladies who would join the D.A.R. along with the United Daughters of the Confederacy.[17] Finally a compromise motion proposed by a Connecticut delegate passed, providing the sum of $2,000 from the National Society to help the Augusta Chapter purchase the property.[18]

The question of National Society ownership of historic sites would certainly have come up at some time or other in the history of such a large and active organization. It is unfortunate that the house which first claimed the attention of the National Society was of only moderate historic importance, so moderate, in fact, that even the Augusta Chapter had originally questioned the advisability of the purchase.[19] In addition, the property was in the Deep South, an area where the Daughters were especially anxious to prove themselves. Add to these sore points the most divisive question of all: Why shouldn't every state have some claim to the National Society's treasury for its own historic spots? When the debate over the humble farm of George Walton is viewed in this light, it is not surprising to see that the D.A.R. left the work of preservation to local chapters or, in rare instances, to state societies.

Individual D.A.R. chapters entered the field of preservation before the turn of the century. In the spring of 1896 an organization called the Revolutionary Memorial Society of New Jersey was formed with a membership drawn largely from patriotic groups, including the D.A.R. The Memorial Society's sole object was the preservation and restoration of landmarks and buildings connected with the Revolution. One of its first acts was to secure an option on the Washington Headquarters in Somerville, better known as the Wallace house.[20] The society purchased the building a year later and opened it to the public as a museum. As their contribution to the society, four D.A.R. chapters furnished some of the rooms in the house.[21] Any number of other examples of D.A.R. chapters working with preservation groups could be cited; the Wallace house happened to be one of the first.

Occasionally a state society of the D.A.R. united to save a significant building, such as the home of William Henry Harrison in Vincennes, Indiana. The state regent reported in 1909 that the regent of the Frances Vigo Chapter in Vincennes had seen the house falling into ruin and had asked the Indiana legislature to make the house state property. Her petition had failed.[22] In October of 1916 the Vincennes Water Company, which had bought the land for settling tanks, offered the mansion to the Frances Vigo Chapter for $2,000, an amount smaller than the price the company had originally paid for it. The D.A.R. organized a Harrison house committee and began a lively campaign. Contributions came in from several groups and individuals outside the state, as well as from every part of Indiana. Early in 1917, the chapter became the owner of the Harrison house.[23] Later, in 1926 the Indiana State Society of the D.A.R. raised over $10,000 in a state-wide effort aimed at endowing the homestead.[24]

Over a period of thirty-five years, a sizable number of historic buildings were saved by individual chapters of the D.A.R. as chapter houses. These were often gifts from members or from friends since it was such a burden on a small chapter to pay the purchase price on a house in addition to furnishing and maintaining it. These chapters were frequent contributors to other preservation projects. By 1906 articles began to appear in the D.A.R. magazine concerning a number of historic properties that the Daughters were saving. After listing about ten of these houses that were already owned by D.A.R. chapters—or were under their care—one writer prophesied, "Before long these freeholdings will gem the states like jewels in a diadem." She may have been too optimistic, but the D.A.R. did continue to gain one or two old buildings each year in different sections of the country.[25]

Another patriotic women's organization founded at almost the same time as the D.A.R. was the National Society of the Colonial Dames of America. There was a period in the early 1890's when two groups of women were fighting a court case over the use of the name "Colonial Dame." An older organization (by one year), the Colonial Dames of America, sued for the use of the title. The courts decided that as long as the words "National Society" preceded the title of the one organization, it was permissible for both groups to be known as Colonial Dames. The Colonial Dames of America centered mainly in New York and Philadelphia and remained a small exclusive group.[26]

The National Society of Colonial Dames, unlike the D.A.R., included in its field of interest almost any historic site associated with the history of our country. The organization was divided into state societies rather than into local chapters. The Colonial Dames had one goal in common with the D.A.R.—the education of children and immigrants.

> A nation cannot fail of nobility that reveres high ideals, and holds them up for the admiration and emulation of its children. . . . In preserving such landmarks as this [Mount Vernon], in cherishing the associations that belong to them, and in holding them up for reverence of the rising generation, our Societies will find their highest and most compensating work.[27]

One of the first houses saved by the National Society of the Colonial Dames of America was the Van Cortlandt Mansion in Van Cortlandt Park, New York City. The house became city property in 1889, but it was not cared for as a historic museum at that time.[28] In 1896 Mrs. Mary N. Church, president and founder of the National Society of Colonial Dames in the State of New York, succeeded in convincing the state legislature and the City Park Board that they should lease the house to her society for thirty years.[29] The mansion was carefully restored and opened to the public in 1897.[30] Mrs. J. V. R. Townsend, who was also regent of the Mount Vernon Ladies' Association, served as chairman of the Van Cortlandt House Committee in 1900. She reported that the building already had attracted a number of children from New York City. ". . . Americanizing of the children, enlisting their interest in historical sites and characters has a great significance to every thinking mind—the making of good citizens of these many foreign youths." [31]

Not long after they had acquired the house, the ladies reasoned that proper use of the Van Cortlandt Mansion would help to counteract criticism of patriotic organizations. One way was to emphasize the educational value of the house.

. . . The sign-manual of the Colonial Dames of the State of New York, which all can see and read, is Van Cortlandt House. It shows that it is time for the world to cease gibing at our society for being composed of women who only live to count their ancestry and to call themselves aristocrats, and to acknowledge that, aristocrats or no, we can do and are doing, unaided, a work which is unique as a factor towards educating the youth of a great city in Americanism and patriotism.[32]

Other state organizations within the National Society saved old houses in various localities—and the stories of these preservations were not very different from that of the New York group. Some received their properties as gifts from individuals; others leased them from cities or private organizations.

There was only one nationwide preservation effort made by the National Society of Colonial Dames, and oddly enough, it was not for an American building. It was the successful campaign to endow Sulgrave Manor in England. Sulgrave, the ancestral home of the Washington family, had been bought by some Englishmen in 1914 for more than $50,000. They had then presented it to the people of the United States as a "memorial of their common inheritance." [33] The Colonial Dames, whose historical emphasis was on the colonial period, were deeply interested in strengthening our ties with Britain in any way possible. After helping the Sulgrave Institution during World War I, the Dames decided in 1923 to make the manor house financially independent. Their motivation was indeed noble:

We hope through this friendly gift to make a great many Americans interested in Sulgrave and in what we call the Sulgrave Spirit —which is one of goodwill and helpfulness among people of one language, and through them, among mankind; and also to relieve the British Committee of the burden of maintaining the Manor House and grounds.[34]

In two years the Colonial Dames raised $112,000—a sum far exceeding the expectations of those who had originally proposed the idea.[35] The next year, 1926, the Colonial Dames built a replica of

Sulgrave at the Sesquicentennial Fair in Philadelphia. The building was sold after the fair, and the proceeds were sent to England for the restoration of a ruined wing of the manor house.[36]

The D.A.R. had many more members than the Colonial Dames, and the Daughters had a greater variety of activities. Most D.A.R. members regarded the Dames as "too snobbish and far less constructive" than they were.[37] There is evidence that a great economic gulf existed between the average Daughter and the typical Colonial Dame. Few D.A.R. chapters could have found five members who would subscribe a total of $1,000 toward the restoration of an old house in 1896, yet the small New York Society of Colonial Dames did just that! [38] Nor would the following description of a gathering of Colonial Dames apply to most D.A.R. meetings: "Lines of motor cars were parked along the block and chauffeurs and footmen chatted in groups." [39]

Log cabins have always had a peculiar fascination for the American people; in the eyes of the public cabins reflect the qualities that marked great men who rose from humble beginnings. Showmen found that "carefully authenticated" log cabins connected with famous Americans were a profitable investment for display at fairs. Tourists enjoyed seeing the birthplace of a national hero—or a home where he had lived during a particularly trying period in his life, before moving on to a brighter destiny. At the Louisiana Purchase Exposition in St. Louis in 1904 no less than four transplanted log cabins were on exhibition. One guidebook said:

> Log cabins of famous men are among the most interesting relics of the Exposition. The one in which Lincoln lived as a child in Kentucky bears exterior and interior evidences of its age. The Grant cabin built in the 50's is in excellent condition. The best preserved of the presidential cabins is that which was built for Theodore Roosevelt on his ranch in the Bad Lands of Eastern North Dakota a short distance from Medora. . . .
>
> When he was four years old Abraham Lincoln lived in a log cabin in what was then Hardin County, Kentucky. That cabin, duly authenticated, has been brought to the World's Fair and rebuilt under cover. . . . It is a shrine to approach for contrast in spectacle; for realization of the nation's development; for reminder of the country's history through tribulation to triumph.[40]

The fourth cabin was believed to have been built in 1803 on a farm owned by Patrick Henry. There were similar exhibitions at other fairs; the Buffalo Exposition in 1901 had an "Old Plantation" with six historic log cabins.[41]

The most famous log cabin in the country was the traditional birthplace of Abraham Lincoln. The historians of the National Park Service (the present owner) have had great difficulty in tracing the origins of the cabin now resting inside of the memorial building in Hodgenville, Kentucky. They believe that much of the cabin on exhibition was standing in 1861 on the farm where Lincoln was born (in 1809).[42] One Lincoln scholar maintains that the cabin we now see in Hodgenville was not erected until 1895.[43] Whatever its real history, the cabin became the property of A. W. Dennett of New York, the inventor of the "quick lunch." Dennett hired the Reverend James W. Bigham, an evangelist, to aid him in showing the cabin and the birthplace farm to the public.[44] They hoped to have the farm and cabin ready in time for the encampment of the Grand Army of the Republic in Louisville in the fall of 1895. The admission fee was so high that very few veterans made the pilgrimage to Hodgenville.[45] Bigham did not give up easily; he dismantled the cabin and had it exhibited in Nashville in 1897 at the Tennessee Centennial. Bigham also provided a cabin supposed to be the birthplace of Jefferson Davis.[46] A young reporter in Nashville interviewed Bigham in front of the Lincoln cabin in an effort to find out more about the history of the little building. Many years later the reporter remembered Bigham's reply, "Lincoln was born in a log cabin, weren't he? Well, one cabin is as good as another." [47] By 1902 the logs of the Lincoln and Davis cabins were in storage somewhere on Long Island, possibly at Coney Island; and the Lincoln farm was involved in a bankruptcy suit brought on by Dennett's unwise business practices.[48]

Richard Lloyd Jones, editor of *Collier's,* observed a newspaper article in 1904 which depicted the Lincoln birthplace farm as a badly neglected spot. Jones and Robert Collier, publisher of the magazine, took an interest in the fate of the farm. They reasoned that if Mount Vernon could be preserved as a national shrine, the Lincoln farm, too, could be saved. Jones went to Hodgenville to find out if the property could be purchased. He learned that it was tied up in litigation over Dennett's bankruptcy, so he commissioned a local lawyer to notify him if the farm should ever be up for public sale.[49]

In August of 1905 the sheriff advertised the sale of the Lincoln farm. The Hodgenville lawyer telegraphed Jones, who in turn notified Collier. Collier was so convinced that the property must be saved that he sent Jones as his personal representative to the sale. In true journalistic style, Jones pictured for Collier's his battle to win possession of the farm. He arrived in Elizabethtown, near Hodgenville, the day before the sale and met several other men who wanted the farm. In dark hues he painted a verbal portrait of some men who wanted to manufacture whisky on the property. Apparently the pure spring waters on the place were of commercial value, and the distillery in question had visions of a bottle with a flag-draped label which proclaimed "Lincoln Birthplace Whisky." [50]

The next day (August 28, 1905) Jones' two competitors in Elizabethtown were so full of patriotic enthusiasm over the impending success of their mission—and so full of Kentucky whisky —that they were unable to leave for the auction. With one eye cocked toward the road from Elizabethtown (the probable route of the two commercial exploiters), Jones began bidding. The farm was finally knocked down to him for $3,600. He rode back down the road to Elizabethtown and happened to meet one of the men who represented the distillery. The distraught businessman offered Jones $10,000 for the farm. Jones described his feelings about the offer: ". . . Posterity had a better use for the place, and it was not handed over." [51]

Jones also refused offers from local patriotic groups—for he believed that the farm belonged to the nation, not just to Kentucky. "In these years, so crammed with eager life and so possessed with appetite for gain, the lesson of the Lincoln farm becomes the nation's imperative need. Democracy is ever humble." [52] He announced that the property had been deeded to the newly created Lincoln Farm Association, whose motive was to make it "a garden spot in the nation's history, a trysting-place whence North and South, East and West may find the inspiration of national unity." [53]

The Lincoln Farm Association was unusual in that it was the only organization of its type to ever set a maximum limit on donations. The explanation appeared in the 1907 appeal for funds:

Rather than make it possible for a few men of great wealth to contribute large sums to the development of this national shrine it was decided to receive into membership in the Society anyone who contributed to the general fund of the Association as small a sum as twenty-five cents, and to limit all contributions to twenty-five dollars—thus making the great memorial to Lincoln represent the tributes of all the people, whom he loved and served, and not that of a privileged few.[54]

This idealism withered when the association's directors saw the results of the first two years of campaigning. It had cost the Lincoln Farm Association $76,083.45 to raise $105,630.31! Advertising, mailing and other office costs had eaten up the thousands of quarters given by school children; only $29,546.86 remained from the contributions that had come in.[55] Reluctantly the board voted to dispense with the maximum limit on donations in 1908. As soon as the change had been made, Mrs. Russell Sage, Clarence Mackay, and Robert Collier each gave $25,000.[56]

The association's plans for the farm included the return of the original cabin, the cleaning and protection of the old spring, the erection of a monument to Lincoln, the building of a historical museum, and better care of the farm itself. The historical museum was to be, in the words of Theodore Roosevelt, "A Temple of Patriotic Righteousness." *Collier's* conservatively predicted that the Lincoln birthplace would become, because of its central location, the most accessible and beautiful of our historical parks.[57]

The next problem was the purchase of the wandering Lincoln birthplace cabin. A member of the board bought the logs in 1906 from one of Dennett's creditors, who had been storing them in the cellar of a building in Long Island City.[58] The general manager of the association, eager to get some publicity, decided to stage a triumphal tour for the cabin on its return trip to Kentucky. Stops were arranged all the way to Louisville, with side trips to such cities as Columbus and Indianapolis. The governor of Kentucky even provided a military guard for the logs.[59]

The association decided that 1909 (the one hundredth anniversary of Lincoln's birth) would be a perfect year to end its work in Hodgenville. President Roosevelt agreed to lay the cornerstone for the memorial building in which the cabin would be placed. These plans went awry, largely because the money was not on hand to begin construction until 1909. Even with newer and more efficient fund-raising techniques, only $65,000 was available in 1908 for the building program. The memorial building was supposed to cost $250,000, and the association hoped to endow the farm with $150,000 more.[60]

Reluctantly the board turned to Congress for help. The January 2, 1909, issue of *Collier's* carried an article announcing that Congress was considering a bill (H.R. 21848) that would give the association $100,000 for completion of the work at Hodgenville. The bill passed the Senate and reached the floor of the House in amended form—asking for $50,000. Speaker Cannon would not recognize the bill in order to bring it to a vote. *Collier's*, no friend of Speaker Cannon, complained:

> The gist of what the Speaker says against the bill, stripped of any definite misrepresentation into which he may be misled, is that it is a Collier enterprise. That is true only in the sense that the purchase of the farm was originally made by one of the owners of this paper, and that since the formation of the Lincoln Farm Association we have been interested in its success. . . . We have been but one paper supporting the enterprise. It has been encouraged by weeklies, monthlies, and dailies.[61]

Collier's even included a printed letter that could be clipped from the magazine and sent to Speaker Cannon, urging passage of the bill.

The memorial building was ready for dedication in 1911. The association succeeded in getting its former board member, President William Howard Taft, to participate in the ceremony. In announcing the success of the association at that time, the treasurer, Clarence Mackay, said that $383,000 had been raised altogether. Mackay described the response of the American people to the patriotic call of Robert Collier: "Once the plans of the association were formulated, the people of the Nation promptly did the rest." Mackay's optimism does not match the figures given in *Collier's*, which show that the association had only $120,000 in 1910. How did this sum grow to be $383,000 in a little more than a year? The answer seems to lie with the "few men of great wealth" who had been permitted to donate more than $25 after 1908. The obvious inference from the figures given above is that the Lincoln

Farm Association had exhausted the generosity of the American people and had been unable to enlist Congressional help. Wealthy socialites provided the money necessary for completion of the memorial building and a small endowment.[62]

One more task remained for the Lincoln Farm Association. The real intention of Collier and Jones had been the development of a historical park that would eventually be turned over to the federal government. It took several years to accomplish this final objective, but success came on April 5, 1916, when the House Committee on the Library reported favorably on a bill for the creation of a national park at Hodgenville. It was to be the gift of the Lincoln Farm Association and would include a $50,000 endowment that would give the park an income of around $2,000 a year.[63] The bill passed and became law that summer. The federal government thus acquired its fourth historic house—a companion for Arlington, the Shirley house and the House Where Lincoln Died.[64] In September, 1916, President Wilson and Robert Collier, together with a number of other important people, attended ceremonies marking the presentation of the Lincoln farm to the nation.[65]

Even while the celebration was in progress in Kentucky a *New York Times* editorial suggested that there might not be enough historical evidence for accepting the cabin enshrined in the memorial building as the actual birthplace of Abraham Lincoln.[66] At one time or another this problem had haunted the men who directed the Lincoln Farm Association, and they resorted to scholarly means for settling the issue.

Affidavits as to its authenticity were taken from old settlers in the vicinity and those who had moved to adjoining States. These were carefully reviewed by Professors Hart of Harvard, Adams of Yale, and Turner of Wisconsin—officers of the American Historical Society—and Miss Ida M. Tarbell, Lincoln's biographer. They agreed that the logs were genuine beyond a reasonable doubt.[67]

The officers of the association kept these precious affidavits in a safe-deposit box in New York, yet there is no conclusive proof that any of the distinguished professors ever declared the cabin authentic.[68] A number of people, including Lincoln's son Robert, denounced the cabin as a fraud.[69] The most recent report made by the National Park Service historians ends with the statement that the "evidence against the cabin's supporting tradition is over-whelming." [70]

Whether or not the cabin was the right one, the Lincoln Farm Association certainly raised a considerable sum of money, some of it by public subscription. In fact, the association accumulated the largest amount dedicated to the cause of preservation since the people of Boston saved Old South Meeting House in the 1870's.

The influence of the association's publicity was powerful. All over the nation, people wrote and talked about the Lincoln birth-place. One Lincoln collector in Milton, Massachusetts, Miss Mary Bowditch Forbes, went even further. She hired a carpenter to go to Hodgenville in the early 1920's to measure the cabin and study the soil on the Lincoln farm. In March of 1924 Miss Forbes announced to the newspapers that she had supervised the building of a replica of the original cabin in her yard. Its logs were hand-hewn and the clay between them matched the color of the soil at Hodgenville. She opened the replica to the public as a museum with a few simple furnishings and some pictures of the Great Emancipator.[71]

Just as World War I was ending, a new phase in historic preser-vation began. For the first time, groups of people organized to re-construct significant buildings that had ceased to exist. One of the earliest examples was the effort to re-create the lost village of New Salem, Illinois, and make it into a state park. The site of the town had been given by William Randolph Hearst to the Old Salem Chautauqua Association in 1906.[72] G. E. Nelson, who had been elected to the board of the association, noted in the fall of 1916 that the area was fast returning to farmland.

> The idea of Lincoln's old home town serving as a hog pasture, and of the auditorium from the Chautauqua Park being made into a cattle barn on a farm, provoked me into serious considera-tion as to whether or not something could be done to restore New Salem as it was in Lincoln's time, and to resurrect and save the Old Salem Chautauqua.[73]

Nelson was instrumental in reorganizing the Chautauqua Asso-ciation in order to offer an effective summer program. More im-portant, he helped to found the Old Salem Lincoln League, whose goal was the reconstruction of the village Lincoln had known. The league began its activities by holding a picnic on the site of New

Salem on July 4, 1917. Among the guests were many old people who had known Lincoln's New Salem and who wrote down their recollections as a basis for the restoration. The next summer the Old Salem Lincoln League helped with the celebration of the Illinois Centennial by building several cabins on the village site in preparation for a pageant. The performance was a success, and it was followed by a dinner for the entire Illinois legislature. The lawmakers were so impressed with the possibilities of the reconstructed village of New Salem that they passed a bill in the spring of 1919 which created Old Salem State Park. This act put the land under the control of the Department of Public Works and Buildings and assigned to this department the duty of completing "the restoration of, as far as possible, all buildings which were standing thereon during the time that Abraham Lincoln resided in the town of New Salem." [74]

Although William Randolph Hearst and the Old Salem Lincoln League had given the village site to the state, much remained to be done. The league moved the one extant original building back to the park in 1922. During the decade after World War I, the Illinois legislature did not appropriate enough money to complete the restoration, so the Lincoln League had to send out booklets all over the country in an attempt to generate national interest in New Salem. The actual reconstruction of the village did not come until the depression of the 1930's.[75] In spite of the delay in completing New Salem, one must not forget that the Illinois legislature was ready as early as 1919 to rebuild a whole town.

A more elaborate and immediately successful reconstruction took place at almost the same time in New York City where a group of women proposed the rebuilding of Theodore Roosevelt's birthplace at 28 East 20th Street. Soon after the sudden passing of Roosevelt in January of 1919, two organizations formed to perpetuate his memory: the Roosevelt Memorial Association, a men's group created by the Republican National Committee, and the Women's Roosevelt Memorial Committee. The former selected three goals: (1) the erection of a memorial to Roosevelt that would rank with the Washington Monument, (2) the propagation of the ideals of Theodore Roosevelt through books dealing with his life, and (3) the creation of a memorial park in Oyster Bay, New York, Roosevelt's former home.[76]

The Women's Roosevelt Memorial Committee, within two months of his death, announced that it had purchased the late President's birthplace. *The New York Times* described the building: "Before the house was sold several years ago for commercial uses it was a four-story brownstone, but alterations to make it useful for a restaurant and shops made it of only two stories, so that the interior will have to be restored entirely." The ladies intended to accomplish this, using descriptions furnished by members of the family along with some passages from Roosevelt's autobiography.[77]

In March the committee adopted the formal title of Woman's Roosevelt Memorial Association. The new organization hoped that the restored house (the ladies did not use the word "reconstruction" until later) would be a "living thing," a place where youth could come together to deepen its understanding of America.[78] Later that spring Mrs. Roosevelt gave the project her blessing by announcing that, of all the proposed memorials to her husband, this one pleased her most.[79]

Meanwhile, the men's organization was having a fruitful year. It, too, was taking advantage of the nation's grief over "Teddy's" unexpected demise. Roosevelt obviously still held a place in the hearts of many of his fellow citizens, for Americans gave over one million dollars to the men's group that first year. The Memorial Association sponsored a "Roosevelt Week" in October of 1919, during which nearly 300,000 meetings were held throughout the country. No Roosevelt appeal in the years that followed ever met with such success.[80]

The women's group started a newspaper called the *Woman's Roosevelt Memorial Bulletin* for the purpose of carrying its mission to the public. The first issue of the little paper indicated that a national organization had been formed—with committee chairmen in eighteen different states.[81] The material in this first paper ranged from an appeal for funds for the birthplace to a letter from the "grateful" people of Cuba asking for a new two-cent coin with Roosevelt's image on it.[82] The February, 1920, *Bulletin* brought the news that a woman architect, Theodate Pope of Farmington, Connecticut, had been chosen to design the Roosevelt house, together with a building next door on property that the association had also purchased.[83] The *Bulletin* had features that were reminiscent of the format of the *Mount Vernon Record,* which had served a similar function sixty years earlier. There were detailed accounts from different state chairmen of activities within their particular areas, quotations from letters that accompanied donations, lists of notable people who had allied themselves to the cause, and, above all, the names and addresses of all the state chairmen.[84]

During 1919 the Woman's Roosevelt Memorial Association raised $121,344, but it spent $86,177 in the acquisition of the two properties on East 20th Street. Other expenses incidental to the organization left the relatively small sum of $7,175 in the association's treasury.[85] In the spring of 1920 the ladies launched their drive in New York City with an intensive two-week campaign to raise $250,000. Volunteer teams worked through every means at their disposal to reach the public. Small cardboard banks in the shape of the completed birthplace were handed out to children. Medallion pins were offered to all adults who contributed one dollar or more and to children who gave twenty-five cents.[86] The treasurer's reports lead one to believe that the campaign was not very profitable. After the rich harvest of 1919, Americans had become less interested in giving to Roosevelt memorials.

The ladies had ambitious plans for their center for Roosevelt Americanism. One idea, which never came into being, was the creation of a number of national scholarships based on prize essays dealing with Theodore Roosevelt. Naturally, these scholarships could not be set up without a $25,000 trust fund. Another plan that shows how deeply these ladies were interested in education was the proposal that copybooks in the schools include the sayings of Roosevelt—and that advanced textbooks be made to conform to Rooseveltian ideas on Americanism and the "square deal." [87]

As their separate campaigns lagged, the two Roosevelt organizations found strength in unity. Friends of the two groups had been urging a union for several years. The men's association had been unable to have a Roosevelt memorial built in Potomac Park in Washington, D. C., and it was involved in a legal hassle over the land in Oyster Bay that was intended for a park. The men had published one book on Roosevelt, and they still possessed most of the million dollars raised during 1919. The ladies, on the other hand, had a workable project that was standing still for lack of funds; in addition, their building could serve as a museum for both organizations.

In the fall of 1922 the two groups negotiated a partial union. The Roosevelt Memorial Association gave the women $150,000 toward the completion of the reconstructed birthplace. The men also placed their collection of Roosevelt memorabilia in the hands of the Woman's Roosevelt Memorial Association along with $15,000 for installing the objects in the exhibit rooms of Roosevelt House. The new birthplace included an auditorium where the men could show their films of Theodore Roosevelt's life.[88] The relationship seemed ideal for both groups. The Roosevelt Memorial Association later reported that over the years it had become entirely satisfied with the idea of working in Roosevelt House. The cost of maintaining the building, when divided between the two organizations, had been reasonable, although the Woman's Roosevelt Memorial Association did not solve all of its financial problems right away.[89] Mrs. Hammond, president of the women's group, issued a call in 1923 for $30,000 to furnish the house and $13,000 for finishing the auditorium.[90]

The patriotic work being done on the reconstruction of Roosevelt House came under attack from an unusual source. The May 1, 1923, New York Times (p. 23) printed a letter from Albert A. Volk, a man who claimed to have supervised the wrecking of the birthplace. Volk said that when the original building was in the process of demolition in 1916 (only three years before the movement to rebuild it!), he had written to Colonel Roosevelt to ask if he wanted any of the old doors or mantels from the house. Roosevelt's secretary had answered that the colonel could not remember anything from that house which he wanted for himself. So, according to Volk, all of the original material had been carted over to the Lower East Side to be used for firewood. The point of the letter was that the memorial house would not contain a single portion of the birthplace; it was to be entirely new with some original family furniture.[91]

Hermann Hagedorn, managing director of the Roosevelt Memorial Association, replied to Volk's attack in behalf of the two organizations. He said that the ladies had never pretended to be rebuilding the structure from original materials—although they had found one of the old mantels—but they were doing considerable research in order to re-create the appearance of the birthplace. He concluded on a lofty note: "Roosevelt House is only incidentally a building. It is a rallying place, a spiritual headquarters for those Americans who look on their country as Roosevelt looked on it, and believe in the American idea and are not too indolent to fight for it. First and foremost, Roosevelt House is a challenge." [92]

During the speechmaking at the dedication of Roosevelt House on October 27, 1923, Mrs. Hammond listed some of the accomplishments of her association.[93] Prominent among the good works was the formation of Roosevelt clubs in many schools throughout the country. These clubs with their membership of over 25,000 students must have contributed a large sum of money toward the purchase of the lot and the reconstruction of the house. In one issue of the *Roosevelt House Bulletin* the ladies cited a "point system" that pupils had worked out in Bryant High School, Long Island City, New York. Members of that Roosevelt Club were given examinations on certain topics and then were advanced in the club through a series of emblems. Among the activities whereby members could earn "points" were: a visit to Roosevelt House with written impressions, attendance at a Roosevelt mass meeting, special services in the school, special services in the club or home, the reading of two books about Roosevelt, organization of another Roosevelt club in some other school, and placement on the honor roll. These activities were certainly geared toward good citizenship, an important objective of the program that the Woman's Roosevelt Memorial Association had originally envisioned.[94]

Financial problems continued to plague the association. Only four states reported contributions to Roosevelt House early in 1924.[95] That year the women started a campaign to raise a $250,000 endowment to finance their many-sided program. A year later, in the spring of 1925, the president sadly reported that only $62,000 had been collected, with a possibility of $5,000 more to come. She also mentioned that there was still a first mortgage of $50,000 which needed to be paid off.[96]

The inevitable question that one has to ask in reviewing the work of a patriotic crusade of the type that rebuilt the Roosevelt birthplace is whether or not it succeeded in carrying out its objectives. A careful study of the issues of the *Roosevelt House Bulletin* during the years 1925 and 1926 provides some revealing figures about the number of school groups that passed through the house. During these two years many school children saw the museum, but the attendance figures were not as large as one might expect in a great metropolitan area such as New York City. Relatively few student groups used the auditorium; rather, D.A.R. chapters and fraternal or patriotic organizations held frequent meetings there. Instead of serving as a center for Americanism, Roosevelt House became more of a center for patriotic societies and social affairs. This does not imply that the whole effort was a failure; it simply means that the ladies did not achieve all the noble goals that they set for themselves. By 1925 the editor of the *Bulletin* admitted that there were only 412 subscribers to the association's magazine.[97] Enthusiasm had waned; the spirit of the campaign was gone. The operation became a housekeeping job, rather than a crusade for Americanism.

The tone of discouragement evident in the later reports of the Woman's Roosevelt Memorial Association actually pointed toward one of the great challenges that faced most of the preservation groups that tried to appeal to the American people as a whole. Almost every historic building, no matter what hopes its would-be preservers might have cherished, turned out to be a local museum. Even houses connected with nationally important figures were finally rescued by people who lived near the buildings themselves (except for the Lincoln cabin). Large national patriotic organizations found that state societies and chapter groups had to handle almost all of the preservation work, for expenditure of national funds for historic houses was a divisive issue. Whether it originated with national organizations or not, preservationism invariably terminated as a local activity in the hands of dedicated amateurs.

VIII

Monticello — the Second Mount Vernon

THE STORY OF THE PRESERVATION OF MONTICELLO encompasses the
entire period covered by this book. Although the home of Jefferson was one of the first buildings to be bought for preservation, it
was not finally saved until the late 1920's. During the ninety years
between 1836 and 1926 a number of people attempted to make
Monticello public property, and some of them even went so far
as to urge Congress to make it one of the first national historic sites.
A great variety of important political and philosophical questions
arose during the battles over the fate of Monticello, most of which
had some bearing upon the Levy family, who controlled the property prior to 1923.

There are circumstances connected with Uriah Phillips Levy's
acquisition of Monticello in 1836 which would lead one to believe
that Levy was in some ways an early preservationist. Uriah Levy
was a lieutenant in the United States Navy who had come into a
fortune. His record in the Navy was somewhat uneven, for he
went through a series of courts-martial, usually caused by minor
clashes with fellow officers who had found him difficult to work
with.[1] Both the manner in which Levy came to own Monticello
and his reasons for buying it are shrouded in mystery. Years afterward his nephew claimed that Levy had been ordered to save
Monticello by President Andrew Jackson.[2] An enemy of the Levys
denied this story, implying that Uriah had beaten a friend of the
Randolph family (Jefferson's descendants) in a race to see who
would get Monticello.[3] Probably neither story has much foundation in fact, and the only certainty is that Uriah Levy did purchase
the house and 218 acres by a deed dated May 21, 1836.[4]

As a Jew, Levy may well have been impressed by Jefferson's ideas on religious freedom. Before a court of inquiry in 1857, while trying to regain his rank of captain in the United States Navy, Levy declared:

> Remembering always that the great mass of my fellow-citizens were Christians; profoundly grateful to the Christian founders of our republic, for their justice and liberality to my long persecuted race; I have earnestly endeavored, in all places and under all circumstances, to act up to the wise and tolerant spirit of our political institutions.[5]

In the fall of 1858 Uriah Levy wrote his lawyer in Charlottesville about the Fourth of July celebration at Monticello. Wishing that he could have been in Virginia for the festivities, Levy referred to Jefferson as "the man who was among the first . . . to call the nation into being, who guided its infant footsteps and taught its infant tongue to lisp no other sentiments than those which were truly Republican." [6]

Further evidence that Uriah did not buy Monticello merely as a summer residence can be found in Benson Lossing's description of a visit to the house in 1853. According to Lossing the mansion was in good condition and a few of Jefferson's belongings were still there. In addition, Lossing noticed a copy of a statue of Jefferson that Levy had presented to Congress years before.[7]

The most convincing and unusual proof of Uriah's preservationist intent was his will, in which he left Monticello to the "People of the United States." One book on the subject implies that Levy's will had been colored by strained family relations, and adds that had he lived one day longer, the will might not have been worded as it was (i.e., giving Monticello to the nation).[8] There is some strength in this argument, since Levy had been a wealthy bachelor who married a much younger woman.[9] There is another possible explanation for Levy's bequest, for he may have been influenced by the Mount Vernon movement, which was particularly strong at that time. Perhaps the rough treatment given John Washington had led Levy to give his home to the nation rather than to his family.[10]

Which of these theories regarding Levy's motives is valid? The best evidence is contained in the will itself. It provided for the disposition of several Virginia farms and some New York real estate. The Virginia lands were willed to a nephew, Asahel Levy, and the New York property went to his wife. Monticello itself was offered to the American people as an agricultural school for the orphaned children of warrant officers of the United States Navy. Should this bequest be refused, the estate was to go to the people of Virginia and then to three Hebrew Congregations.[11] Levy died in New York City on March 22, 1862. The fact that the will was dated May 13, 1858, makes the story of a family squabble that might have been settled if the "Commodore" had lived for one more day seem unlikely. Surely a disagreement that had existed for four years would not melt away so suddenly.[12] However, the omission of a large number of Levy's close relations from the will lends force to the idea of a prolonged family battle over his late marriage. There is no significant evidence of the influence of the Mount Vernon movement on Uriah Levy.

It was unfortunate that Congress and the Department of Justice were compelled to decide upon the Levy will under the stress of the Civil War. A resolution to accept the gift of Monticello did not reach the floor of the Senate until the last day of the session, March 3, 1863. Since no bequest of this particular type had ever been considered before, the debate was short but enlightening. One of the supporters of the resolution argued that the legacy had to be accepted within a reasonable length of time, or the federal government would lose its option. An opposing speaker warned his colleagues that the will was currently the subject of a heated litigation in the New York courts. Other Senators urged further investigation of the matter if the government wished to avoid involvement in the impending lawsuit. Nevertheless, the resolution did pass, making it clear that the majority stood ready to accept Monticello on Levy's terms.[13]

While the Senate went on record as prepared to assume the trust set up under the Levy will, the executive branch of the government had to consider the wisdom of operating Monticello as an agricultural school. The United States District Attorney for the Southern District of New York, E. Delafield Smith, wrote to his superior, Attorney General Bates, inquiring whether or not the government should make itself a party to the suit then in progress. After explaining that the Levy family was contesting the will, Smith asked if the government was likely to accept the trust—expressing his private opinion that the terms were so "onerous" that Congress would probably not agree to them. He enclosed a copy of the proceedings of the New York State Court of Appeals.[14] Two days later came a reply saying that in the judgment of the Attorney General, the bequest had not been accepted by act of Congress and that therefore it did not make the government a party to the court proceedings over the will.[15] Bates also sent a letter to Vice-President Hamlin stating that he believed the government could not be a party to the Monticello controversy because the suit would probably be long and costly, and he was not sure that the federal government could "assume the execution of purely charitable trusts." [16] As far as the government was concerned, disposition of the Levy will was now up to the State of Virginia or to the Portuguese Hebrew Congregations of New York, Philadelphia and Richmond, for all of these had been named as contingent successor beneficiaries of the trust.

In New York the will was the subject of deep legal cogitation. During November of 1863 the New York Supreme Court decided by a vote of two to one that the will was void, thus favoring the disinherited branch of the Levy family, led by Uriah's brother Jonas. The court ruled that the gift was not for a specific object and that the beneficiaries were not clearly named. In addition, the judge who wrote the majority opinion argued that Levy's scheme could never have worked anyway, because the governments of the United States and of Virginia could not have acted as trustees of such a grant.[17] The New York State Court of Appeals, in 1865, by a vote of six to two, upheld the decision of the lower court, stressing the fact that Levy's purpose had been too indefinite. The Levy family then had to find some way of dividing up the property.[18]

While this legal battle was raging between Levy's widow and the rest of the family, a new factor entered the already complicated story of Monticello. Uriah Levy had been an officer in the Union Navy, with a summer home in Confederate territory. Although there is dispute as to the exact date, it seems clear that sometime between 1862 and 1864 the Confederate Government confiscated Monticello. Levy's nephew, who was a minor at the time, claimed that Jonas had gone down to Monticello to save it and had been held as hostage by the Confederates.[19] In any event, it appears that the plantation, slaves and furnishings were sold, and the careful work of Uriah Levy in reassembling the Jefferson articles was to no avail.

The Monticello case moved to the Circuit Court of the City of Richmond in November of 1868. The Levy family initiated a partition suit which pitted one faction led by Jonas Levy against Mrs. Ree (Uriah's widow) and others mentioned in the will.[20] For the next year it appeared that Monticello would soon be offered up for sale in order to settle the case, but Jonas Levy and his son Jefferson Monroe Levy had other ideas. They wanted to clear up all the outstanding issues regarding the property.[21] During the early and middle 1870's Jefferson Levy began buying out the many heirs named in the suit. He faced a very difficult task, for Uriah Levy had seven brothers and sisters, and many of them had a number of children. By 1878 Jefferson Levy had acquired more than half of the ownership of Monticello by this slow process.[22] The next year he consented to a public sale of Monticello, and on March 20, 1879, he appeared in Charlottesville and bought the farm for $10,050, to be paid in three annual installments. Therefore in March of 1881 he became the sole owner of Monticello after a long and costly search for heirs; at last Monticello was again a home.[23]

The tragedy of Monticello was almost complete, for the litigation over the Levy will consumed nearly two decades and caused frightful ruin in the house that everyone was trying to "save." Joseph Wheeler, Uriah's old overseer, remained as tenant; and the Levy family tried to remove him several times.[24] Apparently Wheeler took advantage of the insecure legal status of Monticello, as shown by the following report made in 1878 by a Congressman who had made a recent visit:

> Desolation and ruin mark everything around the place. I went through the house in which Jefferson lived. There is scarcely a whole shingle upon it, except what have been placed there within the last few years. The windows are broken, everything is left to the mercy of the pitiless storm. The room in which Jefferson died is darkened; all around it are the evidences of desolation and decay—a standing monument to the ingratitude of the great republic.[25]

Wheeler's successor as superintendent of the estate left this description of the same era:

During this period Monticello went into decay and near ruin. Wheeler permitted the young people of Charlottesville, in the early days of his occupancy, to use the mansion for balls and entertainments, and the lawns for picnic parties, always charging a fee for use. The Monticello Guards used to come to the place for target practice and were quartered in the mansion. On the spacious lawn which Jefferson had leveled at so much trouble and expense of labor, Wheeler had a shabby vegetable garden, and at one end a pen for his pigs. Cattle were stabled in the basement during the winter, and in the beautiful drawing salon with its handsome parquet floors, Wheeler had a granary where he set up a hand fanning mill and winnowed his grain.[26]

A professor at the University of Virginia reminisced in 1916:

I can remember in my first years as a student there when Monticello was wide open to anybody. There was an old fellow named Wheeler there who would give a right of way all over Monticello. My first view of Charlottesville and all that beautiful country there when I was a boy at college, was gained from the roof of Monticello. We were allowed to parade all up through the house, and we went wherever we wanted, and a lot of boys would go up and watch the sunset from the roof.[27]

The new owner of Monticello, Jefferson Levy, defended his part in the whole regrettable situation:

It was my good fortune to be accorded the opportunity of restoring this historical place at almost the last moment when restoration to its original state was possible. In this work of restoration I spent a great deal of time and money. . . . I have kept it up, at my own expense, not as a place of residence, but as a place where admirers of Jefferson could go and find, as near as possible, the conditions which obtained at the time Jefferson lived there.[28]

Levy apparently believed in the virtues of private ownership of Monticello, and he was convinced that he had done a praiseworthy job on the restoration of the estate. He was unwilling to accept any blame for the conditions which had brought about its near collapse in the 1870's.

There has been a debate over just how far Jefferson Levy carried his restoration, and over the nature of his motives. His superintendent later claimed that Levy had attempted to recover the Jefferson objects sold at the time of the Confederate confiscation of the property.[29] The Dean of the Department of Engineering at the University of Virginia testified in 1916 before a Congressional committee:

> I only know what Mr. Levy did with it [Monticello] after he got it; he put it in order and restored it, and he did not alter any thing about it. I do not know of any one thing Mr. Levy has done to make Monticello different from what it was at the time of Jefferson, and I know of hundreds of things he has done to make it the same.[30]

In order to document his testimony, the Dean proceeded to describe Levy's restoration of some Wedgwood plaques on the dining-room mantel.

It is possible that Levy's restoration of Monticello may not have been quite as exact as his defenders claimed it was. A description of the house in 1887 seemed to prove that the "whole establishment has been put in excellent order by the present owner, . . . and is now as sound and substantial a country mansion as it ever was." But there is an odd note to mar Levy's contention that he had created a Jefferson shrine, for the same account continued: "There is a modern air about its furnishings and fittings which is not Jeffersonian." [31] The obvious conclusion is that Monticello had become a comfortable country home. For instance, Jefferson Levy may have attempted to retain architects from the firm of McKim, Mead and White to add some rooms onto the house because he believed he needed space for entertaining.[32]

Although there has been no general agreement on the thoroughness of the restoration done by Levy, all those who have known Monticello have acknowledged that he had chosen a reliable and devoted man as his superintendent in Thomas L. Rhodes. Rhodes was a local resident who came to Monticello in 1889 and remained for nearly half a century, devoting his time to preserving the house as best he could. He was in complete charge of the restoration until the Thomas Jefferson Memorial Foundation took over the place in 1923; then he continued as superintendent without direct control over restoration policy.[33] During the many years that Levy owned Monticello, Rhodes had been paid some of the time—and at other times he had loaned Levy money. Apparently Levy had periodic financial reverses, though he was usually affluent.[34]

Jefferson Levy enjoyed Monticello for about a decade and a half before he was approached by anyone suggesting that the home of Thomas Jefferson should be a public shrine. In 1897 William Jennings Bryan, taking advantage of a period of increased interest in Jefferson, wrote to Levy asking what price he would charge the government for Monticello. Levy retorted that all the money in the Treasury could not pay for the mansion. Both letters were printed in the Richmond *Dispatch* of April 9 and 15, 1897.[35] Levy and Bryan apparently misinterpreted the true meaning of their exchange, for each of them later ascribed a different reason for Bryan's willingness to let Levy live in Monticello undisturbed. In 1912, while making a public statement regarding Bryan's earlier inquiry, Levy reasoned: "Mr. Bryan was disposed, at one time, to ask the Government to buy it, but after giving the matter full consideration he changed his mind, and assured me that Monticello was in safe hands." [36] Five years later he again implied that he had convinced Bryan that "were it not for me the home of Jefferson would have disappeared and there would now be no Monticello." After this, according to Levy, Bryan "did not press the matter." [37] Bryan had a completely different impression of their correspondence. As Secretary of State in 1914, he wrote to Levy:

> You will remember that several years ago I suggested to you the propriety of selling Monticello to the National Government. You then declined, on the ground that you did not like to have it go out of the possession of your family. I have never relinquished the hope that you would some day yield to the popular desire that the Government should own Monticello. . . .[38]

There is an important dissimilarity between the two accounts. Bryan said that he had desisted from further requests for public ownership because he respected Levy's wish to keep the estate in the family. Levy, on the other hand, believed that he had persuaded Bryan that private ownership would insure better care of such an important historic spot.

Firmly convinced that he could continue to live in the mansion "as trustee for the people Jefferson loved," Levy continued to act as host for groups of patriotic pilgrims who came to Charlottesville to see the home of Thomas Jefferson.[39] Unfortunately, some did not readily acknowledge Levy's position of "trustee." An article entitled "A National Humiliation," by Amos J. Cummings, appeared in the August 24, 1902, issue of the New York *Sun*. Cummings, a former member of Congress, pictured his recent visit to Monticello in scathing terms. He had been stopped at the gate by a colored man who demanded payment of twenty-five cents for entrance to the grounds. The gatekeeper then declared that no one could see the inside of the house; but, as Cummings added, there was really nothing of Jefferson's in the house anyway. The ex-Congressman was furious to find that Levy charged this fee of "patriotic Americans," and to find that Levy valued the house at the grossly inflated price of $100,000. "Possibly he imagines that he can eventually sell it to either the State or Federal Government for this sum," was Cummings' wry comment. He clearly favored public ownership of the property to preserve it from decay—and, one might suppose, from the admission fee as well.

At almost the same time as the Cummings attack, a small book was published privately by Jefferson Levy (it probably was more than a coincidence). It was supposedly written by George Alfred Townsend, but the comments in the introduction and the general tone of the book lead one to believe that Levy had a definite influence on its viewpoint. The text was in the form of two long letters from Townsend reporting on a pleasant weekend at Monticello. The actual reason for the publication of the book can be found in Levy's Introduction:

> In the almost three-quarters of a century since Commodore Levy and his heirs have possessed Monticello, they have made no publication of their almonry, desiring to have Mr. Jefferson's great benignity ever at the front. . . . Late frivolous biographies, however, treat Monticello as if it were but incidentally or recently held; not in the possession of an uncle and his nephew longer than of the original proprietors. . . . The need of some short account of the preservation of Monticello, to answer the inquiries of its numerous visitors, is at least enforced by the swift railroads which put Monticello in the suburbs of Washington. "Gath's" [Townsend's] letters come near enough to the events to supply a *souvenir* and relieve the owner of Monticello from daily interrogations.[40]

Even if this booklet were not intended to answer Cummings' charges specifically, it certainly served that purpose. The account of the condition of Monticello and the selfless hospitality of its proprietor appears to be unduly laudatory: "[Jefferson Levy] is mild, constant, patient but of discrimination. It is difficult to see how a property like this could have been conserved better in one family seventy years, under only two possessors, with no mistakes." [41]

For several years Levy's ownership of Monticello remained unquestioned; then, in 1911 a new figure appeared on the scene to plead with him to help make the home of Jefferson national property. This person was the most ardent and persistent lover of Monticello to emerge up to that time: Mrs. Martin Littleton, the vivacious and able wife of a Congressman from New York. Mrs. Littleton found that the city of Washington lacked any real memorial to Thomas Jefferson—and she decided that the only proper memorial would be Jefferson's own home. Going right to the heart of the matter, Mrs. Littleton decided to spearhead a campaign to persuade Jefferson Levy to sell Monticello to the United States Government.

Her initial salvo in the struggle was a short booklet entitled *One Wish.* During the winter of 1911–1912 she mailed copies of this appeal to influential people throughout the United States.[42] In her introduction Mrs. Littleton declared that the preservation of Monticello would be the most fitting tribute that the people of the nation could offer to the memory of Jefferson. She stressed that Jefferson was not "one man's man"—referring to the fact that Levy was the only person outside the Jefferson family who had legal access to the house and tomb. Mrs. Littleton was firm in her conviction that Jefferson belonged to all the people, and that their wish was also hers—to "lay upon his grave a nation's tears." She presented some details of Uriah Levy's will in order to convince her readers that he, too, had had that "one wish." [43]

During the first months of 1912 Mrs. Littleton was occupied with organizing a group to be known as the Jefferson-Monticello Memorial Association, which was to assist in the movement to make Monticello a public shrine. If one can believe her later statements, Mrs. Littleton was attempting to contact Jefferson Levy personally at this time; for she claimed that she had approached him three times concerning the public ownership of Jefferson's home. She even had a tablet designed by Tiffany's which would commemorate Levy's public spirit in giving Monticello to her association. But this effort did not move Levy in the least.[44]

(Photograph by Robert R. Sisson, © 1948 National Geographic Society)

Touro Synagogue, Newport, R. I.

Ann Pamela Cunningham. Portrait by James Reid, c. 1871, at Mount Vernon.

Soldiers at Mount Vernon
during the Civil War.

Meeting of the Council, 1873, Mount Vernon. Last photograph of
Ann Pamela Cunningham.

Arlington House, Arlington, Va. General Samuel P. Heintzelman,
staff and ladies on east portico steps of mansion, c. 1861.

The Hermitage, Nashville, Tenn., March, 1856.

Independence Hall, Philadelphia, Pa. Vestibule of Congress Hall and the Senate Chamber on the second floor, as restored 1913.

Independence Hall, Philadelphia, Pa. Ground floor hallway, c. 1901.

Independence Hall, Philadelphia, Pa. Senate Chamber on second floor, as restored 1913.

Graff House, Philadelphia, Pa., where Jefferson drafted the Declaration of Independence. McAlles photograph taken in 1855.

(Thomas Jefferson Memorial Foundation)

Hamilton Grange, New York, N. Y.

(American Scenic and Historic Preservation Society)

John Hancock House, Boston, Mass. 1859 photograph.

Old South Meeting House, Boston, Mass. Exterior.

Hartford State House, Conn., 1961. Designed by Charles Bulfinch, completed in 1796.

El Palacio Real de Santa Fe, Santa Fe, N. M. Interior court.

Mission Carmel, Carmel, California. Showing earthquake damage in 1906.

Mission Carmel, Carmel, California. After restoration.

Abraham Lincoln Birthplace National Historical Park, Hodgenville, Ky. Shrine containing the log cabin reputed to be Lincoln birthplace, 1935.

(National Park Service)

Abraham Lincoln Birthplace National Historical Park, Hodgenville, Ky. Traditional Abraham Lincoln Birthplace log cabin, 1959.

(National Park Service)

Theodore Roosevelt
Birthplace, New
York, N. Y.

(National Park Service)

(Library of Congress)

Mrs. Martin W. Littleton in 1914.

(Corcoran Gallery of Art)

Commodore Uriah P. Levy.
Artist unknown, oil.

Monticello. Water color by Peticolas, 1826.

Monticello,
c. 1870.

Monticello. View from garden.

The Octagon, Washington, D. C. Street façade.

1634 house of East Street, Ipswich, Mass.
Edwin Whitefield Collection.

Essex Institute, Salem, Mass., a 17th century house, 1912.

William Sumner Appleton.
Taken in the 1930's.

Abraham Browne House, Watertown, Mass. April 1919, before restoration.

Abraham Browne House, Watertown, Mass. December 1919, during restoration.

Abraham Browne House, Watertown, Mass. January, 1924, following restoration.

(National Trust for Historic Preservation, photo by Mellow, 1962)

Shadows-on-the-Teche, New Iberia, La. Street façade.

(National Trust for Historic Preservation, photo by Mellow, 1962)

Shadows-on-the-Teche, New Iberia, La. Interior, dining room.

Sometime that spring Mrs. Littleton must have decided that further direct appeals to Levy were useless, so she turned to Congress. She succeeded in having a resolution introduced that would create a committee of ten—five Senators and five Representatives. These men were to "inquire into the wisdom and ascertain the cost of acquiring" Monticello so that it might be preserved for all Americans.[45] Mrs. Littleton's resolution, which became the focus of the battle over Monticello in 1912, represented a new strategy on her part. Certain that Levy would not give the house to her association, she anticipated that a tidal wave of popular sentiment would force him to sell the estate to Congress. Little did she know the man she was fighting.

In her first testimony before the Senate Library Committee on July 9, Mrs. Littleton apparently attempted to shame Jefferson Levy into selling Monticello to Congress, hoping that he would give in. After pointing out the importance of Thomas Jefferson, Mrs. Littleton bluntly assumed that Levy would sell Monticello in order to fulfill the terms of Uriah's will! ". . . No doubt, Mr. Levy would do his part toward the public ownership of Monticello, thereby honoring his ancestor who believed it should belong to the people. . . ." [46]

At this point she directed her heavy artillery toward Levy, going out of her way to put him in an unfavorable light. For example, she cited a reference (probably paid for by Jefferson Levy) in the *National Cyclopedia of American Biography,* Volume III, which gave the reader the impression that Levy was the grandson of Thomas Jefferson. She denied this inference and added that the article was equally inaccurate when it implied that Levy had inherited the estate from his uncle.[47] Then Mrs. Littleton attacked Levy's care of Monticello. She offered as her evidence some photographs of the house and the roads leading up to it. She suggested, without saying so outright, that Levy was allowing the estate to run down steadily. The chairman of the committee, somewhat confused by her onslaught, turned to R. T. W. Duke, Levy's lawyer, who was an interested spectator at the hearing. Duke denied the charges made by Mrs. Littleton and added that Levy had always allowed free access to the house and grounds. Mrs. Littleton countered by saying that she could never agree with Duke's testimony.[48]

Mrs. Littleton and Duke traded threats about the future of Monticello. Duke clearly saw that Levy might not sell to Congress, especially as long as Mrs. Littleton's association was tied up with the resolution under consideration.

> I think he would just as soon sell the kingdom of heaven as to sell Monticello. If properly approached, I think he might take the patriotic view of it and sell it to the United States Government. But he looks at the place as the apple of his eye.[49]

Mrs. Littleton then added her trump card. She read a long letter that she had just received from James M. Beck of Pennsylvania, former Solicitor General of the United States. In his letter Beck traced the history of the case in which the federal government had taken some of the lands in the Gettysburg battlefield area by condemnation proceedings. He argued that the same principle applied in the case of a shrine of such importance as the home of Jefferson. In other words, if Jefferson Levy would not sell Monticello to the nation, it would be perfectly legal for the government to condemn the property and give him just compensation for its loss.[50]

Mrs. Littleton's resolution for the creation of the Congressional committee to consider the wisdom of purchasing Monticello passed the Senate on July 17, 1912. It went from there to the House Committee on Rules. Since Levy and Mrs. Littleton's husband were both Democratic Congressmen from the State of New York at that time, the committee sessions were certain to be charged with tension. Mrs. Littleton came to the hearing armed with many of the letters she had received from notable people who had read *One Wish*.

She probably realized that her attack on Levy's care of the estate had been a mistake, for he was very sensitive on this particular issue.[51] However, she used a new argument that further increased the ire of Levy. Now she claimed that he had made Monticello a memorial to Uriah Levy rather than to Thomas Jefferson. Mrs. Littleton went back to 1909, when she and her husband were guests of Jefferson Levy, relating glowingly how she had waited all her life to see the second Mount Vernon—the other "treasure house," as she called it.

. . . We drove through the black night and deep mud up that

steep road to the top of the little mountain. Nothing could be seen. Only above our heads a thick mass of bare limbs of trees, like serpents coiled above us. I can remember nothing now of the house and my visit, except that I have a vivid impression of portraits —big, oil portraits of the Levys—and ships—models of ships in which Uriah Levy was supposed to have sailed. . . . Everything was disappointing. I had a heavy-hearted feeling. There was nothing of Jefferson to me in Monticello. He had dropped out and the Levys had come. One could hear and see only the Levys and the Levy family, their deeds of valor, their accomplishments, their lives.[52]

Mrs. Littleton announced that Levy was standing in the way of the wishes of the American people. She described the discomfort that Levy's attitude had caused for pilgrims approaching Monticello:

> He has seen them pause at its entrance with humiliating sense of intrusion. He has seen them hesitate, reluctant to enter. He has seen proud and sensitive people shrink from asking his permission. He has seen them turn away from the doors without a glance into the rooms where Jefferson lived and died.
> Does he wish to keep this up? Is it not as humiliating to him as to them? And by what right must the people ask Mr. Levy's permission to visit the home and grave of Thomas Jefferson? . . . Is he insensible to all emotions of patriotism and unselfishness? Does he want a whole Nation crawling at his feet forever for permission to worship at this shrine of our independence? Could he submit his feelings to the mortification of saying no? Would not the world cry out shame upon him, and where could he find a place to hide his head? [53]

In concluding her appeal to Congress and Levy, Mrs. Littleton painted an impressive picture of John Washington, the Lees and the Jacksons as examples of those who had given up their homes to the nation. (Actually the Lee Mansion was confiscated, and the Jacksons and Washingtons sold their homes!) While it is easy to question some of her choices, Mrs. Littleton's point was clear— Levy should emulate the model provided him by other people who had sold their historic homes in order to permit the public to enjoy them.[54] Once more she concluded by mentioning the Beck letter and the possibility of condemnation proceedings.

On August 7, 1912, the House Rules Committee held a second

hearing in order to give Jefferson Levy a chance to present his side of the controversy. He began by declaring that everything at Monticello was sacred to him; then he emphatically stated that he would never "listen to any suggestion for disposing of it, whether coming from a private or a public source." At the end of the hearing, Mrs. Littleton took the stand and offered an impassioned plea for her project. According to the *New York Times* correspondent, she burst into tears at the end of her testimony. Whatever she said, combined with her histrionics, must have convinced the gentlemen of the House Rules Committee that hers was a worthy cause, for the committee favorably reported the resolution to the House. But this was a mere preliminary skirmish; the real battle was to take place on the floor of the House of Representatives in December of that year.[55]

During the fall of 1912 Mrs. Littleton continued publicizing her cause. She endeavored to obtain resolutions and petitions from individuals and organizations—all of which she eventually planned to present to Congress. Her correspondence with one preservation leader, William Sumner Appleton of the Society for the Preservation of New England Antiquities, shows that she did not always meet with success in her efforts to gain votes of confidence from the interested public. Appleton, who was, as a New Englander, a foe of governmental preservation, warned Mrs. Littleton that she had better form a "society . . . for the particular purpose of preserving [Monticello] . . . as was done in the case of Mount Vernon." Appleton advised her to copy the Mount Vernon organization "absolutely," for interest in Jefferson was certainly great enough to enable her to find "one or more ladies" in each state who would be willing to work for Monticello. Appleton added that he would not like to see Monticello serve as the football of Congressional politics; action or nonaction by Congress would often create lapses of authority or lack of funds at times when Monticello might need it most.[56] Mrs. Littleton replied to Appleton that if an association of the Mount Vernon type had been possible, it would have been formed long before; "but Mr. Levy refuses to sell Monticello, and there is no power under the sun that could make the place public property, under those circumstances, except the government itself—that is why we have gone to the House of Congress. . . ."[57]

Appleton answered with a blast at the basic philosophy behind acquisition of historic properties by condemnation:

> I am a tremendous believer in buying Jefferson's home for preservation, but as luck will have it I am also an ardent Jeffersonian in my principles, and can't help feeling that Jefferson would turn in his grave at the mere suggestion that the Federal Government should buy his home by right of eminent domain. . . . Frankly, I don't like the method or the result, and am not at all clear in my own mind that it might not be better for the preservation of the home if its acquisition were postponed until such time as the owner or his descendants might make a reasonable propposition to a voluntary association.[58]

In the same letter Appleton complimented Mrs. Littleton on her "desirable letterhead" which he considered very well adapted to her cause. It was a superb example of fervent preservationist stationery of the 1912 period, covered with inspirational statements about Jefferson and his home. All of the printed material left Mrs. Littleton little space to write her letters, but perhaps from the advertiser's viewpoint this was not so important.

As the months passed by and the Congressional debate on Mrs. Littleton's resolution drew nearer, Representative Levy, too, stepped up his efforts to make his arguments known. Levy made a public statement to newsmen on November 12, 1912. He opened it by advising the American people that Mrs. Littleton and her association were gathering funds from the general public to no avail, since he had repeatedly declined offers to sell Monticello. Then he expressed his injured feelings about the type of strategy that Mrs. Littleton was using.

> If the campaign were founded on a real affection and reverence for the memory of Jefferson, I could look on it with different eyes, and however unpleasant it might be for me to see an effort to wrest this property away from me, it would be some consolation to me that I could respect the motives behind the scheme. But this campaign has been attended with numberless and wholly unnecessary misstatements about Monticello, about my Uncle, Commodore Levy; those about myself I suppose I must overlook.
>
> In her second book, which Mrs. Littleton is now sending out, she abandons—absolutely without a word of apology—her old charge that Monticello has not been properly kept up.[59]

Levy then defended his position from another angle. He said bluntly that he had not been involved in the suit which broke his uncle's will; but once in possession of Monticello, he had lavished his care on the estate. He also claimed that the public always had free access to the estate—as far as the safety and preservation of the place would permit. He declared that the whole condemnation scheme was unfair, and that it had been worked out by a woman whose interest in Monticello was of the "briefest" nature. He then brought up one of the most delicate issues of the controversy:

> Public ownership, or quasi-public management, by managing directresses has still to prove its efficiency. At Monticello the atmosphere of the home of Jefferson is maintained, and a feeling of reverence for Jefferson is fostered. At Mount Vernon an admission fee is charged and the home atmosphere is lost.[60]

In spite of Levy's opposition, Mrs. Littleton went boldly ahead with her campaign. She issued a fifty-two-page booklet which told her story as completely as possible, including many pages devoted to a lurid description of the manner in which Uriah Levy's will had been broken. The last section was an idealistic second "chapter" to the earlier appeal, *One Wish*. Then in a letter inserted in the booklet, Mrs. Littleton asked every person or group interested in the Monticello movement to do several things: (1) write to as many Congressmen and Senators as possible, telling them how the public favored government ownership of the Jefferson shrine; (2) pass resolutions asking Congress to buy Monticello, and send them to her in Washington; (3) secure the interest of newspaper publishers in the movement, so that favorable publicity could be given in different sections of the country; (4) join the Jefferson-Monticello Memorial Association and form local branches; (5) send contributions to Miss Laura Littleton (her daughter), who was treasurer of the association. Mrs. Littleton added that she was in the process of collecting as many petitions as possible to present to Congress, therefore she would gladly send blanks to those who were interested in gathering signatures.[61]

Finally, on December 9, 1912, the issue of Monticello's ownership burst upon the floor of the House of Representatives. Chairman Henry of the Rules Committee attempted to get a special rule adopted that would permit immediate consideration of the Senate resolution on Monticello. His motion became the focal point of the great test between the forces marshaled by Mrs. Littleton and Congressman Levy. Representative Henry and some others defended the idea of public ownership of Monticello. Then Representative Dalzell arose and declared that the resolution calling for a committee to study the problem served no purpose, for no committee could tell Congress how "wise" it would be to purchase Monticello—each individual member would have to decide the wisdom of the transaction himself. In addition, Dalzell pointed out that it was equally foolish to look into the price of the estate because Congressmen Levy, who was sitting with the House at that time, had repeatedly declared that he would not sell it.[62]

Levy had other potent allies in his battle against the Senate resolution. Representative Moore stated that the proposal ran directly counter to the long-established Congressional precedent of refusing to accept historic spots. He presented an unromantic argument against the acquisition of such property:

> All over the eastern coast we have sites hallowed by the lives of distinguished men, which would at once command the attention of Congress, and every one of them would have an equal claim upon this body. It would mean additions to the pay rolls of thousands of caretakers at salaries that would have to be provided by the people of the United States.[63]

Moore continued by pointing out that similar bills for federal acquisition of other historic houses had been defeated in the House in recent years because Congress was unwilling to take on the work being done by patriotic groups organized for that very purpose, such as the Daughters of the American Revolution.[64]

Representative Saunders, who was from the district in Virginia that included the Monticello estate, tried to minimize Mrs. Littleton's claims to public support (based on letters and petitions). He pointed out that many of the influential people who had written to Mrs. Littleton in support of her cause were led to believe that she merely favored government purchase of Monticello, not federal seizure. Saunders knew that a number of people who had loaned their prestige to the Monticello movement had withdrawn their endorsement once they saw the real intent was confiscation of private property.[65]

As the debate neared its conclusion, Representative Ferris described the group headed by Mrs. Littleton as "some well-meaning persons, wrought up by emotion and commotion," whom he was sure Congress would have to disappoint.[66]

The vote was taken, and the resolution from the Rules Committee was defeated by a vote of 141 to 101, with many abstentions, including Representative Littleton.[67] Although this vote was not a total victory, Levy appeared to be jubilant. Mrs. Littleton had been watching the debate from the galleries of the House and refused to comment publicly on the outcome. Instead, she telegraphed the governor of Virginia that a prominent Virginian (probably Thomas Fortune Ryan [68]) had authorized her to offer Levy four times the assessed value of the estate—an amount approaching $100,000, if Mrs. Littleton's figure of $25,403 as the assessed value had been correct.[69] Under the terms of the new offer the title to Monticello would rest with the State of Virginia. Representative Levy, fresh from his victory in the House of Representatives, quickly squelched Mrs. Littleton's new move: "I will sell Monticello under no circumstances. I have repeatedly refused $1,500,000 for the property. My answer to any proposition seeking the property of Monticello is: When the White House is for sale, then I will consider an offer for the sale of Monticello, and not before." [70]

The vote in the House spelled defeat for Mrs. Littleton's efforts in that session of Congress. Even with the perspective of time, it is not easy to fix any "blame" for her failure. Probably both Mrs. Littleton and Levy were at fault. He was obstinate in his desire to keep Monticello at all costs, and he may have been a bit too unwilling to recognize the honesty of Mrs. Littleton's motives. Mrs. Littleton was so eager to see Monticello a public property that she grasped at any method that would ensure this result. As a consequence, she failed miserably in her attempts to win Levy's confidence. It would have been easy for her to credit him with saving Monticello from absolute destruction in the late nineteenth century.

In view of the fact that Mrs. Littleton used the example of John Washington in her testimony, it may be worthwhile to compare her work with that of Ann Pamela Cunningham. There are certain similarities: Mrs. Littleton had some literary talents—as did Ann Pamela Cunningham—and she had the added advantage of starting the Monticello movement at a time when the position of women had vastly improved in the public mind. Here differences begin to arise. Miss Cunningham had begun her crusade with the intention of raising enough money to enable the State of Virginia to purchase Mount Vernon from the Washingtons. When later circumstances forced her to change the object of her drive, Miss Cunningham willingly accepted a charter that would give the Ladies' Association ownership of Mount Vernon.

In the case of Monticello, Mrs. Littleton, the wife of an important member of Congress, determined that the federal government should own Monticello. After failing to get the intransigent owner of the estate to give it to an association that she had formed or to the government, she addressed herself to the task of inducing Congress to pay Jefferson Levy for the home. At no time did Mrs. Littleton seriously expect that her association could ever raise the purchase price of Monticello. She put whatever money was collected into the publicity campaign that was to force Jefferson Levy to submit to the will of the American people.

Mrs. Littleton's expression of animosity toward Levy was a crucial difference between the Monticello and Mount Vernon movements. Miss Cunningham's primary objective had been a workable agreement with John Washington. She had great difficulty dealing with this sensitive man who was sure that the Mount Vernon Ladies' Association and the State of Virginia wanted to insult him. Miss Cunningham was sufficiently dedicated to the cause of Mount Vernon to swallow her pride, forget her health, and go see John Washington. She finally succeeded in convincing him that she was doing all she could to treat him fairly. After that initial persuasion, Washington became an important ally of the successful Mount Vernon movement.

Mrs. Littleton, on the other hand, evidently began her enterprise with the mistaken impression that Jefferson Levy had enough regard for the memory of Jefferson to give Monticello to the nation. Failing in her effort, she took her problem to the halls of Congress rather than to Levy. As a final gesture of disgust with Levy's recalcitrant attitude, she threatened him with the specter of condemnation proceedings. The passages quoted above from Mrs. Littleton's testimony before Congress do not show any desire to obtain Levy's goodwill. Probably the master of Monticello was a difficult man to approach, but Mrs. Littleton's remarks were not designed to please him. Unlike Miss Cunningham, Mrs. Littleton apparently decided that one could only go so far in trying to accommodate a private owner; and if he remained stubborn, the only recourse was to find legal means of taking the property away from him. Mrs. Littleton's testimony shows that she believed Levy owned Monticello by a twist of fate and had no right to keep a public shrine. Miss Cunningham never took such an approach with John Washington; she always acknowledged his right of ownership, but also hoped that he would see the wisdom of protecting Mount Vernon by some form of public control. In addition, the controversy which raged between Levy and Mrs. Littleton in late 1912 indicated that Monticello had not yet become a financial burden to its owner; yet John Washington had affirmed that he considered Mount Vernon a constant financial drain long before Miss Cunningham had her fateful meeting with him.

Another vital difference between the methods used by the two ladies lay in the field of administration. Miss Cunningham had expert help in the formulation of the charter of the Mount Vernon Ladies' Association. She devoted nearly all of her time to organizational problems, particularly the choosing and training of viceregents. Mrs. Littleton's Monticello Association appears to have been a family affair whose main purpose was to use every lobbyist device to convince Congress that numerous influential people were in favor of her ideas.

Mrs. Littleton refused to accept her setback in the House of Representatives as final, so the battle entered a new phase. In March of 1913, she held a meeting in New York to build additional support for her association. A *New York Times* reporter who covered this gathering does not seem to have taken Mrs. Littleton very seriously. The audience he described as a small but enthusiastic group. The walls of the theater which Mrs. Littleton had rented for her meeting were plastered with long petitions— all supporting her stand. Names of some of the petitioners were reserved for projection on a screen. "Supreme Court justices were obviously Mrs. Littleton's especial favorites and as the slides showing their signatures appeared on the screen, she would murmur with a delight that would be reflected in a sympathetic flutter in the auditorium." In a short interview after this meeting, Mrs. Littleton expressed a great determination to continue the fight, for Jefferson Levy alone had been responsible for the defeat of her resolution in the House.[71]

One year later, in February of 1914, Mrs. Littleton did succeed in getting the Virginia legislature to pass a resolution which said that private ownership of Monticello had denied access to the public and that public ownership would be a fitting memorial to Jefferson. Again Levy claimed to be the victim of an undemocratic maneuver, for he made it plain that the Virginia legislators had not given him a chance to present his side of the question.[72]

The action of the Virginia legislature, together with Mrs. Littleton's relentless campaign, produced other interesting reactions. Dorothy Dix challenged the American people and the Democratic Party to save Monticello from being "swept away." In an article entitled "Monticello—Shrine or Bachelor's Hall?" she employed a definite anti-Levy tone.[73] The American Scenic and Historic Preservation Society devoted a large section of its 1914 *Report* to the issues involved in the Monticello controversy. The society placed itself somewhere between the two extremes by favoring public control of Monticello, but not by means of condemnation proceedings.[74] In "Appendix F" of the same *Report,* the society offered equal space to Mrs. Littleton and Representative Levy. The views of the Jefferson-Monticello Memorial Association closely resembled the testimony that Mrs. Littleton had given before Congressional committees. However, Levy provided a new account entitled "The Care of Monticello by Its Owner," by W. K. Semple. It was an apologia for Levy similar to the Townsend book of 1902. The Semple article added an argument that Levy had hinted at when he claimed that he had "repeatedly refused $1,500,000 for the property." [75] According to Semple, Levy had once declined an offer of one million dollars for Monticello from the "head of the Vanderbilt family" who had been a guest there.[76]

Following the lead of the Virginia legislature, the Senate Lands Committee favorably reported a bill which called for the purchase of Monticello or, if necessary, its condemnation. The *New York Times* article which described the bill mentioned that Mrs. Littleton was still the energetic leader of the movement to gain governmental control of the house.[77]

A sharp change in the Monticello situation occurred in the fall of 1914, for Levy suddenly announced himself willing to sell Monticello to the government for $500,000! Secretary of State William Jennings Bryan had written Levy a letter on September 23, 1914, renewing his old plea that Levy consider selling the property to the federal government, subject to a life interest for himself. Bryan appealed to Levy as an American and a Democrat: he assured Levy that President Woodrow Wilson, a Virginian and also a Democrat, would pay a visit to dedicate the estate as public property. On October 5, 1914, Levy wrote Bryan that, although he did not want to part with Monticello, the time was opportune for such a sale. Levy added that he hoped Jefferson's home would never be a museum, but rather a summer home for the Presidents of the United States. Levy justified his price of $500,000 by reasoning that it would make him more than half the donor of Monticello, for it had cost him at least twice that amount to buy, restore and keep it up. Most observers treated Levy's offer as a victory for Mrs. Littleton.[78]

The brief exchange of letters between Levy and Bryan settled one of the thorniest points in the fight over Monticello: condemnation was to be a dead issue. The new problem, created by Levy's letter, was the price of half a million dollars and Levy's insistence that he would be half donor of the estate even at that. It must be remembered that Congress had seldom faced the issue of sentimental value attached to a piece of property. In 1896 when Congress voted to buy the House Where Lincoln Died, the legislators made sure that they were paying only for the commercial value of the building.[79] Now the same issue had arisen with Monticello.

On February 23, 1915, the House Rules Committee held a hearing on the first of many bills that were to call for the purchase of the property for $500,000. The initial payment was to have been $100,000 and the remaining $400,000 would be paid in United States Bonds over a period of eight years. The first witness at this hearing was none other than ex-Congressman Levy who explained that he was willing to sell Monticello because the call from the people seemed imperative. He added that the sale, as provided in the bill under consideration, represented a sacrifice on his part "both from a sentimental and monetary standpoint." [80]

At this juncture Levy's new ally, Mrs. Littleton, took the stand.

(She conveniently forgot that in 1912 she had estimated Monticello could not be worth over $80,000.[81])

. . . At first sight the sum of $500,000 for 700 acres of land, with only a brick home and office, a few ancient and crumbling buildings upon it, and a simple and humble tombstone nearby, may appear to be an exorbitant price. But no real American who takes into consideration the patriotic memories that must be forever associated with the property . . . can regard it so.

. . . And it is but fair to say that during the number of years it has been in Mr. Levy's possession he has gratuitously entertained many of the visitors to the place, has guarded the property, and watched over the remains of Mr. Jefferson probably as well as such an exacting public task could be done by an individual.[82]

Mrs. Littleton's speech represented an important tactical change. Now that Jefferson Levy had named a price, she was eager to cooperate. One may doubt that they were ever friendly after the "war of 1912," but Mrs. Littleton had indeed withdrawn her former charges against Levy. Gone were the demands that he stop holding back the adoring pilgrims from the home of Jefferson; gone were the lurid descriptions of Monticello as a Levy shrine or as a building falling back into ruin. And what is more, she did not even attempt to persuade Levy to lower his price. Rather, she bent all her efforts toward winning approval of any bill in Congress that would meet Levy's demands.[83] In addition, President Wilson himself sent a message to a friend in Congress and wholeheartedly defended the proposal,[84] but even his help was not enough to persuade Congress, and the question had to be brought up once more.

In 1916 bills were introduced in both houses of Congress authorizing the purchase of Monticello for $500,000. By this time Mrs. Littleton had been able to make the purchase of Monticello more palatable by convincing the Daughters of the American Revolution that they should volunteer to be the custodians of the property. In July she accompanied a D.A.R. delegation on a visit to President Wilson in order to ask his support. Wilson responded by writing to Mrs. William C. Story, the D.A.R. President General, renewing his endorsement of the proposed purchase.[85]

The House Committee on Public Buildings and Grounds held a hearing on the subject of Monticello on August 8, 1916. Representative J. Charles Linthicum of Maryland, whose wife was influential in the D.A.R., testified that he had been favorably impressed with a recent visit to Monticello. He went into a minute description of Levy's efforts to create a Jefferson shrine. He further illustrated Levy's patriotism by telling how Levy came down from New York each Fourth of July and took Jefferson's music stand outside and used it as a lectern from which he would read the Declaration of Independence to his neighbors. Linthicum was certain that the only money the government would have to expend on Monticello after buying it would be the cost of constructing a better road up to the mansion. His eyewitness account of Levy's care did not convince Congress that Monticello was worth $500,000 any more than did the letter from President Wilson.[86]

That spring the D.A.R. Continental Congress had passed a resolution favoring acquisition of the estate by the government. In order to persuade the Daughters that his cause was a worthy one, Levy and his sister, Mrs. Mayhoff, invited the National Board of Management of the D.A.R. to come to Monticello in October of 1916.[87]

As 1916 wore on, it became increasingly clear that some members of Congress were becoming disgusted with Levy's inability to give them any help in arriving at an exact value for Monticello. Mrs. Story of the D.A.R. wrote to Levy asking him to estimate what Monticello had actually cost him and how much it would cost the government to operate the whole estate. Levy chose to evade the question by saying that any correct appraisal of the property would be impossible.

> I ask, Is the same rule of thumb to be applied here as when the Government buys a site for a post office or a customshouse? Certainly not, after my long stewardship, without my consent. I ask again, If an appraisal be asked, where is the appraisal to stop? What limit be put on a place with such a founder, with such associations, with such a history? . . . I have gone into these matters at, perhaps, unpardonable length, so that I will not seem to be lacking in courtesy if I decline to be drawn into an examination as to who made me offers for the purchase of Monticello, how much offered, the amount of the yearly taxes, etc. The idea of selling Monticello was always abhorrent to me; I never could bear to consider its sale. If my statement be not sufficient that I was offered and refused

$1,000,000 for the property, then it would be useless after this lapse of years to offer in corroboration further testimony on that point. If my statement on that point be not accepted without further evidence, I am content to abide by the consequences.[88]

Levy probably did not foresee the consequences of his letter, for he appears to have been a proud man. The unconvinced members of the committee remained unconvinced—and began questioning Mrs. Story and Levy's lawyer, Judge Duke, as to the probable value of Monticello. The longer the hearing went on, the more impatient the legislators became with Levy's unwillingness to supply them with exact figures of any kind. Few Congressmen were willing to spend half a million dollars in 1916 for sentiment.[89]

The last hearing on the bill to purchase Monticello was held on January 9, 1917, before the Senate Committee on Public Buildings and Grounds, with Mrs. Story and other Daughters of the American Revolution present. The same arguments about Levy's selling price appeared—and no conclusion was reached. In addition, the Senate Committee proceeded to question Judge Duke at some length on possible uses for the 700 acres that the government would buy along with the mansion.[90] In February the House Committee went down to Monticello to inspect the property and investigate some of the claims made in the hearings. Newspapers reported that, as a result of this trip, the Committee might recommend a $400,000 purchase price. But Congress adjourned without taking action on the bill.[91]

While the House and Senate committees were busy considering all the aspects of the proposed purchase, the D.A.R. made its last great endeavor to help Mrs. Littleton in her quest. The March, 1917, issue of the *D.A.R. Magazine* carried an article favoring the purchase because of the historical and architectural importance of Monticello. A month later, at the D.A.R. congress, 3,000 petitions were distributed to state regents, who were to obtain signatures and send the completed forms to members of Congress.

However, all of this feverish effort was laid aside as World War I broke upon the country.[92] Mrs. Littleton later told a friend that she had been close to success in 1917, but the war was the real enemy that had finally halted her campaign. One chapter in the long struggle over Monticello had come to a close.[93] Mrs. Littleton and

Jefferson Levy were no longer at odds, for both favored federal purchase of the house. The resolution that failed in Congress in the spring of 1917 was the last serious attempt to work directly through the government in saving Monticello.

Shortly after the First World War, Jefferson Levy found that he was forced to sell Monticello. He had been unable to interest Congress or Virginia, and no private organizations had appeared that were willing to meet his price. He therefore did exactly what he said he would never do—he put his summer home up for public sale. His agent was H. W. Hilleary of Washington, D. C., a broker who dealt in large Virginia estates. The first thing Hilleary did was to mail a form letter to a number of wealthy individuals around the country. It said (in part):

> The present owner, for sentimental and other reasons, has never before consented to part with it. I am allowed now to bring it to the attention of those who can appreciate and are able to own a property of such distinction and merit.[94]

If one of the prospective purchasers had been interested enough to inquire about Levy's asking price, he would have been told that Hilleary had been authorized to quote $400,000 for Monticello, but "if, after examination," an interested individual might offer less, Hilleary was prepared to send any such communications to Levy. This must have meant that Levy wanted to sell the property in a hurry, for the price had come down $100,000, and lower figures were being invited.[95]

Although no wealthy individual wanted Monticello for a country home, a new movement appeared on the horizon a year later. An organization known as the Thomas Jefferson Memorial Association declared itself willing to purchase the estate for one million dollars. (This group was apparently unaware of Levy's $400,000 price.) Levy, however, had agreed to donate half of that amount as well as the Jefferson relics in the house. The secretary of the association, Charles W. Swan, thought that the whole amount could be raised in a short time without a public subscription, for some of the money had already been pledged, and "influential citizens" had offered to pay the remainder. The founder of the new group was Miss Ruth R. Cunningham, who claimed to be a descendant of Ann Pamela Cunningham. In view of the fact that Miss Cunningham had no children, this assertion was interesting, to say the least! [96]

The new association was no more successful than its predecessors, so Levy again gave up the battle and offered the house for sale through Hilleary's office.[97] *The New York Times* responded to the announcement of the sale in an editorial of July 28, 1921. It defended Monticello as a work of art (as well as a historic monument) and decried continued private ownership of such a building as "unthinkable." In an interview the same day Jefferson Levy admitted that "the place has become a great care and expense to me." He added that he wanted it to be a national shrine, but could not present it to the government himself. He stated that he had turned down offers from Andrew Carnegie and Jacob H. Schiff, both of whom had wanted to buy the estate from him in order to donate it to the nation. Levy hoped that a Schiff or a Carnegie would again consider buying the house as a memorial to Jefferson.[98]

During this period Miss Ruth Cunningham was still at work, attempting to save the reputation of the Thomas Jefferson Memorial Association. Her group, now composed mainly of women, had its headquarters in Richmond. Miss Cunningham went to New York City during the spring of 1922 in order to organize that area for a drive to raise funds. She carried letters from such notables as former Presidents Wilson and Taft, who gave their support to the enterprise. In a *Times* article describing Miss Cunningham's campaign, it was "reported" that in 1912 Thomas Fortune Ryan had offered Levy $750,000 for Monticello, but Levy had turned down his proposal.[99]

By November of 1922, in spite of optimistic reports by the officials of the Thomas Jefferson Memorial Association, the future looked gloomy. Virginia members of the organization had only three weeks left in which to raise $50,000 to bind their contract with Levy. As an inducement, certain New York financiers were rumored to have volunteered to underwrite the $500,000 purchase price if the initial payment could be raised, but the attempt failed.[100]

Early in 1923 a new organization, dedicated to the purpose of acquiring Monticello, was formed by some ladies in Washington,

D.C. Mrs. Marietta Minnegerode Andrews served as president of the newly created National Monticello Association, and a descendant of James Monroe, Mrs. Rose Gouverneur Hoes, was secretary. Mrs. Hoes announced that the association had the blessing of Jefferson Levy, for he had learned that its purpose was the creation of a shrine similar to Mount Vernon.[101] In spite of high hopes, neither of these two groups of ladies—in Richmond or in Washington—seemed to have any clear idea of how to amass $500,000. Still another solution was necessary.

The answer soon appeared. The organization that finally succeeded where so many had failed was the Thomas Jefferson Memorial Foundation.[102] It was born in New York City, rather than in Charlottesville, Richmond, or Washington, D. C. In February of 1923 some prominent New Yorkers interested in saving Monticello held a meeting in the Vanderbilt Hotel. Stuart Gibboney, a Virginian practicing law in New York, was selected from the group to head a small planning committee. A month later Gibboney met at the Lawyer's Club with two other men—John Henry Ranger, representing Levy, and Moses H. Grossman. Ranger convinced the other two men that the owner of Monticello was deep in debt and must sell the house soon. After talking with Ranger, the other two men decided on the formation of the Thomas Jefferson Memorial Foundation, which would serve to unite all of the people working for the cause of Monticello.[103]

Shortly after this meeting, George Gordon Battle, another New York lawyer, Alton Brooks Parker, former Democratic nominee for the Presidency, and Dr. Edwin A. Alderman, president of the University of Virginia, all agreed to work with Gibboney and Grossman in forming a nonprofit patriotic corporation, with Gibboney as president. Theodore Fred Kuper, national director of the new foundation, journeyed to Washington where he obtained the endorsement of Mrs. Andrews and Mrs. Hoes of the Monticello organization of that city. Then he went on to Richmond where he interviewed Mrs. Hotchkiss (of the Richmond group) and Governor E. Lee Trinkle. They both approved. The Thomas Jefferson Memorial Foundation could then incorporate in New York State and domesticate in Virginia—where it could hold property.[104]

On the fifth of April, 1923, *The New York Times* carried the first announcement of the formation of the new organization. It simply stated that the foundation consisted of a unification of the Richmond and Washington groups and added that it would come into existence on April 13, the 180th birthday of Jefferson.[105] On that date the foundation was officially incorporated in Albany while a banquet was being held at the same time at the University of Virginia.

Many important and influential people were among the incorporators. Some had worked hard for Monticello over a period of years, such as Mrs. Littleton, Mrs. Andrews and James W. Gerard; others had expressed interest in the project in a general way, such as Dr. Alderman and Governor Trinkle; a few were financiers, such as Felix Warburg, who represented the vital place of New York City in the work for Monticello. Theodore Fred Kuper has recalled Warburg's reactions to the Monticello idea:

> He understood from me that when Jefferson wrote his epitaph ... he wanted that to be a beacon light for the future: civil liberty, religious freedom, and universal education. I explained that our campaign would be geared on an educational basis and that that would keep on inculcating these ideas. He gave $10,000 originally and he persuaded [William H.] Woodin to match it. He said that these ideals and ... education were what he wanted.[106]

As soon as the formation of the foundation was announced, Jefferson Levy declared his support of it (as he had with other attempts to buy Monticello).[107] However, the foundation did not find Levy easy to work with. One of the first big hurdles it had to cross was the agreement on an option to buy the property, since Levy wanted more than $500,000 for the house and grounds. The men who represented the foundation refused to exceed their original offer: a payment of $100,000 in December of 1923 upon which title would pass to the foundation, a second payment of $100,000 by taking title, subject to a first mortgage given to a New York bank, and the balance of $300,000 to be paid off over a period of years with bonds of the foundation—secured by a second mortgage on the property. In order to persuade Levy to accept an offer below his own idea of the value of Monticello, Gibboney and Grossman advanced $10,000 on the first $100,000 and paid him with their personal checks.[108]

Kuper had to prepare the bonds and the mortgage for the

foundation and also arrange a meeting of the directors who were to decide whether or not to accept the terms of the option. If the directors should have turned down the option, Gibboney and Grossman would have lost the money they had paid Levy. Kuper prepared ballots before the meeting and mailed them to each of the directors. The approval was unanimous.[109]

Now the foundation faced the formidable task of raising $90,000 before December in order to take title to the property. On April 23, 1923, the members of the foundation held a meeting in the Lawyer's Club. One of the most important results of this meeting was the election of Manny Strauss as chairman of the Ways and Means Committee. Strauss made it his business to supervise the raising of the remainder of the $100,000 first payment, and it was not long before the nature of his plan for the campaign became known.[110]

The foundation announced that it was going to conduct a "spiritual pilgrimage" to Monticello. In June the sale of tickets for the pilgrimage was inaugurated at a dinner held on a train in Grand Central Station. Senator Royal S. Copeland, chairman of the New York Committee for the Pilgrimage, went through the train wearing a ticket agent's cap and selling tickets at one cent a mile. The foundation showed movies in the train depicting the trip to Monticello. *The New York Times* estimated that Senator Copeland sold $60,000 worth of mileage books, but the real figures were much smaller.[111]

Money did not come in as Strauss had expected, so he created an underwriter's program. Gibboney and Strauss obtained signatures from people who agreed to pay the difference between what was needed for the first payment in December and what would actually be raised. These men signed promissory notes for amounts of $1,000 or multiples thereof; Herbert Lehman signed for more than $11,000.[112]

The campaign reached the newspapers more prominently in July. George G. Battle, chairman of the Finance Committee, declared that the foundation's ultimate goal was one million dollars —half of which would buy Monticello and the other half endow it. He appealed to the nation to square its debt with the author of the Declaration of Independence, hoping that Monticello would be an inspiration to the people, and a mirror of their gratitude for Jefferson's work.[113]

Meanwhile the year was rolling by, and it was nearly time to pay the initial $100,000. In September, Strauss arranged for a transcontinental speaking tour for the purpose of raising funds. The tour was to cover more than twenty-five different cities and was to be led by such distinguished people as Trinkle, Copeland and Alderman. Before plans for the tour had fully matured, Kuper was told that he would have to make the entire tour for the foundation in person, because the governor of Virginia and the other notables did not have time for it. So Kuper moved out across the West and South, speaking as many as seven times a day—often in areas very hostile to Jeffersonian ideas.[114]

Finally, with money borrowed from banks on the strength of the underwriters' pledges, the foundation paid Levy the balance of the first payment and took the first mortgage for the second $100,000.[115] Kuper described the ceremony:

> The cash and the bonds and mortgage were delivered to Levy, and Levy signed the deed conveying full title to the property and all belongings to the Foundation. This was a very emotional scene and he burst out crying. He said that he never dreamt that he would ever part with the property.[116]

So ended the Levy ownership of Monticello after nearly ninety years. One *New York Times* article, dated December 4, 1923 (page 1), referred to the amount paid to Levy as a contribution from New York. This was essentially correct, for almost the entire sum had been raised in New York City. However, what the papers did not know was that after the payment was made, Kuper had to call upon all the underwriters who had signed promissory notes and collect nearly 80 percent of the value of those notes. The foundation had failed to raise the necessary $100,000 and it had to repay the banks. Each of the men who had signed the notes gladly paid his share of the debt.[117]

Jefferson Levy died on March 6, 1924, but his demise did not affect in any way the plans of the foundation. The estate was already legally in the possession of the organization as long as the foundation discharged its debts to the Levy estate. Mrs. Mayhoff, the heiress of Jefferson Levy, announced that she would carry out her brother's wishes with respect to the purchase of Monticello.[118]

Once the house came into the possession of the foundation, great changes were made, for "the Foundation did not want it to be a Levy shrine." Monticello was to be a memorial to Jefferson; therefore everything having to do with the Levys was removed. Needless to say, this did not please the Levy family.[119]

The job that faced the foundation was a double challenge. The directors not only had to raise the money for continuing the payments to Levy, but, now that they had the title to the property, they had to supervise the estate. Kuper and Gibboney went to Monticello shortly after the title passed and found that it was necessary to rearrange the system for admitting visitors. They instructed Rhodes, the old superintendent, to register visitors in a book and to charge them a minimum fee of fifty cents. The admission fee was to be a donation to the cause of saving Monticello. Kuper and Gibboney also advised Rhodes to stop flying the Confederate flag over the house he occupied at Monticello.[120]

That year, according to Kuper, the foundation began to chart its course for the future:

> In the meantime, we found that it was practically impossible to obtain the large donations which usually characterize these public drives. We also found out that at that same time [ca. 1924] there was a great need in this country for a nation-wide program of patriotic education, not only in the life and works of Jefferson, but in basic democratic ideals which he served and championed. We found that there had been practically no modern publications on the life of Jefferson. We also found that the textbooks passed over Jefferson by mere mention of his Presidency and his signing the Declaration, and even second-hand book shops were surprised when anybody inquired for a book on Jefferson. For these reasons we planned to direct the campaign on an educational basis through the children and their teachers, with the children contributing even a penny.[121]

This testimony to the ignorance of Jefferson's place in our history stems from the apathy on the subject of Jefferson that had faced Uriah Levy when he first bought Monticello in 1836. Unlike the Mount Vernon movement, those who wanted to save Monticello had to establish the place of their hero in the American mind before they could successfully save the home itself. The program followed by the foundation during the next three or four years served the dual function of raising money for Monticello, mainly through small donations, and educating the public to understand the impact of Jefferson on American ideals.

In its mixture of idealism and practical hardheadedness, the Thomas Jefferson Memorial Foundation used techniques that would have been unbelievable in the days of Edward Everett and Ann Pamela Cunningham. A brief study of its campaign methods reveals this. In March of 1924 the officials of the foundation announced the inauguration of a technique that they were to use for several years—Jefferson's Birthday parties in the schools. All gifts brought to these parties were to be donations to the preservation of Monticello.[122] Governor Alfred E. Smith of New York was one of the first of many state officials over the country who proclaimed a "Jefferson Week." Many other cities and states followed by setting aside certain days or weeks for the same noble purpose.[123]

One highly interesting example of the educational work done by the foundation was the free transportation of school children to Charlottesville. As early as March 17, 1924, *The New York Times* (page 8) carried a news items that outlined David A. Ansbacher's plans to take fifty boys and girls to Monticello on Jefferson's Birthday. Kuper gave his recollection of this journey:

> I explained to him [Mr. Ansbacher] the educational goals which we were hoping to achieve, and I suggested that it would be wonderful if we could have a group of New York City elementary school children taken to Monticello. . . . He liked the idea and told me to go ahead and arrange it. The superintendent of schools of the City of New York, at the request of Dr. Ryan, then president of the Board of Education, arranged for each district superintendent to select one boy and one girl who were to represent the district and who, on return, were to report to their schoolmates in school assemblies. We reserved two Pullman cars. . . . Many of these children came from the poorest families. Some had never crossed the Hudson River; some had never been on a train before. . . .
>
> They stayed overnight in a hotel in Charlottesville. . . . On their visit to Monticello, through the streets of Charlottesville and to the University of Virginia, they had their notebooks in their hands, and they were all busy making notes from what the guides said.[124]

Ansbacher told Kuper, who had accompanied him, that he "felt like a thief" because he had gained so much enjoyment from such a small donation (around $1,500).[125]

In 1925 the foundation formed a Centennial Committee to prepare for the observance of the one hundredth anniversary of Jefferson's passing. Franklin Simon, as chairman, said that it would be a "shame" if the people of the United States would permit that date to pass in 1926 and leave Monticello "swamped in debt and . . . tossed about by real estate speculators." [126] Simon announced that during the period from May 11 to June 14, 1925, his committee would conduct an election that would net over half a million dollars. Candidates for the election were to be young ladies, most of whom represented organizations. Those girls who received 50,000 votes would be taken on a free trip to Paris during the month of July.[127] The officials of the foundation had figured that, with each vote costing ten cents, a winner would bring in $5,000 for her 50,000 votes; the foundation would then spend about $1,000 of that amount for her European trip. Kuper arranged the tours in France to be educational, especially from the standpoint of democratic ideals.[128] The New York newspapers began to carry day-to-day totals on the balloting. By the twenty-third of May *The New York Times* (page 2) announced that one girl already had reached the required number of votes.

As the campaign grew hotter, a voice was raised in protest against such a proceeding. Gregory Doyle, who had played a minor role in establishing the foundation, declared that buying votes—even at ten cents—was no way to teach citizenship. He was sure that this type of election would favor girls having more money and that young people would grow to feel that they could buy anything.[129] As the election entered its last day, *The New York Times* came out with a strong editorial supporting the whole election idea. It expressed pleasure at the multitude of small contributions and compared the effort to the "classic" manner in which Mount Vernon was saved.[130]

Simon announced that, before expenses—which were considerable—the election had amassed over $300,000, more than half of which had been raised in New York City alone.[131] As a result of the campaign, a group of fifty-eight girls went to Europe and eleven more, who fell just short of the necessary 50,000 votes, toured Charlottesville as guests of the foundation.[132]

In 1926 Kuper planned what he termed an "educational program" in the New York City schools, with the approval of the Board of Education. On February 17th of that year, at 11:00 A.M., every school child in the city stood up in his room and repeated the "Patriot's Pledge of Faith" which had just been published by the Thomas Jefferson Memorial Foundation:

> I do hereby pledge and declare my sincere belief and devout faith in the fundamental ideals of my country so bravely proclaimed to the world by the immortal signers of the Declaration of American Independence; and in their words so noble, "we pledge to each other our lives, our fortunes and our sacred honor," to the support of those ideals;
>
> And as a token of my sincerity and as an evidence of my gratitude for the blessings which that immortal document has assured to all Americans, I do hereby make this contribution for the preservation of Monticello, the home of Thomas Jefferson, as a National Memorial to the Author of the Declaration of Independence and as a Patriotic Shrine for the Children of America.[133]

The children placed their contributions in envelopes, which were later presented to an official at an assembly. In this manner the pupils of New York City gave $34,864 to Monticello's preservation in one day! [134]

Later that year the foundation used another technique to bring the campaign for Monticello into the spotlight. When the foundation had first taken possession of the house early in 1924, one of the Jefferson relics was still stored in the attic. It was the body of the gig that Jefferson was believed to have driven to Philadelphia when he was a member of the Continental Congress that drafted the Declaration of Independence. The foundation brought the gig to New York City in 1924 for the Democratic National Convention.[135] Two years later the men decided to use it again at the head of a procession that would go from Charlottesville to Philadelphia for the Sesquicentennial Exposition, as a re-enactment of Jefferson's original trip. Kuper secured the cooperation of the committee in charge of the Sesquicentennial and then invited the mayors of over one thousand American cities to send a representative to be in the cavalcade. The American Automobile

Association helped to publicize the tour by offering travel information to the participants. The gig, under military escort and followed by its caravan, moved slowly from Charlottesville up to Philadelphia. It paused in Washington, D. C., so that President Coolidge could make a small donation to the fund. The whole venture may not have raised too much money, but it gave the foundation excellent publicity.[136]

Although the Thomas Jefferson Memorial Foundation tried its best to remain nonpartisan, it did have one unfortunate experience with national politics. In April of 1926 the directors asked Governor Smith of New York to speak at the Fourth of July exercises at Monticello. It was an innocent request—except that Al Smith was an unannounced Presidential candidate, and this was to have been his first speech in the South. Nevertheless, he accepted, and plans went ahead. In early June a printed letter signed "A Daughter of the American Revolution" made its appearance all over the country. It was a bigoted blast attacking the foundation (and Gibboney in particular) for being a willing tool of a Jesuit plot to get a Catholic candidate into the South. Governor Smith promptly withdrew his acceptance of the invitation. Gibboney protested that he had been a McAdoo man at the 1924 Democratic Convention. In some embarrassment, the president general of the D.A.R. repudiated the whole attack and declared that she was seeking the culprit, whoever he or she might be.[137]

At times the foundation received good advertising from unusual sources. As Theodore F. Kuper put it, "Throughout our publicity and educational campaign we were always ready to work with other agencies and organizations that had the funds to spend for publicity in which we could take part with dignity and without any embarrassment to the Foundation and to the cause of Monticello." Not long after the purchase of the estate, Kuper had arranged to have the company that made an enamel called "Barreled Sunlight" paint the exterior of the mansion. However, the foundation attached two conditions to this agreement: the company had to paint one other historic house, preferably Mount Vernon, and then would have to finance a nationwide advertisement showing both houses. Kuper helped to persuade the Mount Vernon officials to accept this part of the agreement, and so the two buildings took on a new white luster and received some fine publicity in nationally circulated magazines.[138]

One other important figure in the Monticello movement deserves mention here although, by some standards, he belongs more clearly in the next chapter. Fiske Kimball was an architectural scholar who had made his initial reputation through a study of Jefferson as an architect. When the foundation was seeking a chairman for its Restoration Committee in 1924, Kimball seemed the natural choice. At that time he was teaching architecture in New York and was also serving as chairman of the Committee on Preservation of Historic Monuments and Scenic Beauties of the American Institute of Architects. In his 1924 report to the institute, Kimball described in great detail the magnificent work being done by the foundation; and he sponsored a resolution which placed the institute squarely behind the Monticello movement. He argued effectively that Jefferson was one of the first notable American designers and that during his Presidency he had helped the profession of architecture in many ways.[139] In the spring of 1924 Kimball published a long article that was intended to impress his readers with the artistic significance of Monticello and the great need for restoring and preserving it. He proclaimed at the end of the essay, "The place waits only to be reclaimed by the nation and restored with loving hands." His hands, naturally, were the ones to do the job.[140]

Kimball became chairman of the Restoration Committee for Monticello in 1924, with R. T. Haines Halsey of the Metropolitan Museum of Art and Charles Moore of the Commission of Fine Arts in Washington, D. C., serving with him.[141] Here and there one can find accounts of Kimball's work as he went about the country, attempting to check on every detail in the restoration and furnishing of Monticello. The following is an example from the New York *World* of February 1, 1925:

> ... Prof. Fiske Kimball, Chairman of the Architect's Committee, hopes not only to restore the lawns and gardens as they were in Thomas Jefferson's period, but also to return to the historic mansion much of the furniture bought by the author of the Declaration of Independence for the rooms he loved so well.
>
> "My visit to Boston was very fruitful," says Prof. Kimball. "I picked out at the Massachusetts Historical Society a large number

of sketches showing the hangings of window curtains, furniture and features of the grounds of Monticello, as well as bills and accounts for the purchase of furniture which gives us some clue to things now vanished."

Unfortunately, Mount Vernon had not possessed such a dynamic scholar when its restoration was first begun, simply because no one in the United States was qualified for that sort of work in 1860. Kimball was very successful in his contacts with members of the Jefferson family who owned pieces that had once been in Monticello—so successful, in fact, that one elderly Jefferson descendant gave Monticello some valuable furniture, although she was in financial need herself.[142]

By the end of 1926 the foundation had not achieved its objective of freeing Monticello from debt, but it had accomplished a remarkable victory. President Gibboney reported in December of that year that $392,411 had been raised since the founding of the organization, of which $265,000 had been applied to the purchase price. Presumably the difference between the two amounts went into continued repairs and upkeep of the mansion, as well as the purchase of Jefferson relics.[143]

A few years later William Sumner Appleton, who was about to start a large fund-raising campaign of his own, wrote to the Thomas Jefferson Memorial Foundation in order to find out how it had raised such a large sum. Gibboney's answer was revealing:

> It has been a very hard up-hill task. . . . For your information I am pleased to advise that we do not use the services of any firm of professional financial solicitors. We have a very small office and we only employ two people who take care of all the publicity, raising of funds, restoring Monticello, etc.[144]

A mere handful of people had accomplished a stupendous task. The job of saving Monticello was so overwhelming that in 1924 Fiske Kimball bluntly warned the American Institute of Architects that, should the efforts of the foundation fail, it would be many years before any other group would attempt the task again.[145] In spite of all its best efforts, the foundation did not make the last payments on the mortgage until 1940.[146]

While the preservation of Monticello ranks with the success of the Mount Vernon Ladies' Association seventy years earlier, there were great differences between the people involved in the two organizations and the times in which their campaigns flourished. Although the Monticello group had some Virginians in its membership, New Yorkers did the real spadework. In fact, the foundation's headquarters remained for many years at 115 Broadway in New York City. A tremendous proportion of the money raised to save Monticello came from the New York area, with school children and financiers as the major contributors. The Mount Vernon organization had branches in each state, though Miss Cunningham herself often acted as a roving main headquarters. The contributions to both crusades were mainly small ones, but the Mount Vernon movement had a more even spread over the country.

Each organization labored to pay an unprecedented sum of money for an old house—and each had to justify the amount paid. The Thomas Jefferson Memorial Foundation appeared to handle this issue better than did the Mount Vernon ladies, setting its goals in terms of $100,000 payments to Levy, rather than stressing the whole purchase price in every appeal. It must be remembered that the delicate issue of "real" versus "sentimental" value was raised frequently in the Congressional hearings on the subject of government ownership of Monticello.

The various groups which tried to save Monticello at one time or another never produced an orator who was able to fill the position of Edward Everett in the Mount Vernon story, although Mrs. Littleton did a pioneer job of popularizing her cause with letters and petitions. No single dominant figure emerges from the Monticello story that exerted the leadership of Ann Pamela Cunningham. The policies of the foundation seem to have been the product of several individuals working together, rather than the inspired ideas of one leader.

The comparison between the two movements becomes even more valid when one realizes that Monticello is probably the only house in America that can be compared to Mount Vernon from the standpoint of criteria for preservation. Both houses are of great historic interest, having been the homes of important men during much of their respective lives. Both mansions possess some beauty in an architectural sense and also have fine locations from the scenic standpoint. They each retain a number of original outbuildings, although those at Monticello were more closely attached to the main house than the ones at Mount Vernon. Possibly the only major advantage that Mount Vernon had at one time over Monticello was its proximity to a center of tourism. As the twentieth century has moved along, the relative isolation of Monticello has become less of an obstacle to travelers.

The Monticello movement marked a transition in the thinking of some Americans toward preservation. The people who were trying to save Mount Vernon dwelled upon its sacredness as a historic shrine. Those who preserved Monticello took two paths to achieve their goal, depending upon the type of individual they hoped to interest. Many saw in Monticello only its connection with history; others appreciated its classic design and influence on the evolution of American styles. Individuals who thought along architectural lines were probably not so numerous as those who were historically minded, but they were indeed a vital minority who have become increasingly important as time has moved on. The next chapter is devoted to a study of this small group of pioneers who developed a sensitivity to the architectural importance of old buildings.

IX

Antiquaries, Architects and Museum Directors

THE STORY NOW SHIFTS ABRUPTLY from an emphasis on history and patriotism to a cultural or artistic point of view. The chapter title suggests a discussion of three extremely different groups of people. Actually there were many similarities among these amateur and professional preservationists. Most of the people who saved buildings of architectural significance were well-educated men (rather than women!) who had traveled widely for that day and age. These men preserved buildings in different ways from their historically oriented brethren. Architects frequently "preserved" structures by means of sketches, floor plans and measured drawings. Museum directors "preserved" by moving houses and woodwork to new locations. Antiquaries recorded buildings in books through sketches or photographs. Though antiquaries were the least professional of the three groups, they made the most important contribution in saving historic buildings on their original sites. The history of architectural preservation does not fall readily into any clear chronological progression; the three stories in this chapter run parallel, with some overlapping.

It is best to begin with antiquaries, for their interest in old houses dates from the early nineteenth century. Norman Isham, himself a pleasant mixture of architect, scholar and antiquary, described the first local historians:

> Years ago there were always, in New England, at least, people known as the oldest inhabitants. They were not collectors but they were curious and, as I remember them, agreeable. . . . Some were genealogists; all had a deep interest in the ways of the past and in the history of the neighborhood.[1]

One of the first students of the New England past was John W. Barber of New Haven, who lived from 1798 to 1885. Isham pictured him as "a quaint figure in a long cloak and tall hat, . . . [who] wanders, sketchbook in hand, over the hills of New England." Although Barber's woodcuts of old buildings and scenes had little or no detail, he was one of the first persons to show any curiosity about the relics of the American past. His work was useful, but it was only a start.[2]

"The real pioneer in the study of New England's ancient buildings," in Isham's estimation, was Edwin Whitefield of Reading, Massachusetts.[3] Even today libraries that have collections of Whitefield's works prize them highly, for his drawings provide a remarkable record of early New England architecture as it appeared in the 1870's and 1880's.

He made his own drawings in lithograph on stone, and, while they are not wonderful and are somewhat uneven in merit, they tell the story and are, generally, to be relied upon . . . as, alas, in many cases they have to be. [These houses were later destroyed.] . . . He knew nothing and apparently cared nothing about the construction of these old dwellings; he like all laymen looked at the form. . . . Whitefield's great merit was his record of the oldest houses, the plain type of the seventeenth and early eighteenth centuries.[4]

Whitefield published five books of his sketches after 1880. He justified these efforts in the preface to his 1892 volume on Massachusetts houses:

The object of this book is to preserve and hand down to all future posterity representations of the Homes of their Forefathers. From a variety of causes they are rapidly disappearing; and before long the places that now know them will know them no more. It has been a labor of love to the undersigned to collect these mementoes of the past; having spent the greater portion of twelve years in visiting the various towns of the six New England States and making sketches of nearly eight hundred buildings, which are more or less interesting. Of these he has published in the five volumes thus far issued, about one-half that number, at a heavy expense to himself. . . .[5]

Whitefield's statement of purpose leads one to believe that he was interested in all kinds of ancient buildings, not merely the select few that had superlative historic importance. Those who have studied Whitefield's works note that he sketched many houses that have been destroyed or radically changed since the late nineteenth century.[6]

Another antiquary who deserves mention along with Whitefield was Dr. Irving Whitall Lyon of Hartford. Isham paid a visit to Dr. Lyon in 1893 to ask assistance in publishing a book on Rhode Island houses. Isham knew that Lyon was recognized as an authority on antique furniture. Lyon considered the idea of joint authorship, but he finally told Isham to publish the work on his own, which he did in 1895. Lyon then did all he could to help the sale of Isham's book in Connecticut. Thus the good doctor gave his blessing to one of the first scholarly architectural monographs printed in this country.[7]

Few antiquaries saved old buildings directly, preferring to collect furniture and books. Wallace Nutting, an antiquary with a keen business sense, actually bought a number of houses for preservation. Nutting lived much of his life in Framingham, Massachusetts, but he made the whole of New England his field of study. He had been a clergyman, then he turned to photography as a career. He eventually published picture books on certain states that might be called guidebooks.[8] Shortly before the First World War, just as the automobile was becoming popular, Nutting embarked upon a remarkably ambitious project. He described it in a leaflet intended for tourists.

> Mr. Nutting has had great difficulty in finding a proper setting for quaint pictures with attractive background and furnishings. He has therefore given his hobby the rein and has just carried out a daring and unique plan. He has purchased four houses, each notable for some outstanding merit and, out of hundreds examined, the best available early American house of the types desired. All are furnished with correct pieces of the period of the house or earlier.[9]

William Sumner Appleton, a friend of Nutting, announced the formation of the "Chain of Houses" in the April, 1915, issue of the *Bulletin of the S.P.N.E.A.* (pages 11-12). Appleton commented hopefully, "Mr. Nutting's antiquarian interest has grown with the extension of this work, so that now the commercial side bids fair to be subordinated to it." Nutting's chain consisted of three houses in Massachusetts and one, the Wentworth-Gardner, in Portsmouth, New Hampshire. A year later he added the Webb house in Wethersfield, Connecticut. In spite of the twenty-five-cent admission charge that Nutting required of all visitors, Appleton saw the more noble aspects of the chain idea. "This undertaking, which started partly as a commercial enterprise, has ended in a labor of love and Mr. Nutting has made the public inestimably his debtor by his invaluable services to the cause of preservation work." [10]

Nutting was not modest in telling the public what could be gained from a visit to his houses (four of them could be seen on a sixty-four-mile motor trip from Boston):

> More can be learned in one day's careful examination of these houses and their furnishings than a considerable course in architecture and the rummaging of shops for years could give.
>
> Anyone who desires to be informed and not at the mercy of the unscrupulous can easily learn the forms and materials not only of edifices and their finish, but of their appropriate furnishings. The benefit of a very costly experience is offered to the public. [11]

The decline in tourist trade after America's entrance into World War I convinced Nutting that the public was not yet ready for the scheme he had worked out. He found he was losing money on the upkeep of his far-flung historic properties. Nutting later admitted that he had embarked on a "vast program for a private person" and had been forced to "trim sails" in order to prepare for whatever economic conditions might follow the war. [12] In 1918 he put the five houses up for sale, and within a year sold them all. [13] The chain had proven to be a noble experiment, but not a commercial success.

The foregoing survey of the work and influence of antiquaries in the preservation movement does much less than justice to their contribution. These men were by nature studious and retiring, which makes it difficult to pull any one of them out from his anonymous position as a hard-working member of a small historical society. Perhaps it is sufficient to say that without these tireless students of the past, the preservation movement would never have had its foundation so secure on the rock of local enthusiasm.

Architects should have been the most active professional group in the preservation movement, yet the contribution of individual architects and the American Institute of Architects (A.I.A.) has been disappointing. Architects were usually essential when delicate restoration projects required guidance. Many of these men popularized elements of "colonial" styles through magazine articles and through designs that were reminiscent of the American past.

The Harvard lectures of Arthur Gilman in 1844 contained some of the earliest indications of an academic interest in the history of American architecture. These lectures were not preservation appeals; they were efforts to inform people about a subject that was not yet respectable for study.[14]

At the 1869 national convention of the A.I.A. Richard Upjohn, president and founder of the institute, sounded the same note, but more clearly. He proposed an investigation of early American buildings in order to make architects think deeply about their own progress: Had they really improved upon the work of their predecessors? Upjohn gave a short description of his own renovation of the Van Rensselaer manor house in Albany in the early 1840's. He then proposed that:

> The talented members of the Academy of Design would do well, when sketching and painting their fine landscapes, to make careful studies of some of the old houses yet remaining,—houses that will be buried in oblivion in the course of another century, unless faithful records are kept of them by all hands. . . . And let me ask, may we not gain a valuable lesson while contemplating these works of our forefathers?[15]

Upjohn's speech inaugurated a learned discourse by Richard Morris Hunt and some other architects on the materials used in the construction of the Old Feather Store, a seventeenth-century building that had recently been torn down in Boston. Isham, in studying the *Proceedings* of this convention, believed that the ideas expressed were far ahead of their time.[16] The speech and the debate which followed bore no direct results, but they may well have served to plant a seed in the minds of the gentlemen present.

In 1878 a Boston architect, Arthur Little, published a book entitled *Early New England Interiors*. It consisted of line drawings (with a curious "old-fashioned" perspective) showing rooms from houses in Salem, Marblehead and the Portsmouth area. None of the illustrations represented the earliest homes, for at that time only eighteenth-century interiors were considered distinguished enough for architectural study. In spite of the uneven quality of these illustrations, the book was a landmark; it was the first publication on colonial buildings by a trained architect.[17]

Soon more books by architects began to appear, offering interesting photographs or drawings of eighteenth-century houses. These works did influence the practice of architecture, though not the preservation movement. Isham, who was trained during this period, remembered these books:

> Thus the architects who bought these publications used them at first in a way which, while it was artistic, at least in some cases, was very unscientific. They copied more or less slavishly from the forms the photographs and drawings put before them. I doubt if they cared to keep separate types which in time were years apart. . . . Their purpose was to build a house in the usual way, but in colonial form—using all our modern ways of woodworking and masonry, but making the windows, doors and so on in Colonial or "near Colonial" forms.[18]

Isham was speaking of a movement we now know as the "Colonial Revival," which flourished just before the turn of the century.

Some architects began to heed Upjohn's advice and found that colonial buildings were indeed worthy of study. Around 1876 a group of young architects traveled into New England "for the purpose of seeing and making drawings of the best examples of Colonial work." These gentlemen were none other than McKim, Mead, Bigelow, and White, three of whom were later to become partners in the great New York architectural firm of McKim, Mead, and White.[19] At the A.I.A. convention the following year, R. S. Peabody reasoned that early American work was honest and served as a harmonious background for furniture of the same period.[20] At the 1879 convention a committee was appointed to investigate the practices of colonial architects and builders. The report, which was printed a year or so later, included the committee's judgment that colonial work was valid in its own time, but it should only influence, not govern, contemporary architects.[21]

The first major preservation effort on the part of any group of architects came in Boston, a city which had already saved Old South and the Old State House. Early in the 1890's officials began to notice signs of decay in the Bulfinch State House which stands at the top of Beacon Hill. The fate of Charles Bulfinch's work became the principal concern of the Boston Society of Architects under the leadership of Charles A. Cummings. In 1895 Cummings and a number of other interested citizens succeeded in getting the legislature to appropriate $375,000 for the restoration and refurnishing of the older portion of the building. Cummings became a consultant while the restoration work was in progress, and Boston gained another refurbished landmark. People in Hartford and other New England cities began to refer to the preservation of the Bulfinch State House in Boston as a precedent to be followed in their own communities.[22]

The American Institute of Architects entered the preservation field weakly in 1890. At its convention that year, Richard M. Upjohn of New York offered a resolution setting up a Committee of Conservators of Public Architecture of the Country. His plea was directed mainly toward some public buildings that were in danger of destruction or alteration at the hands of city and state governments. He believed that these structures, if saved, would someday be monuments in the history of American architecture. The convention passed the resolution, and Upjohn became chairman of the new committee.[23] Over the next seven years the committee gave the cause of preservation some valuable publicity, but it did not rescue any buildings. When the institute convened in 1897, Upjohn was surprised when he was asked to report on his committee of "conservators." He saw no further use for it because the main cause for creation of the committee had disappeared when New York's Customs House was torn down.[24] So ended the first of several preservation committees formed by the A.I.A.

The only house saved by the institute claimed the attention of that organization for many years, and the problems involved in its rescue show why architects were not leaders in preservationism. In the 1880's, while designing a Washington residence for Mrs. Leland Stanford, Glenn Brown took her to see a building called the "Octagon." It had been built by the Tayloe family as a town house around the year 1800. Mrs. Stanford was so pleased with one of the mantels that she wanted to purchase it for her new home, but Brown was unable to persuade the owners to sell the coveted woodwork. From that time on, Brown's interest in the building grew steadily. At the 1889 convention of the institute, he presented a motion that the A.I.A. make its headquarters in Washington at the Octagon. His proposal was tabled.[25] In 1897 when the subject of a national headquarters came up again, the Washington Chapter of the A.I.A. argued:

> . . . [Washington] offered the broadest field for the Institute to arouse interest in and secure national legislation in relation to Art and construction. . . . It would be in a position to make its influence felt in methods adopted by the Government in procuring designs for National buildings, which had been so successfully inaugurated by the Secretary of the Treasury.[26]

The A.I.A. would thus have an effective lobby in the Capital. On February 11, 1898, the board of directors of the institute voted to rent the Octagon for five years at an amount not exceeding $360 a year.[27] The owners were agreeable, so the architects renovated the structure to suit their needs and moved in a few months later.[28]

The Octagon was not yet preserved, for the A.I.A. did not own the property. In 1901 the president, Charles F. McKim, decided that the Octagon would make an excellent permanent headquarters. Glenn Brown recorded a conversation that he had with McKim on this subject. McKim began:

> "We need a recognized home to give us dignity and standing. The Octagon is an ideal house for this purpose. Don't you think the majority of the members would like it? How much do the owners ask for it?"
>
> "I believe the members would unanimously approve the Octagon as their future home," the answer was, "although the owners have fixed no price, I believe we can get it for thirty thousand dollars."
>
> "Make them an offer," he replied, "of thirty thousand dollars, ten thousand to be paid in cash upon their showing a clear title."
>
> "But, Mr. McKim," I said, "we have only five hundred dollars in the treasury."
>
> "I will see," he replied, "that you get the ten thousand cash payment. If I cannot get others to join me, I will send you my check for the amount as soon as they show a clear title and are ready for the first payment." [29]

Within ten days McKim's efforts bore fruit. His prestige was such that he simply told five of the largest architectural firms in the country that he needed two thousand dollars from each of them.

For years the institute had vainly asked these same firms to subscribe a few hundred dollars for the purchase of the same house![30]

McKim did not stop at this point. He set out to convince the institute that the Octagon had real architectural excellence. "It is cause for rejoicing that the institute which has urged upon governments, national, state and municipal, the duty of preserving historic monuments, has itself secured possession of one of the historic houses of America." In great detail he listed the notable events that had taken place in the building; for instance, James Madison had signed the Treaty of Ghent in one of the rooms.[31] Brown was certain that McKim's persuasive influence made the house a place of pilgrimage in the years that followed.[32]

There were some financial problems that the A.I.A. had to face in regard to its new home. At the 1903 convention, George B. Post, chairman of the Committee for Securing Funds for the Purchase of the Octagon, announced that $12,896 had been paid, leaving a debt of $18,000. John M. Carrere of New York proposed that those at the convention subscribe the rest of the debt right there as a testimonial to McKim, who was retiring as president of the institute.[33] Carrere reported sadly to the 1905 convention that he had only collected $3,967 out of a total of $9,000 that had been promised.[34] Finally, in 1907 Cass Gilbert, reporting for the Octagon Fund Committee, announced that the debt had been paid.[35] It had taken six years to clear the house of indebtedness.

Now the most difficult question of all faced the institute: How would the largest organization of architects in the United States treat its only historic house? At the 1914 convention the board recommended the expenditure of up to $2,500 from the emergency fund for repairs that they considered necessary for keeping the building usable. The recommendation won approval, bolstered by the following argument:

> The Institute is accustomed to lend its influence and support to all movements looking to the preservation of historic monuments, and several of the Chapters have been active in bringing about the restoration of historic buildings in their localities. But the Institute, which owns a building, notable both architecturally and historically, has taken no adequate steps to preserve it.[36]

These repairs evidently did little more than prevent actual disintegration of the building.

Two years later the board suggested that the institute vacate the Octagon and restore it as a memorial to the "persuasive enthusiasm and generosity" of Charles F. McKim. The directors admitted that this was a bold program since the institute would be forced to erect a fireproof office building on an adjoining lot. As an inducement, they mentioned that in the past ten days John Russell Pope had succeeded in securing $1,000 in pledges from six architects. The pledges were to take effect only if the board's recommendation passed.[37] During the debate on the proposed memorial Brown estimated that it would certainly cost $100,000 to construct a new office building and properly restore the Octagon. He warned that the sum was so great that the institute would have to resort to soliciting money from the general public.[38] Nevertheless, a motion committing the A.I.A. to this ambitious venture did pass. The directors were not required to take any action until sufficient funds had been collected, and it became increasingly evident as time went on that the institute was unable to match the splendid vision of the men who wanted to restore the Octagon.[39] Finally in 1922 the chairman of the Building Committee, D. Everett Waid, proposed repeal of the motion to set aside the Octagon as a museum building. He argued that such an exhibit might better belong to the federal government, for it would only have a remote connection with the activities of the institute. In addition, maintenance costs would eventually tax the resources of the A.I.A. Waid then proposed a compromise measure: restore the first two floors as museum rooms and offices; make the refurnished drawing room a meeting place for members of the institute, especially those who were visitors to Washington; erect office buildings and a convention hall on the grounds. Waid's suggestion was approved *in toto*.[40]

Instead of entering an era of peace, the A.I.A. experienced a new and bitter controversy over the fate of the Octagon stable. At the 1923 convention, Waid reported that the Building Committee was about to begin repairs on the exterior of the Octagon. He recommended that a recent gift of $5,000 from the Allied Architects of Los Angeles be used in furnishing the drawing room with reproductions of furniture from the period when the house was built. Unfortunately, he also proposed that the stable be torn down to make room for the much-needed convention hall. Since this was only a recommendation, there was no debate and his report was approved.[41] When the A.I.A. convened in 1924, Waid again proposed that the stable be eliminated in order to make way for the convention hall. One member entered a strong plea to save the tottering stable. "We have a committee on the Preservation of Historic Monuments that is looking after everyone else's historic monument but our own (Applause), and it is high time that we preserved our own." His comment set the stage for a heated debate. Many feared that an auditorium on the property would dwarf the Octagon by its size. Others sympathized with the view that the stable was just as important to the architectural harmony of the Octagon lot as the main house. In any event, the convention did not come to a conclusion.[42] During 1925 and 1926 the Building Committee wisely refrained from further discussion of razing the stable or erecting any new buildings on the property.[43]

So ends the troubled story (up to 1926) of the only historic house saved by the American Institute of Architects. Twenty-five years after it had formally acquired the Octagon, the institute was still not completely sure what it would do with the property. Several grandiose plans had been set aside because the board of directors had not raised enough money. It is gratifying to know that the busy A.I.A. did manage to save this important building, and it has served well as a headquarters over the years. McKim had been correct in his decision to force the issue and buy the house for the institute. But when one surveys the battles that raged over the final disposition of the Octagon, it becomes clear why the institute did not buy any other old buildings for preservation.

The A.I.A.'s interest in historic preservation did not terminate with the disappearance of the Committee of Conservators of Public Architecture in 1897. Around the turn of the century the officers of the A.I.A. joined in an effort to prevent any projected disfigurement of the White House.[44] Although the institute had no national preservation committee for several years, some local chapters were active in preservation work. In most cases these efforts were centered on public buildings. Architects were making what they considered to be their unique contribution to the cause of preservation; they wanted to save buildings that were important in the development of American architecture, though some of them lacked historic associations.

The Philadelphia Chapter of the A.I.A. formed its own Committee on Preservation of Historic Monuments in 1898 when T. Mellon Rogers' work on Independence Hall came under criticism.[45] After the work on the hall had ended in 1898, the committee turned to Congress Hall and began a thorough study of the building's history as a prelude to restoration. In 1910 the chapter passed a resolution offering the fruits of its study to the city if the city would undertake a restoration.[46] The Committee on Historic Monuments went to see the mayor in an effort to get his support. During the interview the mayor fell asleep while an irate citizen spoke on the significance of Congress Hall. Carl Ziegler, chairman of the A.I.A. committee, relates how he himself saved the day:

> Suddenly the Mayor's elbow slipped on the polished surface of the table top and he awoke with a start. He too was embarrassed, so in a loud voice I quickly asked him, "Don't you agree with us, your Honor, that it will bring great credit to the City and to your administration if we restore Congress Hall and re-dedicate on its completion with a National celebration." He slowly nodded his his head and said, "yes I do." [47]

On April 6, 1910, Ziegler offered the services of the Philadelphia Chapter of the A.I.A. free of charge if the city would pay for drafting the plans.[48] The actual work did not begin until July of 1911, and from that time onward the Philadelphia architects had a representative at Congress Hall nearly every day to supervise the restoration.[49] After two years of diligent service, Frank Miles Day, the architect in charge of most of the restoration, basked in the praise of his fellow citizens. Congress Hall was reopened to the public with fitting ceremonies on October 26, 1913.[50] A few years later the chairman of the national Committee on Preservation of Natural Beauties and Historic Monuments reported to the A.I.A. convention that the Philadelphia Chapter was "becoming the recognized authority on such matters" as restoration.[51] The Philadelphia architects helped the city again in the early 1920's by drawing the plans for the restoration of the John Bartram Mansion, and then by supervising the work.[52] During 1926 and 1927 the chapter advised the Valley Forge Park Commission on some changes in the Washington Headquarters.[53]

Another A.I.A. chapter active in the preservation movement had its headquarters in New Orleans. The Louisiana Chapter enlisted public support in cataloging all the remaining historic buildings in New Orleans and asked to be warned whenever one of these structures was in any danger.[54] In one case the architects went to the aid of a man whose home had been condemned as a threat to public health. The cost of making the old house safe seemed to be prohibitive, so the architects proposed inexpensive but sound repairs which enabled the owner to keep his home. The Louisiana Chapter also planned a program for students of architecture from Tulane University who recorded architectural details from notable buildings through measured drawings.[55] The chapter showed civic pride by requesting the creation of a municipal art commission in New Orleans to supervise future improvements that might affect the older portions of the city.[56] In late 1926 and early 1927 the architects began gathering material for the drafting of an ordinance that would establish a special zoning system for the Vieux Carré, or Old City. This was the first effort to create a municipal historic preservation law in the United States.[57]

Other chapters of the A.I.A. were active in preservation work in one way or another during the first quarter of the twentieth century. The Boston Chapter, which had fought so well for Bulfinch's State House in the 1890's, set up an agreement with the Society for the Preservation of New England Antiquities to help that society record old buildings by means of measured drawings and photographs.[58]

Not until 1906 did some members of the A.I.A. attempt to set up another national committee on the preservation of historic buildings. This movement failed because the institute was so involved in paying off the debt on the Octagon property.[59] The 1909 convention passed a mild resolution urging individual chapters to keep a watchful eye on all architectural monuments in their respective areas.[60] Two years later another appeal for a "Committee on the Preservation of Historic Structures" fell on deaf ears. The institute also failed to enact a recommendation that architectural students in colleges be asked to assist in a systematic cataloging of historic buildings all over the country by means of measured drawings.[61]

By 1913 the A.I.A. was ready to create a Committee on the Conservation of Natural Resources, and sometime the next year this committee took on preservation work as well—with a new title of tremendous length that implied the institute was watching over both natural resources and historic monuments. The chairman, William M. Ellicott, told the 1914 convention of his hopes for the future: "There must be some well-defined, organized effort looking to the protection of historic buildings, fortifications, and so forth. This work should be systematized by the Institute and carried on by all Chapters." In the same report Ellicott urged the formation of a Bureau of National Monuments in the Interior Department, which would care for "artistic and historic" buildings—thus prophesying the growth of the History Branch of the National Park Service in the early 1930's.[62]

Although the work of the revived Preservation Committee consisted mainly of gathering reports from local chapters, one architectural scholar had a broader view of the mission of the profession. Richard Franz Bach, curator of the School of Architecture at Columbia University, began a series of articles in the *Architectural Record* in 1915 under the title "Books on Colonial Architecture." Bach offered a challenging assignment to architects, for he envisioned a comprehensive catalog of historic buildings. He gave a sense of urgency to the project: "The buildings disappear rapidly, almost monthly, and many are repeatedly altered, converted into taverns and museums or turned to other purposes, which almost invariably involve important structural changes." [63] In later articles Bach continued to hammer away at the great need for a program right at that time, not at some future date. He looked upon the A.I.A. as the best agency for supervising the catalog, and Avery Library at Columbia University as the logical place to deposit drawings and photographs.[64] The chairman of the Committee on Preservation of Historic Monuments and Scenic Beauties in the United States reported to the 1918 convention that he favored Bach's proposal, but he warned that a nationwide program would require more A.I.A. branches and more cooperation between existing chapters and other civic groups.

Your Committee is of the opinion that while such a record or catalogue might be compiled by antiquarian and similar societies, it is certainly within the province of the architect having technical knowledge of the several periods of architectural development to judge and properly classify such buildings, and if the effort of local committees and other agencies can be coordinated as suggested it would seem appropriate to undertake the task under the auspices and advice of the Institute.[65]

Architects were entirely willing to offer their skills to the cause of preservation, but they did not wish to lead it. The reports of the Preservation Committee for the next three or four years revealed that the chairman had to spend all his time trying to organize local chapters into subcommittees that would work in the national effort. Each year up to 1923, the chairman optimistically stated that he was almost ready to begin recording colonial architecture.

In 1923 the emphasis abruptly changed when Fiske Kimball, another architectural scholar, became chairman of the institute's Preservation Committee. Kimball quickly dropped the idea of a catalog, probably considering it too ambitious for the institute at that time. In any event, he described in detail where he believed the committee's influence should be used:

. . . (i) where monuments of really national importance are threatened, either with destruction, or with harmful modification . . . ; (ii) in the initiation and support of policies which may be of general benefit; and (iii) in the conduct of a campaign of education both of architects and of the public as to the proper methods of treatment of old buildings.[66]

Kimball added a new item to the list of responsibilities of his committee—that of correcting errors that architects were making in their restoration of old buildings. His reports for the next two years were replete with news of the whole preservation field as he saw it, with emphasis on the work at Monticello. He also mentioned his efforts to save a house that was on an island in the federal reservation at Fort Eustis, Virginia. He had contacted the military authorities in an attempt to make the building a historic monument under the provisions of an Act of Congress of 1906, and he believed that he had been successful in keeping the house standing.[67] Kimball announced in 1924 that the institute's Preservation Committee had one member in each of the chapters charged with protecting the architectural treasures of his particular area.[68]

When Kimball moved on to the directorship of the Pennsylvania Museum in 1926, A. Lawrence Kocher, an architect and educator, followed him as chairman of the Committee on Preservation of Historic Monuments and Scenery. Kocher's ideas were much like those of his predecessor. He intended to serve as a clearinghouse for information on the subject of preservation: "Public attention is drawn to an endangered building and your chairman has cooperated in arousing public sentiment with a view to checking the destruction." Kocher revived the discarded plan for an extensive catalog of colonial buildings.[69] He also opposed some of the methods of restoration then in use, lamenting that many old buildings had taken on a "forbidding museum character." [70]

The A.I.A. could be accused of negligence in the cause of preservation since the Octagon was the only house it ever saved. Actually the organization was influential, not powerful. Individual chapters were not large enough to take on the responsibility of maintaining historic buildings, a fact made obvious by the difficulties that beset the national organization in its efforts to restore the Octagon. The major contribution of the chapters lay in the field of restoration and publicity for architectural preservation.

Architects performed a valuable service for preservationism by popularizing older styles through books and magazine articles. The first large-scale treatment of colonial buildings came with the publication of the *Georgian Period,* a three-volume set of articles, measured drawings and photographs that came from the *American Architect and Building News* between 1900 and 1902. The set was later published in six volumes as a reference work. [71] One significant periodical that came out later was issued by the White Pine Bureau as an advertisement. The *White Pine Series,* with Russell Whitehead as its editor, began publication in 1915. It was sent out to architects who lived in the area where white pine might be purchased as a building material. The first edition numbered 5,500 copies; ten years later, when the White Pine Bureau severed its connections with the magazine, the circulation had nearly doubled.[72] The first issue gave the reader a clear idea of what the series was intended to do:

Appreciating that most architects prefer to form their own conclusions from good photographs, the pictorial side of the work will be the dominant feature, being in charge of Mr. Julian Buckly, architectural photographer. In selecting subjects the highest standard will be maintained, and they will be chosen with special reference to their usefulness to the architectural designer. By this discriminating choice of subject matter and the quality of its plate reproductions, the Monograph Series hopes to earn a place as a valuable addition to the literature on architecture. . . . The object of the Monograph Series is to further acquaint the architect with "White Pine—Its Qualities—Its Availability—Its Cost." . . .[73]

Although the *White Pine Series* was an advertisement, the publisher wished that it might also serve as a reference work. An early issue included a study of colonial cottages by Joseph Everett Chandler, a well-known restoration architect of that time. In later issues there were descriptions of various towns possessing a large number of surviving early buildings, along with views of contemporary suburban homes built in the colonial style. During the ten years that it was published by the White Pine Bureau, the *Series* consisted almost entirely of photographs of buildings and architectural details. When Russell Whitehead became publisher in 1925, he concentrated on individual houses, and included more measured drawings in each issue. There were still some advertisements, but the detailed treatment of modern suburban homes had disappeared.

When he took over the *Series* Whitehead gave it a challenging goal:

To catch and retain for our descendants this elusive thing, the personality of our ancestors, as expressed in their buildings, we have studied their architecture from the earliest shelters of the colonists to the charming and sophisticated "mansions" of the early Republic. We find them a fascinating and inspiring record of the growth of the germ of our native art,—a germ that grew and throve in the face of great hardships and handicaps.[74]

Whitehead believed that the 1920's were an "American Renaissance" because he saw that the fundamentals of beauty (formerly expressed by the colonial builders) were again appreciated. He heaped scorn on those who had worked in the early days of the "Colonial Revival." The great buildings of the past that had survived the "restorer" and the "improver" were the best models for present-day taste and design. Whitehead found eighteenth-century builders to be men with broad experience, and he hoped that "through the study of their work, our modern world can learn much of design, of thoroughness and of the creation of beautiful buildings that will live to give pleasure in the years to come." [75] The *Monograph Series* (the new name for the *White Pine Series*) certainly introduced America's architectural heritage to an influential audience. Whitehead's magazine, long out of print, is still in demand today.

In 1921 Horace Wells Sellers, chairman of the A.I.A. Preservation Committee, spoke to the institute about the study of colonial buildings. "The growing interest in the subject as evidenced by the publication of measured drawings in architectural journals is suggestive of agencies which might join in the more comprehensive and organized movement which your committee has under consideration." [76] He was referring again to the much-heralded catalog of old buildings. A few years earlier Richard Bach in his articles on "Books on Colonial Architecture," had said:

> The books available in the field of colonial dwellings are chiefly of two kinds: those most readily classified as general historical or as popular works and those which devote themselves to a more definite architectural purpose, carried out through the agency of photographs or measured drawings with details of construction or decoration. Not a few bold spirits have undertaken a general treatment of domestic buildings throughout the thirteen States, and have confined themselves to but one or two volumes. Such studies have invariably been entirely non-architectural and they have, furthermore, in many cases savored of the popular tendency of a certain type of talkative guide books. [77]

The "guide book" appears to have been much more in evidence than the thorough, carefully documented architectural study. The existence of both types of books proved that the reading public was willing to purchase material on the general topic of old buildings. Architects had been a potent force in educating the public, even if they saved very few historic houses.

Before the year 1926 several art museums in the United States had begun to install "period rooms" containing woodwork removed from old houses as a background for antique furnishings. Henry W. Kent of the Metropolitan Museum of Art in New York City concluded that the birthplace of period rooms was northern Europe. Late in the nineteenth century, museum officials in Bavaria and Switzerland pioneered the concept of displaying objects that were related in time. A logical setting for this type of exhibition was a room taken from a building of the period being illustrated. By 1898 the Swiss National Museum in Zurich had sixty-two such rooms, and a few years later Munich's Bavarian National Museum installed almost as many. The idea did not immediately take hold in England and France, though it had some influence in the Scandinavian countries.[78] Earlier, in 1891, Dr. Artur Hazelius, the founder of the Nordiska Museet in Stockholm, had begun assembling a group of buildings in a park he called "Skansen." It was the first of many "open-air museums" that eventually appeared throughout Germany and Scandinavia.[79]

The practice of moving old paneling to private homes came to this country by an indirect route. Early in the nineteenth century a young American traveling in England with his parents went to Abbotsford to visit Sir Walter Scott. This New Englander, Ben: Perley Poore, was impressed with the romantic air of antiquity that pervaded Scott's mansion. According to family tradition, Poore promised Scott that when he grew up he would build such a home in America. Sir Walter tried his best to encourage the young man, and evidently succeeded. Over a period of thirty years beginning around 1850, Poore constructed a country seat at West Newbury, Massachusetts, which he named "Indian Hill." One man who wanted to save Indian Hill in later years described it:

> Its nucleus is a barn made over as a house and greatly added to in an amazing congeries of rooms that seem almost numberless, while attached to, or adjoining the house are extensive barns of interesting construction. The whole is a monument to the genius of Benjamin Perley Poore who built it about the middle of the

nineteenth century, being perhaps the first American to appreciate the importance of picking up parts of houses being destroyed here and there. . . .[80]

Poore's house museum contained, among other mementos, pieces of paneling from two of Boston's most famous early buildings, the old Province house and the John Hancock Mansion. Poore also had a large heterogeneous collection of antique furniture which he proudly showed to interested visitors. His influence must have been wide, for he was reputed to be a genial host.[81]

During the two decades before the First World War, Henry Davis Sleeper, an interior decorator, built "Beauport," an architectural maze on a rocky point at the entrance to the harbor of Gloucester, Massachusetts. His summer home contained woodwork taken from dismantled houses, and it was furnished in a great variety of styles. A friend of Sleeper believed that Beauport had been inspired by visits to Indian Hill.[82]

Neither Indian Hill nor its stepchild Beauport was a scholarly effort to re-create a picture of the past. Both were private collections reflecting the whims of their owners. The influence of Poore and Sleeper on public museums is uncertain, though it is significant that two such men devoted themselves to the acquisition of early American furnishings at a time when they were clearly out of fashion.

Not until eighteenth-century furniture came back into vogue did the concept of period rooms make much of an impression on public institutions in the United States. In 1904 Charles Pendleton presented his large collection of furniture to the Rhode Island School of Design. Since the school did not have a place suitable for exhibiting these items, S. O. Metcalf gave funds for the construction of a fireproof Georgian building designed to house the Pendleton Collection. No old paneling was put into the new building, but the woodwork was as historically accurate as architects could make it in 1904. The idea of providing a period setting for the exhibition of antiques had indeed crossed the Atlantic.[83]

The Essex Institute in Salem, Massachusetts, was the first American institution to take full advantage of both the outdoor museum of Hazelius and the period-room installations of the Swiss and Germans. The fact that this small organization was devoted to the study of the history and geography of Essex County gave it greater latitude than most museums in the selection of material for exhibition. As early as 1899 an official of the institute, Francis Henry Appleton, suggested:

> Besides collecting our relics in-doors, let us be the medium of preserving relics out-of-doors. So far as is possible, and besides some interesting houses in old Salem Village, let spots in nature's landscape . . . be preserved to continue to help us by a bright remembrance of the lives there lived.[84]

Although his appeal did not bear fruit for several years, at least one person in Salem believed that the antiquities of the area should be preserved in an outdoor museum atmosphere.

The pioneer work of the Essex Institute came in the first two decades of the twentieth century while George Francis Dow was its secretary. Dow was a master antiquary and a thorough student of the life of the past. He constantly urged the institute to use exhibition techniques that would be considered modern today, and he usually succeeded in his quest. Just after he became secretary, Dow announced to the members of the institute in 1900 that the museum had expended some money for a collection of old views of Salem and its immediate surroundings. He commented, "The value of such a collection is inestimable when preserved for reference and the inspection of future generations. . . . We are the builders and the preservers for those who are to come after us." [85]

Two years later the president of the institute, Robert S. Rantoul, asserted that the museum of antiquities then being assembled by Dow was already becoming famous throughout New England; people from all parts of the nation were coming to Salem to see the Essex Institute on the basis of its reputation.[86] Francis Appleton, the next president, said in 1905, "It would be well if another ancient, and typical house of early days should be placed in the keeping of the Institute, so furnished as to clearly represent the early life in Essex County." He also thought that a merchant ship's cabin would make an excellent exhibit depicting conditions that faced Salem's captains in the days of the China trade.[87] During 1906 and 1907 Appleton's wish was partially realized, for the institute doubled its exhibition area.

George Francis Dow now had a rare opportunity to explore

concepts of museum installation that had not been tried in the United States. In justice to Dow, it should be made clear that at that time antiquities were still regarded as curiosities to be found only in historical society exhibits and dusty attics. No art museum in the country had any substantial collection of colonial rooms or furniture. Dow was more concerned with the mission of the institute than he was with prevailing tastes:

> Now if the museum has possessed an educational influence in the past, particularly during the congested conditions of recent years, it is most certain that much more effective work will be possible in the future, for the rearranged collections will illustrate, in an almost unique manner, the every-day life of our forefathers. . . .[88]

Dow was familiar with both new types of museum installation in use in Europe and he was impressed with their possibilities. Without concerning himself with the artistic merit of his collection, he began the renovation of the exhibit rooms in 1907 by setting up a staircase from a Salem house that had just been demolished. Soon he brought in architectural fragments from other vanished buildings to adorn his museum.[89]

The most revolutionary change came when Dow constructed three alcoves along one side of the institute's large hall.

> These consisted of a kitchen (1750), bedroom (1800), and parlor (1800), and pains were taken to embody in the trim of these rooms original wood finish taken from a building about to be dismantled or to reproduce carefully architectural details from existing houses. In this way a fine wooden mantel by McIntire was preserved in the parlor, and the wainscot, cornice and other woodwork of the room were reproduced from the finish of a house known to have been designed by him. The clear white pine sheathing in the kitchen came from a farmhouse built in 1730 and the timbered ceiling of this room reproduced in effect the unplastered ceilings of hundreds of houses existing in New England. . . . An effort was made to heighten the illusion by casually placing on the table before the fireplace in the parlor a Salem newspaper printed in the year 1800 and on it a pair of silver-horned spectacles, as though just removed by the reader.[90]

The rooms in the Essex Institute were "three-sided"; that is, the fourth wall of each was a glass partition which permitted the visitor to view the entire room without actually entering.[91] Even today one may walk up to these alcoves and see one of the first American efforts to re-create historical reality.

Dow's use of old woodwork was to have two unforeseen results as time went by. First, museums that followed his example began removing rooms from houses that were intact, rather than from those that were to be destroyed. Second, those in charge of historic houses often sought to imitate Dow's scholarly grouping of furniture and other objects.

Dow was interested in testing the possibilities of the outdoor museum along with period rooms. In 1909 he expressed the wish that the lot behind the institute could be cleared so that the museum could "preserve on its own land one of Salem's oldest houses now standing." He was speaking of the John Ward house, built around 1685. The property on which the Ward house stood had been bought by Essex County to make way for an enlargement of its jail. The building had then been offered to the institute for removal. Dow could not overlook such an opportunity, so he continually reminded the membership that the preservation and restoration of the Ward house would be "eminently" within the province of their organizations.[92] A year later Dow managed to persuade sixteen "friends" of the institute to put up the money for moving the Ward house from its former location to the yard of the museum. The structure needed a great deal of restoration work—and it had no furnishings at all. Dow planned to use the lean-to of the house as an old-time apothecary shop, a "cent shop" (or general store) and a spinning room. He succeeded in finding an old shoemaker's shop in Lynn and had it moved next to the Ward house. He hoped through this addition to be able to illustrate a craft that was fast disappearing.[93]

The Ward house was rebuilt on the inside in order to give it a seventeenth-century appearance, with many details copied from well-known homes in Essex County. Dow then opened the building as a true outdoor museum in the Skansen tradition:

> In furnishing these rooms an effort has been made to present a truthful picture of an interior of the year 1700. Where original furniture or utensils of the period have not been available, reproductions have been made, and the finished result is believed to be highly successful, giving much of the atmosphere of live-

ableness. Miss Sarah W. Symonds and her assistants occupy the second floor and act as custodians, showing the house to visitors when the cow bell signals its call from the front entry. They will be dressed in homespun costumes of the time when the house was built.[94]

Dow soon became convinced that his experiment of hiring costumed hostesses had been successful, for people were writing to him for complete descriptions of the costumes. One small moving-picture company came to Salem to photograph the ladies in the Ward house.[95]

The Ward house and the shoemaker's shop were not the only exhibits that the Essex Institute put in its backyard "out-of-door museum" (as Dow referred to it). In 1913 the institute acquired a porch from a home attributed to the wood-carver Samuel McIntire and attached it to the rear of the main building.[96] A few years later the institute added another porch from an earlier house and a cupola from a shipowner's home. Dow succeeded in creating an array of architectural fragments grouped around the seventeenth-century house with its costumed attendants. Although the Essex Institute's outdoor museum has not grown much larger over the years since Dow's secretaryship, it is unquestionably the earliest of a long line of similar exhibitions that now dot the whole United States.[97]

Sometime around 1914 the Public Museum in Milwaukee, Wisconsin, began to install historical and ethnological displays in its building. One of the first of these was the "Colonial Village," which represented a group of early New England homes. The visitor could walk up to these reproductions, peer into the windows, and see wax models depicting various activities common in seventeenth-century New England. The idea of showing colonial life by carefully arranged museum exhibits was beginning to spread.[98]

The first nationally recognized exhibition to present American furnishings to the public was an outgrowth of the efforts of the great collectors of the 1880's and 1890's. The Metropolitan Museum in New York City put on a display of many types of American household objects as a part of the Hudson-Fulton Celebration of 1909. Henry W. Kent, secretary of the Metropolitan, knew that there were a number of antiquaries who had been collecting furniture and silverware for several decades. He believed that the

1909 show served to focus attention on these men. "The amiable amusement with which the seeker after 'antiques' had been regarded now gave place to respectful attention. Expert, intelligent collecting became a thing to be applauded and admired." The Hudson-Fulton Celebration also helped some of these connoisseurs to get acquainted with each other—for they had been working in different parts of the country.[99] Robert DeForest, president of the Metropolitan, considered the decision to exhibit American furnishings a bold departure. "It seemed to me and to my friend, Henry W. Kent, an opportunity to test out the question whether American domestic art was worthy of a place in an art museum, and to test it out not theoretically but visually." [100]

Both Kent and DeForest must have been impressed with the show, for a significant purchase followed. Eugene Bolles, one of those who had loaned furniture to the museum, announced that he was going to sell his entire collection. Kent heard of Bolles' intention and informed the trustees of the Metropolitan. The board was not yet convinced that American domestic arts should be shown in the museum, but Kent was determined by this time. He invited R. T. Haines Halsey (one of the trustees) and Mr. and Mrs. DeForest to New England as his guests in order to see some early American rooms in Topsfield and Salem. They stopped at the Essex Institute to inspect the newly opened period rooms installed by George Francis Dow. Kent believed that this visit "turned the scales and led to the purchase of Bolles' collection." [101] Mrs. Russell Sage, a wealthy friend of the museum, bought the collection soon afterward and presented it to the Metropolitan. Kent summed up the significance of this acquisition:

> It completed what the Hudson-Fulton exhibition had begun in raising these American arts to a position of acknowledged dignity; and it marked the first recognition by a museum of art of the right of such objects to be included among its collections.[102]

The Metropolitan then had to consider new ways in which to exhibit its acquisition. DeForest had seen (partly through his trip to Salem) that the Metropolitan's "attempt to exhibit this collection in our large Museum galleries made it perfectly clear that in such an environment our American art lost its distinctive charm of simplicity and that it could only be adequately shown in the modest rooms for which it was made." [103] Early American wood-work seemed the best answer to the problem. Sometime after 1911 the museum organized a Committee on American Decorative Art with Halsey as chairman. The committee's real search for period rooms began around 1913.[104]

It should be pointed out here that the largest and wealthiest art museum in the country was at work. The Metropolitan's search was much more of a threat to preservationists than George F. Dow's simple request for money to save a mantel from a house that was about to be destroyed. The people who went forth into the United States looking for woodwork for the Metropolitan were instructed to find just the *right* kind. For the first time preservationists had to protect old buildings against destruction in the name of art, for there was reason to believe that museums might buy rooms from houses that were not in danger of destruction. No system of ethics governing the acquisition of paneling had been worked out by 1913, so the field was open to anyone who could finance such a program.

Rumors spread throughout the preservation field as the officials of the Metropolitan started to look for good paneling. Norman Isham, a noted restoration architect, heard that Henry Kent had visited Newport, Rhode Island, in 1913 and had expressed a great interest in the interior of Touro Synagogue. Isham immediately concluded that the museum intended to rip out the woodwork.[105] An official of the Newport Historical Society discovered that the whole story had been badly twisted; Kent had been interested in all the antiquities of Newport, but he did not say he intended to buy any of them.[106] Still the rumor refused to die. In 1916 the director of the Rhode Island School of Design heard that some members of the New York congregation that owned Touro Synagogue had considered selling the paneling. Soon a number of New England preservationists united again to protest any thought of despoiling the old synagogue.[107] Even though the Metropolitan apparently never had any serious ideas about removing the woodwork, preservationists did not fully trust the museum because it was so affluent at a time when old buildings could be had for relatively small sums.

In 1916 an official of the Metropolitan reported to the main office that the owner of the Cook-Oliver house in Salem, Massachusetts, had some handsome nineteenth-century wallpaper that she intended to remove from the wall because of its shabby condition.[108] The director of the museum, Edward Robinson, wrote to William Sumner Appleton, asking if he might know of someone in the Boston area qualified to remove old wallpaper. Naturally, Robinson did not give any details about the location of the Cook-Oliver paper or the immediate possibility of its destruction.[109] Appleton answered within a week and not only supplied the name of a firm that he had employed for this type of work, but also hopefully recommended to Robinson a fine reproduction wallpaper. He warned that the S.P.N.E.A. was committed to the policy of keeping old houses (including interior finish) intact.[110] The museum had merely asked for the name of a workman and had received a brief sermon on the need for preserving buildings *in situ*. Appleton was unaware of the owner's attitude toward the wallpaper and so must have believed himself duty-bound to influence the museum.

The case of a building in Virginia may cast light on the difference between the reactions of Northerners and Southerners toward the Metropolitan's quest for old paneling. In June of 1916 Halsey received a letter from Frank C. Baldwin, an architect in Fredericksburg, Virginia. Baldwin said that he had heard from a friend that Halsey was seeking early American woodwork for the museum. In an effort to prove himself qualified to speak on the subject, Baldwin cited several articles that he had written in architectural periodicals on the colonial mansions of northern Virginia. He described a paneled room in "Marmion," a plantation home near Fredericksburg, which was for sale and seemed to be of museum quality. Baldwin offered to show the room to any representative the museum might want to send down.[111]

One of the assistants in the American department left at once. He wrote back to Robinson that he found the room unusually dignified and full of detail, though it had only one door, which meant that visitors could not walk through it. In spite of this major disadvantage, he concluded that the paneling would be a superb addition to the museum.[112] President DeForest had seen pictures of the room as it appeared in Marmion, and he offered his thoughts on it. He wondered if it might be too European in spirit to serve as a background for American furniture; but should it prove to be a first-class example of Colonial work, he favored its acquisition.[113] Two reports were enough to convince Kent and the other officers of the quality of the woodwork, so they authorized the purchase on July 5, 1916. Kent dispatched two men to dismantle the room and crate it for shipment to New York.[114]

Through all of the Marmion correspondence there was no evidence of an individual or a group protesting the removal of the room. Edwin Barber, director of the Pennsylvania Museum in Philadelphia, congratulated Kent upon the Metropolitan's new acquisition. Barber admitted that his museum had tried to secure the same room earlier in the winter, but the price had been too high.[115]

Early the next fall the officials of the Metropolitan decided that they would need assistance in finding the best colonial rooms available. Kent wrote to Appleton in Boston, telling him that the museum wanted woodwork from old New England houses. He knew that Appleton often came across details from buildings which were being destroyed, and he suggested that Appleton might share some of them with the museum.[116]

Kent's innocent inquiry produced another lecture from Appleton, who was becoming increasingly unsympathetic with the objectives of the Metropolitan. Appleton reiterated the S.P.N.-E.A.'s policy of preserving all old houses intact on their original sites. Should that become impossible, he added, the society would offer the woodwork to local historical and patriotic organizations. If they wanted no part of the paneling, the S.P.N.E.A. would offer it to the state historical society in whatever state the building was located. Appleton then told the Metropolitan Museum where it stood:

> Of course, if all of these and our Society and the Boston Museum of Fine Arts should refuse to take something which would otherwise be destroyed, I see no reason why we should not cooperate with the Metropolitan Museum to get the object, and in conversations with many New Englanders prominent in this line of work, I have always found that this is their point of view. They all prefer that things should go to the Metropolitan rather than be destroyed. . . .[117]

Appleton had implied that destruction of old woodwork was the only thing worse than sending it to the Metropolitan! In the same letter he explained that local pride entered into the case with many old houses; there was a general "feeling" throughout the region that things made in New England should remain there. Appleton even candidly told Kent that many Bostonians regretted the removal of the Bolles collection to New York because it included so many New England pieces.

Henry Kent was a real diplomat. He thanked Appleton for the "friendly" way in which he had received the museum's request. Kent explained, "I should be unwilling to remove any building, or any part of a building, from its original site which could be taken care of by a local museum." [118] Kent's reasoning illustrates the conflict between rabid preservationists and responsible officials of great art museums. The Metropolitan believed that it was justified (as in the case of Marmion) in taking paneling from a house as long as the owner was willing to sell, even though there was no significant danger of destruction. Appleton, on the other hand, did not favor the removal of woodwork from any building that was still standing intact. The museum decreed that it would withdraw from a proposed purchase only if a local preservation group existed. Appleton concluded that museums should be morally obligated to leave a building alone no matter what the owner's attitude might be. Museums, as public institutions, should exert will power. Kent found that he would have to be careful in dealing with Appleton, for he was a crusader who would not compromise.

Kent forwarded Appleton's letter to President DeForest in order to get his reaction. DeForest sympathized with Appleton's desire to save houses on their original sites, but he found the discussion of New England local pride too sectional. DeForest added one more potent argument for the installation of old paneling in city art museums. "I think there is a question about the relative public good accomplished between preservation in a small, sparsely visited, local historical society or museum and such institutions as the Boston Museum of Fine Arts and the Metropolitan." [119] Obviously, New England period rooms in New York would benefit the public in general because more people could appreciate them there.

Evidently Appleton had second thoughts about his grim warn-

222 ✲ PRESENCE OF THE PAST

ing to the Metropolitan, so he wrote an apologetic note to Kent. He sincerely hoped that Kent had not been angered by his attitude, and he assured him that there would be times when he would be able to offer paneling to the museum without transgressing his principles, though some of this woodwork might not be up to the Metropolitan's standards.[120] There does not seem to be any evidence in New York or Boston that Appleton ever offered rooms to the Metropolitan, or to any other museum, save the Museum of Fine Arts in Boston.[121]

The Metropolitan tried to hold to its promises by standing aside whenever local groups made it evident that they intended to preserve historic houses intact. In 1917 the museum considered purchasing a famous home in Portsmouth, New Hampshire, that had once been a boardinghouse where John Paul Jones had been a guest. Shortly before it was to buy the house, the museum received word that the architect Joseph Chandler was leading a movement to keep the "Jones House" in Portsmouth. On the day of the sale Secretary Kent wrote to Chandler telling him that the Metropolitan would retire from the scene, but would appreciate hearing the outcome of the sale.[122] Chandler replied the following day that the people he was working with wanted to thank the museum for withdrawing, for they were then able to buy the property for a reasonable price.[123] From the tenor of Chandler's letter, it appears that the price would have been considerably higher if the owners had suspected that the Metropolitan Museum had been interested. Chandler's associates, who were descendants of the early owners of the Jones house, eventually donated the property to the local historical society for its headquarters.[124]

The detailed story of one house represents the practical and philosophical problems involved in the removal of old paneling for museum display. Once more Appleton and the Metropolitan Museum engaged in a long debate which helped to illustrate the gulf that separated preservationists from museum directors. The most graceful of Wallace Nutting's Colonial Chain of Houses was the Wentworth-Gardner in Portsmouth. Shortly after Nutting acquired the place in 1915,[125] Appleton wrote, "This was a house of extreme beauty and elegant detail before its purchase and is now even better, for the balusters of the original staircase, which were removed many years ago, have been put back." [126] The house and its furnishings were put up for sale by Nutting early in 1918, along with the remainder of his Colonial Chain. It was at this point that the officials of the Metropolitan heard of the sale through the Brooks Reed Gallery, which represented Nutting. If the museum received the same offer that went to Appleton, it was given the opportunity to buy all five houses with their contents for $125,000.[127]

Kent informed Chairman Halsey of the sale, stating that he did not want to purchase the entire lot. He believed that the "Ironworks house" in Saugus, Massachusetts, was the most desirable building of the five.[128] Early in June of 1918 Halsey wrote to the assistant director, Joseph Breck, that the Saugus house should be investigated because it was a fine example of the earliest type.[129] Breck took it upon himself to tell the Brooks Reed Gallery that the Metropolitan might buy some of the paneling, but not the furniture. The gallery immediately replied that the furniture and houses had to be sold as a whole.[130] Halsey, on his own initiative, approached Nutting on the question of buying woodwork from the Saugus house. Nutting confessed that the only thing of significance in the building was the frame; and he added that another one of his properties, the Wentworth-Gardner house in Portsmouth, was "one of the most beautiful in America." [131]

Henry Kent was dumfounded to learn that Nutting did not consider the Ironworks house architecturally significant. He immediately dispatched an urgent letter to the architect Norman Isham, requesting his opinion of the Saugus and Portsmouth houses.[132] Isham replied that Nutting had spoiled the Saugus house in his restoration of it. Kent was indeed perplexed because Joseph Chandler had pronounced the Ironworks house an excellent re-creation. This was not the first time in history that two architects disagreed on the relative value of another man's restoration.[133]

By July of 1918 Nutting obviously had changed his mind about selling the chain as a whole, for he attempted to interest the Metropolitan in the Wentworth-Gardner house. He instructed Wanamaker's store in New York to forward a large picture book on the Wentworth-Gardner to the museum. Nutting told Halsey that he would sell the house to the first person who would meet his price, because he had to "shorten" his holdings "in nonproductive or slow assets." Nutting hinted that two other people were looking at the property,[134] so Halsey reacted swiftly:

> I immediately got in touch with Mr. Breck, then Mr. DeForest. I did not imagine that there would be any hurry in the matter in these war times, but asked Mr. Nutting for a three weeks' refusal in order that I might have the opportunity to work on the proposed purchase.[135]

Two weeks later Nutting called Breck and told him that he must have a prompt answer from the museum, for there was another interested party.[136]

The next day, July 25, 1918, was a busy one in the office of Henry Kent. It began with a disquieting letter from Halsey: a friend of the museum had questioned the authenticity of Nutting's restoration of the Wentworth-Gardner house, though President DeForest had been so impressed with Isham's detailed architectural report on the building that he wanted Kent to inspect the place himself. Nutting had offered the museum the choice either of buying the whole structure or of stripping it of all its woodwork. DeForest and Halsey both favored the purchase of the entire house so that "it should remain intact until we are ready to set up the rooms in the proposed new building, which of course would be some months after the war." [137]

Kent responded to Halsey's letter by sending an urgent telegram to Isham asking his professional advice (probably for a second time). Isham replied that there had indeed been some restoration by Nutting, but he pronounced the Wentworth-Gardner house "a *very* good one." [138]

Sometime during the last week in July the Metropolitan Museum took stock of all the scholarly opinions it had received, along with the reports made by staff members who had inspected the place. There must have been a decision to purchase the whole structure, for on August 2, Kent wrote to Halsey, "I hope that you have been able to settle the Portsmouth matter satisfactorily." [139] On August 30, 1918, the museum took title to the property. One eventful chapter of the Wentworth-Gardner story had ended.[140] Despite considerable sales pressure from Nutting, the museum had taken the time to obtain expert judgment in regard to the artistic value of the building *before* purchasing it. Appleton

wrote of the events surrounding the sale of the Wentworth-Gardner house in the October, 1919, *Bulletin of the S.P.N.E.A.* (p. 15):

> Shortly before the sale our Society was warned that this hope
> could not be realized [the purchase of all five Nutting houses by
> the S.P.N.E.A.], and it had as good an opportunity to buy the
> Wentworth-Gardner house as had the Metropolitan Museum in
> all respects save one—that it lacked the money for the purchase.
> . . . It also was the feeling among the Trustees that the people of
> Portsmouth would certainly themselves protect the Wentworth-
> Gardner house, for the impending sale was called to the attention
> of Governor Keyes, the Mayor of Portsmouth and other prominent
> citizens. That this was not done was due partly to the high price
> for which the property sold and partly because the exigencies of
> the occasion made it impossible for Mr. Nutting to allow the time
> necessary for the somewhat ponderous machinery of public sub-
> scription to be set in motion.

Appleton's correspondence tells the story in a different light.
Several days after the title passed, he wrote to the director, Edward
Robinson, saying that he had heard a "rumor" that the Metropolitan had bought the Wentworth-Gardner for removal to New
York. He asked Robinson if the museum would give the S.P.N.E.A.
trustees time to consider redeeming the property by paying the
Metropolitan the original purchase price. He was sure that if
the museum would adopt this procedure, it would clear itself of
the charge of vandalism. Appleton, at his diplomatic best, offered
to help bridge the gap between his own views and those of the
New Yorkers.

> I am not one of those to raise the cry of vandalism whenever
> a museum secures something, but as pointed out above, I much
> prefer that a museum should get something good than it should
> go to the junk heap. What I find myself wondering about is whether
> some chance of redemption as I have suggested can't be made the
> rule in all such cases. If that can be done I don't see but that
> museums will clear themselves of all possible accusation as de-
> stroyers rather than preservers of artistic work. If on the other hand
> should they destroy what others might prove to be willing and able
> to preserve, it seems to me that a museum's course of action would
> become questionable.[141]

Appleton sent his letter to Robinson, who had had very little to do with the acquisition of the Wentworth-Gardner house. This circumstance caused Robinson to ask R. T. Haines Halsey to help him formulate a reasonable reply.[142] Halsey was full of ideas. He began by giving Robinson a short sketch of the process by which the Metropolitan happened to buy the house. Halsey had recently met the private individual who had been bidding against the Metropolitan. He turned out to be a wealthy New Yorker who had intended to float the Wentworth-Gardner house on a barge down to his estate on Long Island Sound where he would have used it as a residence. This meant, Halsey argued, that the museum was saving the house from removal to a place where the public would probably never see it. Then Halsey defended the museum from an ethical standpoint. He reasoned that the American section of the Metropolitan needed to include the arts and crafts of New England and that the Wentworth-Gardner woodwork would serve admirably as the central exhibit. He mentioned that the house was located in a rundown section of Portsmouth, where it "could never find the vast audience which it will find in its future home." Here again was the idea that period rooms in a museum could be seen by more people. As a final argument Halsey cited the John Paul Jones house sale as evidence of the museum's willingness to withdraw in the face of any local preservation effort.[143]

Robinson now had ammunition for his reply. He wrote to Appleton with the firm conviction that the museum had saved the house, in view of the plans of the other prospective buyer. Robinson added that the museum had always been willing to stay out of the way of any "bona fide effort being made to preserve an old American home *in situ*," but he knew of no such movement for the Wentworth-Gardner house. Then he injected Halsey's argument that New England should be well represented in the Metropolitan's American collection. He assured Appleton that, although the S.P.N.E.A. trustees might not want to redeem the property, he would submit the matter to the officers of the Metropolitan. Robinson's letter closed with the comforting thought that there was no need to hurry, since the woodwork would not be removed for some time.[144]

Appleton had to fall back on arguments that he had used before. He regretted that local preservation groups did not have enough money to act quickly in emergencies. He asked a few questions about the future of the Wentworth-Gardner woodwork and then promised to present the idea of repurchase to his board in October.[145] Robinson replied that he was not in a position to outline the museum's plans for the house, since the amount of material taken from the building would govern its eventual resale value.[146] In October Appleton dejectedly wrote Robinson that the S.P.N.E.A. trustees had turned down the proposal of redeeming the house. As a last wish, he pleaded for the removal of the entire building to New York.[147]

Opinion in Portsmouth was sharply divided on the issue of the Wentworth-Gardner purchase. Robinson wrote his friend Professor Barrett Wendell, who lived in Portsmouth, asking how the citizens of that city regarded the Metropolitan's sudden action, for the director was evidently concerned about local pride. Wendell replied that Nutting had offered the house to organizations in Portsmouth, but no one had been willing to give a substantial amount of money to such a cause during the war. Wendell was sure that many people in Portsmouth were glad that the museum thought enough of the Wentworth-Gardner to preserve parts of it in New York.[148] Appleton heard the other side of the story. Even two years after the sale he was still receiving letters from irate Portsmouth residents who maintained that Nutting had sold the property in such a hurry that no one in town had had a chance to save it.[149] Appleton concluded that the Wentworth-Gardner house, like the Hancock Mansion before it, was a victim of war, which had turned public attention to other things.[150]

In February of 1919 the Metropolitan finally announced to the public its purchase of the Wentworth-Gardner house. *The New York Times* carried a short article simply noting that eight Portsmouth rooms would be part of a wing of the museum that would house beautiful early American furniture.[151] Newspapers in other cities reacted in several ways to the announcement. Mervin Curl, writing for the Boston *Herald,* bewailed the loss to Portsmouth and then commented wryly that perhaps the teeming millions of people in New York City were starved for lack of colonial beauty.[152] The Philadelphia *Record* hoped that the example of the New York museum would galvanize Philadelphians into taking better care of their own architectural treasures.[153] The Metropolitan itself briefly stated in its *Bulletin* that, while it did not favor tearing down historical landmarks, it had chosen that alternative rather than permit removal of one of the best Portsmouth houses to another state by a private buyer.[154]

Once the news was out, the museum began receiving unusual offers. One came from a Boston firm, I. H. Bogart and Son. According to William M. Bogart, his workmen had been responsible for much of the restoration work that had been done in New England during the previous decade. Bogart listed all the buildings repaired by his firm and then offered Appleton's name as a reference, along with the names of several Boston architects who had supervised restorations. Evidently he was seeking a contract from the museum for the removal of the Wentworth-Gardner woodwork to New York.[155]

During the summer of 1919 Appleton mailed Kent the text of a rather long article on the subject of the museum's purchase that he intended to publish that fall in the *Bulletin of the S.P.N.E.A.* Kent politely thanked him for this gesture and told him that he did not see anything in the article that could be called incorrect. He informed Appleton that the museum was still not certain what it would do with the house itself. Although the museum officials had discussed the possibility of moving the entire building to New York for re-erection in the Metropolitan's courtyard, Kent personally doubted that this would be done.[156]

Appleton's article defended the museum from the charge of vandalism, but it did not allow the Metropolitan to escape completely:

> In Portsmouth, for instance, the Metropolitan Museum would, in the writer's opinion, have greatly strengthened itself against criticism had it publicly announced that it would give the people of that city a reasonable time in which to buy the house from the Museum for the purchase price plus reasonable interest on the amount temporarily invested in the building. . . . In this way a museum would, owing to the power of quick action which its comparative wealth gives it, be able to do an enormous amount of good in preservation work of all kinds and endear itself more than ever to the sympathies of that public on which it must always depend for its support.[157]

Appleton concluded by expressing the hope that someday museums would try to operate chains of houses of their own. He admitted that most museums would be hard put to justify such a procedure, even if it was the best answer from the preservationist's standpoint. Appleton's ideas were visionary for the early 1920's, for it was several years before the Pennsylvania Museum restored some homes in Fairmount Park.

Appleton continued to be concerned with the fate of the Wentworth-Gardner house. In 1920 the Reverend Donald Miller, a close friend of Appleton's and an amateur architect, had visited the Metropolitan. He reported to Appleton that he had talked with Halsey "who has charge of the 'Colonial' section." Halsey had informed him that the future looked bright. ". . . They plan a wing to be built to contain many type-rooms, to show furniture and paneling, etc. In a court will be the Gardner House, set up *entire*—with an old garden before it with flowers, etc." This news must have cheered up the Boston preservationist.[158]

Edward Robinson spent the better part of the summer of 1921 in Portsmouth studying the Wentworth-Gardner in order to discover what parts of the building were original and what parts had been repaired. He talked at great length with the craftsmen who had done the restoration for Nutting. His conclusion was that almost all of the paneling was old, and that the exterior woodwork was either original or a good copy of what had been there. Nutting freely admitted to the museum that he had been compelled to create a new doorframe because there was hardly a trace of the original; he had simply used some local doorways as his models.[159]

As the plans for the great new American Wing of the Metropolitan began to take shape, the officers of the museum arrived at a crucial decision: the Wentworth-Gardner house was a better exhibit in Portsmouth than it was in New York. It is difficult to judge what influenced this course of action. Perhaps it was the excessive cost of moving the house, or it may have been the feeling that the rooms already in the museum's warehouses represented the pre-Revolutionary period satisfactorily. The first indication of President DeForest's change of attitude came in a letter which Appleton received from a New York attorney, F. Kingsbury Curtis. Curtis evidently had learned that DeForest intended to keep the Wentworth-Gardner house intact. Curtis wanted to know if Appleton could help to raise a fund large enough to guarantee the preservation of the building *in situ*. The museum also contacted people in Portsmouth for the same reason.[160]

Appleton had been away on vacation when Curtis' letter arrived, so he acted with a great sense of urgency upon finding it. He telegraphed Curtis to learn all of the details, and wrote to Henry Kent, asking him if he was aware of DeForest's decision. Appleton was most anxious to find out whether the museum intended to sell the house or to permit a Portsmouth group to endow it for the museum.[161] Curtis immediately answered Appleton by telling him not to be alarmed and to keep the whole matter quiet, for all the trustees of the Metropolitan did not yet know about it. He added that his request for help had been based on a personal conversation with DeForest, who hoped that an endowment for the house could be raised by charging a small admission fee. Curtis strongly urged that there be no public subscription of funds,[162] and Appleton agreed although he had some doubts about an appeal to people of great means. He stressed that Portsmouth was one of the few towns on the East Coast where one could study the whole history of American architecture, and the Wentworth-Gardner house was a vital link in that sequence.[163]

In the meantime, some heated discussion took place in New York. Curtis had to write Appleton that the museum had again changed its mind and would definitely move the house to New York. Appleton saw further evidence of this decision in the special issue of the *Bulletin of the Metropolitan Museum of Art* where he read that the Wentworth-Gardner would occupy an interior court in the enlarged museum building. Appleton plaintively wrote to Kent asking when the move was to take place.[164] Kent replied that the operation would "depend upon many things, appropriations, etc., etc.," all of which meant that the museum was still undecided.[165] The Metropolitan continued to vacillate for more than a year, and then it offered the property to the city of Portsmouth for a fair price. Apparently the city did not accept.[166] Soon the construction of the American Wing reached the point where the officers of the museum would have to move the whole house or radically change their plans. They decided on the latter, and so the Wentworth-Gardner was left on its original foundations. Today it is still in Portsmouth, and will probably remain there. The Metropolitan no longer owns it—but can certainly take some of the credit for saving it, even if that had not been the original intention.

The story of the Metropolitan's problems in regard to the Wentworth-Gardner house illustrates the difficult decisions that art museum officials faced when they tried to buy houses that could yield paneling for exhibition purposes. They had to consult experts to find out if the house in question was suitable. Once a purchase was made, they had to meet the charge of vandalism. Because it depended upon the public for support, the museum had to convince everyone that the house had been bought for the public good. Fortunately for the Metropolitan, the board's decision to leave the house in Portsmouth permitted the museum to claim that it was the real preserver of one of America's finest buildings.

These ethical considerations seemed secondary in November of 1922, when the museum announced in a special issue of its *Bulletin* that Mr. and Mrs. DeForest had offered to finance the construction of the American Wing. R. T. Haines Halsey, who had done so much to build up the collection of Americana, declared that he and his friends had had this dream for twelve years, ever since the purchase of the Bolles collection.[167] Two years later, on November 10, 1924, the Metropolitan officially opened its new wing. In a long article introducing the American Wing to the public, Charles O. Cornelius and Halsey each mentioned that the restoration of many of the period rooms had been the work of two leading experts: Norman Isham, who had helped on the eighteenth-century New England rooms, and George Francis Dow, who had supervised the reconstruction of two of the seventeenth-century rooms. In addition, Halsey and Cornelius pointed with pride to the research that had been done:

> In furnishing and equipping the rooms a great effort has been made to insure historical accuracy. The aim has been to show these rooms as they might well have been furnished at the time when the original woodwork was constructed. The general stylistic quality of the rooms has been further fortified from the historic point of view by an exhaustive study of the inventories and newspaper advertisements of the early days. . . .[168]

Isham later stated his objectives in working on museum reconstructions using old woodwork.

> It is not enough to put certain rooms together and fit them with ancient paneling, hangings and paint. To be of use we must show how the work was done at the time chosen for illustration, the time to which the paneling or room or drapery belongs. And the demonstration should not fit the curious only, nor yet the amateur restorer. It should show the architect who has met a puzzle just how his window frames should be made, how wide his sash bars ought to be at a given date, all about hearths and fireplace facings.[169]

Such a high degree of authenticity required time and research, and the Metropolitan had indeed used both to good advantage.

In his speech at the opening of the American Wing, Halsey said that citizens of New York formerly had no place to go to visualize American history or traditions. Prior to the building of the wing a New Yorker would have had to travel all over the Eastern United States in order to gain the same sense of the past that had been captured in the period rooms. The Metropolitan clearly wanted to impress upon the public that it had a sense of mission.[170]

As a fitting postscript to its efforts, the Metropolitan offered a letter from Appleton in its *Bulletin,* so that all could see the goodwill manifested by preservationists toward the museum and its new wing:

> What a superior and truly superb lot [of rooms] you have brought together. It is particularly pleasing to know that an effort was made to select those pretty much abandoned to their fate by the people of the vicinity. That being the case I feel it is a tremendous gain that what would otherwise have been destroyed has been made available to the whole American public in so far as it chooses to visit New York. I even find myself regretting that you did not get some other rooms that I have seen destroyed.[171]

The same *Bulletin* quoted passages from laudatory reviews of the new rooms, many of which pointed out that the museum had been the pioneer in championing American furniture and paneling as an art form deserving exhibition in large museums. The Essex Institute had shown similar objects, but these had been treated as artifacts illustrating the history of the area around Salem.[172]

Soon the cultural impact of the work done in furnishing the American Wing began to permeate the country. A writer in a 1927 *D.A.R. Magazine* said, "The patriotic Americans who treasure the memory of our forefathers can do no better today than to reproduce in their homes the furniture and decorations which have been so well preserved and arranged by the builders of the American Wing. . . ." [173]

It would be misleading to imply that the Metropolitan was the only museum engaged in the search for period rooms. In the correspondence concerning the paneling from Marmion in Virginia there was evidence that the Pennsylvania Museum in Philadelphia was seeking paneling as early as 1916.[174] A year earlier Appleton had advised the Boston Museum of Fine Arts concerning some old woodwork that he thought it should have.[175] The Brooklyn Museum bought its first architectural fragments in 1916, and by the early 1920's it had accumulated nearly twenty rooms from old houses.[176] In 1923 several of these rooms were arranged for a temporary exhibition.[177] In most cases the Brooklyn Museum had to store its collection of old woodwork until there was space enough to install it (1929–1930). The Carnegie Institute in Pittsburgh asked Appleton for help in 1919 when it was searching for representative woodwork from New England houses that were in danger of destruction. That museum, too, received the same cool treatment that Appleton had originally given the Metropolitan.[178]

Art museums were not alone in this quest, for wealthy individuals were smitten by the desire to adorn their homes with paneling from old houses. Fiske Kimball complained to the A.I.A. convention in 1923:

> The recent effort of museums to house their collections of Americana in rooms with woodwork of the corresponding period, has led to widespread imitation on the part of private collectors, not content with rescuing material from houses already doomed to destruction or in process of demolition. They have not hesitated to purchase and demolish houses in no way threatened, which might otherwise have been preserved indefinitely. It cannot be urged too strongly that the architects should oppose such vandalism to the extent of their power. . . .[179]

The first museum to "collect" a group of early buildings was the Pennsylvania Museum (now the Philadelphia Museum). Although Fairmount Park and its houses had been city property since the middle of the nineteenth century, it was not until the twentieth century that Philadelphia began to discover what a rare inheritance it possessed. In 1915 Harold D. Eberlein, an authority on colonial buildings, discussed the Fairmount Park situation in a nationally circulated magazine. He found that in spite of the many houses in the park area which had been destroyed or hopelessly altered, there yet remained a number of fine colonial country homes.[180]

A dramatic letter from Fiske Kimball to Appleton hinted that the Pennsylvania Museum had finally seen the possibilities of the homes still standing near the new museum:

> You will scarcely have heard of my own new plans which result from my decision to accept the post of Director of the Museum in Philadelphia. They have been generous enough to assign me as a residence the house, Lemon Hill in Fairmount Park. . . . I am to give them my services in its restoration and then I will have the task of furnishing it appropriately out of my own small means.[181]

By appointing one of the country's leading restoration architects as its director, the Pennsylvania Museum had created an ideal atmosphere for restoring and refurnishing some of the great homes in Fairmount Park. The commissioners of the park had begun their own restoration of one of the finest mansions, Mount Pleasant, in 1923. Three years later, through a private donation, the museum assisted the commissioners in the completion of that project. The museum also helped by furnishing Mount Pleasant in a manner which returned it to its former glory.[182]

After a year spent on the resurrection of two or three of the Fairmount Park houses, Kimball philosophized on the opportunity they presented Philadelphia:

> New York has ruthlessly swept away most of its early landmarks. Valuing their lost teaching, the Metropolitan Museum has brought together, in its American wing, a series of single rooms from successive periods, with their appropriate furnishings, which admirably illustrate the history and beauty of American art in the days of the early Republic.
>
> Philadelphia's opportunity is still greater. It has a series of whole houses, mostly in their original setting. Not to mention important houses in other parks, or those in the loving hands of patriotic

organizations, it has a dozen in Fairmount Park, conveniently located a few hundred yards apart, near its Museum. These by themselves are sufficient to illustrate the evolution of American art from the time of William Penn until the nineteenth century. In several cases these houses are the very finest of their respective periods and types.

. . . By the time the great new Museum at Fairmount is finished, there will be, to supplement its own suite of American rooms, a chain of fine old houses, appropriately furnished from every period of the Colonies and the Republic.[183]

In comparing the work of those who preserved old buildings for architectural reasons with that of the groups who went out to save houses for historic inspiration, one must consider the motives of those involved. An amateur historian could be taught to appreciate the fact that General Washington had used a particular house for his headquarters. It took much reading and travel to understand that a building such as Mount Pleasant in Philadelphia was significant as a remarkably unchanged example of an eighteenth-century country home. It required an even greater sense of appreciation acquired through training and research to see Mount Pleasant as a well-designed example of American Georgian architecture, especially in its superb woodwork and its perfect proportions.

The people who preserved for artistic reasons intended to educate the public in a different way from those who saved buildings for patriotic purposes. Architects and antiquaries enjoyed the buildings they saved in a quiet way, hoping the public would come to see them without massive campaigns. Men who appreciated architectural refinements did not expect to change people into patriots; they merely hoped to make them more conscious of the beauty of the work of their forefathers.

Another point of comparison between historic and architectural preservation can be found in a study of the manner in which each group treated buildings once they were saved. Those who preserved architectural monuments generally put more research and care into their restorations. Consequently they often disapproved of the practice of returning a building to a particular date because that process meant destroying valuable work from intervening periods.

All three groups discussed in this chapter contributed to the preservation movement in their own way. The performance of architectural organizations seems a bit disappointing, considering the arguments over the use of the Octagon house and the haphazard manner in which the A.I.A. approached the idea of a great historic buildings catalog for this country. Architects did make a valuable contribution to the cause of preservation through their individual efforts to restore buildings correctly.

Museum directors brought about several revolutionary changes in the preservation movement; and they had an impact all out of proportion to the small number of houses they purchased for old woodwork. They were an educative force in the battle for scholarly restorations, and their period rooms set an example for those seeking information on authentic furnishings or accurate details. Often the mere presence of a representative of an art museum caused local citizens to rally to save a house. Most museum officers were keenly aware of the fact that they could be accused of vandalism, so they made a supreme effort to be polite and patient in dealing with local and regional preservation groups. Museums provided many people with their first opportunity to see rooms that represented different parts of the country, as well as several eras in our history.

Last, but by no means least, were the antiquaries. The first ones were obscure men with sketch pads and cameras. Then came the collectors of furniture and silver. Finally, at the turn of the century, antiquaries became preservers of old buildings. These men were a potent force because they were enthusistic about old things for the sake of antiquity; they had few illusions about teaching great lessons or creating a nation of patriots. They merely hoped that early homes would give visitors some appreciation for the life of the past.

X

William Sumner Appleton and the Society
for the Preservation of New
England Antiquities

WILLIAM SUMNER APPLETON WAS A PROPER BOSTONIAN in every
sense of the word. He was born in 1874 in a fashionable Beacon
Street home built by his wealthy grandfather, Nathan Appleton.
He traveled abroad with his family at the age of thirteen, and he
took a second trip to Europe with his tutor shortly after gradu-
ating from Harvard in 1896. He was not particularly robust, so
he tried to restrict his business activities from time to time. From
1898 to 1901 he was a partner in a real estate firm in Boston, but
he had to give up this work in order to regain his health. By the
time he was ready to return to the business world young Appleton found himself the recipient of a trust fund set up for him by
his father. This bequest gave him a respectable income for the
rest of his life, although he could never touch the principal.
Therefore it was impossible for him to go into any enterprise
requiring a large investment of capital.[1]

At the age of thirty-one Sumner Appleton would never have
to work again, yet he was just at the point of discovering his
purpose in life through his liking for history, art, and objects
of antiquarian interest. He began his career as an antiquary in
March of 1905 as one of the three men who spearheaded the
campaign for the preservation and complete restoration of the
Paul Revere house in Boston. This experience must have shown

him the need for coordinating all the preservation activity in New England in the same way that several European countries had worked on a nationwide scale.[2] On his last extensive tour of Europe in 1909 Appleton was especially impressed with certain historic buildings and made mention of the restoration at Carcassonne.[3]

Upon his return to the United States the same year, Appleton launched into preservation work with renewed zeal. He heard that Leroy Brown, owner of the Harrington house in Lexington, Massachusetts, had planned some sweeping alterations to his home. The building had some historical associations, having witnessed the battle on Lexington Green in 1775. As in the case of the Paul Revere house, Appleton took the course of direct action. In December he went out to Lexington to persuade Brown to leave the house as it was. His visit was partially successful, for Brown did promise that he would not tear the Harrington house down. That was not enough for a perfectionist. Appleton gathered some of his influential friends—he had a great many—and tried to induce Brown to give up his plans for remodeling the house. Again he failed.[4]

Then Appleton turned in an entirely new direction. He began having discussions with prominent New Englanders on the subject of setting up a regional preservation society.[5] Charles Knowles Bolton, who was to serve as president of the S.P.N.E.A. for many years, remembered these talks: "I recall one evening in Brookline when he told me of a society he proposed to create. He had a constitution, but I was skeptical until his earnestness and his common sense convinced me that he would be successful."[6] Societies for various types of preservation work were well known by that time, still our persuasive young man had but one idea. He intended to form a vigorous organization that would attempt to protect old homes throughout New England. One of his first acts —as corresponding secretary of the organization that had not yet been chartered—was to write the owner of the Harrington house to request measured drawings of the building before it was materially altered. Brown assented to the idea even if he did not yield to Appleton's plea for preservation of the house in its original condition.[7] By July of 1910 the Harrington house had been rebuilt to conform to Brown's ideas of comfort.[8] But the house

was to serve the cause of preservation well, for through its unfortunate transformation many other New England antiquities
were to be saved.

Appleton was very busy during the spring of 1910. His diary
shows that after January he spent nearly all of his time working
for the new organization. His first plan was to copy the name of
the Association for the Preservation of Virginia Antiquities for
the New England society. One reference in his diary mentions the
"A.P.N.E.A.," which certainly would have been the Association
for the Preservation of New England Antiquities; a day later,
though, he changed the title to "Society." [9] Appleton also spent
considerable time enlisting notable people as incorporators of
the new society. He was quite successful, largely through his enthusiasm and his connections with old Boston families. On March
22 he appeared before a committee of the Massachusetts legislature to support a bill that would give the S.P.N.E.A. the right
to own property tax-free. He spoke with great feeling, according
to the newspapers: "William Sumner Appleton told of the John
Hancock House and of many other fine examples of Colonial
architecture that had been destroyed for lack of organized public
opinion." [10] The legislative committee was properly impressed
by his approach, and the charter was approved.[11]

Appleton wanted to give his society a firm foundation. He was
convinced that the lesser antiquities of New England were worthy
of preservation, so he studied the methods of registration used by
the Boston Museum of Fine Arts in cataloging art objects.[12] In
addition, he designed a seal for the organization that resembled a
coat of arms containing symbols for each of the New England
states. One of his early sketches for a seal shows a picture of the
John Hancock house with the simple statement "Destroyed
1863." [13] Perhaps he hoped that the fate of the Hancock Mansion
could become a battle cry in all future New England preservation
work.

By the time of the incorporation meeting of the Society for the
Preservation of New England Antiquities on April 23, 1910, Appleton had managed to recruit seventeen friends as members. And
so, with an individual assessment of ten dollars, the society began its career.[14] It was not a particularly auspicious start for a
preservation group that expected to save old buildings throughout

a six-state area. Nevertheless, several factors operated in favor of the new society that had not been immediately evident. New England was an ideal location for the first regional preservation society because it was relatively small in area, and it contained more than its share of antiquaries. Above all, the society was to have the unsalaried services of William Sumner Appleton, whose efforts were to make the difference between success or failure.

The S.P.N.E.A. did not receive unqualified approval from all New England historical groups. One lady wrote to Appleton that she favored his objectives, but thought his society might "perhaps . . . swallow up all the local societies that are poor and struggling—like the big corporations." [15] Actually her statement seems ludicrous when one remembers that the S.P.N.E.A. had only eighteen members and a treasury of $180! Still, letters such as that one must have awakened Appleton to the need for respecting local feelings in preservation work. In the years that followed he rarely attempted anything without consulting the historical society most directly concerned with whatever house he was trying to save.

Appleton did not stand still once the society was chartered. He straightway organized a Committee on the Increase of Membership which distributed a printed circular to prospective members, telling them that the S.P.N.E.A. was to be an organization devoted solely to preserving New England antiquities. The circular also told of the society's hopes for a museum in Boston.[16] Before long Appleton was publishing a *Bulletin* which he mailed out to all interested people. The first issue was the fruit of Appleton's deep thoughts on preservation. It began with a blast at vandalism. On the cover was a picture of the Hancock house, along with a caption that told how negligence on the part of both the state and city had brought about its loss. The magazine contained a number of pictures of old New England buildings that had been saved (explaining who had saved them), as well as views of some others that had been destroyed. The text of the *Bulletin* was biting in its criticism of the work being done by "one-house" organizations, such as the Royall House Association which had saved a notable home in Medford, Massachusetts. In Appleton's eyes such groups were wasteful. Historical societies rarely rescued more than one building and thus ignored all other worthwhile houses in their communities. Family associations were much too restricted by their own objectives, for by their very nature they could save only one homestead. In spite of all the efforts of these groups, Appleton said, the antiquities of New England were rapidly disappearing.

The situation requires aggressive action by a large and strong society, which shall cover the whole field and act instantly wherever needed to lead in the preservation of noteworthy buildings and historic sites. That is exactly what this Society has been formed to do. . . .

It is proposed to preserve the most interesting of these buildings by obtaining control of them through gift, purchase, or otherwise, and then to restore them, and finally to let them to tenants under wise restrictions, unless local conditions suggest some other treatment.[17]

Appleton's blunt appraisal of conditions in New England had its effect, for the S.P.N.E.A. had 321 members by the end of its first year.

For a few years Appleton was the only person employed by the society. With true Puritan thrift, he occupied one half of an office on the fifth floor of a building in downtown Boston. He handled all correspondence, worked on the membership drive and edited the *Bulletin*. It was a tremendous job, especially for a person whose income would have permitted a life of ease, but for Appleton the effort was a labor of love. In 1912 he was rewarded when increases in the membership permitted the addition of a full-time stenographer to the staff.[18]

By early 1911 Appleton had begun to broaden his definition of "preserving" antiquities. He urged that members of the S.P.N.E.A. send in photographs, postcards or other pictures showing old buildings. He asked that each view be clearly labeled and dated so that it would be useful in the future. Appleton began to print the names of all donors and their gifts to the library in the *Bulletin*. The mass of pictorial material collected by Appleton all through his career has since proved to be one of the most highly regarded collections at the S.P.N.E.A. headquarters.[19]

Before many months had passed, Appleton had an opportunity to prove that his new organization could buy an old building. On the strength of advice from the society's lawyer, he persuaded the trustees to purchase the Swett-Ilsley house (ca. 1670) in Newbury, Massachusetts. In seeking funds Appleton wrote to descendants of the builder of the house and met with some success. He eventually used this same genealogical approach on almost every building the society bought. The young S.P.N.E.A. had to take a fair-sized mortgage on the Ilsley house, in addition to using money from the Life Membership Fund (an endowment created from the fifty-dollar payments from life members). Appleton immediately rented out the property so that it would produce some kind of income. The society finally possessed an "antiquity"; it had accomplished one of its prime objectives.[20]

Appleton reviewed the work of the society in March of 1912. In his estimation, the S.P.N.E.A. had had important dealings with the owners of ten different properties during its first year. One house (the Swett-Ilsley) had been bought; another given to the society; a third promised as a gift. Another had been saved by an association formed for that purpose; another the family had retained. Two houses had been bought by appreciative individuals. One had been carefully taken down and rebuilt in another town, and another had been moved to a different location within its own community. Only one building of the ten had been doomed to complete destruction. Appleton had reason to be proud.

> What it seems to show is this: the mere existence of this Society is a safeguard for all our finest old houses. When one such is in danger of destruction the possibility of our intervening seems to occur more and more frequently to those whom ties of residence or family bind to the old building.[21]

By the end of 1912 there was tangible evidence that the society had gained the respect of many New Englanders. Its membership had more than doubled so that annual dues brought in $2,600 a year.[22] Appleton had persuaded one member to donate $1,500 as an emergency fund to be used when important buildings were in immediate danger of destruction. The money was to be replenished by the society within a reasonable time after each use, in order to face new emergencies.[23] Appleton and his secretary moved in March of 1913 to an office in the New England Historic Genealogical Society building where they had more adequate space for the library and museum collections.[24] Appleton began devoting much of his time to improving the properties that the society already owned. He succeeded in purchasing several lots of land that adjoined two of the society's houses, hoping that he could decrease the risk of fire and insure the historical integrity of the old buildings.[25]

Appleton renewed his efforts to enlarge the membership of the S.P.N.E.A. by appealing to persons of culture and wealth.

I would like to interest you in the important educational and historical work being done by the Society for the Preservation of New England Antiquities. . . .

In America, unlike Europe, respect for and interest in antiquities is considered more an individual than a state duty. Massachusetts has given us a liberal charter under which we have enrolled over eight hundred members. We require many more. Will you not join us in our efforts to create a society sufficiently strong to emulate the preservation work of foreign countries? [26]

The most ambitious attempt to win members was his 1913 pamphlet entitled *The Colonial Homes of New England, Shall They Be Saved?* Appleton began by hinting at the number of tourists that the old houses of New England could attract each year. He then turned to the patriotic sensibilities of his readers, and pictured the liberty-loving men who gathered around these hearthstones before the Revolution. Only a society organized for the specific purpose, he stated, could save these buildings.

The Society for the Preservation of New England Antiquities was organized on the theory that eternal vigilance is the price of the preservation of our remaining colonial houses. Its chief purpose is to save for future generations structures of the seventeenth and eighteenth centuries, and the early years of the nineteenth, which are architecturally beautiful or unique, or have special historical significance. Such buildings once destroyed can never be replaced. The loss of such an edifice as the home of John Hancock on Beacon Street, Boston, is irreparable.[27]

Appleton listed every house that the S.P.N.E.A. had bought or helped to save, and then he added a note about the society's museum collections and the growing library of pictures and measured drawings. Not satisfied with one booklet, Appleton mailed out a follow-up letter in January of 1914, in which he complained that a large amount of American money was going abroad for the protection and study of ancient ruins, while our own architectural monuments were in great danger.[28]

These appeals, combined with the reputation of the society, were quite successful; by April of 1915 the membership had reached 1,500, and the library and museum had completely outgrown the new office.[29] Appleton and some volunteer members filled many speaking engagements before patriotic and historic groups in an effort to interest those organizations in acquiring old homes as headquarters or as chapter houses.[30] One local newspaper described the S.P.N.E.A. as an organization that "stands pre-eminent in the knowledge of the delicate task of restoring the old New England landmarks."[31] The society had come a long way from the small group of people who had each contributed ten dollars at the initial meeting in 1910.

Not satisfied with this progress, Appleton soon added a fourth property to the society's holdings. It was the Boardman house in Saugus, Massachusetts. His reason for the purchase was simple: the structure was "a magnificent specimen of our early architecture which has come down to us practically unchanged."[32] In 1914 few people in the United States seriously urged the rescue of any house because it was a well-preserved example of some distant period. Appleton considered the earliest buildings the special province of his society because no other group took much interest in them. He believed that someday the public would appreciate the unusual features of older New England homes. Unfortunately, Americans have yet to realize fully the architectural value of the antiquities saved by the ever-watchful Appleton.

Soon there was a great need for a building large enough to accommodate the society's staff and collections. On August 1, 1916, the S.P.N.E.A. acquired the title to a large residence north of Beacon Hill which had been the first town house of Harrison Gray Otis, a former senator and mayor of Boston. Appleton had convinced fifteen members and friends of the society that the mansion would be ideal as a Boston headquarters (besides being a house worthy of preservation in its own right). These fifteen people contributed $22,725, which left a mortgage of only $8,000 on the property. If for no other reason, the purchase of the Otis house deserves mention because it shows how effectively Appleton had persuaded some New Englanders to support his society.[33] In May of 1917 Appleton and his secretary, together with the museum and library, moved into the Otis house from their small office a few blocks away.[34]

In the field of finance Appleton accomplished a near miracle in the midst of World War I. Through the generosity of some members, a special issue of the *Bulletin* was printed in December of 1917. It was a thorough architectural report by Norman Isham on Colony House in Newport, Rhode Island. This little periodical bore unusual fruit when Samuel P. Avery of Hartford wrote Appleton, telling him how impressed he was with the Preservation Society and its magazine. Avery offered to donate $5,000 as a permanent fund for the general purpose of the society if Appleton could raise $10,000 by the first of July, 1918. If Appleton could raise $15,000, Avery promised to double his gift.[35] In spite of the fact that the war was channeling almost all donations into the Liberty Loan, Appleton set out to accomplish this seemingly impossible task. He told the S.P.N.E.A. trustees that the only way to amass the necessary $15,000 was to ask all members of the society to contribute war bonds or to give money that would be invested in the Third Liberty Loan.[36] Appleton then wrote to those members he thought would understand the importance of the Avery offer. He told one woman that he was sure Avery was testing the society—and might perhaps donate more funds in the future.[37] The campaign, thanks to Appleton's energy, was a complete success. The members of the S.P.N.E.A. gave $18,059 during the spring of 1918, which more than met Avery's conditions. With the addition of Avery's $10,000, the society suddenly had a $28,000 endowment where before there had been only a Life Membership Fund and a few scattered smaller funds. It was a remarkable achievement for an organization that was only eight years old.[38]

Appleton was busy in other areas during 1918. He proposed an amendment to the Massachusetts state constitution making the preservation and maintenance of old houses "a public use." The membership evidently responded favorably to Appleton's appeal for support of the amendment in the November election.[39] Although Appleton could not predict what its future value might be, he thought that the new amendment would eventually serve to protect historic landmarks.[40]

In the spring of 1919 Appleton made his first attempt to initiate an independent fund for the preservation of colonial architecture. He published a long article in the May issue of *Art and Archaeology* proposing the creation of an outdoor museum (after the Swedish model) which would contain old buildings that could not remain on their original sites. Appleton was certain that a privately financed organization would be the best agent for administering this project.

> That part of the public capable of appreciating a handsome building for the sake of its artistic merit is small indeed, and the chance of obtaining support from the public treasury is too negligible to notice, except in the case of public buildings of historic interest like Faneuil Hall in Boston, and Independence Hall, Philadelphia. On the other hand, even if this were not the case, our political system, with almost total lack of responsibility as well as its widespread tendency to the spoils system, makes public action extremely dangerous.[41]

The article was Appleton's only bid for nationwide attention, and it bore some fruit, though his plan for the creation of a large national preservation fund did not materialize.

The story of Appleton's efforts on behalf of one particular house serves to illustrate some of the methods he employed in his preservation work. His determination and persuasive powers were critical in saving this particular property. Early in 1915 he learned of the ruinous condition of the Brown house in Watertown, Massachusetts. His first reaction, as in so many other cases, was to write to any people he thought might be descendants of Abraham Brown, the original builder.[42] By the late spring he had managed to interest enough S.P.N.E.A. members in the fate of the house to offer the Watertown Historical Society an interest-free loan to cover the whole $3,000 purchase price, provided that organization would agree to repair and restore the structure. Unfortunately, the Historical Society rejected his offer.[43] Appleton was so convinced that the citizens of Watertown had erred that he brought the whole issue to the surface in the May, 1916, S.P.N.E.A. *Bulletin.* He estimated that the cost of buying and restoring the building would be about $10,000.

The house, if fitted in the style of its different periods, would be of the greatest educational value—a Mecca for tourists and a joy to all.

We have in New England old houses by the score—picturesque houses and houses of great educational and architectural value. Even so, the Brown house offers a combination of all these desirable elements, surpassed, in the writer's opinion, in no case except that of the Fairbanks house in Dedham.[44]

Apparently his arguments fell upon deaf ears, for the Watertown society did not relent in its decision to abandon the Brown homestead, and no member of the S.P.N.E.A. stepped forward to help.

By 1917 Appleton had decided that he must rescue the Brown house on his own initiative. He was unsure about the manner in which to do this, so he wrote to Norman Isham for advice, offering two alternatives: Appleton could take an option on the property and then pay a rent of $300 a year, or he could buy the building outright and re-erect it somewhere else. He reasoned that if he attempted to rent it, the process of decay would continue unabated, whereas he might preserve more if he took the frame apart and put it back together again.[45] Isham's reply was emphatic, for he doubted Appleton's abilities as a restorer.

My advice is to stick to your lease scheme and keep the old building in situ. It has too many secrets to reveal. . . . *Do not tear it down*, it is too important. And don't work without some architect at your elbow. If you have Chandler get him to stay there as much as he can.[46]

Evidently Isham's letter helped to turn the tide, for Appleton told Joseph Chandler shortly thereafter that he had decided to buy the house. Chandler agreed with Isham, pointing out that the chimney would be lost if the house were to be dismantled. He even suggested to Appleton that the building be covered with sailcloth in order to protect it.[47]

Appleton still searched for other ways in which to save the house. In the spring of 1918 he asked Murray Corse, a New York architect, if he would be interested in buying the Brown house as a residence. Appleton argued that one rarely had a chance to live in such a valuable antiquity. Corse replied that antiquity was the only thing valuable about the house; it simply would not do as a home.[48] Then Appleton decided to approach the S.P.N.E.A.

trustees. In a report to the board he presented an honest picture of the financial burden that the society would assume if it bought the property. Then he contrasted this cost with the importance of the surviving materials in the Brown house. He warned that time was short, since the town authorities had been considering demolition of the building as a fire hazard. He only asked that the board authorize an appeal to the S.P.N.E.A. membership for $10,000 to buy and restore the house. The trustees scrutinized photographs of the structure and decided that it was too dilapidated to preserve.[49]

Having exhausted all other means, Appleton took it upon himself in the spring of 1919 to address a letter to some Massachusetts members of the society in hopes that they would contribute to a personal restoration of the house. He still claimed that the Brown homestead was a rare example of a two-story two-room dwelling. He cited Isham's judgment that the remains of an old window, together with other structural details, could reveal much information about other early New England buildings. Appleton even gave some clues as to his concept of the real mission of the S.P.N.E.A.

> So far as I know there is no house of this type restored in New England and houses of this date . . . are as we all know excessively rare. The agencies for their preservation, apart from our Society, are practically none. Houses of this date lend themselves with great difficulty to the average person's idea of a comfortable home and accordingly the houses are rapidly disappearing. In fact, the number of one room houses still in existence is pitifully small. I can't think of half a dozen. Most societies and individuals wishing an old house incline to take one of the later, more elaborate period, and these are in much less danger of destruction, especially the Georgian houses, which make such comfortable homes. It is the very early house, the original settler's—of which the Brown house seems undoubtedly to be one, and an excellent example at that—that our Preservation Society should particularly aim to save, because no other agency seems to care enough about it.[50]

The letter concluded with a solemn warning that the advanced state of decay then evident at the Brown house would permit only a few more days of hesitation.

A week later Appleton went ahead and signed an agreement

to buy the house and lot for $4,000 in his own name, hoping that some friends would back him up later. At that time he had only received $2,500 in donations from the Massachusetts members, plus two interest-free loans of $500.[51] He began to write long reports on the restoration work to his few faithful followers, always remembering to conclude with another appeal for funds. When financial failure seemed imminent, Appleton turned to one lady who had already given $500 and loaned an equal sum without interest. He asked her to donate the second $500 at a critical time when $1,500 was badly needed. Her assent was a further indication that Appleton had built up a core of goodwill among the members.[52] The bedrock of support among his close friends went even deeper, for two years later, in the winter of 1921, he successfully appealed to the same lady for another $1,000. In fact, before that winter had passed, he persuaded three members to give *second* donations of $1,000 to help complete the restoration.[53]

Evidence of Appleton's infectuous enthusiasm can be found in a brief exchange he had with George L. Gould of Topsfield, Massachusetts. Gould had sent a ten-dollar contribution toward the Brown house preservation, but he noted in his letter that he did not feel a great interest in the building.[54] Appleton immediately responded, as he did with all donations. He said that Gould's lack of zeal could be traced to his own poor command of the English language in describing the house. "I can only say that to my mind it is one of the best worth while preserving of them all and the one the restoration of which will be most accurate." [55] He did not appeal to Gould's emotions or even to his sense of patriotism; he merely tried to pass along his antiquarian taste to others.

The next problem was finding a tenant for the Brown house. Appleton had been a pioneer in his ideas concerning adaptive uses for old houses. He did not believe that all worthwhile buildings should be museums, and the Brown house was no exception. Appleton could never have accumulated so many properties under the S.P.N.E.A. if he had exhibited each one as a period piece. In December of 1919 he wrote to Miss Helen E. Royce, who had asked him about the possibility of opening a tearoom and gift shop in one of the society's properties. He recommended the Brown house as a perfect setting for her enterprise and informed her that it would be habitable within a few weeks.[56]

Three years later Appleton's battle for the Brown house came to a close when the S.P.N.E.A. trustees accepted the restored building along with a $3,000 mortgage, as a gift from the small group that had paid for the restoration. During the summer of 1922 the membership subscribed an additional $3,700 for further repairs to the house. Appleton could rest assured that the homestead was safe in the hands of his Preservation Society.[57] In 1937 he told his sister:

> Between you and me and the corner lamp post, . . . [the Brown house] is my own personal monument and the fact that it is now standing at all is simply because I got mad and decided that it shouldn't be pulled down, but I would hate to tell you how many thousands I had to risk paying myself had my efforts failed. At one time it seemed as though I would have to sell everything I owned.[58]

The Brown house has been selected as one example of the work carried on by this amazing man between 1910 and 1947. Appleton had equally close connections with more than twelve buildings which the S.P.N.E.A. acquired by 1926, and he saved an even greater number of buildings in the years that followed.

An important change in the staff of the society came in the spring of 1919, while Appleton was hard at work on the Brown house. George Francis Dow became curator of the museum and assistant editor of the *Bulletin*. Dow, who had resigned from his position at the Essex Institute, assumed control of the magazine and transformed it into a quarterly under the title *Old-Time New England*. The *Bulletin* had been filled with pictures of restoration work that was being done by the society, along with appealing photographs of houses in need of attention. Appleton had written nearly all of the material that went into the *Bulletin* before 1920. The new publication contained articles dealing with old houses and lesser antiquities written by experts in various fields. Appleton was not at all sure that the emphasis on scholarship was a wise move, for he feared that future members of the S.P.N.E.A. might consider themselves subscribers to a magazine rather than supporters of an active organization. He also suspected that *Old-Time New England* might not include enough news of preservation needs. Appleton solved this problem partially by writing lengthy annual reports as corresponding secretary.[59] Dow's presence on the staff helped to free Appleton to visit local preservation groups and to check on houses at some distance from Boston. Dow came to the society with a considerable amount of experience in museum and library work, so there was no question that the S.P.N.E.A. would prove to be even more useful to the public in the years that followed.

The success of the S.P.N.E.A. in its early years caused people to consider it as a preservation agent when they made out their wills. Appleton had instituted a drive in this direction in 1920. He told the membership in a general letter that the society was an organization designed to care for old family homesteads. He hastened to add that those who might devise buildings to the society should (1) require preservation and nothing more, so that the society would not be tied down to a specific use for a house and (2) provide endowments of at least $5,000 to help with the maintenance costs.[60] Between 1920 and 1926 the society did receive several properties through bequests (though some of them included a life interest). Two members purchased an old home and promised to leave it to the society after they had been given $1,000 to carry out a proper restoration.[61]

The City of Boston announced in 1924 that it was planning to widen Cambridge Street, which ran directly in front of the Otis house. Appleton prevailed upon the S.P.N.E.A. trustees to buy the two structures immediately behind the headquarters in order to protect it. When the actual widening took place in 1925 and 1926, Appleton sent out appeals to the membership for help in purchasing additional land. Two more buildings at the rear of the property were then bought to serve as a museum and office wing, and the Otis house was moved back to cover the site of the first two buildings. The city awarded a considerable sum for the land it had taken from the front of the lot. This amount, combined with the donations from the membership, covered the cost of moving the Otis house and restoring it.[62]

Many people engaged in preservation work began to be amazed at the good the S.P.N.E.A. had done with a small outlay of money. Some were impressed with the comprehensive reports that appeared in the *Bulletin*. In 1920 Horace W. Sellers, an architect, referred to the S.P.N.E.A. as the American counterpart of England's Society for the Protection of Ancient Buildings.[63] The chairman of the A.I.A. Preservation Committee in 1915 reported, "In New England, where many buildings of historic and architectural interest exist, there seem to be no [A.I.A] Chapter committees intrusted with this subject. It is claimed that the necessity is met by the existence of the Society for the Preservation of New England Antiquities. . . ." [64] In 1920 Henry Kent of the Metropolitan Museum included a short note to Appleton with his renewal for membership in the S.P.N.E.A. "You must be aware of the influence you have, and of the interest you are creating. It is bound to increase." [65] A tangible sign of public approval of the society was the continued growth in membership, for there were 2,882 members by 1923.[66]

The society's files are full of letters that give some indication of Appleton's influence on preservationism all along the East Coast of the United States. Sometimes people wrote to him asking advice; sometimes he heard of others' efforts and wrote to them "volunteering" his counsel. His correspondence with preservationists is instructive from another standpoint because it reveals interesting details about the inner workings of the S.P.N.E.A. Appleton was often impelled to write about his own situation in order to illustrate a point he was making.

Some individuals made brave attempts to follow Appleton's footsteps in regions where the distribution of population and the general attitude of the public did not permit organizations such as the S.P.N.E.A. at that time. Edgar G. Miller, a wealthy furniture collector in Baltimore, wrote to Appleton in 1920, saying that he had read the long article in the May, 1919, issue of *Art and Archaeology* on the need for a national preservation program. Miller wanted to assemble some influential people who would be interested in saving the best of Maryland's early buildings. Unfortunately, Miller could not even decide upon a suitable name for his organization, so it never came into existence.[67]

In 1920 Appleton contacted Miss Susan P. Frost, a Charleston (South Carolina) real estate dealer who had been one of the moving spirits in starting the Society for the Preservation of Old Dwellings in that city. He freely offered his advice, but he was sadly disappointed when Miss Frost and her friends violated a prime rule of the S.P.N.E.A. Susan Frost insisted that her society could accomplish more by buying old houses, renovating them, and then either renting or selling them to desirable people. Appleton repeatedly warned Miss Frost that selling a building back into private ownership would again subject it to the dangers from which she had so recently rescued it.[68] His counsel was welcomed, though Miss Frost's efforts in Charleston continued in the direction she had chosen to follow.[69]

An examination of the letters that passed between Appleton and an architect in Philadelphia in 1926 shows why the S.P.N.E.A. model could not be imitated easily in other parts of the country. Clarence W. Brazer wrote to Appleton requesting copies of the S.P.N.E.A. bylaws and charter. He informed Appleton that he was going to organize a society that would cover the territory south of New England, with Philadelphia as a center. Brazer believed that 1926 would be a particularly opportune year for uniting preservationists because the sesquicentennial celebration in Philadelphia that year would stimulate new interest in colonial work.[70]

Appleton responded with a long letter which told Brazer how the S.P.N.E.A. functioned. He cautioned Brazer that the area he had staked out was too vast, for Appleton's experience had proven that properties much more than an hour's trip from Boston became progressively harder to manage. Appleton reminded him that the Association for the Preservation of Virginia Antiquities already covered the field in Virginia and that the American Scenic and Historic Preservation Society was taking care of New York. He pointed out that local pride had become an obstacle once the S.P.N.E.A. moved its activities beyond the borders of Massachusetts. Appleton was convinced that a low membership fee (though not much below three dollars) was preferable, for it could bring together the maximum number of people interested in the new society's work. He advised Brazer to begin collecting pictures of all types of old buildings in the Middle Atlantic States, since this practice had been one of the most valuable services performed by the S.P.N.E.A. In addition, he suggested that Brazer set up a board chosen by the rotating system (used by the S.P.N.E.A.), by which no trustee could be put back on the board until he had been out of office for at least a year. The waiting period permitted the removal of unwanted trustees with a minimum of friction.[71]

Brazer was impressed by the detail and scope of Appleton's letter, but he still had unanswered questions about the staff that his new society would require.[72] Appleton responded with frankness and some pessimism. He warned Brazer of the difficulties that might arise in imitating the New England group exactly. Appleton first mentioned the problem of finding a suitable name for the Middle Atlantic States' group of preservationists. Next, he turned to his own work up to 1926. He honestly admitted that he had been in a position to donate all of his time to the S.P.N.E.A. without compensation. Assuming that his services could be considered worth the salary of a director of a similar organization, Appleton estimated that he had saved the society over $48,000 in the period of time that he had been its corresponding secretary. He then outlined the duties of the other members of his staff. Dow worked on the magazine, did the bookkeeping and inspected nearby properties, while Appleton himself supervised the real estate and the museum work. One of the secretaries handled the library cataloging, and the other managed the filing of photographs, postcards and other materials. As an afterthought, Appleton added that because he had founded the society and received no salary, he had never been obligated to render long reports to his board, nor had he needed to ask permission to take certain kinds of action.[73]

Brazer replied that he would attempt to follow most of Appleton's suggestions except that he would imitate the Pennsylvania Museum's classification of membership. He asked for the names of any people in the Pennsylvania area who might be interested in the new society.[74] Shortly afterward Appleton informed Brazer that another architect, William Edgar Moran, was thinking of forming a preservation organization centered in New York. Through Appleton's help, the two men met each other but were unable to find any way to divide their respective territories.[75] The correspondence with Brazer came to an abrupt halt, and Appleton lost track of him for a number of years.

In 1941 Appleton wrote to Brazer at a New York address, politely inquiring about the fate of his Pennsylvania group.[76] Brazer related a pitiful story. He had interested some important people, including the governor of Pennsylvania, in his proposed society; but he had to restrict his area severely when he found preservationists at work in Maryland and northern New Jersey. Furthermore, the Philadelphia members wanted to confine the scope of the society to their own city. A final blow came with the death of several leading members just as the great depression began to cut contributions. The little society had to be disbanded. Brazer was sure that effective preservation work might have been initiated if he had been able to unite the numberless preservation organizations that were springing up in the Middle Atlantic States.[77]

Lack of unity—the reason for Brazer's failure in Pennsylvania —was the same difficulty that had plagued the preservation movement when C. R. Ashbee had tried to create an American National Trust in 1901. Only Appleton, in his restricted area, had come close to setting up a clearinghouse for people who desired to save old buildings throughout a wide region.

In addition to his voluminous correspondence with antiquaries and architects along the East Coast, Appleton kept in contact with European preservationists. He placed his society on the mailing lists of several foreign organizations in order to collect information on their activities. The December, 1914, issue of the *Bulletin* contained an announcement that the reports of both the Society for the Protection of Ancient Buildings and the English National Trust were on file in the S.P.N.E.A. office for anyone who might want to study them.

Appleton regarded the S.P.A.B. as similar to his own society, particularly in its opposition to any kind of restoration that would destroy old work on a building. He also found that the S.P.A.B. included many techniques in its definition of "repairs" that he would normally consider restoration. Appleton favored ultraconservative restoration—which would place him close to the ideas of Ruskin and Morris, who had established the S.P.A.B.[78]

Appleton was also a student of the outdoor museum idea. He communicated with the director of the Northern Museum in Stockholm in 1918 and began exchanging publications with him.[79] During the years that followed World War I, Appleton stressed the need for an outdoor museum in New England that would preserve old buildings that might not otherwise be saved. In his article for *Art and Archaeology* he discussed the Swedish museum villages and the philosophy behind such re-creations of the past.[80] In 1927 G. Berg, assistant director of the Stockholm museum, wrote to Appleton praising him for the work that he had already done in New England. Berg requested details in regard to preservation organizations and preservation laws in the United States. He explained that he was planning to use this information in an article on the work of the S.P.N.E.A. for some Swedish reviews. Berg's inquiry was a rare international tribute to Appleton's work.[81]

Indications of active correspondence with both British preservation organizations can be found in the S.P.N.E.A. files. A. R. Powys, secretary of the S.P.A.B., inquired if the S.P.N.E.A. members could help his society meet some of its current expenditures. The debt had been incurred in collecting architectural reports. Appleton printed the entire letter from Powys in the October, 1924, *Old-Time New England* with the comment that, although the society could not spend money outside of New England, it could certainly make space available in its bulletin for requests for help from deserving organizations.[82] Powys inserted Appleton's response in the 1925 *Report* of the S.P.A.B.[83] It was treated as a friendly gesture, and the next year's *Report* included another letter from Appleton which complimented the British society on its thorough and effective work. Appleton advised the S.P.A.B. to be sure to photograph buildings before, during and after repairs.[84]

Appleton also exchanged ideas with S. H. Hamer, secretary of the British National Trust. He had read the 1926 *Report* of that organization, and he wanted to know just how the Trust administered its many properties. The S.P.N.E.A. then had twelve of its own (fourteen, if one considers barns as properties).[85] Hamer replied that the National Trust leased some of its houses to tenants who permitted the public to view them at reasonable hours. The arrangement was remarkably similar to that which Appleton had already worked out with some of the S.P.N.E.A. buildings.[86]

Appleton had two methods for collecting news about other societies here and abroad. Either he sent donations that were just large enough to insure him copies of all the periodicals of an organization or he exchanged publications with other groups. His library accession lists show that, year after year, his office received almost all of the leading magazines that dealt with the fields of preservation and restoration. Judging by his correspondence, one can assume that he read most of them.

Before leaving this study of the S.P.N.E.A. and its founder, it should be helpful to pause and consider Appleton from the standpoint of the people who worked with him. Bertram K. Little, his successor as corresponding secretary, and Miss E. Florence Addison, who worked with Appleton in the S.P.N.E.A. office from 1920 until the time of his death in 1947, both regarded him as a singularly dedicated man oblivious to his own needs. His unmarried status and his independent income gave him a peculiar freedom in his work; he was indeed his own boss. Little and Miss Addison remembered him as engaging and quiet in most of his dealings with others.

Appleton's workday was an unusually long one. He spent hours poring over clippings and other types of material gathered from his reading. He often visited the houses which came to his attention and then dictated a résumé of his findings on returning to the office. (The files are still full of these confidential reports.) If a call came into the office concerning a building that was in particular danger, he simply dropped everything and left for the day. He attempted to answer inquiries as quickly as possible, especially if speed was an element in rescuing a house from destruction. Appleton prepared answers to all letters that came to him and even took time to prod preservationists in other areas. Little said that Appleton frequently called him late at night from the Otis house where he had been working for hours over a problem. Once Appleton became engrossed in his work, he lost all sense of time. Both Miss Addison and Little recalled that Appleton talked eagerly about European concepts of preservation. The French *Monuments Historiques* was a subject that interested him, for he hoped that old buildings in New England might be similarly cataloged someday. Skansen was another favorite topic. The William Sumner Appleton who emerges from these reminiscences resembles closely the man found in his writings: a person completely devoted to his lifework.[87]

There are many points of comparison between the careers of Sumner Appleton and Ann Pamela Cunningham. Although they were not contemporaries and lived in different areas of the country, both Miss Cunningham and Appleton were born into wealthy families and enjoyed a certain amount of financial independence throughout their lives. They waited many years before discovering a path in life and then dedicated themselves to the objectives they set. In the case of Miss Cunningham, the nature of her cause and the tremendous obstacles to be overcome in saving Mount Vernon forced her to take a more active public role than Appleton found necessary in the case of the S.P.N.E.A. They both proved to be able administrators who inspired a sense of mission in their assistants. Neither Miss Cunningham nor Appleton had any significant family responsibilities during the period of his greatest labor, so each could give all of his time to his work. Both of them possessed a wide circle of influential friends who were indispensable in promoting their causes. Although both had physical difficulties, Miss Cunningham's crippling invalidism was more of a trial than was Appleton's consistently weak constitution.

Both were innovators. Miss Cunningham was a leader in the field of organization and also a visionary in her insistence that Mount Vernon be kept just as George Washington had left it. She was the first to set up a truly national women's organization, one which became the object of respectful imitation. Appleton was a pioneer in different areas. He took ideas which had already been tried in some isolated instances and applied them on a larger scale; he also borrowed freely from European techniques of preservation and restoration. His work in documenting restorations by research through both written and photographic accounts marks him as one of the first scientific restorers. Appleton was one of the first persons in America to develop an admiration of fine buildings simply because they were well-preserved examples of a particular period. A thorough student of early American architecture, he consulted some of the most learned architects of the day.

Only in the case of Miss Cunningham, whose career covered the early years of the preservation movement, and with Appleton, who is the last major figure in this book, does one see a person dedicated entirely to the task of saving old houses. One of the most serious problems that has faced the movement all through its history has been the fact that preservationists have looked upon their historical efforts as a sideline, not as a main objective. Many organizations which have saved historic sites have wasted considerable time and expense digressing into fields only incidentally related to preservation. This was certainly not true of either the Mount Vernon Ladies' Association or of the S.P.N.E.A.—for these two organizations were created with one specific object, and they have remained faithful to that goal in spite of numerous temptations to deviate onto side paths. They did not have hereditary qualifications and they looked upon education for patriotism as a secondary result of their efforts. Miss Cunningham and Sumner Appleton had a wide influence on the preservation movement, and the two organizations they founded are very much alive today. The officials of both societies take pride in the belief that they are following the paths marked out by their respective founders.

The following excerpt from a letter which Appleton received in 1942 from Fiske Kimball will serve as an appropriate postscript to the early history of the S.P.N.E.A.:

. . . I, particularly, have seen with admiration the immense snowball of your Society growing larger and larger, and bringing more and more houses under its wing. It has been a marvellous work, and the model and admiration of all in that line. It still remains true, as your secretary said to me on my first visit, just before you came in, that "Mr. Appleton *is* the Society"! [88]

XI

Criteria for Selecting Buildings
Worthy of Preservation

ONE OF THE MOST LEGITIMATE QUESTIONS that should be asked about preservationists is: Precisely what did they hope to accomplish by saving buildings that otherwise would have been altered or destroyed? By means of a study of the answers that various preservationists have given, one can see how these people evolved a host of reasons for selecting all types of historic places for preservation. Although it is impossible to discuss all of the reasons, there are certain major groups of criteria that recur constantly: patriotic inspiration, local and civic pride, the need for exhibition areas, family pride, commercial objectives, and architectural or aesthetic enjoyment.

Few topics have attracted more attention at recent meetings concerned with historic preservation than the study of criteria for selecting buildings. Many critics believe that *too many* historic sites have been saved as museums. It has been estimated that as many as 2,000 historic house museums are now operating in the United States, and there are signs that the number is steadily increasing. In 1955 Kenneth Chorley, then president of Colonial Williamsburg, warned: "There is a limit to historic preservation." He explained that the preservation of an old building for exhibition could only be justified if it had real historic or artistic importance. He deplored some of the "landmarks" that had been saved by overzealous preservers of the past.[1] The following year, the Committee on Standards and Surveys of the National Trust for Historic Preservation reported that any building seriously considered for preservation should have "outstanding historical and cultural significance in the nation or in the state, region, or community in which it exists." Appropriately, the committee proposed a checklist of criteria, according to which preference should be given to buildings which had some historic values combined with a "preponderance of original material." [2]

Architects have been more outspoken in their criticism of the motives which guided early preservationists. In 1941 Henry-Russell Hitchcock spoke vehemently of the "regional myopia" which too often had governed the selection of buildings by local preservation organizations. He thought that these groups had committed two terrible errors by: (1) not considering any architectural styles after Greek Revival; and (2) saving too many buildings in New England of the seventeenth and eighteenth centuries "without regard to essential architectural merit." [3]

At the beginning of the twentieth century a number of preservationists directed serious attention to general criteria for the selection of historic buildings. These people fell into two fairly distinct groups: those who favored historic and inspirational values and those who looked mainly for architectural qualities. Andrew Green and Edward Hall of the American Scenic and Historic Preservation Society represent the former and William Sumner Appleton the latter.

When Green first set up his society in 1895 he claimed that preservation of historic monuments was a "duty" because it would "quicken a spirit of patriotism" and help to cultivate an interest in different localities throughout New York State. He lauded the human faculty of memory and warned that civilization could not advance without a better sense of its past. He was confident that places where great tragedies had been enacted would inspire visitors "to lofty undertakings." [4]

Edward Hall, secretary of the American Scenic, had to speak out in 1913 when he was asked if the façade of the old Assay Office in downtown New York was historic. He replied that since the building was less than 100 years old, it was not "historic." The storm of protest that greeted his judgment caused Hall to write at some length on the question of preservation. He prefaced his remarks by saying that he would not discuss architectural monuments because they lacked historic interest as he defined it. Then he went more deeply into the meaning of the word "historic" when that term was applied to a building. Hall said that some places were "use-historic" because famous Americans had been born in them or had lived in them, or because they had been the scene of important events. Such structures, reasoned Hall, could become "historic" within the lifetime of one man. Sites that did not have any connection with particular men or events were only "time-historic," and would therefore have to reach a certain age in order to be worthy of preservation.[5] Hall explained how Mount Vernon had value as a use-historic building.

> . . . One may stand before the modest wooden home of a gentle-man farmer in Mount Vernon, Va., and feel no stirring of the emotion until he knows that here lived Washington. Then the blood tingles, the nerves thrill. Then the building loses its insignificance, and the vision of the great patriot, general and statesman transforms it into a shrine of national patriotism.[6]

In 1925 Hall applied his use-historic criterion in a curious way to the Treason House at West Haverstraw, New York, the scene of Benedict Arnold's attempt to give West Point to the British.

> The preservation of the house is not to honor treason, but partly to save a landmark connected with one of the most critical periods of the war and to keep in mind the patriotic abhorrence of such conduct; also as a pre-revolutionary building that witnessed many important events in that vicinity.[7]

Because patriotic inspiration was so much easier to explain to the public, the American Scenic and Historic Preservation Society rarely took an interest in a house that would have fitted Hall's "time-historic" criterion.

Appleton, on the other hand, had an opposing view. In 1919 he prepared a roster of all the New England buildings he would want to preserve.

> The list would include houses of superlative architectural interest of the type of the Pierce-Nichols house in Salem, Mass., or the Moffatt-Ladd house in Portsmouth, N. H., also houses of supreme historical interest comparing well with the Webb house in Wethersfield, Conn., or Paul Revere's house in Boston, and houses of supreme associational interest of the class represented by Whit-

tier's birthplace in Haverhill or Longfellow's boyhood home in Portland. Even this list takes no account of those excessively old buildings of the early 17th century, of truly mediaeval construction and such history and personal association as comes from the fact of their having housed some rugged pioneer of the earliest days.[8]

Appleton always looked for original features in seventeenth-century houses. In 1915 he was using architectural criteria when he said of the Boardman house in Saugus, Massachusetts, that "no house of the seventeenth century . . . has come down to us so little altered and still retaining so many of its valuable features—such as original chimney, many original doors, much original sheathing, original sills, unplastered ceilings, fine and varied old hinges, etc." [9]

Although Appleton preferred to accept only the best houses for his society, he was flexible at times. He admitted that if organizations other than the S.P.N.E.A. saved the "best" houses, his society might have to save the "second best." He also admitted that the S.P.N.E.A. might accept houses of secondary importance if they were offered on very liberal terms.[10] Appleton also occasionally acquired properties of minor significance in communities distant from Boston in hopes that he might be helping the cause of preservation in those outlying districts—not to speak of adding new members to the society.[11] Lest Appleton be accused of being totally unselective in his preservation activities, it must be said that there were some cases when he advised against saving certain houses. When a group from Brighton, Massachusetts, asked him to pass judgment on an old home in 1919, he replied that he was unable to find anything older than the Revolutionary period in the building and that it "had been so terribly man-handled and altered within recent times that by no possibility would it be worth purchasing for preservation." [12]

It appears that Appleton was ahead of his time in setting up criteria for saving houses. For instance, in 1921 he favored the preservation of an unusual 1854 house in Somerville, Massachusetts. ". . . This would make an ideal period house for the display of mid-Victorian black walnut, but the present is probably fifty years too early for anything of the kind. . . ." He recognized that Victorian architecture and furnishings were definitely out of style and would remain so.[13]

Unlike Appleton and Hall, the majority of preservationists did not spend much time thinking about general criteria for selecting historic buildings to save. To them the most important criterion was usually the element of immediate danger of destruction. Only when it became clear that a particular structure was threatened did people begin to think long and hard about why it should be saved.

At this point it is best to examine some of the reasons that preservationists from all camps have given for saving their landmarks. Although the criteria listed here are described as if they were separate items, most properties possessed a mixture of inspirational and practical advantages that caused people to save them.

If any single factor can be considered the motivating force behind the majority of preservation efforts, it would certainly be the hope that historic house museums would contribute to patriotic education. Many earnest individuals believed that revived patriotism could help to cure some of the social and political ills that were current in the United States. Wendell Phillips told the people of Boston that Old South preserved would be the most "eloquent" school they could provide for the youth of the future.[14] Some of the speakers at the 1879 dedication of Washington's Headquarters at Valley Forge referred to that humble stone building as a "fountain" to which patriots could come and "drink inspiration," and as an "altar" where posterity would recognize its dependence upon God and the efforts of the forefathers.[15] The select committee of the New York legislature that studied the purchase of the Hasbrouck house in 1850 reasoned from several patriotic standpoints. The committee held that any home so closely connected with the Revolution would create a "flame of patriotism" in the bosom of anyone who entered its sacred portals. The legislators also hoped that the old house would be an antidote for thoughts of disunion that were gripping the country at that time.[16] A few years later Ann Pamela Cunningham wrote that a deeper regard for the qualities which made Washington great would help to still the "angry waves of sectional strife and bitterness." [17]

The use of patriotic criteria generally took one of two forms; either the house to be preserved was a reminder of the hardships suffered by revered ancestors, or it was a beautiful exemplification of the peace and harmony of the uncomplicated past. Both of these considerations would promote good citizenship among those who visited the houses. The old homes of Deerfield, Massachusetts, seemed to tell about the trials of the early settlers. The citizens who attempted to save the Old Indian House looked upon it as a "memorial of the dangers and sufferings of our fathers, in the infancy of our country." [18] Many years later Mrs. Jenny Sheldon, wife of the Deerfield antiquary George Sheldon, vividly portrayed the patriotic significance of the Reverend John Williams house:

> The youth who finds himself in a home whose walls echo to the voices of Revolutionary Minute Men catches the inspiration of their deeds and goes forth a stronger man to dare and to do for the righteous cause of human freedom.[19]

Many preservationists widened their definition of patriotism to include nobility of character. They hoped that historic buildings could help to curb the sordid commercialism of the era of big business. President J. D. Moffat of Washington and Jefferson College said in 1893 that places connected with the lives of great men were "the most effective agencies for the cultivation of patriotism —a virtue that is apt to disappear with excessive pursuit of wealth, unless kept alive by historic places and celebrations." [20] Wendell Phillips was sure that if people were "alive to such influences" as patriotism, then he could "laugh at money-rings or demagogues armed with sensual temptations." [21] The people who wanted to save the old Bulfinch State House in Hartford were especially concerned lest future generations should look back on Hartford's citizens as "completely obsessed by . . . frantic commercialism." [22] J. G. Randall, writing in the 1920's, believed that the campaign to save Monticello had a "spiritual significance" because Jefferson's home was a cultural resource that could connect us with our vanishing past.[23]

Some of those who hoped to preserve historic houses as structures embodying the peace and order of colonial life went to great extremes to assign unsuspected virtues to these old buildings. In 1901 Edwin F. Naulty launched an unsuccessful campaign to make a museum out of Harewood, a country seat near Charlestown, West Virginia. According to Naulty:

> The influence exerted toward good citizenship and a love of country by a trip to such an historic spot as Harewood cannot be

calculated. Its educational value upon the young is certain. It helps to keep us in touch with the high ideals of an elder day and brings the romance and beauty of Colonial and Revolutionary life before our eyes as can no spoken or printed word. No one can go to such a place as Harewood and walk through its stately chambers and about its beautiful grounds without becoming a better man or woman.[24]

Preservationists believed that the mere act of stepping inside a historic house would thus produce a mystical change in the visitor and make him, in Naulty's words, "a better man or woman." Just how this was to happen no one ever outlined, though it was generally expected that visitors would be purified by gaining a sense of appreciation for the beauties of colonial life along with a feeling of gratitude for the sacrifices of those who first lived in these early homes.

Another potent criterion used by preservationists was an appeal to local pride. The loss of an important old building could, they argued, actually be a sign that a community had no appreciation for its past. Just such an argument was used when the Washington Association was trying to rescue the Ford Mansion in Morristown, New Jersey. One newspaper reporter, alarmed at the possible destruction of the building, referred to it as the "Mecca of Morris County." [25] A few years later the Reverend W. H. H. Murray told an audience in Old South Meeting House that Boston's "soul" would be taken from her "body" if buildings such as Old South were torn down. In his estimation Boston would be relegated to the ignominious position of "any city that has sprung up within the last twenty years." [26] Many years later the governor of Kentucky issued a proclamation calling for funds to help his state save the house (near Bardstown) known as "My Old Kentucky Home." Writing mainly to people in his own state, the governor carried local pride to a new height.

> You also are privileged and invited to join with the sons and daughters of Kentucky in a contribution to this fund, which shall be used alone to preserve the home of the song that is your song and our song. You have stood with uncovered head and tear-dimmed eyes as the old song tugged at your heart-strings. Now let it tug at your purse strings.[27]

The most practical reason for preserving historic buildings

usually has been kept in the background, but it has appeared frequently enough in preservation appeals to deserve mention. Historical organizations that sprang up in the nineteenth century found that they needed headquarters for meetings and places to display their collections. An excellent illustration of such a motivation was the purchase of the Reuben Brown house in Concord, Massachusetts, by the Concord Antiquarian Society in 1887. The society had selected the Brown house simply because it appeared to be a suitable place for exhibiting the relics that Cummings Davis had given to the society.[28] The American Institute of Architects bought the Octagon in 1901 to serve as a Washington, D. C., headquarters where the organization could influence legislation. The Octagon was indeed a fine building of the Federal period, but if it had not been in downtown Washington, it would hardly have suited the purposes of the institute.[29]

Family associations looked upon their homesteads as landmarks toward which all descendants of distinguished ancestors could look with pride. In 1902 Augustus Alden spoke of the Alden homestead in Duxbury, Massachusetts, as the "Mecca" of all his clan, "for the old house is in a way the symbol of the splendid vitality of those in whose veins the blood of John Alden is perpetuated." [30] Family hearths not only illustrated the vitality of the descendants of pioneers; they also gave a sense of "home" to many people who longed for the magnetic attraction of a picturesque house which they could claim as a part of their own family tradition.

In a few instances minority groups enjoyed commemorating the deeds of their own heroes. Around the turn of the century the Italians of New York City began making pilgrimages to a house on Staten Island that had had a brief connection with Garibaldi and also with Antonio Meucci, who was credited with the invention of the telephone.[31]

In several cases religious groups or individuals interested in the development of a particular religion preserved sites and buildings that figured in religious history. One of the most notable examples was the work of Mrs. Mary Beecher Longyear, of Brookline, Massachusetts. A woman of considerable wealth, Mrs. Longyear spent many years collecting materials dealing with the history of Christian Science. As a part of her project Mrs. Longyear bought and restored four houses connected with the life of Mary Baker Eddy, founder of the religion. She bought the homes "hoping to keep them out of the hands of exploiters" and also because she wanted to use them to illustrate Mrs. Eddy's career factually without creating "shrines where her personality would be worshipped." [32] In 1926 Mrs. Longyear set up a foundation to carry out her purposes, and since 1934 it has been chartered by the State of Massachusetts as a charitable trust.[33] Another instance of a religious motivation occurred in 1923 when the Episcopal Bishop of Connecticut initiated a drive to preserve the Glebe house in Woodbury as a landmark for all Episcopalians who wished to commemorate the consecration of the first American bishop in 1783.[34]

Shortly after the beginning of the twentieth century it became evident that popular historic buildings were bringing tourists into towns that had advertised their antique treasures effectively. Therefore it seems probable that some people saw a real commercial advantage in historic house museums. Governor Curtis Guild of Massachusetts wrote to the Paul Revere Memorial Association in 1907 that the restored Revere house would bring "every year to this city thousands who otherwise would treat Boston merely as a way station." Although it is difficult to ascertain whether or not local merchants contributed to the Memorial Association, the governor's message undoubtedly had some effect.[35] Appleton and other preservationists did not hesitate to use commercial criteria whenever they thought it was worthwhile. On May 15, 1912, Appleton addressed a letter to the merchants of Cambridge, Massachusetts, soliciting donations for the Cooper-Austin house.

> The Preservation of such a house must surely increase the number of visitors going to Cambridge, lengthen the time they stay there, and increase somewhat the amount of money they spend there. All of this is good business, and accordingly we appeal to you as a business man to help this enterprise as a business proposition for Cambridge.[36]

In a few cases buildings of unusual interest came into the hands of people who hoped to gain a profit from them. A bizarre example was the story of the John Brown Fort Company, formed in 1891 for the purpose of exhibiting the small engine house in which John Brown was captured in 1859 after his raid on Harpers Ferry, West Virginia. The incorporators of the company put up a considerable sum of money with the intention of dismantling the structure and moving it to Chicago for the 1893 World's Fair. Although they did succeed in moving it, the incorporators lost all of their money through a series of delays in the erection of a building to house the little fort. The engine house was open to the public for a few days, and there were only eleven paid admissions at fifty cents each! This fiasco immediately ended the John Brown Fort Company, which went into receivership. The John Brown "fort" wandered for several years before it came to rest on the campus of a Negro college in Harpers Ferry.[37]

In at least one case a historic house became the focal point of a public philanthropy. Miss Caroline Emmerton purchased the House of Seven Gables in Salem, Massachusetts, with the hope of converting it into the headquarters for a settlement association. In 1911, after the house had been open to the public for a year, Miss Emmerton discovered that it had great drawing power as a literary landmark (associated with Nathaniel Hawthorne). She moved most of the settlement activities to nearby buildings and opened the house as a museum, reserving some rooms as residential quarters for her social workers. Soon the House of Seven Gables became a source of income for a charitable enterprise.[38]

Only a handful of houses had been saved by 1926 as architectural monuments. These buildings were either associated with a renowned architect or suited the purposes of some institution that wished to display the arts of the past. When the Boston Society of Architects wanted to get the Massachusetts legislature to keep the Bulfinch State House in 1896, they found the money could only be voted "as a matter of sentiment." Aesthetic arguments carried little weight with politicians.[39] The Pierce-Nichols house in Salem was acquired in 1917 by the Essex Institute after a public campaign to raise the purchase money. The 1917 report of President Endicott gave some indication of the criteria that the institute had used in selecting the Pierce-Nichols house for preservation: "Built in the latter part of the eighteenth century by Samuel McIntire, whose fame as an architect, not only in Salem but in the country at large, is greater now than perhaps at any time since his death, the house remains to-day practically unchanged." [40] With the exception of the Bulfinch State House in Hartford, there were few other campaigns for buildings associated with famous architects. St. John's College in Annapolis paid the unprecedented sum of $47,000 for the Hammond-Harwood house in that city in 1926. The college had decided to use this fine eighteenth-century home in conjunction with its department of American history as a museum for the study of colonial "mobiliary arts." [41] There was no significant event or person connected with the Harwood house other than its builder, William Buckland.

Once a group of people saw a notable building in danger, every argument imaginable supporting the idea of preservation came sharply into focus. In 1902 a syndicate of promoters offered to buy the Park Street Church in Boston, since it occupied a valuable downtown location. The price offered was so attractive that the officers of the church seriously considered selling the property. The threat of destruction caused another group within the congregation to publish a lengthy pamphlet offering fifteen reasons why Park Street Church should remain. The criteria listed in the booklet could be narrowed to four major headings: (1) The church occupied a prominent street corner which required a "monumental" building. (2) The edifice represented an architectural type that was becoming rare in Boston. (3) The church had witnessed the formation of a number of reform movements, and it also had some literary associations. (4) The congregation had a debt to the public at large and to posterity to continue caring for the building. No doubt the pamphlet had some effect; yet sober financial considerations ultimately preserved Park Street Church. The promoters could not raise the money they promised. [42]

Perhaps the most imposing array of criteria ever marshaled for one house appeared in 1916 when a varied group of New Englanders united to save the Sargent-Murray-Gilman house in Gloucester, Massachusetts. This dedicated band of preservationists stated its case in glowing terms in a booklet entitled *The Story of an Interesting and Historic Old House in Gloucester, Massachusetts*. The criteria to be used for judging the Sargent house naturally began with the problem of immediate danger: "Parties from New York [perhaps the Metropolitan?] and other places have for some time been anxious to buy the woodwork in this house." Here two criteria were quickly established—outsiders wanted a Gloucester house, and this one had interior woodwork of sufficient quality to create interest in a city hundreds of miles away. In addition, the building had been the birthplace of the Reverend Samuel Gilman, author of "Fair Harvard," and for many years had been the home of the Reverend John Murray, founder of Universalism in America. The booklet concluded by saying that a proper yard in front of the house would help to create a spot of beauty in the heart of Gloucester's business district. The project should appeal to all Universalists, Unitarians, Harvard men, and lovers of early New England buildings.[43] Not to be outdone, Appleton published another reason for saving the house in his *Bulletin* for December, 1916. He had found that several occupants had been involved in lawsuits that eventually established the right of any person in Massachusetts to support the church of his choice. Appleton concluded that the structure should interest people who wished to commemorate a victory for the separation of church and state.[44] Even with so many historical and aesthetic arguments in its favor, the Sargent-Murray-Gilman house was not saved until 1919.[45]

Although people paid lip service to the idea of architectural preservation, the vast majority of houses saved before 1926 had some connection with important events or people. A. Lawrence Kocher, chairman of the A.I.A. Preservation Committee, lamented the neglect of buildings that had architectural significance.

> The public is not readily persuaded where matters of beauty are a concern. People appreciate old buildings for sentimental reasons, such as that they might have housed General Washington for a night. They do not understand, nor treasure, them for their construction or outstanding architectural value. . . .[46]

Preservationists soon found that old buildings usually had to be saved by means of emotional crusades. The American public did not become aroused until it was jolted into the realization that each particular structure would contribute to an understanding of our nation's past. Even up through the 1920's it was not unusual for a mansion as important as Rosewell, in Gloucester County, Virginia, to be destroyed partly through negligence.[47] This magnificent brick home might have been rescued if the public had been more aware of its value as a specimen of Georgian architecture. Unfortunately, the Page family that had built Rosewell did not occupy a sufficiently brilliant place in history to make its homestead memorable.

In spite of the apparently haphazard manner in which preservationists selected the buildings they wanted to save, their record is indeed a creditable one. Present-day architectural scholars may point an accusing finger at the early preservers who rode on the crest of waves of patriotic oratory as they saved the numberless headquarters of Washington. Yet the greatest gift that the preservationist of the past has left for the tourist of today is the large number of ancient buildings that illustrate, among other things, America's architectural heritage.

XII

Techniques of Restoration

ONCE A PRESERVATIONIST HAD SUCCEEDED IN SAVING A BUILDING he was faced with a new problem: What would he do with his newly acquired relic? Would he preserve it intact or remake it into its "old self"? Answers to these questions can be found by surveying the development of restoration techniques. The variety of techniques used on historic structures in the early years of the preservation movement reflects the tastes and objectives of those who devoted themselves to worthy educational causes.

Although most of the earliest restorations were the work of untrained amateurs, preservationists grew to depend upon architects or antiquaries for advice. If the architectural profession did not make a profound contribution to the movement as a whole, it certainly did well in the area of restoration. Here architects appeared to be at home; they assumed that their training had prepared them for the demanding task of returning old buildings to their original state. Unfortunately, most architects began their work without familiarizing themselves with the methods of colonial builders, so their first restorations lacked real authority. Nevertheless, before the end of the First World War a handful of these men were making a definite contribution to scholarly restoration procedures. Many of them had traveled and knew the problems that had faced restorers abroad. In 1902 Professor A. D. F. Hamlin of Columbia University outlined the philosophical struggle that had raged in Europe between those who favored sweeping restorations and those who opposed any alterations that destroyed old materials. Professor Hamlin was not sure he could determine exactly when repairs tended to become restoration; but he knew that it was easy to reach the danger point where the original fabric of a building could be destroyed. Hamlin apparently sided with the conservative policies of Ruskin and Morris.[1]

American architects took restoration work seriously by the early 1920's. Horace Wells Sellers, writing in 1920 for the *Journal of the A.I.A.*, supported the general philosophy of the Society for the Protection of Ancient Buildings in calling for greater respect for the surviving mementos of craftsmen who toiled centuries ago. He quickly added that no restorer should feel obligated to honor the efforts of the workmen of the late nineteenth century, an era he considered a low point in American design.[2] The next year Sellers condemned restorations done by "inexperienced or unsympathetic hands," warning that errors in restorations should be a potent argument for the formation of A.I.A. chapter preservation committees.[3] Two years later Fiske Kimball blasted away at some of the newer restorers:

> It should be realized . . . that restoring an old home or garden is specialized work, and not every architect has the special knowledge and experience—to say nothing of the patience and willingness to devote adequate time—to do this work. . . . It must be acknowledged that in a number of instances the greatest knowledge and experience in such work is possessed by men not architects by profession, athough there are conspicuous instances also of architects who have achieved notable success in this line.[4]

Kimball's successor as chairman of the A.I.A. Preservation Committee, A. Lawrence Kocher, asserted that the institute should do all it could to prevent "so-called 'restoration.' "[5]

In order to have a yardstick for measuring the success of the early restorers, let us note briefly a few of the rules formulated by experienced architects within recent years. During the 1930's the Board of Advisory Architects hired to supervise Rockefeller's restoration of Williamsburg drafted a "Decalogue" of requirements that were to govern that project. Kimball and Kocher drew up the main part of the list, basing it on the thoroughly conservative view that all architects and craftsmen should respect the surviving work of the past. They asked that original materials be retained to the maximum extent, even though this might involve additional expense. Naturally they sanctioned the use of fragments from other buildings if each was clearly marked as such; they also approved the inclusion of new materials, carefully executed in the manner of the old, as long as there was no attempt to "antique" the new.[6]

The Advisory Board on National Parks, Historic Sites, Buildings, and Monuments published a more complete statement of a restoration policy in 1937. The board took into account some of the conflicting forces that could influence a responsible individual charged with a restoration.

> Educational motives often suggest complete reconstitution, as in their heyday, of vanished, ruinous or remodelled buildings and remains. This has often been regarded as requiring removal of subsequent additions, and has involved incidental destruction of much . . . historical evidence, as well as of aesthetic values arising from age and picturesqueness.
>
> The demands of scholarship for the preservation of every vestige of architectural and archeological evidence—desirable in itself—might, if rigidly satisfied, leave the monument in conditions which give the public little idea of its major historical aspect or importance.
>
> In aesthetic regards, the claims of unity or original form or intention, or variety of style in successive periods of building and remodelling, and of present beauty of texture and weathering may not always be wholly compatible.
>
> In attempting to reconcile these claims and motives, the ultimate guide must be the tact and judgment of the men in charge.[7]

The Park Service Advisory Board also made some specific recommendations about restoration techniques. It required that extensive research be done before beginning a project—and that a complete record be kept while the restoration was in progress. There was also a valuable note of caution: ". . . Better preserve than repair, better repair than restore, better restore than reconstruct."[8] It is heartening to realize that some of the first preservationists did subscribe to this theory.

In the long history of American preservationism a great many restorations have been attempted, and almost every conceivable treatment has been given to old buildings. The remainder of the chapter is a survey which covers most of the techniques used by early restorers. The examples range from attempts to place his-

torical markers on buildings to restorations that were based on
sound research and painstaking workmanship. Between these two
extremes one can find reconstructions, radical renovations, re-
movals and all sorts of alterations. Because each effort was influenced by several considerations, it is difficult to arrive at definite
categories. Often a restoration was colored by the experience of
the person supervising the work; at other times patriotic purposes
governed whatever had to be done. Therefore the wide spectrum
of restoration techniques has only one common thread running
through it: each restoration was an effort on the part of one individual or group to make an old building more useful and more
accurate as a representation of the past.

The most radical approach to the problem of restoration was
the idea that buildings did not need restoration at all; they could
be suitably marked as historic places and then be left to take care
of themselves. Before the beginning of the twentieth century a
number of patriotic groups and family associations believed that
affixing tablets to old buildings would re-create a certain amount
of historical reality. They may also have thought that the presence
of a tablet would remind others to leave the structure intact.[9] Professor Hamlin told the American Scenic and Historic Preservation
Society in 1902 that the act of placing a tablet on a building "is
to open a perennial fountain of inspiration, to establish a silent
but effective preacher of virtue." [10]

Others reasoned that the mere act of putting up a historical
marker bore little relation to either preservation or restoration.
Ashbee reported to the English National Trust in 1901 on this
question.

> I think . . . that the placing of tablets is sometimes over done,
> and I have met many Americans who consider that when a tablet
> is once placed somewhere there is an end of the business. But to set
> a tablet where there is nothing left to visualize the past is a some-
> what barren proceeding.[11]

Appleton was proud of the fact that the Society for the Preservation of New England Antiquities had never resorted to markers,
and had saved old homes instead.[12] In a few cases he had to swallow
his pride and permit other groups to install tablets when these
organizations had contributed toward saving S.P.N.E.A. houses.
In 1916 he allowed the Nathaniel Tracy Chapter of the Daughters

of the Revolution to place a marker on the Swett-Ilsley house after the ladies had donated $1,270 to that restoration.[13] Joseph Chandler attacked tablets as "advertisements" put up by societies that gave money here and there. He admitted that patriotic groups had done much good in preservation work, but he thought they should find a better way to memorialize their accomplishments.[14]

Even when buildings were doomed to destruction, some people believed that recording architectural features by means of photographs or drawings was a valuable service. The Philadelphia *Evening Bulletin* for May 20, 1854, noted that "Mr. Richards, the daguerreotypist" had set out to record "objects of interest" before they disappeared. He had taken a view of the Associated Presbyterian Church, which was about to be dismantled.[15] By the end of the nineteenth century architects had taken the lead in this field. The Philadelphia Chapter of the A.I.A. tried in 1913 to get the director of the Department of Public Works to help them begin a picture survey of all colonial buildings left in the city at that time.[16] Shortly after the turn of the century the Colonial Dames of Connecticut began collecting photographs and historical materials on Connecticut houses, and in 1923 they published some of the results of their work in a large volume.[17]

In a few notable cases preservationists refused to consider the destruction of a house as the final act. From the time of the demolition of the Hancock Mansion in 1863 there had been some hope that it might be reconstructed. In 1917 the governor of Massachusetts proposed to the legislature that the state rebuild the Hancock house on its original site as a governor's residence. Nothing came of his recommendation.[18] A few years later a paper manufacturer, Horace A. Moses, offered to build a house in Ticonderoga, New York, that would serve as the headquarters for the New York State Historical Association. He specified that the structure should be a fireproof reproduction of some old house. The officers of the Historical Association decided that the John Hancock house would be ideal, since it had been built of stone and brick. The association proudly opened its replica in 1926, noting that it was as accurate a reconstruction as possible, being based largely on measured drawings made at the time the original mansion was torn down. The building served as a museum and headquarters, with the first floor furnished with reproductions of the best furniture from the American Wing of the Metropolitan Museum. No materials from the Hancock house itself had been used.[19]

From the standpoint of historical reality, people considered an old house on a new site far more satisfactory than a reproduction. The classic use of removal and reconstruction involved the Beniah Titcomb house in Newburyport, Massachusetts. The City of Newburyport bought the land on which the Titcomb house stood in 1911 and began to clear the lot for new municipal buildings. Appleton inspected the tottering ruin and pronounced it an excellent specimen, noting its well-preserved seventeenth-century woodwork. The city offered to give the building to the S.P.N.E.A. if the society would move it. Newburyport's proposal illustrates the fact that often a destructive agency favored preservation when removal was possible. A member of the S.P.N.E.A. asked Norman Isham to make measured drawings of the house and then to remove some of the most valuable portions of the interior. This was done, and the drawings and the woodwork became part of the S.P.N.E.A. museum.[20] Meanwhile the local Daughters of the Revolution tried and failed to raise enough money to move the structure to another lot so that it could serve them as a chapter house.

Ralph Burnham of Ipswich bought the remains of the Titcomb house, dismantled it carefully and moved the timbers to Essex for re-erection.[21] There they rested in storage for nearly six years while the most important parts of the interior woodwork were in Boston in the S.P.N.E.A. museum. When Burnham finally began to rebuild the house in 1917 he asked Appleton to lend him these fragments in order to make his reconstruction complete. The trustees of the society loaned the materials requested, intending that this experiment would set a precedent for future cases. Appleton was pessimistic.

> While great care was given to the re-erection of the staircase, other details were less accurately attended to. Most of these would be unnoticed by the average visitor but in their sum total they go far to deprive the house of value as an antiquarian document.[22]

Sometimes preservationists found that they could move houses in sections or as a whole—in preference to having them dismantled. The obvious advantage was that more original materials would survive if the building were moved in sections. Miss Caroline Emmerton, at Appleton's instigation, fought long and hard with the City Council of Salem, Massachusetts, in order to move the Hathaway house to the grounds of the House of Seven Gables in 1911.

> It was moved by a roundabout way to its present location, through Bridge, Webb and Derby Streets in three sections, and when each section of the house arrived it looked like Birnam Woods, having torn off a great deal of foliage from the overarching elms on the way down.[23]

Several steps had to be taken to preserve the William Damm Garrison house at Dover, New Hampshire. The Annie E. Woodman Institute bought the little log building in 1915 with the idea of moving it into the town of Dover and setting it up as an exhibit. It took one week to move the house, and when it arrived the institute erected a protective pavilion over the whole structure to keep out the elements. Today it is still on the grounds of the Woodman Institute, surrounded by classic columns and latticework.[24]

During the first two decades of the twentieth century a number of wealthy individuals bought old mansions for country homes and "restored" them with the intention of entertaining on a lavish scale. Dormer windows suddenly appeared where rooftops had been plain; servants' quarters grew out of the sides of buildings; partitions fell to make larger rooms; and porches which had never existed before graced the façades of old homes. Historical reality rarely interfered with personal comfort in those days. Westover, the former home of William Byrd II on the James River in Virginia, was a typical private restoration. When Mrs. C. Sears Ramsay purchased the estate in 1898, it included the original house and one of the old dependencies (the other had been burned during the Civil War). Mrs. Ramsay rebuilt the missing dependency in a somewhat newer style and then connected the two smaller buildings to the main house by means of two-story brick hallways which provided needed space for servants. She then removed a partition between two of the first-floor rooms and made a large dining room.[25] On the second floor she removed the original mantels and had more "modern" ones inserted in their places. When she found herself severely criticized for this last step (which could not be justified on the grounds of comfort), Mrs. Ramsay had the original mantels put back. Most of the changes made around 1900 are still in evidence today.[26]

By 1923 Fiske Kimball found it necessary to protest some of the alterations made in old homes by private owners. He requested that architects who supervised these restorations help the owners to see that "their own best interest lies in keeping the building as near as possible in its original condition." He suggested that when wealthy people wanted to add huge wings for servant rooms, they should consider the possibility of separate structures for that purpose.[27]

Not all private restorations were intended to provide comfortable homes for socialites. In 1922 an artist in New Iberia, Louisiana, began a painstaking restoration of his family home, which he had recently inherited. His name was Weeks Hall, and the plantation was "Shadows on the Teche." Hall apparently intended to leave the property to some organization that would open it to students of antebellum Louisiana architecture and culture. Hall began his project by hiring Richard Koch of New Orleans, an expert on the architecture of that area. The two men worked slowly and cautiously on the problem of "making the house habitable without in the least changing its original purpose and condition." Hall wanted a real preservation, not a sweeping restoration. Although heat and light and plumbing had to be installed, almost every piece of surviving material in the house was either repaired or faithfully copied. Hall recorded in his notebook on the restoration that the only change which Koch made was the addition of some latticework on one side of a porch to match older latticework on the other side.[28]

When patriotic and historical organizations bought old buildings to serve as headquarters, they freely altered them to suit their needs. Characteristic of this type of restoration was the case of the Spaulding house in Lowell, Massachusetts. When the Molly Varnum Chapter of the D.A.R. acquired the house in 1906 it had several partitions torn down in order to make one large room across the front of the building. The enlarged room served as a meeting place for the chapter and also as a hall where members and friends could hold parties. No doubt some old woodwork had to be destroyed or moved in this process.[29] The renovation of homes for headquarters occasionally reached a bizarre extreme. In an article in the *D.A.R. Magazine,* the regent of the Wiltwyck Chapter, Kingston, New York, reported that when her chapter had bought an old house in 1908 "the whole interior was removed and altered to make it more suitable for a chapter house, the entrance hall and staircase being copied from those at Mount Vernon." [30]

Some patriotic groups were founded with the specific object of restoring the buildings they saved. This meant that they often had to fight off suggestions from well-meaning amateurs. When the Mount Vernon Ladies' Association purchased the home of the Father of His Country, some people volunteered ideas intended to help the ladies preserve the estate, but some of these proposals were beyond the realm of reason. Shortly before the association took possession of the plantation, Samuel Sloan, an architect, warned that if tourists and the elements continued to treat Mount Vernon as they had in the past, there would soon be no materials left that had anything to do with George Washington. He proposed tearing the mansion down and marking each piece as to its proper location. Then he would have deep stone foundations laid to support brick walls encased in marble. The new building would resemble the old one in every detail, though it would be slightly larger in order to house the original interior woodwork. The roof would be of marble and the balustrade of galvanized iron. Sloan added thoughtfully that his project would cost approximately $1,500,000, but he was sure that the American people would "cheerfully" furnish the money for such a noble undertaking. [31]

The emphatic answer to all such suggestions may be found repeatedly in the writings of Ann Pamela Cunningham. In 1859 she declared that one of the principal tasks of the association was "to provide for the annual maintenance, constant security, constant repair, after we have transformed Mount Vernon *from what it is,* to *what it was,* under the watchful eye of the great Chief." [32] Although she did not have the benefit of modern research techniques or professional opinion, Miss Cunningham was one of the first persons involved in preservationism who considered historical accuracy a prime requisite. Her definition of accuracy was, of course, to return Mount Vernon to its appearance in 1799, the year of Washington's death. Shortly after making her initial statement of purpose, Miss Cunningham saw to it that the new superintendent of the estate, Upton Herbert, made enough repairs to keep the house structurally sound. The major restoration work, which was resumed after a delay caused by the advent of the Civil War, only served to show that Miss Cunningham had been ahead of her time.[33] Under the supervision of an army engineer (instead of Miss Cunningham) all of the rooms on the second floor of the house were repapered and the old paper and plaster were removed wherever they looked worn.[34] This "restoration" has plagued Mount Vernon officials right up to the present time.

Miss Cunningham was not alone, for there were others who aimed for historical accuracy in those early days. In January of 1856 the Carpenters' Company of Philadelphia set out to restore its ancient hall with "especial care to be taken to preserve, as much as possible, every feature in said Hall as it now exists indicative of its original finish." [35]

The story of the 1910 restoration of the House of Seven Gables in Salem, Massachusetts, illustrates the number of conflicting forces at work influencing a restorer. Joseph Chandler, the architect in charge, had to turn the old building into a reasonable recreation of the house in Hawthorne's book and also make it habitable for the settlement association which used it. Chandler also was influenced by his growing respect for the work of eighteenth-century builders. As the Advisory Board of the Park Service later pointed out, only "tact and judgment" could resolve all these forces. Wisely, Chandler attempted a compromise.

> The house . . . being destined for "settlement work" and for a moderate degree of comfort in cold weather there were substituted in the alterations the "double-hung" windows identified with a later date. . . . It was decided to keep much as they were, the interiors of this remarkable addition to an earlier house, they being after slight restorations of some parts, most interesting examples of the second period of Colonial Architecture. . . .[36]

Further evidence of Chandler's tact and good sense can be seen in his working relationship with the owner, Miss Caroline Emmerton. During the intervening centuries the house had lost four of its original gables, so Chandler and Miss Emmerton searched the attic for traces of the vanished gables. Soon they found patched sections of roof, old mortise holes and parts of beams that had been broken off, and they used this evidence in adding four new gables. Chandler also helped to re-create the old chimney with its secret staircase. He persuaded Miss Emmerton to give up the idea of installing an arched window (described by Hawthorne) because the house did not offer a shred of evidence to support such an addition.[37] Only a literary purist could object to Chandler's slight deviation from Hawthorne's settings. For more than fifty years the settlement workers have lived in reasonable comfort. And, more important, examples of two very different periods of American architectural development have been permitted to remain side by side in the same building.

At about the same time that Chandler was completing the restoration of the House of Seven Gables an important new influence began to move into the preservation field. Trained architects and antiquaries, entrusted with the delicate task of returning historic buildings to their former appearance, began to subscribe to the principle that as much surviving old work as possible should remain. One of the first of these restorations was carried out by the Philadelphia Chapter of the American Institute of Architects at Congress Hall, starting in 1911. A chapter committee began an intensive study of the building in 1900, very soon after Independence Hall had reopened. The Philadelphia architects went through journals, letters, newspapers and old engravings for their evidence. They went into the building itself to measure and photograph every significant detail. They removed sections of wallpaper and plaster in order to find evidence of original stairways and partitions. After several years the committee prepared a complete set of plans and specifications for the restoration.[38]

Once the City of Philadelphia voted the money to carry out the restoration of Congress Hall, the A.I.A. committee members went to work with renewed zeal. Under the chairmanship of Frank Miles Day, they provided supervision, setting the tone for the whole operation in a "General Note" which prefaced the specifications for the contractor.

> On account of the historical interest attached to this building and the desirability of recording all facts obtainable regarding its past, any unforeseen conditions, peculiarity of construction or interesting facts uncovered during the progress of the restoration must be brought to the attention of the Architect before removing or

destroying it. Upon notification, the Architect will immediately visit the building for the purpose of making a survey or otherwise adding to the record.

Every precaution shall be taken to save inviolate all old work, and no cutting or removal of old work shall be done without the consent of the Architect. All old material so removed is to be carefully saved and stacked where directed, except any which may be ordered from the site by the Architect, in which case, the Contractor is to promptly remove it.[39]

While the restoration was in progress the committee attempted to find papers in the state archives that might explain original details on the building.[40] The end result was a fine restoration which, while not perfect, has won the respect of the architects of the National Park Service.

Antiquaries often were more willing to retain original materials than were architects because antiquaries did not consider themselves artists; they presented the past just as they saw it, whether it was eye-appealing or not. Therefore a detailed study of Appleton's work at the Abraham Brown house in Watertown, Massachusetts, should serve to illustrate some of the differences between the first scholarly restorers.

During the summer and fall of 1919 Appleton spent many hours each day in Watertown personally supervising the restoration of the Brown house. He maintained a brisk correspondence with nearly every architect who knew anything about seventeenth-century New England buildings. As a consequence, he never lacked advice. For instance, Murray Corse, a New York architect, earnestly wrote Appleton:

> It gives me great satisfaction to hear that Mr. Chandler is going to help you. He seems to be far and away the ablest of our archaeologists, for he has not only knowledge and experience, but what is so often ignored, architectural skill and artistic appreciation. So many restorations are spoiled by lack of these very qualities, restorations that seem otherwise perfectly literal. After all, to revive the feeling, the atmosphere of the old is the most important; and as the old was essentially artistic it stands to reason that only an artist can do so. If we simply turn out a dry literal reconstruction (as the Germans do) the result is worse than useless, for people think: "How ugly those old things were. Why spend money in preserving them?" [41]

Appleton would have none of this. He answered Corse by telling him that *he* was in charge of the restoration and that Isham and Chandler could see him whenever they wished to discuss any controversial points that arose while the repairs were in progress. Appleton had no intention of "doctoring" history. He noted that he was watching every piece of evidence as it was taken out of the house; he had each rafter checked to see if the building had ever been thatched and each part of the framing inspected to find out if it had been half-timbered. The house was supposed to tell its own story. "You will be glad to know that we are having the house copiously photographed as the work progresses, so that there will be lots of evidence to fall back on." [42]

Appleton, acting as a referee in the midst of a number of architects, made all the final decisions.

> Yesterday at the Brown house I had Mr. Isham and Mr. Chandler for the special purpose of settling some doubtful points. It was entertaining to see how they failed to agree and really tragic to see Mr. Isham condemn as 18th century work details which my experience teaches me beyond the shadow of a doubt are of the 17th century. However, the work is in my hands and nobody else's and the 17th century work is safe as a church. I am, in spite of the criticism that I get, the most conservative restorer of the entire lot and a building is in the safest hands when I have charge of it. Kindly observe my modesty! [43]

Appleton admitted his own errors, trusting that others would profit from them. Early in 1919 Isham refused to accept Appleton's date of 1640–1650 for the Brown house; Isham believed it was of a later date. Appleton hired a lawyer to search the deeds and wills connected with the property in order to establish a date. His research indicated that the house was probably built in 1663 by Abraham Brown, Jr.[44] Appleton immediately told Isham that he had been mistaken, for the later date (which has subsequently been changed to 1698) conformed to the architectural evidence brought to light during the restoration.[45] Appleton occasionally found fault with his own restoration methods. In the fall of 1919, when the Brown house project was well under way, he wrote to Isham that he had at first thought enough photographs were being taken at each stage of the repairs, but he lamented, "it is practically impossible to make too many photographs of this sort of work." [46]

During the restoration Appleton chose to hold down the artistic urge to beautify the Brown house artificially. Whenever he found sections of seventeenth-century work, he left them in place and covered them with glass. On the second floor he uncovered the frame of a triple casement window embedded in one wall; and instead of moving it or "restoring" it, he simply left it visible "so that anyone can see the evidence as we found it and draw their own conclusions." [47]

In March of 1920, when the restoration was nearly finished, Appleton again invited Isham to inspect his masterpiece.

> To my great delight he was unable to pick any flaws with the work done to date. Where I had done things he might have done differently, he admitted the evidence as to just what should have been done was not as clear as we might wish and accordingly anyone would be justified in using his own judgment. . . . Praise from such an expert as he is was highly gratifying.[48]

Dr. Abbott Lowell Cummings, a present-day expert in the field of restoration, offered his authoritative opinion of Appleton's work in Watertown.

> At that time there had been fewer restorations than there are now for guidance and inspiration, needless to say, but on the other hand it was a period of ferment with such men as Norman Isham, Joseph Chandler . . . and George Francis Dow . . . very active and very much on the scene. I have always felt quite strongly that as his first formal restoration job (and in a sense his only big job) Sumner Appleton certainly equalled if he did not actually surpass the work of these men. This is especially true in the matter of the restraint he showed: his reluctance to gloss, his refusal to tamper with any essentially important evidence, leaving it instead under glass . . . his liberal (and correct) use of whitewash (which has never been popular with restorers), and, of course, the comprehensive record, both written and photographic which he kept. In all of this his work was done so well that I feel we have hardly surpassed him to this day.[49]

At the Brown house and in other restorations Appleton was deeply concerned with the problem of identifying modern materials put in to replace sections that had decayed. In the Harrison Gray Otis house he used tacks, arranged in small triangles, in the upper right-hand corner of all pieces of new wood. Even today the student of restorations can examine the Otis house stairway and readily detect the pieces of wood that were marked under Appleton's unusual system.[50]

The achievements of the Philadelphia architects and Sumner Appleton prove that before 1926 many of the techniques considered essential for a good restoration were in use. While most of the people charged with restorations continued to commit errors through ignorance, haste or faulty judgment, there were a few men who looked upon the repair of old buildings as a responsibility. Whether these individuals were architects or not, they all became thorough students of the practices of early American builders.

The great tragedy in the history of restoration techniques in the United States is the fact that scientific restorers had little influence on the preservation movement as a whole. Consequently, numerous restorations in the pre-1926 era were marked by needless destruction of early work. Distance was undoubtedly a factor which kept many preservationists from finding out much about restorers working in other sections of the country. There were no magazines that offered much information on this subject other than the *Bulletin of the S.P.N.E.A.* and the *Annual Reports* of the American Scenic and Historic Preservation Society, and the latter publication did not usually discuss restorations at any length. Perhaps the main reason for the poor work that was done was the question of speed. Proper restoration takes thought and patience. It was usually easier to place an informative tablet on the front of a historic house or to remove several old partitions to create space for meetings. Instead of depending upon research in order to achieve authenticity, wealthy individuals found it more enjoyable to buy old mansions and "fix them up" by adding large wings to house servants. The American public obviously did not object to such practices; it was willing to appreciate the historic significance of an old building without expressing concern over how accurate a representation of the past the "restored" structure might be.

XIII

The Economics of Preservation

THE FIRST SUCCESSFUL PRESERVATION EFFORTS revealed that two very important economic considerations would have to be taken into account whenever a historic building was to be saved. In one way or another funds would have to be raised for the purchase of each property. Unfortunately, that was only half of the story—for payment of the purchase price only changed the ownership; it did not insure the stability of the structure for years to come. Few preservationists could see beyond the glorious day when an old house was purchased, nor could they trouble themselves with the sordid, day-to-day maintenance problems. These idealistic lovers of the past did not exhibit any of the characteristics normally associated with the hardheaded businessman.

Since the federal government and most state governments did not take an active interest in buying historic sites before 1926, preservation work remained in the hands of private groups formed for that purpose. These organizations were made up of middle-class people, rather than those of great wealth. The lists of donors printed in the *Bulletin of the S.P.N.E.A.* show that the great majority gave less than twenty dollars to each project of that society. There were a few instances where rich people actually paid the whole purchase price of a historic building, though almost all of these did not come until the early 1920's. Mrs. Longyear purchased the Mary Baker Eddy houses before 1923. That year Henry Ford bought the Wayside Inn in Sudbury, Massachusetts, and then obtained the Botsford Tavern near Detroit.[1] In 1924 J. P. Morgan, Jr., and George F. Baker, Jr., purchased Hamilton Grange in New

York City for the American Scenic and Historic Preservation Society.[2]

Preservationists usually were not realistic about the economic forces that worked against them, especially when they tried to save residences that stood on valuable property near the centers of large cities. Several patriotic organizations attempted in 1919 to rescue the house in New York City where President Monroe had died in 1831, but the building was on a block of land that was becoming increasingly valuable for office space. That November some real estate brokers paid $138,000 for the Munroe house and the two buildings next to it, and within two years the value of the property rose to $300,000. In 1922, in spite of this formidable obstacle, a group of distinguished men banded together for the purpose of saving the house and transforming it into a center for Pan-American friendship. The New York State legislature would not permit the new organization to acquire the land by condemnation proceedings (which would have arrived at a fair price), so the value continued to soar.[3] In retrospect, the effort to save the Munroe house was doomed to failure from the start. Any building that is to be preserved in the business district of a large, growing city has to have transcendent historic importance in order to justify a public campaign of massive proportions which will overcome inflated property values.

Local preservation groups had to use a variety of fund-raising activities in order to be successful. Sometimes a campaign to save a historic house required years of effort. Such a struggle took place between 1924 and 1926 in Jamaica Plain, Massachusetts. A women's group, the Tuesday Club, united to save the old Loring-Greenough house which occupied a large lot that had been set aside for commercial development. This energetic band of ladies agreed to pay $53,000 for the house, although they had only $1,000 in their treasury—a very brave undertaking indeed.

Borrowing from the experience of other women's clubs in the Boston area, the Tuesday Club launched its drive by means of a dramatic meeting where pledges were announced. The members present promised over $4,000 as a start. The club immediately voted its entire waiting list into membership, thereby nearly doubling the size of the force working to save the Loring-Greenough house.[4]

From then on the club began to pursue its goal with vigor and imagination. The president donated the services of her lawyer. One member guaranteed a loan of $16,000. Another woman furnished a room in the building with salable antiques. Various painters and decorators contributed their time for some of the repairs on the house. The Tuesday Club divided itself into teams under "captains," each team promising to give or earn $25 by a certain date. In the fall the ladies amassed $500 from a housewarming and a three-day bazaar. They offered the barn as a garage and collected rental fees (for rooms in the house) amounting to over $249 the first year. The young people of the town patronized the tennis court on the property. A "Trash and Treasure Shop" set up on the main street in town brought in $431 in three weeks. Fashion shows and debutante balls, card parties and a large Christmas celebration all brought in more money. On Thursday nights throughout the winter the club sold dinners in the house. By the next spring the Tuesday Club had raised $18,000 toward the purchase price, above and beyond the expenses of maintaining the building. A wealthy friend of the club had promised to give $5,000 whenever the ladies could raise $18,000; therefore, by March of 1925 the group had actually raised $23,000! During that year they stepped up their activities by opening a tearoom along with the antique shop. Although it took them several years to pay off the huge debt that they had contracted for the property, the Tuesday Club had made the purchase of the Loring-Greenough house a community project.[5]

Frequently local groups found themselves unable to conduct campaigns to save their own landmarks without some sort of assistance. This was a common situation in small New England towns that had a heavy concentration of fine houses. Regional organizations such as the S.P.N.E.A. offered a helping hand by gathering support from a number of societies. In June of 1916, William Sumner Appleton heard that the Hyland house in Guilford, Connecticut, was in great danger of destruction. A wrecking company had already set a date when it was going to demolish the house. At the last minute the Dorothy Whitfield Historical Society in Guilford agreed to take over the property if it could do so with a down payment of $400 and a mortgage of $800. In view of the fact that the asking price was $2,400, someone had to supply the remaining $1,200 to make the project successful. Ex-Governor Woodruff of Connecticut became concerned about the fate of the building and managed to persuade the owners to lower the price by $600. Then the S.P.N.E.A. trustees authorized a contribution of $200, a sum representing approximately one-half of the 1915 dues of the Connecticut members of the society. Appleton and Governor Woodruff guaranteed to provide the remaining $400. Appleton immediately sent out a special appeal to his Connecticut members, and an additional $573 poured in—insuring the preservation of the Hyland house.[6]

Preservationists had to be careful to time their campaigns in order to catch the imagination of the public. They realized that the rescue of historic buildings was in many ways an emotional activity, and so they carefully took advantage of events that put their houses in the news. The Thomas Bailey Aldrich Memorial in Portsmouth, New Hampshire, raised enough money to buy the old home associated with Aldrich's boyhood. The fact that the organization formed within a year of the author's death helps to explain why $10,000 could be raised in a three-year period, ending in 1910. The public was inclined to be generous at a time when Aldrich's name had been brought to their attention by his passing from the scene.[7] In 1919 the Woman's Roosevelt Memorial Association used the same technique when it began its campaign to rebuild Roosevelt's birthplace within two months of his death.[8]

Although few preservation efforts achieved success through speed and determination, there were a few cases where a time limit was used to spur the rescue of an old building. The defect inherent in this technique was the fact that the threat was often all too real and therefore slow-moving patriots frequently lost the landmarks they hoped to save. On February 15, 1911, the Bishop of Albany announced that he would have to order the destruction of the Schuyler Mansion, then being used as an orphanage, unless the building were purchased by the state or some patriotic society before the first of July of that year. He set the price at $40,000.[9] The following day a bill was introduced in the New York State legislature authorizing the purchase of the Schuyler house for the price named by the bishop, and within a month the bill had received the governor's signature. Although it may not have been the only reason for the quick approval of this measure, the time limit set by the bishop had called for speedy action by the legislature.

Preservation groups found that people who desired to commemorate their ancestors were often a willing source for needed funds. The Quincy and Adams County Historical Society in Quincy, Illinois, conceived of a plan that appealed peculiarly to midwestern farmers who were the sons and grandsons of the men who had settled the area around Quincy. When the members of the historical society decided to preserve the Governor Wood house in Quincy early in the twentieth century, they set aside one room in the structure as a memorial room. The society said that it would cover the walls of this particular room with tablets commemorating the worthy pioneers of the area. Descendants of these men could glorify their ancestors by buying a tablet for a price that included a sizable donation toward the purchase of the house. The idea was so successful that the property was paid for within a few years.[10]

Around the turn of the century, preservation groups used certificates and different classes of membership as a means of making donors feel that they "belonged." When Edwin Naulty tried to set up an organization to save Harewood (in West Virginia) in 1901, he promised that "Founders" (who gave five hundred dollars or more) would receive a gold medal and have their names inscribed on a tablet; special "Contributing Members" (who donated twenty-five dollars or more) would get bronze medals cast from old cannons; and regular members who gave at least one dollar would get beautiful certificates.[11] Although there is no yardstick for measuring the effectiveness of these techniques for fund raising, only a few of the larger and more successful preservation groups used medals or certificates in their campaigns.

The most disheartening realization that emerges from a study of the economic side of the American preservation movement is the fact that the majority of people who saved old houses did not understand that the word "preservation" really meant maintenance of these structures throughout the years that followed. It was exciting to embark upon a crusade to "save" a landmark. It must have been a great relief to shout the victory cry, "The old house is ours!" But for many people this was the end of the road. They believed that the building, once it was open to the history-minded public, would take care of itself with the money that came in from admission fees.

Although early attendance figures for historic house museums are rare and generally unreliable, the few we have tell a story of slow increase. Most museums doubled their attendance between 1905 and 1926, but few did better than that. In view of the fact that the automobile had come into wide use by 1926, the increase over a twenty-year period does not seem very sharp. The Ford Mansion in Morristown, New Jersey, had about 8,000 registered visitors in 1887. By 1915 the number had risen to about 11,000, and this total grew to 21,000 by 1926—approximately two and one-half times the 1887 attendance.[12] By today's standards, these totals are exceedingly small. Prior to 1926 fifty cents was considered a high admission fee; many houses charged either a quarter or a dime. When low fees are matched by equally low attendance figures, it is not difficult to comprehend why so few historic buildings were able to support themselves.

Preservationists seldom admitted outright that they were discouraged with low admissions income, but the problem existed. Some organizations hinted that maintenance costs were indeed high. Observe the tone of the 1925 report of the New Hampshire Colonial Dames:

> The preservation of Colonial landmarks is important, and the Moffatt-Ladd house is one of the most beautiful examples of Colonial architecture in America. Its upkeep is no small matter financially, and the Dames often wish they might wave a fairy wand to make it stand still so that they could contribute more generously to other patriotic causes. . . . But it pays, since a stream of people passes through the house during the season. . . . Each of these visitors felt a new reverence for his country's history as he carried away with him the picture of this lovely old house.[13]

There were isolated examples of groups that found their historic buildings to be assets, but these were rare indeed. In 1920 the librarian of the Maine Historical Society estimated that the Longfellow house in Portland had shown a profit for the three previous years. The profit had maintained the society's collections, but it was not sufficient to run the organization.[14]

At times enterprising people found that maintenance costs could be covered by means of a commercial venture. In Marshfield, Massachusetts, around the year 1919, three gentlemen formed a partnership called the Winslow Associates. Their objective was the preservation and restoration of the Winslow mansion in that town. The house presented a challenge since it was in poor condition after years of neglect—the townsfolk had long considered it too large for family use. The three gentlemen looked ahead to 1921, for that year was to be the great celebration of the Pilgrim Tercentenary in nearby Plymouth, and there would be a great number of tourists in the Marshfield area who would want food during their visit. The Winslow house might well be the answer to their problem. The associates borrowed money to restore the house, connect the stable with the main building, and transform the new wing into a large dining room. Visitors could thus eat in a fine old home furnished with excellent antiques (provided by one of the partners). At the end of the first season the Winslow Associates were so pleased with the financial and antiquarian success of the undertaking that they recommended that other communities attempt similar restorations.[15]

Within a few years of the purchase of a historic house, a preservation group usually realized that it was necessary to campaign for some form of endowment to close the gap that existed between admission fees and running expenses. In a few cases—a happy few —an endowment was raised at the time the building was saved. In 1905 General J. Watts de Peyster gave a house in Akin (now Fort Johnson), New York, to the Montgomery County Historical Society. The house, known as Fort Johnson, had been one of the homes of Sir William Johnson prior to the Revolution. Shortly after General de Peyster presented the property to the society, Stephen Sanford donated $15,000 to ensure proper care of the structure. His endowment was an unusual and useful gift.[16]

The general public responded favorably to appeals for funds if a specific object were mentioned, such as the purchase of a historic house; but campaigns for endowment funds ended in failure almost every time. Two factors contributed to this problem. First, announcing the need for an endowment to cover running expenses seemed to be an admission that a preservation organization was a failure because people were not visiting a historic building in large enough numbers to maintain it. Second, the goal of an endowment was simply a sizable sum of money, which really did not have much appeal for potential donors. In most cases, an endowment had to exceed the purchase price of a house in order to be of any use.

In spite of the difficulties involved, nearly every preservation organization attempted to build up an endowment. The most successful campaigns were those that made the process appear to be painless. The Essex Institute in Salem, Massachusetts, set out in 1916 to raise money to buy the Pierce-Nichols house. Appleton wrote to the institute, attempting to check on the price of the property, which he understood to be $18,000. He intended to inform the S.P.N.E.A. membership that the institute would not take on the house unless it had that amount on hand.[17] Stephen Phillips of the institute told Appleton that the actual purchase price was only $10,000, but he did not want the public to know that the officials of the museum had decided to raise nearly $10,000 more to endow the property.[18] The ruse worked, for the $18,000 which was collected included about $8,000 of endowment. Two years later, the president of the institute asked for an additional $2,000 to make the endowment an even $10,000, but this time the public did not respond.[19]

Most organizations that set out to purchase historic buildings could not sustain the momentum built up during a successful preservation campaign. The experience of the New London (Connecticut) County Historical Society illustrates the sad awakening that often followed a battle against the forces of destruction. On February 20, 1907, the president of the society announced to his board that he had taken a three-month option for $33,000 on the Shaw Mansion in New London. He hoped that the house would become a headquarters for the society in the years to come. Immediately the board began to discuss plans for raising the necessary funds. One board member dramatically produced an agreement that had been signed by several people, pledging various amounts of money for the mansion. The first person who had signed the paper had promised to give $10,000![20] By the end of April, the president announced that the society had nearly reached its goal. Six friends had given $28,500, which meant that the people of New London would have to raise $4,500 in a month and a half.[21]

Needless to say, the campaign was a success, but the New London County Historical Society soon found that it had come too far too fast. In the fall of 1907, only a few months after purchasing the house, the board made plans for an endowment fund of $25,000! Not until then did the membership begin to realize how much it was going to cost to maintain the Shaw Mansion.[22] The 1910 annual report revealed the reason for an endowment. Annual membership dues, admission fees from the house, sales of souvenirs and income from invested funds had come to a grand total of $380; upkeep of the property had cost the society $908 for that same year. Therefore $528 had to be made up by donations from interested members.[23] The same organization which had raised $33,000 in three months could not, in the next three years, raise enough to endow its own property. Neither the members nor the general public could understand the need for the endowment.

In 1910 Appleton attempted to endow the S.P.N.E.A. by gathering the fifty-dollar fees required of life members into the Life Membership Fund, which was to be a vital part of the society's income.[24] Still, the fund was never large enough, and Appleton had to resort to annual appeals to his membership in order to purchase more properties for the society.

Appleton's ideas for financing preservation work covered a broader field than those of his colleagues because he had founded his society on the premise that regional organizations would function more effectively than local ones. Only two years after the formation of the S.P.N.E.A., he said that the income from a fund of $200,000 would permit the society to buy a house or two each year.[25] As time went by, it became clear to Appleton that admission fees and periodic appeals for public donations would never really pay for the vital work of systematically preserving architectural monuments. In May of 1919 he proposed that a large national fund be set up under the control of the Archaeological Institute of America, and seven years later he unveiled his master plan.[26]

What is needed in this country is a fund of say five million dollars in the hands of a board of trustees having power to distribute its income up and down the whole country wherever most needed in order to preserve what is best. Probably the most efficacious way of using this would be to pay for the endowment of a property provided local interest attended to the purchase. The endowment is generally the most expensive and difficult part of the undertaking and its application to the house could always be made dependent on its purchase within a certain definite time and its proper care by some local body.[27]

He went on to estimate that the proposed $5,000,000 fund should produce $250,000 a year. He estimated that $50,000 ought to be an adequate endowment for almost any property, so the board of trustees administrating the fund could endow at least five buildings a year.

There were other solutions to the financial problems that plagued preservationists. In the early 1920's Appleton corresponded with Miss Susan Pringle Frost of Charleston, South Carolina. She was a real estate dealer who had been one of the founders of the Society for the Preservation of Old Dwellings. Susan Frost believed that a preservation group should begin a restoration and then sell the building in question to "sympathetic" owners. She was convinced that many more properties could be saved this way —rather than through the path chosen by Appleton and the S.P.N.E.A.[28]

As the years went by, more and more organizations initiated spirited campaigns to save old landmarks and then lapsed into halfhearted attempts to endow these structures because none of the leaders realized that preservation work required a well-developed plan for future maintenance. It was hard to mix sordid economic considerations with something as uplifting as the preservation of buildings that represented the past. Perhaps if preservationists had been more hardheaded in their approach, fewer important buildings would have survived the onward march of civilization. Wallace Evan Davies' estimate of the patriotic movement could certainly apply to all preservationists: ". . . There was no taint of the mercenary in their concept." [29] Preserving landmarks was an educational mission and should not yield material gain. Like the New Hampshire Colonial Dames, struggling to pay the bills for the Moffatt-Ladd house, most preservationists considered themselves well rewarded if visitors to their buildings left with a renewed appreciation for their heritage. That feeling was worth more than a sense of financial security.

Conclusion

By 1926 the preservation movement had come a long way from the accidental rescue of the Hasbrouck house and the great crusade for Mount Vernon. The principal motivation of the preservationists of the nineteenth and early twentieth centuries had been a desire to educate the American people into a deeper regard for their history, only occasionally tempered by aesthetic considerations. In 1926 a new era was at hand for American preservationism; John D. Rockefeller, Jr., decided that he would undertake the plans proposed by the Reverend W. A. R. Goodwin for the complete restoration of colonial Williamsburg.[1] The influence of the Williamsburg restoration was so revolutionary that the American preservation movement has not been quite the same since then.

Throughout this book the efforts of those who sought to preserve historic landmarks have been called a "movement" only because there seemed to be no better way to describe them. Certainly the movement was lacking in unity and coherence. Its leaders had only one thing in common—they all contributed in some way to the rescue of old buildings. Nevertheless, there are certain descriptive conclusions that may be drawn concerning the activities of these people.

In the first place, American preservationism was essentially an indigenous movement. Even while our preservation ideas resembled those of Europe they were actually native in origin, as can be seen in correspondence resulting from the occasional instances of American contact with European preservationists. The indigenous character of the movement is further proven by the interest in historic landmarks which appeared in the United States a decade before the Civil War, before many European nations began taking care of their own antiquities.

Second, preservationism in the United States was a thoroughly romantic movement. Nineteenth-century Americans were highly receptive to proposals for inculcating patriotic love of past glories by setting aside the homes of important figures in our national history as symbols. Having experienced an emotional upsurge of patriotic inspiration from historic spots, would-be preservers fully expected to create a similar renaissance throughout the entire nation.

Third, the changing criteria used for selecting buildings to save indicate that preservationists reflected many of the major changes of current in American social thought. In the 1850's preservers were reformers teaching that disunion could be cured by a greater regard for the sacrifices of our Founding Fathers. After the Civil War (and especially around the time of the 1876 Centennial) they appealed for a new sense of national dedication. As the nineteenth century wore on, preservationists began to talk much like progressives. They believed that a willingness to pause inside a historic house and reflect upon the simple, rugged life of the past would provide an antidote for the materialistic ills of the present. At the turn of the century, many preservationists thought that old buildings might prove to be a most important tool for the Americanization of immigrant children. During the period of the Spanish-American War and World War I, preservers expressed confidence that visits to historic sites would serve to create militant loyalty to American traditions. In the bustling twenties preservationists offered an aesthetic argument, declaring that an appreciation of beauty and harmony could be gained from old homes. Changes in preservationist thinking do not mean that the movement was subject to cycles of activity. Rather, the growth of preservation work after the 1870's was remarkably steady up until the First World War, and after the war interest in old buildings grew at an even faster pace.

There was a strong educational and reformist strain in the movement. It seems beyond dispute that many preservationists gave of their time and money because of an underlying conviction that the public could be educated and regenerated by exposure to homes symbolic of the virtues of the past. These patriots often spoke of their desire to preserve America's historic traditions, and they earnestly hoped to see more signs of cultural maturity in the youth of the nation. In spite of their educational objectives, most groups that saved old buildings had few formal contacts with schools. Two notable exceptions were the Woman's Roosevelt Memorial Association and the Thomas Jefferson Memorial Foundation. To be sure, by present-day standards, the majority of preservationist pioneers badly neglected the job of interpreting their historic buildings to the public. They believed that the buildings themselves would do the teaching. Therefore saving landmarks quickly became an end in itself, with explicit educational programs arising only where the participants had begun to lose faith in the power of historic houses to tell their story unaided.

Surviving lists of donors to preservation activities lead one to conclude that the core of preservationist support was middle-class in character. With very few exceptions philanthropic foundations and people of great wealth did not take a deep interest in historic sites until John D. Rockefeller, Jr.'s transformation of Virginia's colonial capital in 1926. Middle-class enthusiasts, motivated by a desire to enrich the lives of their fellow men, bore the financial burden.

Women were predominant in the preservation movement as long as it stressed history and patriotic inspiration. When architectural preservation began toward the end of World War I, men became equally active. Women apparently were not so enthusiastic about the field of architecture. In addition, women's organizations were gradually shifting to a primary concern with battling subversion and furthering Americanism, and historic buildings were only one avenue in such a crusade. Men's groups tended to save old homes for their own sake, and often de-emphasized the inspirational aspects of preservation.

By 1926 there were signs of a nascent professionalism in certain areas of restoration work. Both Norman Isham and Fiske Kimball were generally known as "restoration" architects, along with the Philadelphia Chapter of the A.I.A. In the field of administration there were almost no signs of professionally trained museum directors, although William Sumner Appleton and

George Francis Dow did approach the status of full-time directors of historical projects. Neither of these men had any formal training in museum work. Instead they combined years of experience with an avid reading of all pertinent literature in the field. Prior to 1926 the principal qualification for administrative responsibility in historic preservation was patriotic enthusiasm.

During the nineteenth and early twentieth centuries the preservation movement developed definite regional characteristics. The private historical society and individual semi-autonomous chapters of patriotic organizations held sway in New England. After the turn of the century, when other parts of the country were looking to state governments for aid in preservation work, New Englanders were supporting a private regional body, the S.P.N.E.A. All through New England's preservationist literature runs a strain of distrust of any type of governmental ownership of historic buildings. A possible cause for this distrust may have been the native New Englander's conviction that state and local governments, under the control of Irish political leaders, would not respect the history of the region. In the South the loose governmental structure and a tendency to remain rural discouraged local preservation organizations. Southerners had to be satisfied with individual participation in national and regional preservation groups because their most important buildings were usually far out in the country. Thus only a few nationally significant homes in the South were saved through vigorous organizations that appealed to the whole country. The small chapters of the A.P.V.A., together with the Ladies' Hermitage Association and some D.A.R. chapters, remained the only local groups in the South seeking to save historic sites. The Middle Atlantic States had some small local historical societies, much like those in New England, but most preservationists in this region turned to the state and city for aid. In the Midwest and the Far West the pattern of the Middle Atlantic area was most common, though there was an even greater emphasis on state-owned historic sites.

Preservationism was an Anglo-Saxon movement, if one can consider extant lists of donors to be an accurate gauge of the support given to historic buildings, but strangely enough, preservation literature does not contain any outspoken nativist declarations.

Preservationists spent their time trying to educate immigrants, rather than condemning the newcomers.

The indigenous nature of the American preservation movement can be seen through the testimony of an observant English visitor. In 1901 C. R. Ashbee noted how astounded he was at the great number of local groups engaged in preservation work in the United States, and he expressed doubt that the whole movement could ever be centralized, as had been done in some European countries.[2] Unlike France, our federal government had not cataloged its historic buildings. Unlike England, we had no national organizations to shape the direction of the movement in the manner of the English National Trust and the Society for the Protection of Ancient Buildings. And, unlike Sweden, there were no great American outdoor museums that pictured some part of our history in the way that Skansen illustrated Swedish life through the ages. Ashbee implied that the preservation movement in the United States had no real sense of direction. He might have concluded that our preservationists looked upon themselves as educators serving the American public, and each and every group had its own particular definition of public service.

Today the fragmented nature of the American preservation movement still concerns the people who are most involved in it. Since 1949 there has been an American National Trust which has attempted to provide some needed coherence for preservation work all over the United States. The trust has served as a valuable force in the field of information and education through meetings, courses, and a national magazine. For nearly thirty years the federal government (through the National Park Service) has been preserving and restoring historic monuments with a large trained professional staff of archaeologists, architects and historians. Many surveys, architectural and otherwise, have been made since 1926. Zoning ordinances and foundations now are working to protect historic districts in some of our older cities. Yet the main problems mentioned in this book are still with us. Optimists persist in looking upon every old house as another Mount Vernon. They still believe that once a historic building has been purchased it has been saved, and that maintenance will be only a minor consideration. And, in spite of the large body of literature on the subject of interpretation, they continue to hope that each building will speak for itself, without benefit of any program for communicating with the visiting public.

The diversity and fragmented nature of the preservation movement had both strengths and weaknesses. Present-day architectural historians argue that too many buildings have been opened as historic house museums that are not of sufficient importance historically or architecturally to warrant such recognition. These critics also point out that some structures that should have been saved have been permitted to fall into decay and ruin. No doubt the great number of untrained amateurs who supervised restorations made irreparable errors of judgment. Nevertheless, in the final balance, the scales tip heavily in favor of the early preservers simply because their basic accomplishment is still with us today— the large number of historic landmarks rescued for posterity. The pioneers of the preservation movement prepared the American people to accept the idea of spending money for the seemingly profitless activity of saving a few of the spots that contributed to the study of history or the enjoyment of beauty. If these people had not launched some of their patriotic crusades, the American public would be much poorer today. Individuals such as William Sumner Appleton and Ann Pamela Cunningham have made sure that a growing, strong America cannot completely ignore the physical remains of its early history.

Notes

INTRODUCTION

1. Two notable exceptions are: Laurence Vail Coleman, *Historic House Museums* (Washington: American Association of Museums, 1933), 187 pp.; and Walter Muir Whitehill, *Independent Historical Societies* (Boston: Boston Athenaeum, 1962), 593 pp.

2. Allan Nevins and Frank Ernest Hill, *Ford: Expansion and Challenge, 1915–1933* (New York: Charles Scribner's Sons, 1957), pp. 496–501; and Rutherfoord Goodwin, *A Brief and True Report Concerning Williamsburg in Virginia* (Richmond: Colonial Williamsburg, Inc., 1940), pp. 92–99.

3. Eugene Emmanuel Viollet-le-Duc, *On Restoration, and a Notice in Connection with Historical Monuments of France* (tr. by Benjamin Bucknall; London: Sampson, Low, Marston, Low, and Searle, 1875), p. 9.

4. Hans Huth, "The Evolution of Preservationism in Europe," *Journal of the American Society of Architectural Historians*, I (October, 1941), pp. 5–9.

5. John Ruskin, *The Seven Lamps of Architecture* (*Everyman's Library*; London: J. M. Dent and Sons, Ltd.; New York: E. P. Dutton and Company, 1907), p. 199.

6. William Morris, "Architecture and History," *7th Annual Meeting of the Society for the Protection of Ancient Buildings* (June, 1884), pp. 49–76.

7. Axel Nilson and Nils Keyland, *Guide to Skansen I, the Historical and Ethnological Department of Skansen* (tr. by Nils Keyland and Edward Adams Ray; 5th edition; Stockholm: Northern Museum, 1923), p. 5.

CHAPTER I

1. Benjamin H. Latrobe, extract from *Pocket Diary*, copied by Fiske Kimball, 1916, and quoted in Thomas Tileston Waterman and John A. Barrows, *Domestic Colonial Architecture of Tidewater Virginia* (New York: Charles Scribner's Sons, 1932), p. 13.

2. *Independent Chronicle* quoted by the Reverend Richard D. Pierce in the preface to *The Records of the First Church in Boston, 1630–1868; Publications of the Colonial Society of Massachusetts*, XXXIX, xlvii; also quoted in Whitehill, *Independent Historical Societies*, p. 550.

3. Minutes of the Select Council of the City of Philadelphia, March 11, 1813, typescript (Independence National Historical Park, Philadelphia).

4. Independence National Historical Park, *Historic Structures Report, Part II, on Independence Hall* (Philadelphia: Independence National Historical Park, April, 1962), pp. 83, 84.

5. *Ibid.*, pp. 81–83.

6. *Ibid.*, pp. 85, 86.

7. *Ibid.*, pp. 94–97.

8. *Ibid.*, pp. 98–103; and Robert G. Stewart, "Restorations at Independence Hall" (Unpublished thesis, University of Pennsylvania, Philadelphia, September, 1953), pp. 1–9.

9. Independence National Historical Park, *op. cit.*, pp. 104–108.

10. John H. G. Pell, "The Restoration of Fort Ticonderoga," Chapter Eleven of Stephen H. P. Pell, *Fort Ticonderoga, A Short History* (Ticonderoga, New York: Fort Ticonderoga Museum, 1961), pp. 93–100; and Alfred C. Bossom, "The Restoration of Fort Ticonderoga," *The Bulletin of the Fort Ticonderoga Museum*, X (No. 2, 1958), p. 125.

11. Morris A. Gutstein, *The Story of the Jews of Newport* (New York: Bloch Publishing Company, 1936), pp. 230–237, 292, 329, 330.

12. Esther I. Schwartz, "Touro Synagogue Restored, 1827–29," *Journal of the Society of Architectural Historians*, XVII (Summer, 1958), p. 25.

13. Gutstein, *op. cit.*, pp. 246–250.

14. See Chapter VIII for fuller treatment of the Monticello story.

15. Clarkson A. Collins, "History of the Rhode Island Historical Society" (Typewritten manuscript, 1952, in the vertical files of Rhode Island Historical Society, Providence), pp. 8, 9.

16. George D. Seymour, "How the Doors of the Rev. Mr. Russell's House in Branford in which the Founders of Yale Assembled 1701–2 Came into the Possession of the University," *Old-Time New England*, XVI (April, 1926), pp. 169–172.

17. J. M. Arms Sheldon, "The 'Old Indian House' at Deerfield, Mass., and the Effort Made in 1847 to Save It from Destruction," *Old-Time New England*, XII (January, 1922), p. 100.

18. *Ibid.*

19. *Ibid.*, pp. 100, 101, 103.

20. *Ibid.*, pp. 103, 106.

21. Letters from the Reverend R. Crawford to Dr. D. D. Slade, October 28, 1863; October 29, 1867; and January 15, 1868, furnished by Denison R. Slade, of Chestnut Hill, Massachusetts (Handwritten copies in drawer #28, Box on Indian House, Archives of Pocumtuck Valley Memorial Association, Memorial Hall, Deerfield, Massachusetts).

22. *History and Proceedings of the Pocumtuck Valley Memorial Association, 1870–1879*, I (1890), pp. 316, 317.

23. Amelia F. Miller, "The Indian House," *Deerfield Alumni Journal*, XVII (Autumn, 1960), pp. 3–12.

24. Robert Emmet Deyo, "The Unsuccessful Attempt of the Trustees of the Village of Newburgh to Make an Improvement Which Involved the Destruction of Washington's Headquarters," Historical Society of Newburgh Bay and the Highlands, *Publication XVII* (Newburgh, New York: The Society, 1916), pp. 17–22.

25. Chapter 181 of the Laws of 1839, found in *Laws of New York, 62nd Session, 1839*, pp. 155, 156, cited in A. Elwood Corning, *The Story of the Hasbrouck House, Washington's Headquarters, Newburgh, New York* (n.p., Board of Trustees, State of New York, of Washington's Headquarters, 1950), p. 55.

26. Richard Caldwell, *A True History of the Acquisition of Washington's*

Headquarters at Newburgh by the State of New York (Salisbury Mills, New York: Stivers, Slauson and Boyd, 1887), pp. 8, 9.

27. *Ibid.,* pp. 10, 11.

28. Quoted in *ibid.,* p. 19.

29. Quoted in *ibid.,* pp. 21, 23.

30. *Ibid.,* pp. 25, 38.

31. Dorothy C. Barck, "Washington's Newburgh Headquarters," *Journal of the Society of Architectural Historians,* XIV (May, 1955), pp. 30–32.

32. Benjamin Robert Winthrop, *The Washington Chair, Presented to the New York Historical Society* (New York: Charles B. Richardson, 1857), pp. 5–9.

33. U. S. Congress, Senate Committee on the Library, *Care and Preservation of the Hermitage,* Report 314, to accompany S. 4797, 60th Cong., 1st Sess., February 28, 1908 (Washington: Government Printing Office, 1908), p. 3.

34. Resolution of the Carpenters' Company, January 17, 1859, quoted in Charles E. Peterson, "Carpenters' Hall," *Historic Philadelphia* (Issued as Volume 43, Part 1, of *Transactions of the American Philosophical Society;* Philadelphia: The Society, 1953), p. 114.

35. "Final Report of the Committee on the Authenticity of the Tradition of the First Church—Built in 1634," *Essex Institute Historical Collections,* VII (1865), pp. 116–118.

36. Walter M. Merrill, *New England Treasury of American Beginnings* (New York: Newcomen Society in North America, 1957), p. 22.

37. *A Historical Sketch of Boston Containing a Brief Account of Its Settlement, Rise and Progress, with a Glance at Its Present Prospective and Prosperity* (Boston: Edward L. Mitchell, 1861), p. 43.

38. Wendell Phillips quoted in Massachusetts Legislature, Committee on Federal Relations, *Arguments in Behalf of Petitions for Aid in the Preservation of the Old South Meeting-House* (Boston: Alfred Mudge and Son, 1878), p. 35.

39. "Governor Hancock's House," *Gleason's Weekly Line-of-Battleship* (Boston), I (March 12, 1859), p. 1.

40. Boston, Joint Special Committee on Hancock House, *Report to Board of Aldermen, City of Boston, June 3, 1863, of Joint Special Committee to Consider the Expediency of Any Measure for the Preservation of the Hancock House, in Beacon Street* (City Document No. 56; Boston: City of Boston, 1863), p. 9; and Thomas C. Amory, address, January 9, 1883, in *Proceedings of the Bostonian Society, 1883,* pp. 15–17.

41. Walter Kendall Watkins, "The Hancock House and Its Builder," *Old-Time New England,* XVII (July, 1926), p. 12.

42. Joseph Everett Chandler, *The Colonial House* (New York: Robert M. McBride and Company, 1924), p. 110.

CHAPTER II

1. Ruth Miller Elson, "American Schoolbooks and 'Culture' in the Nineteenth Century," *Mississippi Valley Historical Review,* XLVI (December, 1959), p. 418.

2. Bushrod Washington, a printed notice, signed and dated July 4, 1822 (Archives of the Mount Vernon Ladies' Association of the Union, Mount Vernon, Virginia; hereafter referred to as M.V.L.A. Archives).

3. *Documents Relating to the Proposed Purchase of Mount Vernon by the*

Citizens of the United States, in Order that They May at All Times Have a Legal and Indisputable Right to Visit the Grounds, Mansion and Tomb of Washington (Washington: T. Barnard, 1846, M.V.L.A. Archives).

4. Typewritten scrapbook in regard to the Centennial of the M.V.L.A. (M.V.L.A. Archives).

5. Letter from Lieutenant Colonel H. L. Scott to John Washington, March 18, 1851, in the Centennial Files (M.V.L.A. Archives).

6. Letter from John A. Washington to Lt. Col. H. L. Scott, March 25, 1851, in the Centennial Files (M.V.L.A. Archives).

7. Letter from Lt. Col. H. L. Scott to John Washington, March 28, 1851, in the Centennial Files (M.V.L.A. Archives).

8. Letter from John Washington to Louis McKenzie, February 2, 1858, in Early Records (hereafter referred to as ER), IX, p. 39 (M.V.L.A. Archives).

9. *Gleason's Pictorial* (Boston), V (October 29, 1853), p. 1.

10. Message of Governor Joseph Johnson, December 5, 1853, quoted in [James B. Sener], *The Report of the Virginia Board of Visitors to Mount Vernon for the Year 1901* (Richmond: J. H. O'Bannon, 1901), pp. 20, 21.

11. Report of the Committee of the House of Delegates, dated March 3, 1854, quoted in [Sener], *op. cit.,* pp. 21, 22.

12. Message of Governor Johnson, December 3, 1855, quoted in [Sener], *op. cit.,* pp. 24, 25.

13. [Sener], *op. cit.,* p. 25.

14. *Ibid.,* pp. 26, 27.

15. Ann Pamela Cunningham, "To the Ladies of the South," *Charleston Mercury,* December 2, 1853, ER I, p. 1 (M.V.L.A. Archives).

16. Diary of Benjamin F. Perry, quoted in Marion R. Wilkes, *Rosemont and Its Famous Daughter* (Washington: The Author, 1947), pp. 5, 17.

17. Letter from Mrs. George W. Campbell to Mrs. S. E. Johnson Hudson, September, 1897 (?), ER IV, pp. 6–11 (M.V.L.A. Archives). Our main source for the story of the birth of the Mount Vernon movement is this letter written nearly forty-five years after the events took place; but it will have to do, for the author appears to have been an eyewitness, and her account does not conflict with the writings of Ann Pamela Cunningham. Mrs. Lily Laughton, Miss Cunningham's successor, remembered Miss Cunningham as saying that she was with her mother on the boat passing Mount Vernon. "Report of the M.V.L.A., 1889," *Reports of the Mount Vernon Ladies' Association of the Union, 1858–1895* (Baltimore: Friedenwald Company, 1896), p. 7 (of that report).

18. Ann Pamela Cunningham, *A Letter from the Founder and First Regent of the Mount Vernon Association,* dated May 28, 1866, from Rosemont to Miss Tracy at Mount Vernon (n.p., n.n., n.d.), pp. 1, 2.

19. Letter from Ann Pamela Cunningham to Eleanor L. Washington, December 19, 1853, ER I, p. 3 (M.V.L.A. Archives).

20. Letter from Eleanor Washington to Ann Pamela Cunningham, June 10, 1854, ER IX, p. 3 (M.V.L.A. Archives).

21. Ann Pamela Cunningham, "To the Ladies of the South," *Washington Union,* April 20, 1854, ER I, p. 2 (M.V.L.A. Archives).

22. Cunningham, *Letter from the Founder,* pp. 2, 3.

23. *Ibid.,* p. 4.

24. Mount Vernon Ladies' Association of the Union, *Catalog of the Centennial Exhibition Commemorating the Founding of the Mount Vernon La-*

dies' Association of the Union, 1853–1953 (Mount Vernon, Virginia: The Association, 1953), pp. 49, 50.

25. Letter from Edward Everett to the Virginia Mount Vernon State Committee, December 12, 1855, ER IX, p. 91; and Edward Everett, "The Character of Washington" (Copy of manuscript in the Massachusetts Historical Society, Boston, speech given before the Massachusetts Historical Society, June 17, 1858, M.V.L.A. Archives).

26. Edward Everett, *Journal,* quoted in Paul Revere Frothingham, *Edward Everett, Orator and Statesman* (Boston: Houghton Mifflin Company, 1925), p. 377.

27. Mrs. Roger A. Pryor, "The Mount Vernon Association," *American Historical Register,* I (January, 1895), pp. 418–420.

28. Letter from Henry S. Randall to Mary M. Hamilton, January 1, 1859, ER XII, p. 217 (M.V.L.A. Archives).

29. Edward Everett, *Oration on the Character of Washington* (Boston: Little, Brown and Company, 1913), pp. 23–25.

30. "South Carolina and Mr. Everett," *Philadelphia Press,* October 30, 1858, quoted in *Mount Vernon Record* (Philadelphia), I (November, 1858), p. 44.

31. Frothingham, *op. cit.,* p. 379.

32. Letter from Edward Everett to Ann Pamela Cunningham, May 30, 1861, quoted in Frothingham, *op. cit.,* pp. 421, 422.

33. Cunningham, *Letter from the Founder,* pp. 6, 7.

34. Letter from Edward Everett to Ann Pamela Cunningham, July 18, 1856, ER IX, p. 109 (M.V.L.A. Archives).

35. Letter from John Washington to Ann Pamela Cunningham, March 13, 1858, ER IX, p. 47 (M.V.L.A. Archives).

36. Letter from Ann Pamela Cunningham to Lily Berghmans, November 22, 1873, ER II, p. 273 (M.V.L.A. Archives).

37. *Mount Vernon Record,* I (August, 1858), p. 15.

38. *Ibid.,* Extra Issue (February, 1859), p. 89.

39. *Ibid.,* I (March, 1859), p. 96.

40. *Ibid.,* (September, 1858), p. 21.

41. *Ibid.,* II, Extra Issue (November, 1859), p. 97.

42. "The Mount Vernon Matinee at Niblo's," *Home Journal,* November 27, 1858, quoted in *Mount Vernon Record,* I (December, 1858), p. 54.

43. *Mount Vernon Record,* II, Special Issue (November, 1859), p. 98.

44. *Ibid.,* II, Extra Issue (December, 1859), p. 1.

45. *Gleason's Weekly Line-of-Battleship,* I (March 12, 1859), p. 1.

46. "Unbalanced Patriotism," *Saturday Evening Post,* January 1, 1859.

47. "Mount Vernon," *Gleason's Weekly,* I (November 5, 1859), p. 1.

48. Letter from Ann Pamela Cunningham to George Riggs, May 27, 1859, ER I, pp. 129–133 (M.V.L.A. Archives).

49. Dorothy Troth Muir, *Presence of a Lady, Mount Vernon, 1861–1868* (Washington: Mount Vernon Publishing Company, 1946), p. 9.

50. Camille Ferri Pisani, "The Tour of Prince Napoleon," *American Heritage,* VIII (August, 1957), pp. 73–75.

51. Letter from Edward Everett to Mary Hamilton, February 13, 1864, ER IX, p. 301; and manuscript by Margaret A. Comegys on the Council of 1864, ER XIV, p. 13 (M.V.L.A. Archives).

52. "Report of the M.V.L.A., 1882," *Reports of the M.V.L.A.*, p. 5 (of that report).

53. "Report of the M.V.L.A., 1888," *Reports of the M.V.L.A.*, p. 4 (of that report).

54. "Proceedings of the Council of the M.V.L.A., November 19, 1866," *Reports of the M.V.L.A.*, pp. 3, 4 (of that report).

55. "Report of the M.V.L.A., 1867," *Reports of the M.V.L.A.*, p. 4 (of that report).

56. Letter from Ann Pamela Cunningham to Mrs. Abby Chace, July 15, 1868, ER II, p. 19 (M.V.L.A. Archives); and M.V.L.A., *Historical Sketch of Ann Pamela Cunningham, "A Southern Matron," Founder of the "Mount Vernon Ladies' Association"* (Jamaica, New York: Marion Press, 1903), pp. 39–45. The text of the letter to Mrs. Chace has been altered by the omission of some rather pointed remarks that can be found in the original letter.

57. Letter from Ann Pamela Cunningham to Abby Chace, July 15, 1868, ER II, p. 239 (M.V.L.A. Archives).

58. Ann Pamela Cunningham, "Farewell Address," in "Minutes of the Council of the M.V.L.A., June 2, 1874," *Reports of the M.V.L.A.*, pp. 6, 7 (of that report).

59. Letter from William Sumner Appleton to *Boston Herald*, May 13, 1918 (Society for the Preservation of New England Antiquities Files, Boston; hereafter referred to as S.P.N.E.A. Files).

60. Lily Berghmans, "Regent's Report," in "Report of the M.V.L.A., 1875," *Reports of the M.V.L.A.*, p. 5 (of that report).

61. Letter from Mrs. Nathaniel Halstead to Colonel James Hollingsworth, January 7, 1876, ER VII, p. 72 (M.V.L.A. Archives).

62. Letter from Mrs. Nathaniel Halstead to Isaac Hinckley, January 7, 1876, ER VI, p. 111 (M.V.L.A. Archives).

63. "Report of the M.V.L.A., 1888," *Reports of the M.V.L.A.*, p. 5 (of that report).

64. Jenny M. Ward, *ibid.*, p. 18.

65. "Report of the M.V.L.A., 1889," *Reports of the M.V.L.A.*, pp. 30, 31 (of that report).

66. "Report of the M.V.L.A., 1892," *Reports of the M.V.L.A.*, p. 14 (of that report).

67. "Report of the M.V.L.A., 1895," *Reports of the M.V.L.A.*, p. 4 (of that report).

68. "Report of the M.V.L.A., 1881," *Reports of the M.V.L.A.*, pp. 6, 7 (of that report).

69. Letter from Abby Chace to Sarah C. Tracy, November 1, 1865, ER XIII, p. 6 (M.V.L.A. Archives).

70. Letter from Mrs. Nathaniel Halstead to Abby Chace, June 25, 1878, ER VII, p. 137 (M.V.L.A. Archives).

71. "Neglected Mount Vernon," *Boston Herald*, November (?), 1883, clipping with comments by Mrs. Lorenzo Sweat, ER XIX, p. 177 (M.V.L.A. Archives).

72. Letter from F. A. Richardson to Mrs. Lorenzo Sweat, June 29, 1886, ER XIX, p. 179 (M.V.L.A. Archives).

73. Letter from William Sumner Appleton to *Boston Herald*, May 13, 1918 (S.P.N.E.A. Files).

74. American Scenic and Historic Preservation Society (hereafter referred to as American Scenic), *27th Annual Report, 1922*, p. 155.

75. Letter from Mrs. William H. Holstein to Mrs. Lorenzo Sweat, May 20, 1878, ER XX, p. 107 (M.V.L.A. Archives).

76. Letter from Mrs. Lorenzo Sweat to Mrs. William Holstein, June 1, 1878, ER XX, p. 108 (M.V.L.A. Archives).

77. Letter from Mrs. William Holstein to Mrs. Lorenzo Sweat, June 8, 1878, ER XX, p. 109 (M.V.L.A. Archives).

78. Letter from David G. Haskins to Mrs. Lorenzo Sweat, July 3, 1878, ER XX, p. 111 (M.V.L.A. Archives).

79. Letter from Mrs. William Holstein to Mrs. Lorenzo Sweat, June 8, 1878, ER XX, p. 109 (M.V.L.A. Archives).

80. Letter from Amy Jackson to Mrs. J. V. R. Townsend, December 8, 1888, Authentication File W-159 (M.V.L.A. Archives).

81. Letter from Philoclea E. Eve to Colonel Andrew Jackson, January 5, 1889, quoted in Mary C. Dorris, *Preservation of the Hermitage, 1889–1915* (Nashville, Tennessee: Ladies' Hermitage Association, 1915), p. 26.

82. Dorris, *op. cit.*, p. 29.

83. *Ibid.*, p. 59.

84. *Ibid.*, pp. 62, 63.

85. *Ibid.*, p. 105.

86. Mary Beecher Longyear, "Diary, March 31, 1920 to June 14, 1921," May 22, 1921 (Files of the Longyear Foundation, Brookline, Massachusetts).

87. Longyear Foundation, *Longyear Foundation, Created Under an Assignment and Declaration of Trust, Dated 5th April, 1926,* Printed copy in Files of the Longyear Foundation, p. 4.

88. *American Monthly Magazine,* XV (July, 1899), p. 43.

89. Richard Lloyd Jones, "The Lincoln Birthplace Farm," *Collier's,* XXXVI (February 10, 1906), p. 13.

90. Richard Lloyd Jones, "The Lincoln Farm Association," *Collier's,* XXXVIII (February 9, 1907) p. 13.

91. Mrs. Martin W. Littleton, quoted in U. S. Congress, House Committee on Rules, *Public Ownership of Monticello,* Hearings, 62nd Cong., 2nd Sess., on S. Con. Res. 24, July 24, 1912 (Washington: Government Printing Office, 1912), p. 6.

92. Mrs. Letitia E. Wright, "The Colonial Garden at Stenton Described in Old Letters," address on January 16, 1914, quoted in Site and Relic Society of Germantown, *Germantown History,* II, 1, p. 19.

93. Mrs. Frank W. Curtis, "Frances Vigo Chapter, Vincennes, Indiana," *D.A.R. Magazine,* L (April, 1917), p. 254.

94. *Christian Science Monitor* (Boston), July 8, 1922.

95. Susan H. Walker, "George Mason of Gunston Hall," *D.A.R. Magazine,* LI (November, 1917), p. 259.

96. Mrs. John Henry Hammond, "We Must Build Roosevelt House," *Woman's Roosevelt Memorial Bulletin,* I (April, 1920), p. 1.

97. Mrs. Roger A. Pryor, "The Mount Vernon Association," *American Historical Register,* I (January, 1895), p. 410.

98. Anne H. Wharton, National Society of Colonial Dames of America, *Historian's Address, April 25, 1900,* p. 25.

99. Bessie S. Childs, "Columbia Chapter, Columbia, South Carolina," *American Monthly Magazine,* XXXIII (October, 1908), pp. 939, 940.

CHAPTER III

1. Murray Nelligan, "Old Arlington, the Story of the Lee Mansion National Memorial" (Unpublished Doctor of Philosophy dissertation, Columbia University, New York, 1954), pp. 464, 465 (cites the Heintzelman Diary for May 26, 1861).
2. *Ibid.,* p. 486.
3. *Ibid.,* pp. 487, 488.
4. *New York Tribune,* January 12, 1864, and *National Republican,* January 12, 1864, quoted in Nelligan, *op. cit.,* p. 489.
5. Nelligan, *op. cit.,* p. 490.
6. *New York Times,* February 19, 1872, cited in Nelligan, *op. cit.,* p. 497.
7. Enoch Aquila Chase, "The Arlington Case," *Virginia Law Review,* XV (January, 1929), pp. 211–214.
8. *Ibid.,* pp. 214, 215, 222–232.
9. *Ibid.,* p. 233.
10. "Plan to Restore Home of General Lee," *Washington Post,* August 7, 1921.
11. Nelligan, *op. cit.,* p. 504.
12. Charles E. Hatch, Jr., "The Moore House: A National Shrine," *William and Mary College Quarterly Historical Magazine,* XXI, Second Series (October, 1941), pp. 293–317.
13. Mrs. J. Enders Robinson, "Origin of the A.P.V.A.," *1900 Yearbook of the Association for the Preservation of Virginia Antiquities,* pp. 4, 5; and letter from Miss Mary J. Galt, quoted in *1911 Yearbook of the A.P.V.A.,* p. 46.
14. Mrs. J. Taylor Ellyson, "Report of First Vice President and Acting President," *1904 Yearbook of the A.P.V.A.,* pp. 10, 11.
15. Mrs. Vivian Minor Fleming, quoted in Lily Lykes Shepard, "Fredericksburg Landmark Restored," *D.A.R. Magazine,* LXV (May, 1931), p. 278.
16. *1896 Yearbook of the A.P.V.A.,* pp. 59, 60.
17. *1900 Yearbook of the A.P.V.A.,* p. 53.
18. *1905/8 Yearbook of the A.P.V.A.,* pp. 49, 50.
19. Mary Newton Stanard, *John Marshall and His Home* (Richmond, Virginia: William Ellis and Sons, Inc., 1913), pp. 34, 35; and *1911 Yearbook of the A.P.V.A.,* pp. 38, 39.
20. *1911 Yearbook of the A.P.V.A.,* pp. 40, 41.
21. *1923 Yearbook of the A.P.V.A.,* p. 10; and *1926/7 Yearbook of the A.P.V.A.,* p. 16.
22. *1911 Yearbook of the A.P.V.A.,* pp. 11, 12.
23. *1925 Yearbook of the A.P.V.A.,* pp. 11, 12.
24. Mary Newton, "The Association for the Preservation of Virginia Antiquities," *American Historical Register,* I (September, 1894), pp. 19, 20.
25. *1900 Yearbook of the A.P.V.A.,* pp. 4, 5.
26. *1923 Yearbook of the A.P.V.A.,* pp. 33, 34.
27. *Ibid.,* p. 13.
28. Letter from William Sumner Appleton to Florence M. Levy, March 1, 1923 (S.P.N.E.A. Files).
29. Confederate Memorial Literary Society, *In Memoriam Sempiternam* (Richmond, Virginia: The Society, 1896), pp. 13–22.
30. The Reverend William Archer Rutherfoord Goodwin, *Historical Sketch*

of *Bruton Church* (Petersburg, Virginia: Franklin Press, 1903), pp. 63–65; and the Reverend W. A. R. Goodwin, *The Record of Bruton Parish Church,* (Edited, with revisions and additions, by Mary Frances Goodwin; Richmond, Virginia: Dietz Press, 1941), pp. 52–70.

31. Dorris, *Preservation of the Hermitage,* p. 13.
32. *Ibid.,* pp. 28–30.
33. *Ibid.,* p. 32.
34. *Ibid.,* pp. 34–36.
35. Mary C. Dorris, in *Nashville American,* February 16, 1889, quoted in *ibid.,* pp. 42, 43.
36. Dorris, *Preservation of the Hermitage,* pp. 44–47.
37. *Ibid.,* pp. 50, 51, 57.
38. *Ibid.,* pp. 52–54.
39. *Ibid.,* pp. 63, 64.
40. *Ibid.,* pp. 76, 77.
41. *Ibid.,* pp. 65–67.
42. *Ibid.,* pp. 78, 79.
43. *Ibid.,* pp. 83, 100.
44. U. S. Congress, Senate Library Committee, *Care and Preservation of the Hermitage,* February 28, 1908, p. 5.
45. Dorris, *op. cit.,* pp. 81, 88, 102.
46. *Ibid.,* p. 92.
47. U. S. Congress, Senate Library Committee, *op. cit.,* pp. 1–3.
48. U. S. Congress, Senate, *The Hermitage,* debate on S. 4797, March 2, 1908, in *Congressional Record,* 60th Cong., 1st Sess., p. 2744.
49. Letters from Osborn H. Oldroyd to Archie L. Bowen, February 9, 1925, and April 15, 1925, quoted in Archie L. Bowen, "A. Lincoln: His House," *Lincoln Centennial Association Papers* (Springfield, Illinois: The Association, 1925), pp. 50–55.
50. Archie L. Bowen, *op. cit.,* 17–73, 103–125; William Burton Benham, *Life of Osborn H. Oldroyd* (Washington: Beresford Press, 1927), pp. 11, 12; and Frank Darneille, *History of the Lincoln Homestead* (Springfield, Illinois: The Author, 1938), pp. 19, 20.
51. Marcus Benjamin (Editor), *Washington during War Time, a Series of Papers Showing the Military Phases during 1861 to 1865; Official Souvenir of the Thirty-Sixth Annual Encampment of the Grand Army of the Republic* (Washington: Byron Adams, 1902), p. 93.
52. U. S. Congress, House Committee on Appropriations, *House in Which Lincoln Died,* Hearing before Subcommittee, 54th Cong., 1st Sess., on H. R. 7664, March 21, 1896 (Washington: Government Printing Office, 1896), p. 255.
53. *Ibid.*
54. *New York Times,* April 26, 1896, p. 28; and Bowen, *op. cit.,* pp. 51–55.
55. U. S. Congress, House Committee on Appropriations, *op. cit.,* p. 258.
56. *New York Times,* April 2, 1896, p. 4.
57. U. S. Congress, House Committee on Appropriations, *op. cit.,* p. 256.
58. Memorial Association of the District of Columbia, *Words from Many Sources Commendatory of Its Work; and Especially of the Plan to Purchase the House in Which President Lincoln Died* (Washington: The Association, ca. 1893), 63 pp.
59. F. F. Wilshin, "The Shirley House" (Typewritten manuscript, October

28, 1939, in General Files, Branch of History, National Park Service, Washington), pp. 30, 73.

CHAPTER IV

1. George B. Tatum, "The Origins of Fairmount Park," *Antiques*, LXXXII (November, 1962), pp. 502–505.

2. *Ibid.*, p. 505; and *Sketch of Fairmount, Lemon Hill, and the Adjoining Grounds, as a Public Park* (Philadelphia: n.n., 1855), p. 28; and Commissioners of Fairmount Park, *First Annual Report of the Commissioners of Fairmount Park* (Philadelphia: The Commissioners, 1869), p. 8.

3. M. Russell Thayer, *The Real Founder of Fairmount Park, a Unilateral Correspondence* (Philadelphia: Dunlap Printing Company, 1903), pp. 4, 5; and Tatum, *op. cit.*, p. 507.

4. Letter from John Cresson, December 11, 1869, quoted in *Second Annual Report of the Commissioners of Fairmount Park* (1870), p. 35.

5. John Cresson, quoted in *Third Annual Report of the Commissioners of Fairmount Park* (1871), pp. 43, 44, 51.

6. Sarah Dickson Lowrie, *Strawberry Mansion, First Known as Somerton, the House of Many Masters* (New York: Committee of 1926 of Pennsylvania, 1941), pp. 196–200.

7. Charles Shearer Keyser, *Fairmount Park, Sketches of Its Scenery, Waters, and History* (Philadelphia: Claxton, Remsen, and Haffelfinger, 1871), p. 65.

8. Pennsylvania, Joint State Government Commission, *Catalog of Historical Buildings, Sites and Remains in Pennsylvania*, report to the General Assembly of the Commonwealth of Pennsylvania (Philadelphia: State of Pennsylvania, 1949), p. 46; and Associate Committee of Women of the Pennsylvania Museum of Art, *The Chain of Colonial Houses* (Philadelphia: The Committee, 1932), p. 3.

9. "The Sale of the Ford Estate," *True Democratic Banner* (Morristown, New Jersey), June 5, 1873 (Files of the Morristown National Historical Park, Morristown, New Jersey).

10. "Sale," *True Democratic Banner*, June 5, 1873 (Morristown National Historical Park).

11. Undated (probably June 28, 1873), untitled clipping (Morristown National Historical Park).

12. Theodore Randolph, quoted in Edmund D. Halsey, *History of the Washington Association of New Jersey* (Morristown, New Jersey: The Author, 1891), p. 11.

13. Halsey, *op. cit.*, pp. 21–24.

14. *Ibid.*, pp. 11, 12; and Washington Association of New Jersey, "Trustees Book," I, p. 36, MSS (Morristown National Historical Park).

15. Washington Association of New Jersey, *op. cit.*, pp. 7, 19.

16. *Ibid.*, p. 19.

17. Text of H. Res. 197, 48th Cong., 1st Sess., March 10, 1884, in Washington Association of New Jersey, *op. cit.*, p. 105.

18. Halsey, *op. cit.*, pp. 13, 15.

19. R. S. Peabody, *Proceedings of the 11 Convention, American Institute of Architects, 1877*, p. 17.

20. Mrs. James B. Clark, Address, *American Monthly Magazine*, VII (December, 1895), p. 521; and Mrs. Effie Hallock, "The Interest in Our Colonial

and Revolutionary Past," *American Monthly Magazine,* XIII (August, 1898), pp. 126, 127.

21. Letter from Colonel Frank M. Etting to John L. Shoemaker, April 29, 1871, in a newspaper clipping in a scrapbook dealing with the 1876 restoration of Independence Hall (Independence National Historical Park, Philadelphia).

22. Frank M. Etting, *Memorials of 1776* (Originally written for *Penn Monthly;* Philadelphia: W. W. Bates, 1873), pp. 3, 12.

23. Philadelphia, Committee on the Restoration of Independence Hall, *First Report* (1873), pp. 2–7; *Third Report* (1875), p. 18.

24. *Proceedings on the Occasion of the Centennial Celebration of the Occupation of Valley Forge by the Continental Army under George Washington, June 19, 1878, and also Dedication of Headquarters, June 19, 1879* (Philadelphia: J. B. Lippincott, 1879), pp. 3, 4.

25. Henry Armitt Brown, oration, quoted in *ibid.,* pp. 82–93.

26. Letter from Mrs. William Holstein to Mrs. Lorenzo Sweat, June 8, 1878, ER XX, p. 109 (M.V.L.A. Archives).

27. *Proceedings on the Occasion,* p. 96.

28. J. Smith Futhey, quoted in *ibid.,* p. 102.

29. Ex-Governor James Pollock, quoted in *Proceedings on the Occasion,* p. 114.

30. "Washington's Headquarters during the Revolution," *Magazine of American History,* III (February, 1879), pp. 157–160.

31. Thomas Donaldson, *The House in which Thomas Jefferson Wrote the Declaration of Independence* (Philadelphia: The Author, 1898), pp. 74, 78.

32. *Ibid.,* p. 77.

33. *Ibid.,* pp. 78, 79.

34. *Ibid.,* pp. 79–81.

35. *Ibid.,* p. 81.

36. *Ibid.,* pp. 1–119.

37. *Ibid.,* pp. 91–93.

38. Richard Tyler, Status finder report, September 2, 1960, typed card (Independence National Historical Park).

39. Alfred S. Eisenhower, "Annual Report of the Bureau of City Property," *Fourth Annual Report of Edwin S. Stuart, Mayor of Philadelphia,* pp. 336–337 in Independence National Historical Park, Design and Construction Division, "Documents Relating to the Physical History of Independence Hall, Period, 1891–1899," Typewritten collection of MSS, 1953 (Independence National Historical Park).

40. Letter from the Colonial Dames to Mayor Edwin S. Stuart, June 14, 1894, Typed copy of Select Council Journal, 1894, I, p. 165 (Independence National Historical Park).

41. "Custody of Independence Hall" (Editorial), Philadelphia *Inquirer,* October 5, 1894, in Philadelphia, Bureau of City Property, Scrapbook Number 2, containing newspaper clippings dealing with the work of the Bureau (Independence National Historical Park).

42. "Within Historic Halls," Philadelphia *Public Ledger,* March 5, 1896, Typed copy; *New York Times,* March 9, 1896, in Independence National Historical Park, "Documents Relating"; and "Pennsylvania Society of the Colonial Dames of America," Letter, June 7, 1898, Typed copy (Independence National Historical Park).

43. Broadside copy of a proposed ordinance, ca. 1895, in Independence National Historical Park, "Documents Relating" (Independence National Historical Park).

44. Letter from Anne Law Hubbell to Mrs. Charles C. Harrison, March, 1896, in Harrison Collection (American Philosophical Society, Philadelphia), also a typed copy in Independence National Historical Park, "Documents Relating"; "Revolutionary Sons Beat a Retreat," Philadelphia *Bulletin,* March 17, 1896, in Philadelphia, Bureau of City Property, Scrapbook Number 2 (Independence National Historical Park).

45. "The Daughters Will Do It," Philadelphia *Bulletin,* March 19, 1896, in Independence National Historical Park, "Documents Relating"; and letter from T. Mellon Rogers to Mrs. Charles Harrison, December 10, 1896, in Independence National Historical Park, "Documents Relating" (Independence National Historical Park).

46. Unidentified clipping, ca. 1897, in Harrison Collection; and letter from Frank M. Riter to Mrs. Charles C. Harrison, June or July, 1898, in Harrison Collection (American Philosophical Society, Philadelphia).

47. "State House Restored," Philadelphia *Ledger,* February 20, 1897, in Philadelphia, Bureau of City Property, Scrapbook Number 2 (Independence National Historical Park).

48. "A Revelation," Unidentified clipping, ca. 1897, in Independence National Historical Park, "Documents Relating" (Independence National Historical Park).

49. Letter from T. Mellon Rogers to Mrs. Charles C. Harrison, December 10, 1896, in Independence National Historical Park, "Documents Relating" (Independence National Historical Park).

50. "Resolution," *Ordinances and City Solicitor Opinions, 1897,* p. 89, in Independence National Historical Park, "Documents Relating" (Independence National Historical Park).

51. Independence National Historical Park, *Historic Structures Report, Part II, on Independence Hall,* pp. 116–130.

52. Robert G. Stewart, "Restoration of Independence Hall under the Committee for the Preservation of Historic Monuments of the American Institute of Architects," Typewritten manuscript, Philadelphia, March 12, 1954 (in the possession of Robert Stewart, Washington, D. C.), p. 12.

53. T. Mellon Rogers, "Diary, 1898," March 9, 1898 (Museum collection of Independence National Historical Park).

54. Letter from T. Mellon Rogers to Frank M. Riter, July 20, 1898, inserted in Rogers, *op. cit.*

55. "Colonial Patterns not of the Period," Philadelphia *North American,* March 4, 1899, in Philadelphia, Bureau of City Property, Scrapbook Number 3 (Independence National Historical Park).

56. "Some Feminine Ideas of State House," Philadelphia *North American,* March 8, 1899, in Philadelphia, Bureau of City Property, Scrapbook Number 3 (Independence National Historical Park).

57. Wallace Evan Davies, *Patriotism on Parade, the Story of Veteran's and Hereditary Organizations in America, 1783–1900* (LXVI of *Harvard Historical Studies;* Cambridge, Massachusetts: Harvard University Press, 1955), pp. 216, 218.

58. Milo M. Quaife, Melvin J. Weig, and Roy E. Appleman, *The History of the United States Flag* (New York: Harper and Brothers, 1961), pp. 94, 97.

59. *Philadelphia Press,* September 11, 1887, quoted in Oliver Parry, *Betsy Ross and the United States Flag,* paper read before the Bucks County Historical Society, at Doylestown, Pennsylvania, January 19, 1909 (n.p., n.n., n.d.), pp. 3, 4.

60. Letter from Charles M. Smith to Oliver Parry, January 11, 1909, quoted in Parry, *op. cit.,* pp. 33, 34.

61. Letter from Charles H. Weisgerber to Edward Brooks, July 3, 1908, in American Flag House and Betsy Ross Memorial Association, File box of letters and papers (Betsy Ross House, Philadelphia).

62. Printed card from Edward Brooks to Philadelphia school principals, May 22, 1895, in File box (Betsy Ross House).

63. Letter from John Quincy Adams to Charles Mund, November 8, 1897, in File box (Betsy Ross House).

64. Addie Guthrie Weaver, *The Story of Our Flag, Colonial and National, with Historical Sketch of the Quakeress Betsy Ross* (Chicago: The Author, 1898), pp. 93, 94.

65. *Ibid.,* p. 94.

66. Letter from Charles H. Weisgerber to Edward Brooks, June 16, 1900, in File box (Betsy Ross House); New York *Tribune,* June 27, 1900, p. 4.

67. *American Monthly Magazine,* XV (August, 1899), p. 206.

68. Letter from John Quincy Adams and Edward Brooks to superintendents, principals and public schools in Indiana, November 21, 1902, in File box (Betsy Ross House).

69. American Flag House and Betsy Ross Memorial Association, *Fifth Annual Report* (1903), File box (Betsy Ross House).

70. New York *Tribune,* June 27, 1900, p. 4; and Theodore D. Gottlieb, *The Origin and Evolution of the Betsy Ross Flag Legend or Tradition* (Newark, New Jersey: The Author, 1938), 8 pp.

71. Washington *Post,* December 15, 1907; and letter from Charles H. Weisgerber to Edward Brooks, July 3, 1908, in File box (Betsy Ross House).

72. Washington *Post,* December 15, 1907; and Philadelphia *Public Ledger,* November 30, 1913, Section 10.

73. Letter from Charles H. Weisgerber to Edward Brooks, October 21, 1910, in File box (Betsy Ross House).

74. Letter from Charles H. Weisgerber to Edward Brooks, July 3, 1908, in File box (Betsy Ross House).

75. Parry, *op. cit.,* pp. 4–33; and Sidney Frank Krauss and Frank H. Mancill, *Philadelphia Forum Magazine,* date unknown (M.V.L.A. Archives).

76. Pennsylvania, Joint State Government Commission, *Catalog,* p. 44.

77. Mrs. Stephen Pell, "The Pavilion and the King's Garden," *The Bulletin of the Fort Ticonderoga Museum,* X (No. 2, 1958), pp. 116, 117.

78. John H. G. Pell, "The Restoration of Fort Ticonderoga," Chapter Eleven of Stephen H. P. Pell, *Fort Ticonderoga, a Short History,* pp. 97, 99.

79. Mrs. Stephen Pell, *op. cit.,* p. 117.

80. Newspaper clippings, 1908 and 1909, dealing with the proposed restoration of Fort Ticonderoga, quoted in *The Bulletin of the Fort Ticonderoga Museum,* X (No. 2, 1958), pp. 100–103.

81. Mrs. Stephen Pell, *op. cit.,* pp. 117, 118.

82. Alfred C. Bossom, "The Restoration of Fort Ticonderoga," *The Bul-*

letin of the Fort Ticonderoga Museum, X (No. 2, 1958), pp. 127–131; John H. G. Pell, *op. cit.,* pp. 100, 101.

83. "Champlain, Ethan Allen and Taft to Shake Hands," New York *Herald,* June 27, 1909, Photostat printed in *The Bulletin of the Fort Ticonderoga Museum,* X (No. 2, 1958), pp. 132, 133.

84. *Ibid.*

85. John H. G. Pell, *op. cit.,* p. 108.

86. *Ibid.,* pp. 108–111.

87. Edward H. Hall, "The Inspiration of Our Founder," *Scenic and Historic America,* II (December, 1930), p. 18; and American Scenic, *18th Annual Report, 1913,* p. 29.

88. Trustees of Scenic and Historic Places and Objects, *Memorial to the Legislature of the State of New York,* January, 1895, and *Act of Incorporation and By-Laws,* March 26, 1895 (n.p., n.n., n.d.), pp. 4–6.

89. *Ibid.,* pp. 8, 9.

90. American Scenic, *12th Annual Report, 1907,* p. 21.

91. C. R. Ashbee, *A Report by Mr. C. R. Ashbee to the Council of the National Trust for Places of Historic Interest and Natural Beauty, on His Visit to the United States on the Council's Behalf, October, MDCCCC, to February, MDCCCCI* (London: Essex House Press, 1901), p. 13.

92. American Scenic, *9th Annual Report, 1904,* p. 189.

93. "Dr. Edward Hagaman Hall," *Scenic and Historic America,* IV (January, 1937), pp. 22–24.

94. American Scenic, *7th Annual Report, 1902,* p. 16.

95. *Ibid.,* p. 18.

96. American Scenic, *13th Annual Report, 1908,* pp. 168, 169.

97. American Scenic, *9th Annual Report, 1904,* p. 214.

98. American Scenic, *12th Annual Report, 1907,* pp. 21–28; and American Scenic, *26th Annual Report, 1921,* p. 141.

99. American Scenic, *16th Annual Report, 1911,* p. 555.

100. American Scenic, *6th Annual Report, 1901,* p. 43.

101. American Scenic, *10th Annual Report, 1905,* p. 109.

102. American Scenic, *18th Annual Report, 1913,* p. 33.

103. American Scenic, *26th Annual Report, 1921,* p. 140.

104. American Scenic, *29th Annual Report, 1924,* p. 9.

105. American Scenic, *5th Annual Report, 1900,* p. 19. This structure is not to be confused with Philipse Castle or Philipsburg Manor in Tarrytown, New York.

106. *Ibid.,* pp. 19, 21.

107. American Scenic, *6th Annual Report, 1901,* pp. 28, 29.

108. American Scenic, *13th Annual Report, 1908,* pp. 38, 39.

109. *Ibid.,* pp. 36, 39–42.

110. American Scenic, *16th Annual Report, 1911,* pp. 59–61.

111. American Scenic, *17th Annual Report, 1912,* pp. 77, 90.

112. American Scenic, *18th Annual Report, 1913,* p. 78.

113. American Scenic, *16th Annual Report, 1911,* p. 61. The book is Appendix "B" of American Scenic, *13th Annual Report, 1908,* p. 165.

114. American Scenic, *30th Annual Report, 1925,* p. 27.

115. American Scenic, *17th Annual Report, 1912,* p. 153.

116. American Scenic, *6th Annual Report, 1901,* p. 25.

117. American Scenic, *7th Annual Report, 1902,* p. 25.

Notes ✻ 319

118. American Scenic, *17th Annual Report, 1912,* pp. 147–153.
119. American Scenic, *19th Annual Report, 1914,* pp. 111, 112.
120. *Ibid.,* p. 112.
121. American Scenic, *30th Annual Report, 1925,* pp. 20, 27, 28; George F. Kunz, "Origin and Record of the Society," *Scenic and Historic America,* II (December, 1930), p. 14; and Raymond H. Torrey, "Hamilton Grange," *Scenic and Historic America,* III (April, 1934), pp. 21, 22.
122. American Scenic, *6th Annual Report, 1901,* pp. 28, 29.

CHAPTER V

1. Similar figures (New England 15, Middle Atlantic 10, South 1, and Midwest 1) can be found in Committee on Handbook of the Conference of Historical Societies, *Handbook of American Historical Societies* (Madison, Wisconsin: Cantwell Printing Company, 1926), 81 pp. My own figures for New England seem more complete because sources having to do with New England are easier to find.
2. Hamilton Andrews Hill, *History of Old South Church (Third Church) Boston, 1669–1884* (Boston: Houghton Mifflin Company, 1890), II, pp. 528–538.
3. Everett W. Burdett, *History of the Old South Meeting-House in Boston* (Boston: B. B. Russell, 1877), pp. 88–90; and Directors of the Old South Work, *Freedom and the Old South Meeting-House,* No. 202 of *Old South Leaflets* (Boston: Directors of the Old South Work, n.d.), p. 28.
4. Directors of the Old South Work, *The Old South Meeting House,* No. 183 of *Old South Leaflets* (Boston: Directors of the Old South Work, n.d.), p. 7.
5. Burdett, *op. cit.,* pp. 90–98.
6. Hill, *op. cit.,* II, p. 545.
7. Burdett, *op. cit.,* pp. 98–99.
8. Boston *Evening Transcript,* September 15, 1876, quoted in *Freedom and the Old South Meeting-House,* p. 26.
9. Boston *Evening Transcript,* October 13, 1876, quoted in *Freedom and the Old South Meeting-House,* p. 26; and Burdett, *op. cit.,* p. 100.
10. *Freedom and the Old South Meeting-House,* p. 26; and Burdett, *op. cit.,* p. 102.
11. *Freedom and the Old South Meeting-House,* p. 26; and Burdett, *op. cit.,* p. 103.
12. Massachusetts Legislature, Committee on Federal Relations, *Arguments in Behalf of Petitions for Aid in the Preservation of the Old South Meeting-House,* pp. 5–43.
13. *Freedom and the Old South Meeting-House,* p. 30.
14. Emma Coleman, Typewritten manuscript on Alice C. Baker (Archives of Pocumtuck Valley Memorial Association, Memorial Hall, Deerfield, Massachusetts), p. 92.
15. Hugh Morrison, *Early American Architecture* (New York: Oxford University Press, 1952), p. 435.
16. George H. Moore, *Prytaneum Bostoniense, Notes on the History of the Old State House,* second paper read before the Bostonian Society, February 9, 1886 (Boston: Cupples, Upham & Co., 1886), pp. 32–33; and Boston, City Council, *Re-Dedication of the Old State House, Boston, July 11, 1882,* third edition (Boston: City Council, 1885), pp. 111, 112.

17. Bostonian Society, *Proceedings, 1908,* p. 49 and *Proceedings, 1882,* pp. 9, 10; and Boston, City Council, *op. cit.,* 163, 164.

18. Bostonian Society, *Proceedings, 1882,* p. 10.

19. George H. Moore, *Prytaneum Bostoniense, Notes on the History of the Old State House,* read before the Bostonian Society on May 12, 1885 (Boston: Cupples, Upham & Co., 1885), 31 pp.; and Boston, City Council, *op. cit.,* pp. 200–210.

20. Morrison, *op. cit.,* pp. 435–439; and Boston, National Historic Sites Commission, *Final Report of the Boston National Historic Sites Commission* (Washington: Government Printing Office, 1961), pp. 100, 101.

21. Bostonian Society, *Proceedings, 1908,* pp. 25, 26; and Boston, National Historic Sites Commission, *op. cit.,* p. 114.

22. J. M. Arms Sheldon, "The Personality of the Rev. John Williams House," *History and Proceedings of the Pocumtuck Valley Memorial Association,* VI (1912–1920), p. 447; and George Sheldon and J. M. Arms Sheldon, *The Rev. John Williams House* (Deerfield, Massachusetts: Pocumtuck Valley Memorial Association, 1918), 32 pp. This pamphlet contains three articles by George Sheldon from the Greenfield (Massachusetts) *Gazette and Courier,* July 2, July 30, and August 6, 1877.

23. Letter from George Sheldon to William Sumner Appleton, summer of 1912, in Jenny Sheldon, "Things to be Remembered about Deerfield and Vicinity," a notebook (Archives of the Pocumtuck Valley Memorial Association, Memorial Hall, Deerfield, Massachusetts); and "Editor's Easy Chair," *Harper's New Monthly Magazine,* LVI (December, 1877), p. 141.

24. Letter from L. W. Thompson to William Sumner Appleton, August 30, 1930 (Files of the Society for the Preservation of New England Antiquities, Boston).

25. Newport Historical Society, *First Annual Report, 1886,* pp. 24–26; and Edith May Tilley, "The Newport Historical Society in Its Earlier Days," *Bulletin of the Newport Historical Society,* No. 12 (April, 1914), pp. 5–11.

26. Newport Historical Society, *Second Annual Report, 1887,* pp. 7, 8; Tilley, *op. cit.,* p. 12; and Mrs. R. Sherman Elliott, *The Seventh Day Baptist Meeting House, Newport, Rhode Island,* read before the Newport Historical Society, November 18, 1929 (Newport, Rhode Island: Newport Historical Society, n.d.), p. 11.

27. George Tolman, *Catalog of a Portion of the Concord Antiquarian Society* (Boston: Thomas Todd Company, 1911), unpaged.

28. *Proceedings of the Lexington Historical Society,* I, pp. xx, xxi.

29. *Ibid.,* II, pp. v, vii, x.

30. *Ibid.,* pp. x, xi; III, p. 138.

31. *Ibid.,* III, p. 139.

32. Dr. Fred S. Piper, "The Lexington Historical Society," in Charles Hudson, *History of the Town of Lexington, Middlesex County, Massachusetts, from Its First Settlement to 1868, Revised and Continued to 1912* (Boston: Houghton, Mifflin Company, 1913), I, pp. 492, 493.

33. American Scenic, *19th Annual Report, 1914,* p. 222.

34. *Proceedings of the Lexington Historical Society,* III, p. 180.

35. Alvin Lincoln Jones, *Under New England Roofs* (Boston: C. B. Webster, 1894), p. 60.

36. "Minutes of Annual Meeting, December 6, 1897," in Ipswich Historical Society, *Publication V,* p. 94.

37. Ipswich Historical Society, *Publication VI*, pp. 3, 39.

38. The Reverend Thomas F. Waters, quoted in *ibid.*, p. 8.

39. J. M. A. Sheldon, "Thomas Franklin Waters," *History and Proceedings of the Pocumtuck Valley Memorial Association*, VI (1912–1920), pp. 538, 540.

40. Sylvester Baxter, "The Hotel Cluny of a New England Village," in William Rotch Ware (Editor), *The Georgian Period* (Boston: American Architect and Building News Company, 1901), II, p. 73.

41. William Sumner Appleton, "Destruction and Preservation of Old Buildings in New England," *Art and Archaeology*, VIII (May, 1919), p. 148.

42. William Sumner Appleton, "Annual Report of the Corresponding Secretary," *Bulletin of the S.P.N.E.A.*, V (April, 1914), pp. 9, 10.

43. Appleton, "Destruction and Preservation," *Art and Archaeology*, VIII (May, 1919), p. 158.

44. [William Sumner Appleton], "The Thomas Lee House at East Lyme, Conn.," *Bulletin of the S.P.N.E.A.*, V (December, 1914), pp. 2, 3.

45. Celeste Bush, quoted in Appleton, "Destruction and Preservation," *Art and Archaeology*, VIII (May, 1919), p. 159.

46. [William Sumner Appleton], "A Summer's Record of Preservation Work in New England," *Bulletin of the S.P.N.E.A.*, VII (December, 1916), p. 21.

47. There were other exceptions outside of New England. See Whitehill, *Independent Historical Societies*, pp. 138, 164, and 171.

48. Nathan Goold, *The Wadsworth-Longfellow House, Longfellow's Old Home, Portland, Maine, Its History and Its Occupants* (Portland, Maine: Maine Historical Society, 1905), pp. 5, 22.

49. W. O. Fuller, *An Old Town by the Sea* (Portsmouth, New Hampshire: Thomas Bailey Aldrich Memorial, 1910), pp. 7–13.

50. Appleton, "Destruction and Preservation," *Art and Archaeology*, VIII (May, 1919), p. 164.

51. Jones, *op. cit.*, p. 191. It appears that John Crowley, a public-spirited citizen of Dedham, bought the house in 1896 in order to help the Dedham Historical Society save it. See Boston, National Historic Sites Commission, *Final Report*, pp. 210, 211.

52. J. Wilder Fairbank, "With the Historian," *Ye Fayerbanke Historial*, I (November, 1903), pp. 35, 36.

53. *Ibid.*, p. 36.

54. *Ibid.*, pp. 36, 37.

55. *Ibid.*, p. 38.

56. Dr. Arthur Fairbanks, *Ye Fayerbanke Historial*, I (November, 1903), pp. 41, 43.

57. *Ye Fayerbanke Historial*, I (June, 1904), pp. 27, 34.

58. *Ibid.* (November, 1904), pp. 14, 15.

59. Charles K. Bolton, "Diary, 1909–1913," August 22, 1912 (Massachusetts Historical Society, Boston).

60. Society of the Descendants of Pilgrim John Howland, *Howland Homestead*, I (July, 1911), p. 2.

61. Pilgrim John Howland Society, *The Pilgrim John Howland House, 1667*, (n.p., The Society, n.d.), unpaged.

62. Edward S. Alden, *Alden Homestead, Duxbury, Mass., Shrine of Millions of Descendants of John Alden and His Wife, Priscilla Mullens* (Holyoke, Massachusetts: Alden Press, 1932), pp. 7–9.

63. Letter from Tristram Coffin to William Sumner Appleton, October 10, 1922 (S.P.N.E.A. Files, Boston); Appleton, "Report," *Old-Time New England*, XV (July, 1924), pp. 30–32.

64. Boston *Sunday Herald*, February 15, 1914, in the clipping collection (Fruitlands Museum, Harvard, Massachusetts).

65. Untitled clipping, June 27, 1914, in the clipping collection (Fruitlands Museum).

66. *The Clinton Courant*, October 17, 1914, in the clipping collection (Fruitlands Museum).

67. Appleton, "Report," *Bulletin of the S.P.N.E.A.*, VI (April, 1915), p. 14.

68. Clara E. Sears, *Revised Catalogue of "Fruitlands" at Harvard, Mass.* (Harvard, Massachusetts: The Author, ca. 1915), p. 23.

69. Clara E. Sears, "First Meeting of Trustees, August 10, 1930," in "Notes, 1915–1941," Typewritten manuscript, unpaged (Fruitlands Museum).

70. Evangeline W. Andrews, "Introduction," J. Frederick Kelly, *The Henry Whitfield House, 1639, The Journal of the Restoration of the Old Stone House, Guilford* (Guilford, Connecticut: Henry Whitfield State Historical Museum, 1939), pp. xvii-xx; Trustees of the Henry Whitfield House, *Proceedings at the Formal Opening of the State Historical Museum, Henry Whitfield House* (Guilford: The Trustees, 1904), p. 36; and Mabel W. Stimson, National Society of Colonial Dames in the State of New York, *Report of the National Society of Colonial Dames in the State of New York, 1903*, p. 10.

71. Appleton, "Report," *Bulletin of the S.P.N.E.A.*, VII (May, 1916), p. 17.

72. Appleton, "Report," *Old-Time New England*, XIII (April, 1923), p. 187.

73. *Ibid.*, XV (July, 1924), p. 30.

74. Municipal Art Society of Hartford, Connecticut, *Bulletin No. 5: Preservation and Restoration of City Hall* (Hartford: The Society, 1906), 16 pp.

75. Municipal Art Society of Hartford, Connecticut, *Bulletin No. 15: The Old State House, Hartford, Why It Should Be Preserved* (Hartford: The Society, 1911), pp. 4, 5.

76. Emily S. G. Holcombe, "Save the Old State House," *ibid.*, p. 3.

77. Letter from George M. Curtis to William Sumner Appleton, October 11, 1913, with enclosure (S.P.N.E.A. Files, Boston).

78. Letter from Louis R. Cheney to George D. Seymour, November 6, 1913, a copy (S.P.N.E.A. Files, Boston).

79. "The New Old City Hall," *Hartford Courant*, September 14, 1916 (S.P.N.E.A. Files, Boston).

80. Letter from William Sumner Appleton to Morgan G. Bulkeley, May 21, 1917; and note from Louis R. Cheney on a printed S.P.N.E.A. donation request (S.P.N.E.A. Files, Boston).

81. Letter from Arthur Perkins to William Sumner Appleton, January 12, 1920 (S.P.N.E.A. Files, Boston).

Chapter VI

1. For further information see Walter Muir Whitehill, *Independent Historical Societies* (Boston: The Boston Athenaeum, 1962), pp. 243–320.

2. Joseph R. Knowland, *California, A Landmark History, Story of the Preservation and Marking of Early Day Shrines* (Oakland, California: Tribune Press, 1941), p. v.

3. Clinton P. Anderson, "The Adobe Palace," *New Mexico Historical Review*, XIX (April, 1944), pp. 98–115.

4. *Ibid.*, pp. 115–118.

5. Knowland, *op. cit.*, p. 14; and Rexford Newcomb, *The Old Mission Churches and Historic Houses of California* (Philadelphia: J. B. Lippincott Company), p. 249.

6. Knowland, *op. cit.*, p. 46.

7. *Ibid.*, pp. 4, 5; Maynard Geiger, O.F.M., "Preservation and Restoration of the California Missions," *Historic Preservation*, XIV (1962), p. 106; and Newcomb, *op. cit.*, p. 262.

8. Knowland, *op. cit.*, p. 107; and Eliza D. Keith, *Report of the Historical Landmarks Committee of the Native Daughters of the Golden West* (San Francisco: The Author, 1902), p. 19.

9. Letter from Charles F. Lummis to Mrs. Eliza D. Keith, quoted in Keith, *op. cit.*, p. 30.

10. Newcomb, *op. cit.*, p. 151.

11. *Ibid.*, p. 207.

12. Knowland, *op. cit.*, pp. 92, 125, 126.

13. *Ibid.*, pp. v, vi; and Keith, *op. cit.*, pp. 29, 32, 33.

14. Keith, *op. cit.*, pp. 3, 29–33.

15. Newcomb, *op. cit.*, pp. 243, 244; and Knowland, *op. cit.*, p. 7.

16. Knowland, *op. cit.*, pp. 60, 61; and Geiger, *op. cit.*, pp. 106, 107.

17. Knowland, *op. cit.*, p. 103.

18. *Ibid.*, pp. 175, 176.

19. *Ibid.*, pp. 22, 56, 57; and Newcomb, *op. cit.*, pp. 160, 235.

20. Knowland, *op. cit.*, p. 29; Geiger, *op. cit.*, p. 107; and Newcomb, *op. cit.*, p. 228.

21. San Francisco *Examiner*, December 1 and 7, 1915.

22. U. S. Congress, Senate, *Army Appropriation*, debate on H. R. 16460, July 24, 1916, *Congressional Record*, 64th Cong., 1st Sess., pp. 11512, 11513.

23. See for example the work of the D.A.R. with the Theodore Roosevelt Log Cabin in Bismarck, North Dakota, cited in Lewis Barrington, *Historic Restorations of the Daughters of the American Revolution* (New York: Richard H. Smith, 1941), Plate 179.

CHAPTER VII

1. William McDowell, letter in Washington *Post*, July 21, 1890 (D.A.R. Library, Washington, D. C.).

2. Mrs. John F. Yawger, "Report of Committee on Preservation of Historic Spots," National Society of the Daughters of the American Revolution, *Report of the National Society of the Daughters of the American Revolution* (Washington: Government Printing Office, 1920), XXIV, pp. 59, 60.

3. N.S.D.A.R., *Report* (1897), I, p. 54.

4. Mrs. Emory Wendell, "Louisa St. Clair Chapter, Detroit, Michigan," *American Monthly Magazine*, XVI (June, 1900), p. 1201.

5. Mrs. Ellen H. Walworth, *American Monthly Magazine*, I (July, 1892), pp. 9, 10.

6. *American Monthly Magazine*, XI (September, 1897), p. 283.

7. *Ibid.*, XII (May, 1898), p. 840.

8. *Ibid.*, p. 843.

9. *Ibid.*, p. 848.

10. *Ibid.*, XIV (April, 1899), pp. 985–988.
11. *Ibid.*, pp. 989–994.
12. *Ibid.*, pp. 994, 1005, 1009, 1013.
13. *Ibid.*, XVI (May, 1900), p. 1020.
14. *Ibid.*, (April, 1900), pp. 621, 630, 632, 634.
15. *Ibid.*, p. 635.
16. *Ibid.*, pp. 636, 637.
17. *Ibid.*, pp. 641, 642.
18. *Ibid.*, p. 644.
19. *Ibid.*, XI (September, 1897), p. 283.
20. *Ibid.*, IX (November, 1896), pp. 467, 468.
21. *Ibid.*, XI (October, 1897), pp. 404–407.
22. *Ibid.*, XXXV (July, 1909), p. 236.
23. *D.A.R. Magazine*, L (April, 1917), pp. 254–256.
24. *Ibid.*, LIX (August, 1925), p. 474.
25. *American Monthly Magazine*, XXVII (December, 1905), pp. 843–854; see also Barrington, *Historic Restorations of the Daughters of the American Revolution.* Not all the historic properties described in the book were actually saved by the Daughters of the American Revolution.
26. Anne H. Wharton, National Society of Colonial Dames of America, *Historian's Address, 1900,* p. 4.
27. *Ibid.*, pp. 24, 25.
28. Mrs. Morris Patterson Ferris, *Van Cortlandt Mansion Erected 1748, Now in the Custody of the Colonial Dames of the State of New York* (New York: National Society of Colonial Dames in the State of New York, 1897), p. 3.
29. National Society of Colonial Dames in the State of New York, *Report, 1897,* pp. 29, 30.
30. N.S.C.D. in the State of New York, *Report, 1898,* pp. 35, 36.
31. Mrs. J. V. R. Townsend, N.S.C.D. in the State of New York, *Report, 1900,* pp. 32, 33.
32. Mrs. Katherine M. Beekman, N.S.C.D. in the State of New York, *Report, 1904,* pp. 32, 33.
33. Mrs. Joseph Rucker Lamar. *A History of the National Society of Colonial Dames of America from 1891 to 1933* (Atlanta, Georgia: Walter W. Brown Publishing Company, 1934), p. 145.
34. National Society of Colonial Dames of America, *The Story of Sulgrave Manor and a Few Reasons Why Americans Should Create This Endowment* (n.p. n.n., ca. 1923), unpaged.
35. Lamar, *op. cit.*, pp. 148, 149, 153, 156–159.
36. Grace Finlay McPherson, *A History of the First Fifty Years of the New Jersey Society of the Colonial Dames of America, 1892–1942* (Somerville, New Jersey: Somerset Press, 1942), p. 37.
37. Davies, *Patriotism on Parade,* p. 103.
38. N.S.C.D. in the State of New York, *Report, 1897,* p. 30.
39. *Roosevelt House Bulletin,* II (Spring, 1924), p. 6.
40. Walter B. Stevens, *The Forest City, Comprising the Official Photographic Views of the Universal Exposition Held in Saint Louis, 1904* (St. Louis, Missouri: N. D. Thompson Publishing Company, 1904), unpaged.
41. Roy Hays, "Is the Lincoln Birthplace Cabin Authentic?" *Abraham Lincoln Quarterly,* V (September, 1948), pp. 143, 144.
42. U. S. Department of the Interior, National Park Service, *Abraham Lin-*

coln *National Historical Park, Kentucky* (Washington: Department of the Interior, 1959), leaflet.

43. Hays, *op. cit.*, p. 134; and Benjamin H. Davis, "Report of Research on the Traditional Abraham Lincoln Birthplace Cabin," Mimeographed manuscript, February 15, 1949 (General Files, Branch of History, National Park Service, Washington), pp. 27–29.

44. Hays, *op. cit.*, pp. 131–134; and Davis, *op. cit.*, pp. 1, 2.

45. Hays, *op. cit.*, pp. 133, 134; and Davis, *op. cit.*, pp. 2, 3.

46. Hays, *op. cit.*, pp. 136, 137; and Davis, *op. cit.*, pp. 34, 35.

47. David R. Barbee, letter to the editor, Washington *Post*, October 11, 1948, quoted in Davis, *loc. cit.*

48. Hays, *op. cit.*, pp. 147–150; and Davis, *op. cit.*, pp. 37, 38.

49. Richard Lloyd Jones, "The Lincoln Birthplace Farm," *Collier's*, XXXVI (February 10, 1906), p. 13.

50. *Ibid.*

51. *Ibid.*, p. 14.

52. *Ibid.*

53. Richard Lloyd Jones, "The Lincoln Farm Association," *Collier's*, XXXVI (February 10, 1906), p. 15.

54. "The Lincoln Farm Association," *Collier's*, XXXVIII (February 9, 1907), p. 13.

55. Lincoln Farm Association, *Second Annual Meeting of the Board of Directors of the Lincoln Farm Association, Report of the Executive Committee, Secretary, Treasurer and General Manager, February 26, 1908* (New York: The Association, 1908), pp. 5, 6.

56. *Ibid.*, p. 6.

57. Jones, "The Association," *Collier's*, XXXVI (February 10, 1906), p. 15.

58. Hays, *op. cit.*, p. 153.

59. *Ibid.*, pp. 153–157; Lincoln Farm Association, *op. cit.*, pp. 18, 32; and "The Association," *Collier's*, XXXVIII (February 9, 1907), p. 13.

60. Lincoln Farm Association, *op. cit.*, pp. 5, 6, 37.

61. "Cannon Versus Lincoln," *Collier's*, XLII (January 2, 1909), p. 5.

62. *New York Times*, November 10, 1911, p. 16.

63. U. S. Congress, House Committee on the Library, Report Number 221, *To Accept Deed of Gift to Homestead of Abraham Lincoln* (H.R. 8351), as quoted in *Congressional Record*, 64th Cong., 1st Sess., pp. 5554, 5555 (April 5, 1916).

64. *New York Times*, July 18, 1916, p. 5.

65. "The Lincoln Farm Becomes the Property of the Nation," *Collier's*, LVII (September 4, 1916), p. 17.

66. *New York Times*, September 5, 1916, p. 8.

67. "The Lincoln Centennial Memorial," *Collier's*, XLIV (February 12, 1910), p. 10.

68. Lincoln Farm Association, *op. cit.*, p. 24; and Hays, *op. cit.*, p. 163.

69. Hays, *op. cit.*, pp. 161–163.

70. Davis, *op. cit.*, p. 37.

71. Margaret Fitzhugh Browne, "A Twin of Lincoln's Birthplace Ten Miles from Boston's State House," Boston *Evening Transcript*, March 12, 1924, III, p. 4.

72. G. E. Nelson, "The Genesis of Restored New Salem," *Journal of the Illinois State Historical Society*, XXXVI (December, 1943), p. 368.

73. *Ibid.,* p. 371.
74. *Ibid.,* pp. 372–376; and Thomas P. Reep, *Lincoln at New Salem* (Petersburg, Illinois: Old Salem Lincoln League, 1927), pp. 137, 138.
75. Reep, *op. cit.,* pp. 108, 140.
76. Roosevelt Memorial Association, *Annual Report, 1919–1921,* pp. 9, 10.
77. *New York Times,* March 13, 1919, p. 24.
78. *Ibid.,* March 18, 1919, p. 10.
79. *Ibid.,* April 17, 1919, p. 11.
80. Roosevelt Memorial Association, *op. cit.,* pp. 11, 14.
81. *Woman's Roosevelt Memorial Bulletin,* I (December, 1919), p. 1.
82. *Ibid.,* p. 2.
83. *Ibid.* (February, 1920), p. 1.
84. *Ibid.,* p. 3.
85. *Ibid.,* p. 4.
86. *Ibid.* (April, 1920), pp. 1, 5.
87. *Roosevelt House Bulletin,* I (June, 1920), pp. 2, 3.
88. *Ibid.* (Spring, 1923), p. 4; and Roosevelt Memorial Association, *Annual Report, 1921–1922,* pp. 14–16.
89. Roosevelt Memorial Association, *Annual Report, 1924,* pp. 14–19.
90. *Roosevelt House Bulletin,* I (Spring, 1923), p. 2.
91. *New York Times,* May 1, 1923, p. 23.
92. *Roosevelt House Bulletin,* II (Summer, 1923), p. 4.
93. *Ibid.* (Fall, 1923), p. 1.
94. *Ibid.* (Fall, 1925), p. 8.
95. *Ibid.* (Spring, 1924), p. 4.
96. *Ibid.* (Spring, 1925), pp. 1, 2.
97. *Ibid.* (Summer, 1925), p. 3.

CHAPTER VIII

1. Abram Kanof, "Uriah Phillips Levy: The Story of a Pugnacious Commodore," *Publications of the American Jewish Historical Society,* XXXIX (September, 1949), pp. 1–66.
2. George Alfred Townsend, *Monticello and Its Preservation Since Jefferson's Death, 1826–1902, Correspondence of George Alfred Townsend, "Gath"* (Washington, D. C.: Jefferson M. Levy, 1902), p. 10.
3. Maud Littleton, *Monticello* (New York: n.n., 1912), p. 12.
4. Kanof, *op. cit.,* p. 10.
5. Uriah Phillips Levy, *Defence of Uriah P. Levy before the Court of Inquiry Held at Washington City, November and December, 1857, Prepared and Read By His Senior Counsel, B. F. Butler, of New York* (New York: C. Bryant and Company, 1858), p. 11.
6. Letter from Uriah P. Levy to George M. Carr, September 17, 1858 (Carr Papers, Alderman Library, University of Virginia, Charlottesville, Virginia).
7. Benson J. Lossing, "Monticello," *Harpers New Monthly Magazine,* VII (July, 1853), p. 149.
8. John S. Patton and Sallie J. Doswell, *Monticello and Its Master* (Charlottesville, Virginia: The Mitchie Company, 1925), p. 58.
9. Kanof, *op. cit.,* pp. 53, 64, 65; and Thomas L. Rhodes, as told to Frank B. Lord, *The Story of Monticello* (Washington, D.C.: American Publishing Company, 1928), p. 85.

10. Rhodes, *ibid.*, pp. 85, 86; and Littleton, *op. cit.*, pp. 16–19.

11. Liber 141, p. 254, Surrogate Court of the County of New York, quoted in Kanof, *op. cit.*, Appendix II, pp. 61–66.

12. Kanof, *op. cit.*, p. 11.

13. U. S. Congress, Senate, *Property Devised by Captain Levy*, debate on S. Res. 137, March 3, 1863, in *Congressional Globe*, 37th Cong., 3rd Sess., p. 1495.

14. Letter from E. Delafield Smith to Attorney General Edward Bates, March 16, 1864, concerning the will of Uriah P. Levy (National Archives, Record Group 60, Washington, D. C.).

15. Letter from T. J. Coffey to E. Delafield Smith, March 18, 1864, concerning the will of Uriah P. Levy (National Archives, Record Group 60, Washington, D. C.).

16. Attorney General Edward Bates, quoted in J. G. Randall, "When Jefferson's Home Was Bequeathed to the United States," *South Atlantic Quarterly*, XXIII (January, 1924), p. 37.

17. Levy vs. Levy, in Oliver Barbour, *Reports of Cases in Law and Equity Determined in the Supreme Court of the State of New York* (Albany, New York: W. C. Little, 1864), XL, pp. 585–626.

18. Levy vs. Levy, *Reports of Cases Argued and Determined in the Court of Appeals of the State of New York* (Albany, New York: W. C. Little, 1866), XXXIII, pp. 97–138.

19. James A. Bear, Jr., *Old Pictures of Monticello* (Charlottesville, Virginia: University of Virginia Press, 1957), p. 4; Townsend, *Monticello*, pp. 17, 18; *Frank Leslie's Illustrated Newspaper* (New York: February 8, 1862), p. 182; and letter from Jonas P. Levy to George Carr, December 28, 1868 (Carr Papers, Alderman Library, University of Virginia, Charlottesville, Virginia).

20. Jonas P. Levy et al vs. Mary Jane Hastings et al, report in the Circuit Court of the City of Richmond, November 30, 1868 (Carr Papers, University of Virginia, Charlottesville, Virginia).

21. Letter from Jonas Levy to George M. Carr, June 13, 1869 (Carr Papers, University of Virginia, Charlottesville, Virginia).

22. Letters from Jonas Levy to George Carr, April 7, 1873; from Jefferson Levy to George Carr, July 17, 1876, September 22, 1877, and December 16, 1878; and undated list of Levy heirs (Carr Papers, University of Virginia, Charlottesville, Virginia).

23. George M. Carr, report on the sale of Monticello, March, 1879, to Circuit Court of the City of Richmond; and letter from Jefferson Levy to George Carr, March 3, 1879 (Carr Papers, University of Virginia, Charlottesville, Virginia).

24. Letters from Jonas Levy to George Carr, December 28, 1868, and from Jefferson Levy to George Carr, May 6, 1879 (Carr Papers, University of Virginia, Charlottesville, Virginia).

25. Representative A. A. Hardenbergh of New Jersey, quoted in U. S. Congress, House, *The Grave of Thomas Jefferson*, debate on H. R. Res. 141, April 13, 1878, in *Congressional Record*, 45th Cong., 2nd Sess., p. 2494.

26. Rhodes, *Monticello*, p. 91.

27. Professor William M. Thornton, quoted in U. S. Congress, House Committee on Public Buildings and Grounds, *Purchase of Monticello*, Hearings, 64th Cong., 1st Sess., on H. J. Res. 269, December 15, 1916 (Washington, D. C.: Government Printing Office, 1917), p. 28.

28. Letter from Jefferson M. Levy to Mrs. William C. Story, December 7, 1916, quoted in U. S. Congress, House Committee on Public Buildings and Grounds, *ibid.,* p. 17.

29. Rhodes, *op. cit.,* p. 92.

30. Professor William Thornton, quoted in U. S. Congress, House Committee on Public Buildings and Grounds, *Purchase of Monticello,* December 15, 1916, p. 28.

31. Frank R. Stockton, "The Later Years of Monticello," *The Century Magazine,* XXXIV (September, 1887), p. 657.

32. Prof. William Thornton, quoted in U. S. Congress, House Committee on Public Buildings and Grounds, *op. cit.,* p. 27.

33. Patton and Doswell, *Monticello,* p. 60; and Theodore Fred Kuper, "Collecting Monticello," *Manuscripts,* VII (Summer, 1955), pp. 222, 223.

34. Interview with Theodore Fred Kuper concerning the work of the Thomas Jefferson Memorial Foundation, in the Fashion Institute of Technology, 227 West 27th Street, New York, May 3, 1960, transcript written in his presence, in the possession of the author.

35. Merrill D. Peterson, *The Jefferson Image in the American Mind* (New York: Oxford University Press, 1960), pp. 382, 512.

36. Jefferson M. Levy, quoted in *New York Times,* November 12, 1912, p. 22.

37. Letter from Jefferson M. Levy to Mrs. William C. Story, December 7, 1916, quoted in U. S. Congress, House Committee on Public Buildings and Grounds, *op. cit.,* p. 18.

38. Letter from William Jennings Bryan to Jefferson M. Levy, September 23, 1914, quoted in U. S. Congress, House Committee on Public Buildings and Grounds, *Purchase of Monticello,* Hearings, 64th Cong., 1st Sess., on H. J. Res. 269, August 8, 1916 (Washington, D. C.: Government Printing Office, 1916), Part II, pp. 4, 5.

39. The Jefferson Club of St. Louis, *The Pilgrimage to Monticello, the Home and Tomb of Thomas Jefferson, by the Jefferson Club of St. Louis, Mo., October 10 to 14, 1901* (St. Louis: Con. P. Curran Printing Company, 1902), pp. 6, 7.

40. Townsend, *Monticello,* pp. 3, 4.

41. *Ibid.,* p. 22.

42. Maud Littleton, "One Wish," letter dated August 30, 1911, reprinted from *Congressional Record* (Washington, D. C.: Government Printing Office, 1912), 16 pp.; Interview with Kuper, May 3, 1960; and Mamie Downard Peck, *Thomas Jefferson and His Home, Monticello* (Corsicana, Texas: Marr Publishing Company, 1928), pp. 5–7.

43. Littleton, *op. cit.,* pp. 7, 10, 13–16.

44. *New York Times,* March 19, 1913, p. 9.

45. Senate Concurrent Resolution 92, 62nd Cong., 2nd Sess., quoted in U. S. Congress, Senate Committee on the Library, *Public Ownership of Monticello,* Hearings, 62nd Cong., 2nd Sess., on S. J. Res. 92, July 9, 1912 (Washington, D. C.: Government Printing Office, 1912), p. 3.

46. Mrs. Martin W. Littleton, quoted in U. S. Congress, Senate Committee on the Library, *ibid.,* p. 7.

47. *Ibid.,* p. 19.

48. *Ibid.,* pp. 31, 48, 50.

49. R. T. W. Duke, quoted in U. S. Congress, Senate Committee on the Library, *ibid.*, p. 50.

50. Letter from James M. Beck to Mrs. Martin Littleton, quoted in U. S. Congress, Senate Committee on the Library, *ibid.*, pp. 50–52.

51. U. S. Congress, House Committee on Rules, *Public Ownership of Monticello,* Hearings, 62nd Cong., 2nd Sess., on S. Con. Res. 24, July 24, 1912 (Washington, D. C.: Government Printing Office, 1912), p. 7.

52. *Ibid.,* pp. 6, 36.

53. *Ibid.,* p. 37.

54. *Ibid.,* p. 38.

55. *New York Times,* August 8, 1912, p. 8.

56. Letter from William Sumner Appleton to Mrs. Martin Littleton, October 28, 1912 (Files of the Society for the Preservation of New England Antiquities, Boston, Massachusetts).

57. Letter from Mrs. Martin Littleton to W. S. Appleton, early November, 1912 (S.P.N.E.A. Files, Boston).

58. Letter from W. S. Appleton to Mrs. Martin Littleton, November 4, 1912 (S.P.N.E.A. Files).

59. Jefferson Levy, quoted in *New York Times,* November 12, 1912, p. 22.

60. *Ibid.*

61. Littleton, *Monticello,* pp. 5–21, 33, 34, and "To Those Who Have Read This Little Story of Monticello," pp. 3–6.

62. U. S. Congress, House, *Monticello,* debate on H. Res. 740, December 9, 1912, in *Congressional Record,* 62nd Cong., 3rd Sess., p. 347.

63. *Ibid.*

64. *Ibid.,* p. 348.

65. *Ibid.,* pp. 348, 349.

66. *Ibid.,* p. 349.

67. U. S. Congress, House, *Monticello,* December 9, 1912, *ibid.,* pp. 349, 350.

68. R. T. W. Duke, quoted in U. S. Congress, House Committee on Public Buildings and Grounds, *Purchase of Monticello,* December 15, 1916, p. 31.

69. U. S. Congress, House Committee on Rules, *Public Ownership of Monticello,* July 24, 1912, p. 35.

70. Jefferson Levy, quoted in *New York Times,* December 10, 1912, p. 3.

71. *New York Times,* March 19, 1913, p. 9.

72. *Ibid.,* February 17, 1914, p. 20; and February 26, 1914, p. 7.

73. Dorothy Dix, "Monticello—Shrine or Bachelor's Hall?" *Good Housekeeping,* LVIII (April, 1914), pp. 538–541.

74. American Scenic and Historic Preservation Society, *Annual Report, 1914,* p. 233.

75. *New York Times,* December 10, 1912, p. 3.

76. American Scenic, *op. cit.,* Appendix F, "Monticello, Virginia," pp. 519–541.

77. *New York Times,* March 20, 1914, p. 5.

78. *Ibid.,* October 6, 1914, p. 6.

79. U. S. Congress, House Committee on Appropriations, *House in Which Lincoln Died,* Hearing before Sub-committee, 54th Cong., 1st Sess., on H. R. 7664, March 21, 1896 (Washington, D. C.: Government Printing Office, 1896), p. 258.

80. U. S. Congress, House Committee on Rules, *Purchase of Monticello,*

Hearings, 63rd Cong., 2nd Sess., on H. J. Res. 390 and H. J. Res. 418, February 23, 1915 (Washington, D. C.: Government Printing Office, 1915), pp. 4, 7.

81. U. S. Congress, Senate Committee on the Library, *Public Ownership of Monticello*, July 9, 1912, p. 30.

82. U. S. Congress, House Committee on Rules, *op. cit.*, p. 10.

83. *Ibid.*, pp. 11–13.

84. *New York Times*, February 26, 1915, p. 11.

85. *Ibid.*, August 1, 1916, p. 16.

86. U. S. Congress, House Committee on Public Buildings and Grounds, *Purchase of Monticello*, August 8, 1916, Part II, pp. 10, 11; and *New York Times*, August 8, 1916, p. 6.

87. National Society of Daughters of the American Revolution, *Report* (1916), XX, p. 136.

88. Letter from Jefferson M. Levy to Mrs. William C. Story, December 7, 1916, quoted in U. S. Congress, House Committee on Public Buildings and Grounds, *Purchase of Monticello*, December 15, 1916, pp. 17, 18.

89. U. S. Congress, House Committee on Public Buildings and Grounds, *ibid.*, pp. 34–36.

90. U. S. Congress, Senate Committee on Public Buildings and Grounds, *Purchase of Monticello*, Hearings, 64th Cong., 1st Sess., on S. J. Res. 153, January 9, 1917 (Washington, D. C.: Government Printing Office, 1917), pp. 14–22.

91. American Scenic, *Annual Report, 1917*, pp. 352, 353.

92. Fanny Harnit, "Monticello," *D.A.R. Magazine*, L (March, 1917), pp. 158–162; and *New York Times*, April 20, 1917, p. 13.

93. Interview with Kuper, May 3, 1960; and Kuper, "Monticello," *Manuscripts* (Summer, 1955), p. 216.

94. Letter from H. W. Hilleary to W. S. Appleton, April 1, 1919 (S.P.-N.E.A. Files).

95. Letter from H. W. Hilleary to W. S. Appleton, April 12, 1919 (S.P.N.E.A. Files).

96. *New York Times*, June 19, 1920, p. 14.

97. *Ibid.*, July 27, 1921, p. 17.

98. *Ibid.*, July 28, 1921, pp. 12, 13.

99. *Ibid.*, April 13, 1922, p. 40.

100. *Ibid.*, November 3, 1922, p. 12.

101. *Ibid.*, March 2, 1923, p. 12.

102. During my study of this organization and its campaigns through the years 1923–1926, I had the privilege of meeting Theodore Fred Kuper, who was national director of the foundation for the first ten years of its existence. He provided an unusually clear insight into its methods and purposes, as well as fresh viewpoints on some of the important people who united to save Jefferson's home. Probably my thinking about the objectives of the Thomas Jefferson Memorial Foundation will reflect in some degree the deeper feelings expressed by Mr. Kuper as he looked back over the years at his connection with this great movement.

103. Patton and Doswell, *Monticello*, pp. 70, 71; and interview with Kuper, May 3, 1960.

104. Interview with Kuper; and Kuper, "Monticello," *Manuscripts* (Summer, 1955), pp. 216, 217.

105. *New York Times*, April 5, 1923, p. 19.

106. Interview with Kuper; and Kuper, *op. cit.*, p. 219.
107. *New York Times,* April 16, 1923, p. 16.
108. Interview with Kuper; Kuper, *op. cit.,* p. 217; and Patton and Doswell, *Monticello,* pp. 73, 74.
109. Interview with Kuper; Kuper, *op. cit.,* p. 218; and Patton and Doswell, *op. cit.,* p. 74.
110. *New York Times,* April 23, 1923, Section I, Part II, p. 5; and interview with Kuper.
111. *New York Times,* May 27, 1923, p. 20; and June 16, 1923, p. 2; interview with Kuper; and Kuper, *op. cit.,* p. 218.
112. Interview with Kuper; and Kuper, *op. cit.,* pp. 218, 219.
113. *New York Times,* July 15, 1923, Section II, p. 2.
114. *Ibid.,* September 2, 1923, Section II, p. 2; interview with Kuper; and Kuper, *op. cit.,* p. 218.
115. *New York Times,* December 4, 1923, p. 1.
116. Interview with Kuper.
117. *Ibid.;* and Kuper, *op. cit.,* p. 219.
118. *New York Times,* March 7, 1924, p. 15; March 8, 1924, p. 3; and March 11, 1924, p. 4.
119. Interview with Kuper.
120. *Ibid.;* and Kuper, *op. cit.,* p. 221.
121. Interview with Kuper.
122. *New York Times,* March 9, 1924, Section X, p. 2.
123. *Ibid.,* March 20, 1924, p. 21.
124. Interview with Kuper. See also *New York Times,* April 12, 1924, p. 18; April 13, 1924, p. 6, and Section II, p. 15; and Kuper, *op. cit.,* p. 220.
125. Interview with Kuper, May 3, 1960.
126. *New York Times,* May 11, 1925, p. 15.
127. *Ibid.,* May 1, 1925, p. 3.
128. Interview with Kuper.
129. *New York Times,* May 24, 1925, Section IX, p. 14.
130. *Ibid.,* June 13, 1925, p. 14.
131. *Ibid.,* June 15, 1925, p. 17.
132. *Ibid.,* July 3, 1925, p. 5; and July 14, 1925, p. 22.
133. Thomas Jefferson Memorial Foundation, *The Story of the Thomas Jefferson Memorial Foundation,* Number 4B of "Monticello Papers" (n.p., The Foundation, ca. 1925), unpaged.
134. *New York Times,* February 18, 1926, p. 3, and March 25, 1926, p. 12; interview with Kuper; and Kuper, "Monticello," *Manuscripts* (Summer, 1955), p. 220.
135. *New York Times,* April 6, 1924, p. 9; April 8, 1924, p. 3; and July 1, 1924, p. 21.
136. *Ibid.,* June 20, 1926, p. 1; June 26, 1926, p. 5; June 27, 1926, p. 1; and June 29, 1926, p. 4; and interview with Kuper.
137. *New York Times,* April 29, 1926, p. 1; May 20, 1926, p. 4; June 15, 1926, p. 3; and June 16, 1926, p. 27.
138. Interview with Kuper.
139. *Proceedings of the 57th Convention, American Institute of Architects, 1924,* pp. 129, 130.
140. Fiske Kimball, "Monticello," *Journal of the A.I.A.,* XII (April, 1924), p. 181.

141. Thomas Jefferson Memorial Foundation, *op. cit.*, unpaged.
142. Interview with Kuper; and Kuper, *op. cit.*, p. 219.
143. *New York Times,* December 22, 1926, p. 11.
144. Letter from Stuart Gibboney to W. S. Appleton, June 2, 1928 (S.P.N.E.A. Files).
145. *Proceeedings of the 57th Convention, A.I.A., 1924,* p. 130.
146. Thomas Jefferson Memorial Foundation, *Report of the President, February 1, 1941* (New York: The Foundation, 1941), pp. 1, 5.

CHAPTER IX

1. Norman Isham, *In Praise of Antiquaries* (n.p., Walpole Society, 1931), p. 3.
2. *Ibid.,* pp. 5, 6.
3. *Ibid.,* p. 9.
4. *Ibid.,* pp. 9–11, 19.
5. Edwin Whitefield, *Homes of Our Forefathers in Massachusetts* (new edition; Boston: The Author, 1892), unpaged.
6. Richard Franz Bach, "Books on Colonial Architecture, Part III," *Architectural Record,* XL (July, 1916), p. 92.
7. Isham, *op. cit.,* pp. 11–13; and Norman Isham and Albert F. Brown, *Early Rhode Island Houses* (Providence, Rhode Island: Preston and Rounds, 1895), 100 pp.
8. Wallace Nutting, *Wallace Nutting's Biography* (Framingham, Massachusetts: Old America Company, 1936), pp. 283–285.
9. [Wallace Nutting], *The Wallace Nutting Colonial Chain of Picture Houses* (n.p., n.n., 1915), unpaged.
10. William Sumner Appleton, "Report," *Bulletin of the S.P.N.E.A.,* VII (May 1916), pp. 19, 21.
11. [Nutting], *The Wallace Nutting Colonial Chain,* unpaged.
12. Nutting, *Biography,* p. 95.
13. Appleton, "Report," *Bulletin of the S.P.N.E.A.,* X (October, 1919), pp. 15–17; XI (July, 1920), p. 35.
14. W. Knight Sturges, "The Long Shadow of Norman Shaw," *Journal of the Society of Architectural Historians,* IX (December, 1950), p. 16.
15. *Proceedings of the 3rd Convention, American Institute of Architects, 1869,* pp. 47–49; and Marcus T. Reynolds, "The Colonial Buildings of Rensselaerwyck," *Architectural Record,* IV (June, 1895), pp. 425–433.
16. Isham, *Antiquaries,* pp. 15–17.
17. *Ibid.,* p. 17; Sturges, *loc. cit.;* and Arthur Little, *Early New England Interiors, Sketched in Salem, Marblehead, Portsmouth and Kittery* (Boston: A. Williams and Company, 1878), unpaged.
18. Isham, *op. cit.,* pp. 19, 20.
19. Letter from William R. Mead to Charles Moore, April 11, 1918, quoted in Charles Moore, *Daniel H. Burham, Architect, Planner of Cities* (Boston and New York: Houghton Mifflin Company, 1921), I, p. 67.
20. *Proceedings of the 11th Convention, A.I.A., 1877,* p. 17.
21. *Proceedings of the 13th Convention, A.I.A., 1879,* p. 65; and George C. Mason, "Colonial Architecture," *American Architect and Building News,* X (August 13, 1881), p. 72.

22. "The Massachusetts State House, Boston," in Ware (Editor), *The Georgian Period*, III, p. 119.

23. *Proceedings of the 24th Convention, A.I.A., 1890*, pp. 33–35.

24. *Proceedings of the 31st Convention, A.I.A., 1897*, p. 27.

25. Glenn Brown, *1860–1930 Memories, a Winning Crusade to Revive George Washington's Vision of a Capital City* (Washington: The Author, 1931), pp. 235, 236.

26. *Ibid.*, p. 236.

27. *Proceedings of the 32nd Convention, A.I.A., 1898*, p. 12.

28. *Proceedings of the 33rd Convention, A.I.A., 1899*, p. 18.

29. Brown, *op. cit.*, pp. 238, 239.

30. *Ibid.*, p. 239.

31. *Proceedings of the 36th Convention, A.I.A., 1902*, p. 9.

32. Brown, *loc. cit.*

33. *Proceedings of the 37th Convention, A.I.A., 1903*, pp. 56, 58.

34. *Proceedings of the 39th Convention, A.I.A., 1905*, p. 53.

35. *Proceedings of the 41st Convention, A.I.A., 1907*, p. 61.

36. *Proceedings of the 48th Convention, A.I.A., 1914*, pp. 13, 23.

37. *Proceedings of the 50th Convention, A.I.A., 1916*, pp. 18, 19.

38. *Ibid.*, p. 25.

39. *Ibid.*, pp. 38, 39.

40. *Proceedings of the 55th Convention, A.I.A., 1922*, pp. 48, 86, 87.

41. *Proceedings of the 56th Convention, A.I.A., 1923*, pp. 37, 38.

42. *Proceedings of the 57th Convention, A.I.A., 1924*, pp. 56–58.

43. *Proceedings of the 58th Convention, A.I.A., 1925*, p. 106; and *Proceedings of the 59th Convention, A.I.A., 1926*, p. 125.

44. *Proceedings of the 35th Convention, A.I.A., 1901*, p. 17.

45. Horace Wells Sellers, "Origin of the Committee on Preservation of Historic Monuments," Typescript in American Philosophical Society (Copy in Files of Independence National Historical Park).

46. Typed copy of the resolution, January 20, 1910, in A.I.A. papers, Historical Society of Pennsylvania (Microfilm at Independence National Historical Park).

47. Letter from Carl A. Ziegler to Alfred Bendiner, November 1, 1950 (Independence National Historical Park).

48. Letter from Carl A. Ziegler to Mayor John E. Reyburn, April 6, 1910, in A.I.A. papers, Historical Society of Pennsylvania (Microfilm in Independence National Historical Park).

49. Letter from Ziegler to Bendiner, November 1, 1950.

50. Philadelphia *Record*, October 26, 1913, cited in Edward M. Riley, "The Independence Hall Group," *Historic Philadelphia*, p. 40.

51. *Proceedings of the 50th Convention, A.I.A., 1916*, p. 92.

52. *Proceedings of the 57th Convention, A.I.A., 1924*, p. 129; and *Proceedings of the 59th Convention, A.I.A., 1926*, p. 157.

53. *Proceedings of the 60th Convention, A.I.A., 1927*, p. 154.

54. *Proceedings of the 49th Convention, A.I.A., 1915*, p. 123.

55. N. C. Curtis, "The Work of the Louisiana Chapter in Urging the Preservation of the Historic Architecture of New Orleans, and in Seeking to Restore Its Influence in Modern Building," *Journal of the A.I.A.*, IV (May, 1916), pp. 219, 220.

56. *Proceedings of the 50th Convention, A.I.A., 1916*, p. 92.

57. *Proceedings of the 60th Convention, A.I.A., 1927,* p. 155; William Henry Hanckel, "The Preservation Movement in Charleston, 1920–1962" (Unpublished Master's thesis, University of South Carolina, Columbia, South Carolina, 1962), pp. 29–33; and Jacob Morrison, *Historic Preservation Law* (New Orleans, Louisiana: Pelican Publishing Company, 1957), pp. 86, 101.

58. *Proceedings of the 56th Convention, A.I.A., 1923,* pp. 103, 104.

59. *Proceedings of the 40th Convention, A.I.A., 1906,* pp. 179, 180.

60. *Proceedings of the 43rd Convention, A.I.A., 1909,* p. 145.

61. *Proceedings of the 45th Convention, A.I.A., 1911,* p. 114.

62. *Proceedings of the 48th Convention, A.I.A., 1914,* p. 49.

63. Bach, "Books on Colonial Architecture, Part I," *Architectural Record,* XXXVIII (August, 1915), p. 693.

64. Bach, "Books on Colonial Architecture, Part VIII," *Architectural Record,* XLII (November, 1917), pp. 488–491.

65. *Proceedings of the 51st Convention, A.I.A., 1918,* p. 119.

66. *Proceedings of the 56th Convention, A.I.A., 1923,* p. 103.

67. *Ibid.,* p. 105.

68. *Proceedings of the 57th Convention, A.I.A., 1924,* p. 126.

69. *Proceedings of the 59th Convention, A.I.A., 1926,* p. 157.

70. *Proceedings of the 60th Convention, A.I.A., 1927,* p. 153.

71. William Rotch Ware (Editor), *The Georgian Period* (Boston: American Architect and Building News Company, 1901), 3 v.

72. "Valedictory and Felicitation," White Pine Bureau, *White Pine Series of Architectural Monographs,* X, 6 (1924), p. 16.

73. "Salutation," *White Pine Series,* I, 1 (1915), unpaged.

74. "The White Pine Series of Architectural Monographs," *White Pine Series,* XII, 1 (1926), p. 11.

75. "The American Renaissance," *White Pine Series,* XII, 3 (1926), p. 5.

76. *Proceedings of the 54th Convention, A.I.A., 1921,* p. 157.

77. Bach, "Books on Colonial Architecture, Part III," *Architectural Record,* XXXIX (February, 1916), p. 188.

78. Henry W. Kent, "The American Wing in Its Relation to the History of Museum Development," *Bulletin of the Metropolitan Museum of Art,* XVII (November, 1922, Part II), pp. 14, 15.

79. Nilson and Keyland, *Guide to Skansen I,* p. 5; and F.A. Bather, "The Triumph of Hazelius," *Museums Journal,* XVI (December, 1916), p. 132.

80. Appleton, "Report," *Old-Time New England,* XXX (April, 1940), pp. 114, 115; and XXIX (April, 1939), p. 144.

81. Josephine P. Driver, "Ben: Perley Poore of Indian Hill," *Essex Institute Historical Collections,* LXXXIX (January, 1953), pp. 10–12.

82. Appleton, "Report," *Old-Time New England,* XXIX (April, 1939), p. 144.

83. L. Earle Rowe, "The Pendleton Collection and Its Setting," *Bulletin of the Metropolitan Museum of Art,* XVII (November, 1922, Part II), pp. 22, 23.

84. Francis Henry Appleton, "Address of the President," *Annual Report of the Essex Institute* (May 6, 1912), p. 8.

85. George F. Dow, "Report of the Secretary," *Annual Report of the Essex Institute* (May 7, 1900), p. 20.

86. Robert S. Rantoul, "President's Address," *Annual Report of the Essex Institute* (May 5, 1902), p. 7.

87. Francis H. Appleton, "President's Address," *Annual Report of the Essex Institute* (May 1, 1905), pp. 8, 9.

88. Dow, "Report," *Annual Report of the Essex Institute* (May 6, 1907), p. 17.

89. *Ibid.*, pp. 14, 15; and George F. Dow, "Museums and the Preservation of Houses," *Bulletin of the Metropolitan Museum of Art*, XVII (November, 1922, Part II), pp. 16, 17.

90. Dow, *op. cit.*, pp. 17, 18.

91. Isham, *Antiquaries*, p. 21.

92. Dow, "Report," *Annual Report of the Essex Institute* (May 3, 1909), p. 18.

93. *Ibid.* (May 2, 1910), pp. 16, 17.

94. *Ibid.* (May 1, 1911), p. 18; and (May 6, 1912), p. 16.

95. *Ibid.* (May 5, 1913), pp. 17, 18.

96. *Ibid.*, p. 18.

97. *Ibid.* (May 1, 1916), p. 17.

98. Cora Hinkley Atwell and Marcia B. Ferguson, "Milwaukee Past and Present," *D.A.R. Magazine*, XLIX (December, 1916), pp. 367–371.

99. Henry W. Kent, "The Walpole Society, 1910–1935," quoted in Walpole Society, *The Twenty-Fifth Anniversary Meeting of the Walpole Society* (Boston: The Society, 1935), pp. 16–19.

100. Robert W. DeForest, quoted in Metropolitan Museum of Art, *Addresses at the Opening of the American Wing* (New York: The Museum, 1925), p. 4.

101. Letter from Henry W. Kent to the Walpole Society, October 3, 1947, quoted in Walpole Society, *Walpole Society Notebook, 1947*, pp. 20, 21.

102. Henry W. Kent, "Walpole Society," quoted in Walpole Society, *Twenty-Fifth Anniversary*, p. 20.

103. Robert W. DeForest, quoted in Metropolitan Museum, *op. cit.*, p. 5.

104. *Ibid.*

105. Letter from William Sumner Appleton to Edith May Tilley, October 27, 1913 (S.P.N.E.A. Files)

106. Letter from Edith May Tilley to William Sumner Appleton, October 29, 1913 (S.P.N.E.A. Files).

107. Letter from L. Earle Rowe to William Sumner Appleton, September 25, 1916; letter from William Sumner Appleton to L. Earle Rowe, September 26, 1916; and letter from L. Earle Rowe to William Sumner Appleton, September 29, 1916 (S.P.N.E.A. Files).

108. Letter from Harriet Faxon to the Metropolitan Museum, February 19, 1916 (Metropolitan Museum Archives, New York).

109. Letter from Edward Robinson to William Sumner Appleton, February 25, 1916 (Metropolitan Museum Archives).

110. Letter from William Sumner Appleton to Edward Robinson, March 4, 1916 (Metropolitan Museum Archives).

111. Letter from Frank C. Baldwin to R. T. Haines Halsey, June 14, 1916 (Metropolitan Museum Archives).

112. Letter from D. Friedley to Edward Robinson, June 22, 1916 (Metropolitan Museum Archives).

113. Letter from Robert DeForest to R. T. Haines Halsey, June 19, 1916 (Metropolitan Museum Archives).

114. Letter from Henry Kent to Mr. Reynolds, July 5, 1916 (Metropolitan Museum Archives).

115. Letter from Edwin Barber to Henry Kent, July 19, 1916 (Metropolitan Museum Archives).

116. Letter from Henry Kent to William Sumner Appleton, September 26, 1916 (Metropolitan Museum Archives).

117. Letter from William Sumner Appleton to Henry Kent, September 29, 1916 (Metropolitan Museum Archives).

118. Letter from Henry Kent to William Sumner Appleton, October 4, 1916 (Metropolitan Museum Archives).

119. Letter from Robert DeForest to Henry Kent, October 6, 1916 (Metropolitan Museum Archives).

120. Letter from William Sumner Appleton to Henry Kent, October 5, 1916 (Metropolitan Museum Archives)

121. Letter from William Sumner Appleton to Morris Gray, March 16, 1915 (S.P.N.E.A. Files).

122. Letter from Henry Kent to Joseph Chandler, April 16, 1917 (Metropolitan Museum Archives).

123. Letter from Joseph Chandler to Henry Kent, April 17, 1917 (Metropolitan Museum Archives).

124. Appleton, "Report," *Bulletin of the S.P.N.E.A.*, IX (November, 1918), p. 33.

125. *Ibid.*, VI (April, 1915), p. 11.

126. *Ibid.*, VII (May, 1916), p. 20.

127. *Ibid.*, X (October, 1919), p. 15.

128. Letter from Henry Kent to R. T. Haines Halsey, May 31, 1918 (Metropolitan Museum Archives).

129. Letter from R. T. Haines Halsey to Joseph Breck, early June, 1918 (Metropolitan Museum Archives).

130. Letter from Joseph Breck to Brooks Reed Gallery, Inc., June 5, 1918; and letter from Brooks Reed to Joseph Breck, June 6, 1918 (Metropolitan Museum Archives).

131. Letter from Wallace Nutting to R. T. Haines Halsey, June 15, 1918 (Metropolitan Museum Archives).

132. Letter from Henry Kent to R. T. Haines Halsey, June 18, 1918; and letter from Henry Kent to Norman Isham, June 18, 1918 (Metropolitan Museum Archives).

133. Letter from Henry Kent to R. T. Haines Halsey, June 25, 1918 (Metropolitan Museum Archives).

134. Letter from Wallace Nutting to R .T. Haines Halsey, July 6, 1918, in Wallace Nutting, "The Wentworth-Gardner House," portfolio of photographs with some comments, ca. 1917 (Metropolitan Museum Library).

135. Letter from R. T. Haines Halsey to Edward Robinson, September 7, 1918 (Metropolitan Museum Archives).

136. Telegram from Joseph Breck to R. T. Haines Halsey, July 24, 1918 (Metropolitan Museum Archives).

137. Letter from R. T. Haines Halsey to Henry Kent, July 25, 1918 (Metropolitan Museum Archives).

138. Message to Henry Kent from M. H. Warren, July 25, 1918 (Metropolitan Museum Archives).

139. Letter from Henry Kent to R. T. Haines Halsey, August 2, 1918 (Metropolitan Museum Archives).

140. Letter from DeForest Brothers to Henry Kent, August 30, 1918 (Metropolitan Museum Archives).

141. Letter from William Sumner Appleton to Edward Robinson, September 3, 1918 (S.P.N.E.A. Files)

142. Letter from Edward Robinson to R. T. Haines Halsey, September 5, 1918 (Metropolitan Museum Archives).

143. Letter from R. T. Haines Halsey to Edward Robinson, September 7, 1918 (Metropolitan Museum Archives).

144. Letter from Edward Robinson to William Sumner Appleton, September 9, 1918 (S.P.N.E.A. Files).

145. Letter from William Sumner Appleton to Edward Robinson, September 15, 1918 (S.P.N.E.A. Files).

146. Letter from Edward Robinson to William Sumner Appleton, September 18, 1918 (S.P.N.E.A. Files).

147. Letter from William Sumner Appleton to Edward Robinson, October 18, 1918 (S.P.N.E.A. Files).

148. Letter from Barrett Wendell to Edward Robinson, October 15, 1918 (Metropolitan Museum Archives).

149. Letter from Susan Wentworth to William Sumner Appleton, November 7, 1920 (S.P.N.E.A. Files).

150. Letter from William Sumner Appleton to Edward Robinson, September 3, 1918 (Metropolitan Museum Archives).

151. *New York Times,* February 12, 1919.

152. Mervin J. Curl, "New York Art Centre Buys Historic New Hampshire House," Boston *Herald,* March 2, 1919.

153. "Preserve the Landmarks" (Editorial), Philadelphia *Record,* March 9, 1919.

154. Charles O. Cornelius, "The Wentworth-Gardner House," *Bulletin of the Metropolitan Museum of Art,* XIV (February, 1919), p. 24.

155. Letter from William M. Bogart to the Metropolitan Museum, February 24, 1919 (Metropolitan Museum Archives).

156. Letter from Henry Kent to William Sumner Appleton, July 10, 1919 (S.P.N.E.A. Files).

157. Appleton, "Report," *Bulletin of the S.P.N.E.A.,* X (October, 1919), p. 16.

158. Letter from the Reverend Donald Millar to William Sumner Appleton, February 19, 1920 (S.P.N.E.A. Files).

159. Edward Robinson, "Notes on the Wentworth-Gardner House," Typewritten report dated 1921, 4 pp. (Metropolitan Museum Archives).

160. Letter from F. Kingsbury Curtis to William Sumner Appleton, November 14, 1922 (S.P.N.E.A. Files).

161. Night letter from William Sumner Appleton to F. Kingsbury Curtis, November 20, 1922; and letter from William Sumner Appleton to Henry Kent, November 22, 1922 (S.P.N.E.A. Files).

162. Letter from F. Kingsbury Curtis to William Sumner Appleton, November 21, 1922 (S.P.N.E.A. Files).

163. Letter from William Sumner Appleton to F. Kingsbury Curtis, November 23, 1922 (S.P.N.E.A. Files).

164. Letter from William Sumner Appleton to Henry Kent, November 29, 1922 (S.P.N.E.A. Files).
165. Letter from Henry Kent to William Sumner Appleton, December 4, 1922 (S.P.N.E.A. Files).
166. Letter from Charles Walker to William Sumner Appleton, April 16, 1923 (S.P.N.E.A. Files).
167. "The Wing of American Art," *Bulletin of the Metropolitan Museum of Art*, XVII (November, 1922), p. 243; and R. T. Haines Halsey, "Early American Rooms in the Museum," *Bulletin of the Metropolitan Museum of Art*, XVII (November, 1922, Part II), pp. 6, 7.
168. Charles O. Cornelius and R. T. Haines Halsey, "The American Wing," *Bulletin of the Metropolitan Museum of Art*, XIX (November, 1924), p. 251.
169. Isham, *Antiquaries*, pp. 21, 22.
170. R. T. Haines Halsey, quoted in Metropolitan Museum, *Addresses*, pp. 9, 10.
171. "The American Wing: A Letter," *Bulletin of the Metropolitan Museum of Art*, XX (January, 1925), p. 28.
172. *Bulletin of the Metropolitan Museum of Art*, XX (February, 1925), pp. 43, 44.
173. Emily Frelinghuysen, "Early American Exhibition," *D.A.R. Magazine*, LXI (January, 1927) p. 13.
174. Letter from Edwin Barber to Henry Kent, July 19, 1916 (Metropolitan Museum Archives).
175. Letter from William Sumner Appleton to Morris Gray, March 16, 1915; and letter from Morris Gray to William Sumner Appleton, March 18, 1915 (S.P.N.E.A. Files).
176. Brooklyn Institute of Arts and Sciences, *Museums of the Brooklyn Institute of Arts and Sciences, Reports, 1914*, p. 36; *1915*, p. 40; *1916*, p. 48; *1917*, p. 44; *1918*, p. 24; *1920*, p. 24; *1922*, p. 16; *1923*, p. 13; *1924*, p. 15.
177. Luke Vincent Lockwood, "The Secretary House," *Brooklyn Museum Quarterly*, X (July, 1923), p. 103.
178. Letter from Robert Harsche to William Sumner Appleton, June 27, 1919; and letter from William Sumner Appleton to Robert Harsche, July 2, 1919 (S.P.N.E.A. Files).
179. *Proceedings of the 56th Convention, A.I.A., 1923*, p. 105.
180. Harold Donaldson Eberlein, "Colonial Seats in Fairmount Park, Philadelphia," *American Homes and Gardens*, XII (August, 1915), pp. 255, 256.
181. Letter from Fiske Kimball to William Sumner Appleton, June 14, 1925 (S.P.N.E.A. Files).
182. Fiske Kimball, "Mount Pleasant," *Pennsylvania Museum Bulletin*, XXII (September, 1926), pp. 197–200.
183. Fiske Kimball, "Philadelphia's 'Colonial Chain,'" *Art and Archaeology*, XXI (April, 1926), pp. 198, 199, 203.

CHAPTER X

1. "William Sumner Appleton, 1874–1947," *Old-Time New England*, XXXVIII (April, 1948), pp. 71, 72.
2. *Ibid.*; and Paul Revere Memorial Association, *Handbook of the Paul Revere Memorial Association* (Boston: The Association, 1956), p. 6.

3. William Sumner Appleton, "Diary, 1906–1910," March 23, 1909 (S.P.N.E.A. Files, Boston).

4. *Ibid.,* December 18, 20, 22, and 23, 1909.

5. *Ibid.,* December 28, 1909.

6. Charles K. Bolton, "Address," *Old-Time New England,* XXX (April, 1940), p. 108.

7. Letter from Leroy Brown to William Sumner Appleton, January 11, 1910, Scrapbook dealing with the early history of the S.P.N.E.A., I, unpaged (S.P.N.E.A. Files).

8. *Lexington Minute Man,* July 9, 1910, clipping in Scrapbook on S.P.N.E.A., I (S.P.N.E.A. Files).

9. Appleton, "Diary," January 20, 21, 1910 (S.P.N.E.A. Files).

10. Boston *Transcript,* April 23, 1910 (S.P.N.E.A. Files).

11. *Ibid.;* Appleton, "Diary," March 22, 1910; and Senate Bill, No. 281, March 4, 1910, Scrapbook on S.P.N.E.A., I (S.P.N.E.A. Files).

12. Museum of Fine Arts, "Method of Registration Employed by the Museum of Fine Arts, Boston" (S.P.N.E.A. Files).

13. Scrapbook on S.P.N.E.A., I (S.P.N.E.A. Files).

14. William Sumner Appleton, "A Brief Account of the Society for the Preservation of New England Antiquities," Typewritten manuscript for Charles Messer Stowe, ca. 1930 (S.P.N.E.A. Files).

15. Letter from Fanny C. Stone to William Sumner Appleton, April 26, 1910, Scrapbook on S.P.N.E.A., I (S.P.N.E.A. Files).

16. Circular to prospective members, Scrapbook on S.P.N.E.A., II (S.P.N.E.A. Files).

17. *Bulletin of the S.P.N.E.A.,* I (May, 1910), pp. 1, 4–6.

18. Appleton, "Report," *Old-Time New England,* XI (April, 1921), p. 186.

19. *Bulletin of the S.P.N.E.A.,* II (March, 1911), p. 6.

20. [Appleton], "The Ilsley House," *ibid.* (August, 1911), pp. 11, 12.

21. Appleton, "Report," *Bulletin of the S.P.N.E.A.,* III (July, 1912), p. 20.

22. [Appleton], "Our Greatest Need—New Members," *Bulletin of the S.P.N.E.A.,* III (February, 1913), p. 26.

23. [Appleton], "The Helen F. Kimball Emergency Fund," *Bulletin of the S.P.N.E.A.,* III (February, 1913), p. 11.

24. Appleton, "Report," *Old-Time New England,* XI (April, 1921), p. 186.

25. [Appleton], "The Campaign to Buy the Corner Lot," *Bulletin of the S.P.N.E.A.,* III (February, 1913), pp. 18, 19.

26. Appleton, printed letter to prospective members, ca. May, 1913, Scrapbook of printed forms, I, unpaged (S.P.N.E.A. Files).

27. [William Sumner Appleton], *The Colonial Homes of New England, Shall They Be Preserved?* (Boston: Society for the Preservation of New England Antiquities, 1913), pp. 6, 7.

28. Appleton, printed letter, January 5, 1914, Scrapbook of printed forms, I (S.P.N.E.A. Files).

29. Appleton, "Report," *Bulletin of the S.P.N.E.A.,* VI (April, 1915), pp. 18, 19.

30. *Ibid.,* V (April, 1914), pp. 8, 9.

31. Clinton (Massachusetts) *Courant,* October 17, 1914, in the clipping collection (Fruitlands Museum, Harvard, Massachusetts).

32. [Appleton], "The Bennett-Boardman House, Saugus, Mass.," *Bulletin of the S.P.N.E.A.,* V (December, 1914), p. 1.

33. [Appleton], "The Harrison Gray Otis House," *Bulletin of the S.P.N.E.A.,* VIII (March, 1917), p. 7.

34. Appleton, "Report," *Old-Time New England,* XI (April, 1921), p. 186.

35. Letter from Samuel P. Avery to William Sumner Appleton, February 19, 1918 (S.P.N.E.A. Files).

36. [Appleton], "Third Liberty Loan Endowment Fund," *Bulletin of the S.P.N.E.A.,* IX (February, 1919), p. 8.

37. Letter from William Sumner Appleton to Mary Ware, April 18, 1918 (S.P.N.E.A. Files).

38. Appleton, "Report," *Bulletin of the S.P.N.E.A.,* IX (November, 1918), p. 25.

39. Appleton, printed letter to Massachusetts members, October 28, 1918, Scrapbook of printed forms, II (S.P.N.E.A. Files).

40. Appleton, "Report," *Bulletin of the S.P.N.E.A.,* X (October, 1919), pp. 18, 19.

41. Appleton, "Destruction and Preservation," *Art and Archaeology,* VIII (May, 1919), pp. 176–179.

42. Letter from William Sumner Appleton to George Peabody Wetmore, January 11, 1915, Scrapbook dealing with the history of the preservation and restoration of the Abraham Brown house, Watertown, Massachusetts, I, p. 4 (S.P.N.E.A. Files).

43. Letter from William Sumner Appleton to Charles Abbott, June 8, 1915, Brown House Scrapbook, I, p. 6 (S.P.N.E.A. Files); and Appleton, "Report," *Bulletin of the S.P.N.E.A.,* VII (May, 1916), p. 15.

44. Appleton, *op. cit.,* p. 16.

45. Letter from William Sumner Appleton to Norman Isham, October 4, 1917, Brown House Scrapbook, I, p. 14 (S.P.N.E.A. Files).

46. Letter from Norman Isham to William Sumner Appleton, October 5, 1917, Brown House Scrapbook, I, p. 14 (S.P.N.E.A. Files).

47. Letter from Joseph Chandler to William Sumner Appleton, October 8, 1917, Brown House Scrapbook, I, p. 15 (S.P.N.E.A. Files).

48. Letter from Murray Corse to William Sumner Appleton, May 22, 1918, Brown House Scrapbook, I, p. 18 (S.P.N.E.A. Files).

49. Appleton, "Report to the Trustees," December 30, 1918, Brown House Scrapbook, I, pp. 21, 22 (S.P.N.E.A. Files); and Appleton, "Report," *Old-Time New England,* XI (July, 1920), p. 24.

50. Letter from William Sumner Appleton to some Massachusetts members, April 12, 1919, Brown House Scrapbook, I, p. 34 (S.P.N.E.A. Files).

51. Letter from William Sumner Appleton to Heloise Meyer, April 21, 1919, Brown House Scrapbook, I, p. 26 (S.P.N.E.A. Files).

52. Letter from William Sumner Appleton to Mary C. Wheelright, May 24, 1919, letter from William Sumner Appleton to Mary C. Wheelright, November 10, 1919, and letter from Mary C. Wheelright to William Sumner Appleton, ca. November 19, 1919, Brown House Scrapbook, I, pp. 53, 130, 132 (S.P.N.E.A. Files).

53. Letter from William Sumner Appleton to Mary C. Wheelright, February 2, 1921, Brown House Scrapbook, II, p. 34 (S.P.N.E.A. Files).

54. Letter from George L. Gould to William Sumner Appleton, August 26, 1919, Brown House Scrapbook, I, p. 105 (S.P.N.E.A. Files).

55. Letter from William Sumner Appleton to George L. Gould, August 29, 1919, Brown House Scrapbook, I, p. 109 (S.P.N.E.A. Files).

56. Letter from William Sumner Appleton to Helen E. Royce, December 1, 1919, Brown House Scrapbook, I, p. 135.

57. Appleton, "Report," *Old-Time New England*, XIII (April, 1923), pp. 176, 177.

58. Letter from William Sumner Appleton to his sister Mrs. Eleanor Standen, December 14, 1937 (S.P.N.E.A. Files).

59. Appleton, "Report," *Old-Time New England*, XI (April, 1921), pp. 185, 187.

60. Appleton, printed letter to members, April 1, 1920, Scrapbook of printed forms, II, unpaged (S.P.N.E.A. Files).

61. Appleton, "Report," *Old-Time New England*, XII (April, 1922), pp. 164, 165.

62. *Ibid.*, XV (July, 1924), p. 20; and [Appleton], "The Otis House and Proposed Fireproof Museum," *Old-Time New England*, XVII (October, 1926), pp. 90–92.

63. Horace Wells Sellers, "Protection of Historic Buildings," *Journal of the A.I.A.*, VIII (February, 1920), p. 63.

64. *Proceedings of the 49th Convention, A.I.A., 1915*, p. 123.

65. Letter from Henry Kent to William Sumner Appleton, July 13, 1920 (S.P.N.E.A. Files).

66. Appleton, "Report," *Old-Time New England*, XIII (April, 1923), p. 193.

67. Correspondence between Edgar G. Miller and William Sumner Appleton, 1920–1926 (S.P.N.E.A. Files).

68. Correspondence between Susan P. Frost and William Sumner Appleton, 1920–1925 (S.P.N.E.A. Files).

69. Hanckel, "The Preservation Movement in Charleston," pp. 8–12.

70. Letter from Clarence W. Brazer to William Sumner Appleton, February 17, 1926 (S.P.N.E.A. Files).

71. Letter from William Sumner Appleton to Clarence Brazer, February 19, 1926 (S.P.N.E.A. Files).

72. Letter from Clarence Brazer to William Sumner Appleton, February 24, 1926 (S.P.N.E.A. Files).

73. Letter from William Sumner Appleton to Clarence Brazer, February 27, 1926 (S.P.N.E.A. Files).

74. Letter from Clarence Brazer to William Sumner Appleton, March 11, 1926 (S.P.N.E.A. Files).

75. Letter from William Sumner Appleton to Clarence Brazer, March 19, 1926; and letter from Clarence Brazer to William Sumner Appleton, April 16, 1926 (S.P.N.E.A. Files).

76. Letter from William Sumner Appleton to Clarence Brazer, March 21, 1941 (S.P.N.E.A. Files).

77. Letter from Clarence Brazer to William Sumner Appleton, March 24, 1941 (S.P.N.E.A. Files).

78. [Appleton], "Notes," *Bulletin of the S.P.N.E.A.*, V (December, 1914), pp. 18, 19.

79. Letter from William Sumner Appleton to the Director of the Northern Museum, Stockholm, September 5, 1918 (S.P.N.E.A. Files).

80. Appleton, "Destruction and Preservation," *Art and Archaeology*, VIII (May, 1919), pp. 176, 177.

81. Letter from G. Berg to William Sumner Appleton, August 2, 1927 (S.P.N.E.A. Files).

82. Letter from A. R. Powys to William Sumner Appleton, February 4, 1924, quoted in *Old-Time New England,* XV (October, 1924), pp. 91, 92.

83. A. R. Powys, "Ancient Buildings in America," *48th Annual Report, Society for the Protection of Ancient Buildings* (June, 1925), pp. 18, 19.

84. Letter from William Sumner Appleton to A. R. Powys, May 21, 1926, quoted in *49th Annual Report, S.P.A.B.* (May, 1926), pp. 16, 17.

85. Letter from William Sumner Appleton to S. H. Hamer, July 17, 1926 (S.P.N.E.A. Files).

86. Letter from S. H. Hamer to William Sumner Appleton, July 28, 1926 (S.P.N.E.A. Files).

87. Interview with Miss E. Florence Addison and Bertram K. Little concerning William Sumner Appleton, in the Harrison Gray Otis house, Boston, Massachusetts, February 5, 1960, typewritten transcript of tape recording, in the possession of the author.

88. Letter from Fiske Kimball to William Sumner Appleton, December 10, 1942 (S.P.N.E.A. Files).

CHAPTER XI

1. Kenneth Chorley, "What's Wrong with Historic Preservation," in National Trust for Historic Preservation, *Primer for Preservation: A Handbook for Historic-House Keeping* (Historic-House Keeping Series No. 1; Washington: National Trust for Historic Preservation and New York State Historical Association, 1955), p. 21.

2. Committee on Standards and Surveys, *Criteria for Evaluating Historic Sites and Buildings* (Washington: National Trust for Historic Preservation, 1956), pp. 3, 4, 6.

3. "Summary of the Round Table Discussion on the Preservation of Historic Architectural Monuments, Tuesday, March 18, 1941, at the Library of Congress," *Journal of the American Society of Architectural Historians,* I (April, 1941), p. 22.

4. Trustees of Scenic and Historic Places and Objects, *Memorial to the Legislature of the State of New York* (January, 1895), p. 6; and American Scenic, *5th Annual Report, 1900,* pp. 51, 52.

5. American Scenic, *18th Annual Report, 1913,* pp. 158, 159.

6. American Scenic, *19th Annual Report, 1914,* p. 19.

7. American Scenic, *30th Annual Report, 1925,* p. 113.

8. Appleton, "Report," *Bulletin of the S.P.N.E.A.,* X (October, 1919), pp. 24, 25.

9. *Ibid.,* VI (April, 1915), p. 5.

10. *Ibid.,* VII (May, 1916), p. 14.

11. Interview with Miss E. Florence Addison and Bertram K. Little, February 5, 1960.

12. Appleton, "Report," *Old-Time New England,* XI (July, 1920), pp. 34, 35.

13. *Ibid.* (April, 1921), pp. 173, 175.

14. Directors of the Old South Work, *The Old South Meeting House,* No. 183 of the *Old South Leaflets,* p. 6.

15. J. Smith Futhey and James Pollock, quoted in *Proceedings on the*

Occasion of the Centennial Celebration of the Occupation of Valley Forge, pp. 102, 113.

16. Select Committee of the New York State Legislature, quoted in Richard Caldwell, *A True History,* pp. 20–23.

17. *Mount Vernon Record,* I (July, 1858), p. 1.

18. J. M. A. Sheldon, "The Old Indian House," *Old-Time New England,* XII (January, 1922), p. 102.

19. J. M. A. Sheldon, "The Personality of the Rev. John Williams House," *History and Proceedings of the Pocumtuck Valley Memorial Association,* VI (1912–1920), p. 449.

20. J. D. Moffat, quoted in Memorial Association of the District of Columbia, *Words from Many Sources,* p. 31.

21. *The Old South Meeting House,* p. 8.

22. Municipal Art Society of Hartford, Connecticut, *Bulletin No. 15: The Old State House, Hartford, Why It Should Be Preserved,* p. 7.

23. James G. Randall, "When Jefferson's Home Was Bequeathed to the United States," *South Atlantic Quarterly,* XXIII (January, 1924), p. 39.

24. Edwin Fairfax Naulty, *Historic Harewood, Of Pleasant Memory and Patriotic Association* (Philadelphia: Washington Manor Association for the Purchase and Preservation of Historic Harewood, 1901), p. 29.

25. "Sale," *True Democratic Banner,* Morristown, New Jersey, June 5, 1873 (Morristown National Historical Park).

26. *The Old South Meeting House,* p. 12.

27. Governor Edwin P. Morrow, quoted in Willard Rouse Jillson, *The "Old Kentucky Home"* (Reprint from *Register of the Kentucky State Historical Society,* May, 1921, Vol. 19, No. 56; n.p., n.n., n.d.) p. 10.

28. Tolman, *Catalog of a Portion of the Concord Antiquarian Society,* unpaged.

29. *Proceedings of the 32nd Convention, A.I.A., 1898,* p. 12.

30. Augustus E. Alden, *Pilgrim Alden, the Story of the Life of the First John Alden in America* (Boston: James H. Earle and Company, 1902), p. 173.

31. American Scenic, *10th Annual Report, 1905,* pp. 142, 143.

32. Mary Beecher Longyear, quote from her diary in Longyear Foundation, *Longyear Foundation, Its Purpose and Unfoldment* (Boston: Trustees of Longyear Foundation, 1946), p. 8.

33. Longyear Foundation, *op. cit.,* pp. 7–14.

34. Henry Kent, "The Glebe-House, Woodbury, Connecticut," *Old-Time New England,* XIII (April, 1923), p. 173.

35. Letter from Governor Curtis Guild, Jr., to the Paul Revere Memorial Association, November 29, 1907, quoted in Paul Revere Memorial Association, *Handbook,* pp. 9, 10.

36. Letter from William Sumner Appleton to the merchants of Cambridge, Mass., May 15, 1912, Scrapbook on S.P.N.E.A., III, unpaged (S.P.N.E.A. Files).

37. Charlotte J. Fairbairn, "John Brown's Fort" (Typewritten manuscript, August 15, 1961, Files of Region 5, National Park Service, 143 South Third Street, Philadelphia), pp. 16–43.

38. Caroline O. Emmerton, *The Chronicles of Three Old Houses* (Boston: Thomas Todd Company, 1935), pp. 30, 39.

39. "The Massachusetts State House, Boston," in Ware (Editor), *The Georgian Period,* III, p. 119.

40. William C. Endicott, "Address of the President," *Annual Report of the Essex Institute* (May 7, 1917), p. 7.

41. Letter from Edgar G. Miller to William Sumner Appleton, September 28, 1926; and letter from Dr. James Bordley, Jr., to Edgar G. Miller, September 29, 1926 (S.P.N.E.A. Files).

42. Committee for the Preservation of Park Street Church, *The Preservation of Park Street Church, Boston* (Boston: The Committee, 1903), pp. 3–18.

43. [L. M. Powers], *The Story of an Interesting and Historic Old House in Gloucester, Massachusetts* (Boston: Murray Press, ca. 1916), pp. 5–15.

44. [Appleton], "A Summer's Record of Preservation Work in New England," *Bulletin of the S.P.N.E.A.,* VII (December, 1916), pp. 11–13.

45. Appleton, "Report," *Bulletin of the S.P.N.E.A.,* IX (November, 1918), pp. 28, 29.

46. *Proceedings of the 59th Convention of the A.I.A., 1926,* p. 158.

47. Thomas T. Waterman, *The Mansions of Virginia, 1706–1776* (Chapel Hill, North Carolina: University of North Carolina Press, 1945), p. 112.

CHAPTER XII

1. American Scenic, *7th Annual Report, 1902,* pp. 79, 80.

2. Horace Sellers, "Protection of Historic Buildings," *Journal of the A.I.A.,* VIII (February, 1920), pp. 62, 63.

3. *Proceedings of the 54th Convention, A.I.A., 1921,* p. 157.

4. *Proceedings of the 56th Convention, A.I.A., 1923,* p. 105.

5. *Proceedings of the 59th Convention, A.I.A., 1926,* p. 157.

6. A. Lawrence Kocher, typewritten manuscript on the history of restorations, given to the author during an interview in Williamsburg, Virginia, December 27, 1959, in the author's possession; and William Graves Perry, "Restoration of Williamsburg, Notes on the Architecture," *Architectural Record,* LXXVIII (December, 1935), p. 370.

7. U. S. Department of the Interior, National Park Service, *National Park Service Restoration Policy Statement* (Washington: U. S. Department of the Interior, 1956, mimeographed), p. 1.

8. *Ibid.,* p. 2.

9. Letter from Mrs. Henry Ferguson to William Sumner Appleton, January 27, 1912 (S.P.N.E.A. Files).

10. American Scenic, *op. cit.,* p. 70.

11. Ashbee, *A Report by Mr. C. R. Ashbee to the Council of the National Trust,* p. 5.

12. *Old-Time New England,* XVIII (July, 1927), p. 48.

13. Appleton, "Report," *Bulletin of the S.P.N.E.A.,* VII (May, 1916), p. 5.

14. Chandler, *The Colonial House,* p. 160.

15. Philadelphia *Evening Bulletin,* May 20, 1854 (Independence National Historical Park).

16. Letter from Horace Sellers to Morris L. Cooke, June 14, 1913, copy on microfilm dealing with Congress Hall restoration (Independence National Historical Park).

17. Letter from Mrs. Henry Ferguson to William Sumner Appleton, January 27, 1912 (S.P.N.E.A. Files); Bertha Chadwick Trowbridge (Editor), *Old Houses of Connecticut* (New Haven, Connecticut: Yale University Press, 1923), 519 pp.

18. American Scenic, *22nd Annual Report, 1917,* p. 347.

19. Elizabeth A. Tower, *The John Hancock House* (Ticonderoga, New York: New York State Historical Association, 1926), pp. 1–4.

20. [Appleton], "The Beniah Titcomb House," *Bulletin of the S.P.N.E.A.,* II (August, 1911), pp. 15–17.

21. Appleton, "Report," *Bulletin of the S.P.N.E.A.,* III (July, 1912), pp. 15, 16.

22. *Ibid.,* IX (November, 1918), pp. 29, 30.

23. Emmerton, *Chronicles of Three Old Houses,* p. 47.

24. John Scales (Editor), *Catalog of Articles in Ye William Dam Garrison at Woodman Institute, Dover, N.H.* (Dover, New Hampshire: Woodman Institute, 1917), p. 5.

25. "Westover Restored," *Country Life in America,* XXX (August, 1916), pp. 25–27.

26. Waterman, *The Mansions of Virginia,* pp. 160, 163.

27. *Proceedings of the 56th Convention, A.I.A., 1923,* pp. 104, 105.

28. Weeks Hall, "A Record of 'Shadows on the Teche,' at New Iberia, Louisiana," two scrapbooks of photographs and comments on the history and restoration of the plantation, 1940 (Files of the National Trust for Historic Preservation, Washington); and letter from Richard Koch to the author, November 5, 1963, in the author's possession.

29. *American Monthly Magazine,* XXXI (November, 1907), p. 715; and Ada McClelland, "Some D.A.R. Houses," *D.A.R. Magazine,* L (March, 1917), p. 155.

30. *D.A.R. Magazine,* LXIX (April, 1935), p. 220.

31. Samuel Sloan, "How to Restore Mount Vernon," *Architectural Review and Builder's Journal,* I (August, 1868), quoted in Charles Peterson, "American Notes," *Journal of the Society of Architectural Historians,* X (December, 1951), pp. 33–35.

32. *Mount Vernon Record,* II (December, 1859), p. 108.

33. Letter from Sarah C. Tracy to Ann Pamela Cunningham, March 13, 1861, quoted in Muir, *Presence of a Lady,* p. 19.

34. Letter from Mrs. S.A.W. Tiffey to Philoclea Eve, February 13, 1884, ER IV, pp. 75–78 (M.V.L.A. Archives).

35. Charles E. Peterson, "Carpenters' Hall," *Historic Philadelphia,* p. 113.

36. Chandler, *op. cit.,* p. 64.

37. Emmerton, *op. cit.,* pp. 30–36.

38. Letter from Carl A. Ziegler to Mayor John E. Reyburn of Philadelphia, April 6, 1910, copy on microfilm in Congress Hall restoration file (Independence National Historical Park); and "The Restoration of Congress Hall," *Old Penn* (November 1, 1913), p. 204.

39. *Specifications: Structural Portion of the Restoration of Congress Hall,* July 22, 1911, p. 25, copy on microfilm in Congress Hall restoration file (Independence National Historical Park).

40. Letter from Horace W. Sellers to Thomas L. Montgomery, February 9, 1912, copy on microfilm in Congress Hall restoration file (Independence National Historical Park).

41. Letter from Murray Corse to William Sumner Appleton, May 13, 1919, Brown House Scrapbook, I, p. 44 (S.P.N.E.A. Files).

42. Letter from William Sumner Appleton to Murray Corse, May 14, 1919, Brown House Scrapbook, I, p. 45 (S.P.N.E.A. Files).

43. Letter from William Sumner Appleton to Murray Corse, May 16, 1919, Brown House Scrapbook, I, p. 46 (S.P.N.E.A. Files).

44. Letter from G. Andrews Moriarty, Jr., to William Sumner Appleton, July 30, 1919, Brown House Scrapbook, I, pp. 74–79 (S.P.N.E.A. Files).

45. Letter from William Sumner Appleton to Norman Isham, August 2, 1919, Brown House Scrapbook, I, p. 85 (S.P.N.E.A. Files).

46. Letter from William Sumner Appleton to Norman Isham, October 15, 1919, Brown House Scrapbook, I, p. 124 (S.P.N.E.A. Files).

47. *Ibid.*

48. Letter from William Sumner Appleton to Harry V. Long, March 20, 1920, Brown House Scrapbook, II, p. 1 (S.P.N.E.A. Files).

49. Letter from Abbott Lowell Cummings to the author, March 2, 1960, in the author's possession.

50. Appleton, "Report," *Bulletin of the S.P.N.E.A.,* IX (November, 1918), pp. 34, 35.

Chapter XIII

1. Nevins and Hill, *Ford: Expansion and Challenge, 1915–1933,* pp. 498–500; and *Old-Time New England,* XV (July, 1924), pp. 26, 28.

2. George F. Kunz, "Origin and Record of the Society," *Scenic and Historic America,* II (December, 1930), p. 14.

3. American Scenic, *25th Annual Report, 1920,* pp. 169, 170; and *28th Annual Report, 1923,* pp. 262, 265, 266.

4. Tuesday Club, *The Story of the Loring-Greenough House* (Jamaica Plain, Massachusetts: Tuesday Club, ca. 1939), pp. 1, 4, 5.

5. *Ibid.,* pp. 5–9.

6. [Appleton], "A Summer's Record of Preservation Work in New England," *Bulletin of the S.P.N.E.A.,* VII (December, 1916), pp. 3, 4.

7. Fuller, *An Old Town by the Sea,* pp. 7, 8.

8. *New York Times,* March 13, 1919, p. 24.

9. Letter from Bishop Thomas M. A. Burke to Mrs. Daniel Manning, February 15, 1911, quoted in American Scenic, *16th Annual Report, 1911,* p. 126.

10. David F. Wilcox (Editor), *Quincy and Adams County History and Representative Men* (Chicago: Lewis Publishing Company, 1919), I, p. 523.

11. Naulty, *Historic Harewood,* p. 28.

12. Washington Association of New Jersey, "Trustees Book" (Morristown National Historical Park); and letter from Francis Ronalds to the author, April 4, 1960, in the author's possession.

13. National Society of Colonial Dames of America, *Historian's Report, 1925,* pp. 23, 24.

14. Letter from Evelyn L. Gilmore to William Sumner Appleton, March 6, 1920 (S.P.N.E.A. Files).

15. Thomas P. Robinson, "The Historic Winslow House at Marshfield, Mass., and Its Restoration," *Old-Time New England,* XI (January, 1921), pp. 107–112.

16. American Scenic, *11th Annual Report, 1906,* p. 90.

17. [Appleton], "A Summer's Record," *Bulletin of the S.P.N.E.A.,* VII (December, 1916), pp. 8, 9.

18. Letter from Stephen W. Phillips to William Sumner Appleton, November 1, 1916 (S.P.N.E.A. Files).

19. William C. Endicott, "Address of the President," *Annual Report of the Essex Institute* (May 5, 1919), p. 9.

20. Elizabeth Gorton, "Records, 1905–1911," *Records and Papers of the New London County Historical Society*, III, Part II (1912), pp. 289–291.

21. Ernest E. Rogers, "Circular Letter to the Society," *Records and Papers of the New London County Historical Society*, III, Part II (1912), pp. 330, 331.

22. Gorton, "Secretary's Report, 1906–1907," *Records and Papers of the New London County Historical Society*, III, Part II (1912), pp. 296, 297.

23. Gorton, "Records, 1905–1911," *Records and Papers of the New London County Historical Society*, III, Part II (1912), pp. 317, 319.

24. [Appleton], "The S.P.N.E.A.," *Bulletin of the S.P.N.E.A.*, I (May, 1910), p. 7.

25. Appleton, "Report," *Bulletin of the S.P.N.E.A.*, III (July, 1912), p. 21.

26. Appleton, "Destruction and Preservation," *Art and Archaeology*, VIII (May, 1919), pp. 180, 181.

27. Letter from William Sumner Appleton to Edgar G. Miller, September 29, 1926 (S.P.N.E.A. Files).

28. Letter from Susan Pringle Frost to William Sumner Appleton, July 30, 1920; and letter from William Sumner Appleton to Susan Pringle Frost, May 14, 1925 (S.P.N.E.A. Files).

29. Davies, *Patriotism on Parade*, pp. 354, 355.

CONCLUSION

1. Goodwin, *A Brief and True Report Concerning Williamsburg*, p. 93.

2. Ashbee, *A Report by Mr. C. R. Ashbee to the Council of the National Trust*, p. 4.

Bibliography

LETTERS AND INTERVIEWS

(Names with an asterisk are represented by more than five letters)

American Flag House and Betsy Ross Memorial Association, File box of letters and papers dealing with the early work of the Association, in the Betsy Ross House, Philadelphia, Pennsylvania, containing letters from:

Adams, John Quincy
Brooks, Edward

*Weisgerber, Charles H.

Carr Papers, Correspondence of George M. Carr, dealing with the litigation over Monticello, in the Manuscripts Division, University of Virginia Library, Charlottesville, Virginia, containing letters or manuscripts from:

*Carr, George
Caldwell, Rand
*Levy, Asahel S.
*Levy, Jefferson M.
*Levy, Jonas P.
Levy, Uriah P.

Lockwood, G. W., Jr.
Ree, W. J.
Smith, Edward Flair
Tillotson, G.
*Wheeler, Joel N.

Harrison Collection, Papers of Mrs. Charles C. Harrison, American Philosophical Society, Philadelphia, Pennsylvania.

Metropolitan Museum of Art, New York City, Archives containing letters from:

*Appleton, William Sumner
Baldwin, Frank Conger
Barber, Edwin
Bogart, William M.
Breck, Joseph
Chandler, Joseph
Chauncey, Mary Porter
Cornelius, Charles O.
DeForest, Robert W.
Downs, Joseph
Faxon, Harriet

Friedley, D.
*Halsey, R. T. Haines
Howe, Winifred
Isham, Norman
*Kent, Henry W.
Nutting, Wallace
Reed, Brooks
*Robinson, Edward
Warren, M. H.
Wendell, Barrett
Wood, Naomi

Mount Vernon Ladies' Association of the Union, Mount Vernon, Virginia, Archives containing letters and papers from:

Campbell, Mrs. George W.
Chace, Abby

Comegys, Margaret A.
*Cunningham, Ann Pamela

349

Eve, Philoclea E.
*Everett, Edward
*Halstead, Nancy Wade
Hamilton, Mary M.
Haskins, David G.
*Holstein, Mrs. William H.
Jackson, Amy A.
Lossing, Benson J.
Poore, Ben: Perley

Randall, Henry S.
Richardson, F. A.
Scott, Lt. Col. H. L.
*Sweat, Margaret J. M.
Taylor, Van Campen
Tiffey, Mrs. S. A. W.
Washington, Bushrod
Washington, Eleanor
Washington, John A.

Society for the Preservation of New England Antiquities, Boston, Massachusetts, Files and scrapbooks containing letters from:

*Appleton, William Sumner
Avery, Samuel P.
Balch Family Association
Berg, G.
Bordley, Dr. James, Jr.
*Brazer, Clarence W.
Brock, Susan E.
Brown, Leroy V.
*Chandler, Joseph
Cheney, Louis R.
Coffin, Tristram
Commerford, Arthur B.
Committee of S.P.N.E.A. Trustees
Committee on the Increase of
    Membership
*Corse, Murray
*Covell, Elizabeth
Curtis, F. Kingsbury
Curtis, George M.
Day, Joseph P.
Director, Northern Museum,
    Stockholm
*Dow, George Francis
Eliot, Charles W.
Elliott, Gertrude E.
Ellyson, Lora H.
Endicott, William C.
Erving, H. W.
Fairbanks, Arthur
Ferguson, Mrs. Henry
Fisher, William R.
*Frost, Susan Pringle
Fullerton, F. N.
Gannett, W. H.
Gardner, Arthur H.
Gibboney, Stuart G.
Gilmore, Evelyn L.
Glenn, Maj. Gen. E. F.
Gould, George L.

Gray, Morris
Hall, Edward H.
Hall, Weeks
Hamer, S. H.
Harsche, Robert B.
Hilleary, H. W.
Hipkiss, Edwin J.
*Isham, Norman
Kent, Henry W.
Kimball, Fiske
Levy, Florence M.
Littleton, Maud
Mason, Philip A.
Meyer, Heloise
Millar, Rev. Donald
Miller, Edgar G.
Moran, William Edgar
Moriarty, G. Andrew
Perkins, Arthur
Phillips, Stephen W.
Robinson, Edward
Rowe, L. Earle
Schutz, Walter S.
Seymour, George Dudley
Simes, Frank
Smith, Annie Fleming
Smith, Emily B.
Starbuck, Alexander
Stone, Fanny C.
Sturgis, R. Clipston
Terry, Roderick
Thompson, L. W.
Tilley, Edith May
Towne, Omar A.
Upshur, F. W.
Walker, Charles
Ware, Mary L.
Warner, Herbert O.
Wentworth, Susan

Coffey, T. J. Letter to E. Delafield Smith, March 18, 1864, concerning the will of Uriah P. Levy. National Archives, Record Group 60, Washington, D. C.

Crawford, the Reverend R. Letters dealing with the recovery of the Indian house door from Dr. D. D. Slade, furnished by his son Mr. Denison R. Slade, of Chestnut Hill, Massachusetts, 1863–1868. Handwritten copies in drawer #28, Box on Indian house, Archives of the Pocumtuck Valley Memorial Association, Memorial Hall, Deerfield, Massachusetts.

Cummings, Abbott Lowell. Letter to the author, March 2, 1960, concerning the restoration of the Abraham Brown house. In the author's possession.

Cunningham, Ann Pamela. *A Letter from the Founder and First Regent of the Mount Vernon Association,* dated May 28, 1866. N.p., n.n, n.d. 11 pp.

Fuller, Melville, et al. Letter to Hon. Daniel Lamont, Secretary of War, February 3, 1897, concerning Senate Document 113, 54th Cong., 2nd Sess. National Archives, Record Group 46, Washington, D. C.

Independence National Historical Park. Files containing microfilms and typescripts of documents from the Historical Society of Pennsylvania and the American Philosophical Society, and original documents from the City of Philadelphia dealing with the restoration and care of Independence Hall, Congress Hall and Old City Hall. Files of Independence National Historical Park, Philadelphia, Pennsylvania.

Koch, Richard. Letter to the author, November 5, 1963. In the author's possession.

Lamont, Daniel. Letter to Vice-President Adlai Stevenson, February 5, 1897, concerning Senate Document 113, 54th Cong., 2nd Sess. National Archives, Record Group 46, Washington, D. C.

Ronalds, Francis S. Letter to the author, April 4, 1960, concerning attendance figures at the Ford Mansion. In the author's possession.

Smith, E. Delafield. Letter to Attorney General Edward Bates, March 16, 1864, concerning the will of Uriah P. Levy. National Archives, Record Group 60, Washington, D. C.

Waters, T. Franklin. Letter to George Sheldon, October 23, 1902. Personal Correspondence of George Sheldon, 1–29, Archives of the Pocumtuck Valley Memorial Association, Memorial Hall, Deerfield, Massachusetts.

Wells, George. Letters to George Sheldon, August 4, 1877. Williams Papers, Archives of the Pocumtuck Valley Memorial Association, Memorial Hall, Deerfield, Massachusetts.

Addison, E. Florence, and Little, Bertram K. Interview concerning William Sumner Appleton, in the Harrison Gray Otis house, Boston, February 5, 1960. Typewritten transcript of tape recording, in the author's possession.

Kuper, Theodore Fred. Interview concerning the work of the Thomas Jefferson Memorial Foundation, in the Fashion Institute of Technology, 227 West 27th Street, New York, May 3, 1960. Transcript written in his presence, in the author's possession.

Miscellaneous Manuscript Material

Alexander, Edward P. "Wanted: Historical Interpreters." Typewritten manuscript of speech given before the National Trust in 1958. Files of the National Trust for Historic Preservation, Washington, D. C. 7 pp.

Appleman, Roy Edgar. "Report on Ashland, Home of Henry Clay, Lexington, Kentucky." Typewritten manuscript, September 25, 1937. General Files, Branch of History, National Park Service, Washington, D. C. 51 pp.

Appleton, William Sumner. "A Brief Account of the Society for the Preservation of New England Antiquities." Typewritten manuscript for Charles Messer Stowe, ca. 1930. Files of the Society for the Preservation of New England Antiquities, Boston. 2 pp.

———. "Diary, 1906–1910." Files of the S.P.N.E.A., Boston, 183 pp.

———. "Harry Dean's Work in Connection with the S.P.N.E.A." Typewritten manuscript, ca. 1919. Files of the S.P.N.E.A., Boston. 4 pp.

———. Three scrapbooks dealing with the early history of the S.P.N.E.A. Files of the S.P.N.E.A., Boston. Unpaged.

———. Three scrapbooks dealing with the history of the preservation and restoration of the Abraham Brown house, Watertown, Massachusetts. Files of the S.P.N.E.A., Boston.

———. Three scrapbooks of printed forms, 1910–1919. Files of the S.P.N.E.A., Boston. Unpaged.

Bolton, Charles K. "Diary, 1909–1913." Massachusetts Historical Society, Boston. Unpaged.

Coleman, Emma. Typewritten manuscript on Alice C. Baker. Archives of the Pocumtuck Valley Memorial Association, Memorial Hall, Deerfield, Massachusetts. 106 pp.

Collins, Clarkson A. "History of the Rhode Island Historical Society." Typewritten manuscript, 1952. Vertical Files of the Rhode Island Historical Society, Providence, Rhode Island. 35 pp.

Davis, Benjamin H. "Report of Research on the Traditional Abraham Lincoln Birthplace Cabin." Mimeographed manuscript, February 15, 1949. General Files, Branch of History, National Park Service, Washington, D. C. 39 pp.

Dean, Henry Charles. "The Restoration of Olde New England Houses." Typewritten manuscript of address given at the Munroe Tavern, Lexington, Massachusetts, February 12, 1917. Files of the S.P.N.E.A., Boston. 4 pp.

Everett, Edward. "The Character of Washington." Copy of manuscript in the Massachusetts Historical Society, Boston. Speech given before the Massachusetts Historical Society, June 17, 1858. Archives of the M.V.L.A., Mount Vernon, Virginia.

Fairbairn, Charlotte J. "John Brown's Fort." Typewritten manuscript, August 15, 1961. Files of Region 5, National Park Service, 143 South Third Street, Philadelphia, Pennsylvania. 148 pp.

Hall, Weeks. "A Record of 'Shadows on the Teche' at New Iberia, Louisiana." Two scrapbooks of photographs and comments on the history and restoration of the plantation, 1940. Files of the National Trust for Historic Preservation, Washington, D. C. Unpaged.

Hanckel, William Henry. "The Preservation Movement in Charleston, 1920–1962." Unpublished Master's thesis. University of South Carolina, Columbia, South Carolina, 1962. 80 pp.

Independence National Historical Park, Design and Construction Division. "Documents Relating to the Physical History of Independence Hall, Period, 1891–1899." Typewritten collection of manuscripts, 1953. Files of Independence National Historical Park, Philadelphia, Pennsylvania. Unpaged.

Kocher, A. Lawrence. Typewritten manuscript on the history of restorations, given to the author during an interview in Williamsburg, Virginia, December 27, 1959. In the author's possession.

Levy, Jonas P. "Account of a Visit to Monticello, ca. 1835–6." Typewritten manuscript in "Descriptions of Monticello." Files of the Thomas Jefferson Memorial Foundation, Charlottesville, Virginia. 1 p.

Longyear, Mary Beecher. "Diary, March 31, 1920, to June 14, 1921." Files of the Longyear Foundation, Brookline, Massachusetts.

————. Typewritten copy of Diary, 1918–1919. Files of the Longyear Foundation, Brookline, Massachusetts.

McCoy, Charles S. "Personal Recollections of Louis Hertle, 1860–1949." Typewritten manuscript. Archives at Gunston Hall, Fairfax County, Virginia. 7 pp.

Mount Vernon Ladies' Association of the Union. Typewritten scrapbooks in regard to the Centennial of the M.V.L.A. Archives of the M.V.L.A., Mount Vernon, Virginia. Unpaged.

Museum of Fine Arts, Boston. "Method of Registration Employed by the Museum of Fine Arts, Boston," with comments by William Sumner Appleton. Files of the S.P.N.E.A., Boston.

Nelligan, Murray. "Old Arlington, the Story of the Lee Mansion National Memorial." Unpublished Doctor of Philosophy dissertation. Columbia University, New York, 1954. 524 pp.

Nutting, Wallace. "The Wentworth-Gardner House." Portfolio of photographs with some comments, ca. 1917. Library of the Metropolitan Museum of Art, New York City. Unpaged.

Pardee, Walter Stone. "Pardee's Old Morris House, Public Museum and Civic Center." Typewritten manuscript, Chicago, 1923. Original in New Haven Colony Historical Society, New Haven, Connecticut; copy in the Library of Congress, Washington, D. C. 10 pp.

Philadelphia Chapter of the American Institute of Architects. Papers dealing with the restoration of Congress Hall. Historical Society of Pennsylvania; copies on microfilm in Independence National Historical Park, Philadelphia, Pennsylvania.

Robinson, Edward. "Notes on the Wentworth-Gardner House." Typewritten report dated 1921. Archives of the Metropolitan Museum of Art, New York City. 4 pp.

Rogers, T. Mellon. "Diary, 1898." Museum collection of Independence National Historical Park, Philadelphia, Pennsylvania.

Sears, Clara Endicott. "Notes, 1915–1941." Typewritten manuscript. Files of the Fruitlands Museum, Harvard, Massachusetts. Unpaged.

Sheldon, George. "Historical and Genealogical Gossip about the Old Parson Williams Homestead and Its Occupants, I." Typewritten manuscript with corrections by J. M. Arms Sheldon. Williams Family Papers, 211:451–469, Archives of the Pocumtuck Valley Memorial Association, Memorial Hall, Deerfield, Massachusetts. 6 pp.

Sheldon, Jenny. "Things to be Remembered about Deerfield and Vicinity." Notebook. Archives of the Pocumtuck Valley Memorial Association, Memorial Hall, Deerfield, Massachusetts.

Stewart, Robert G. "Restoration of Independence Hall under the Committee for the Preservation of Historic Monuments of the American Institute of

Architects." Typewritten manuscript, March 12, 1954. In the possession of Robert G. Stewart, Washington, D. C. 14 pp.
———. "Restorations at Independence Hall." Unpublished thesis, University of Pennsylvania, Philadelphia, September, 1953. 24 pp.
Stover, Charles B. "Some Historical Notes Concerning the Old Dyckman Farmhouse." Typewritten report submitted to Cabot Ward, Commissioner of Parks, Manhattan and Richmond, ca. 1915. Vertical Files of Avery Memorial Library, Columbia University, New York City. 6 pp.
Washington Association of New Jersey. "Trustees Book." Manuscripts, 1874–1915. Files of the Morristown National Historical Park, Morristown, New Jersey. 2 v.
Wilshin, F. F. "The Shirley House." Typewritten manuscript, October 28, 1939. General Files, Branch of History, National Park Service, Washington, D. C. 73 pp.

GOVERNMENT DOCUMENTS

Boston. City Council. Re-Dedication of the Old State House, Boston. July 11, 1882. (Third Edition.) Boston, City Council, 1885. 216 pp.
———. Joint Special Committee on Hancock House. Report to Board of Aldermen, City of Boston, June 3, 1863, of Joint Special Committee to Consider the Expediency of Any Measure for the Preservation of the Hancock House, in Beacon Street. City Document No. 56. Boston, City of Boston, 1863. 14 pp.
Boston National Historic Sites Commission. Final Report of the Boston National Historic Sites Commission. Washington, U. S. Government Printing Office, 1961. 261 pp.
Illinois. Department of Conservation. Division of Park and Memorials. The Home of Abraham Lincoln. Springfield, Illinois, State of Illinois, n.d. Unpaged.
———. Department of Public Works and Buildings. Illinois State Parks. Springfield, Illinois, State of Illinois, 1941. 37 pp.
Independence National Historical Park. Historic Structures Report, Part II, on Independence Hall. Philadelphia, Pennsylvania, Independence National Historical Park, April, 1962. 150 pp. plus notes and illustrations. Mimeographed.
Jones, Richard Lloyd. Letter to Senator Robert LaFollette, April 18, 1916. Quoted in Congressional Record, 64th Cong., 1st Sess., p. 9236.
Levy vs. Levy. Reports of Cases Argued and Determined in the Court of Appeals of the State of New York. Albany, New York, W. C. Little, 1866, XXXIII, pp. 97-138.
Levy vs. Levy. In Oliver Barbour, Reports of Cases in Law and Equity Determined in the Supreme Court of the State of New York. Albany, New York, W. C. Little, 1864, XL, pp. 585–626.
Littleton, Maud. "One Wish." Letter dated August 30, 1911. Reprinted from Congressional Record. Washington, Government Printing Office, 1912, 16 pp.
Massachusetts General Court. Committee on Cities. Report of Hearing before the Committee on Cities, March 8, 1907 on the Bill, Senate 189, To Preserve the Old State House as an Historic and Patriotic Memorial, and to

Prohibit Its Use for any other Purpose. Boston, Rockwell and Churchill Press, 1907. 22 pp.

Massachusetts Legislature. Committee on Federal Relations. *Arguments in Behalf of Petitions for Aid in the Preservation of the Old South Meeting-House.* Boston, Alfred Mudge and Son, 1878. 48 pp.

Pennsylvania. Joint State Government Commission. *Catalog of Historical Buildings, Sites and Remains in Pennsylvania.* Report to the General Assembly of the Commonwealth of Pennsylvania. Philadelphia, State of Pennsylvania, 1949. 58 pp.

————. Washington Crossing Park Commission of Pennsylvania. *Brief Itinerary of a Trip from Philadelphia to Washington's Crossing and Other Points of Historical Interest in Bucks County, Pennsylvania.* Philadelphia, The Commission, 1926. 54 pp.

Philadelphia. Committee on the Restoration of Independence Hall. *Reports, 1873–1875.* Philadelphia, The City of Philadelphia, 1873–1875. 3 pamphlets.

Schneider, J. Thomas. *Report to the Secretary of the Interior on the Preservation of Historic Sites and Buildings.* Washington, Department of the Interior, 1935. 185 pp.

[Sener, James B.]. *The Report of the Virginia Board of Visitors to Mount Vernon for the Year 1901.* Richmond, Virginia, J. H. O'Bannon, 1901. 88 pp.

[Service, C. M. (Compiler)]. *Parks and Memorials of the State of Illinois.* Springfield, Illinois, Department of Public Works and Buildings, ca. 1925. 64 pp.

Stevens, Sylvester K., and Kent, Donald H. *Conserving Pennsylvania's Historic Heritage.* Harrisburg, Pennsylvania, Pennsylvania Historical and Museums Commission, 1947. 64 pp.

U. S. Congress. House. *Monticello,* Debate on H. Res. 740, December 9, 1912. *Congressional Record,* 62nd Cong., 3rd Sess., pp. 345-349.

————. ————. *The Grave of Thomas Jefferson.* Debate on H. R. Res. 141, April 13, 1878. *Congressional Record,* 45th Cong., 2nd. Sess., p. 2494.

————. House Committee on Appropriations. *House in Which Lincoln Died.* Hearing before Subcommittee, 54th Cong., 1st Sess., on H. R. 7664, March 21, 1896. Washington, Government Printing Office, 1896, pp. 255-258.

————. House Committee on Public Buildings and Grounds. *Purchase of Monticello.* Hearing, 64th Cong., 1st Sess., on H. J. Res. 269, August 8, 1916. Washington, Government Printing Office, 1916. Part I, pp. 3–8; Part II, 16 pp.

————. ————. *Purchase of Monticello.* Hearing, 64th Cong., 1st Sess., on H. J. Res. 269, December 5 and 15, 1916. Washington, Government Printing Office, 1917. 37 pp.

————. House Committee on Rules. *Public Ownership of Monticello.* Hearing, 62nd Cong., 2nd Sess., on S. Con. Res. 24, July 24, 1912. Washington, Government Printing Office, 1912. 78 pp.

————. ————. *Purchase of Monticello.* Hearing, 63rd Cong., 2nd Sess., on H. J. Res. 390 and H. J. Res. 418, February 23, 1915. Washington, Government Printing Office, 1915. 16 pp.

————. House Committee on the Library. Report No. 221. *To Accept Deed of Gift to Homestead of Abraham Lincoln* (H. R. 8351). Quoted in *Congressional Record,* 64th Cong., 1st Sess., April 5, 1916, pp. 5554, 5555.

———. Senate. *Army Appropriation.* Debate on H. R. 16460, July 24, 1916. *Congressional Record,* 64th Cong., 1st Sess., pp. 11512, 11513.

———. ———. *Final Report of the Louisiana Purchase Exposition Commission, 1906.* Senate Document No. 202, 59th Cong., 1st Sess. Washington, Government Printing Office, 1906. 550 pp.

———. ———. *Property Devised by Captain Levy.* Debate on S. Res. 137, March 3, 1863. *Congressional Globe,* 37th Cong., 3rd Sess., p. 1495.

———. ———. *The Hermitage.* Debate on S. 4797, March 2, 1908. *Congressional Record,* 60th Cong., 1st Sess., p. 2744.

———. Senate Committee on Public Buildings and Grounds, *Purchase of Monticello.* Hearing, 64th Cong., 1st Sess., on S. J. Res. 153, January 9, 1917. Washington, Government Printing Office, 1917. 26 pp.

———. Senate Committee on the Library. *Care and Preservation of the Hermitage.* Report No. 314, to accompany S. 4797, 60th Cong., 1st Sess., February 28, 1908. Washington, Government Printing Office, 1908. 7 pp.

———. ———. *Public Ownership of Monticello.* Hearing, 62nd Cong., 2nd Sess., on S. J. Res. 92, July 9, 1912. Washington, Government Printing Office, 1912. 57 pp.

U. S. Department of the Interior. National Park Service. *Abraham Lincoln National Historical Park, Kentucky.* Washington, Department of the Interior, 1959. Leaflet.

———. ———. History Division, General Section. *Minutes of the Conference of Regional Historians and Architects, January 20–26, 1951, Williamsburg, Jamestown, Virginia and Washington, D. C.* Mimeographed booklet. Files of the National Park Service, Washington, D. C. 2 pp.

———. ———. *National Park Service Restoration Policy Statement.* Washington, D. C., Department of the Interior, 1956. 5 pp. Mimeographed.

———. ———. *Ruins Stabilization* (Vol. XXIII, *National Park Service Administrative Manual*). Washington, Department of the Interior, 1956. Unpaged. Mimeographed.

Young, Rogers W. Letter to Chief of Mission 66 Staff, concerning glossary of National Park Service Terms. U. S. Department of the Interior. National Park Service. History Division, General Section. *Definitions.* Files of the National Park Service, Washington, D. C. Unpaged. Mimeographed.

MAGAZINES, NEWSPAPERS, PROCEEDINGS AND REPORTS

American Heritage, Vols. VI–XII, December, 1954–1961.

American Homes and Gardens, Vols. V, XII, 1908, 1915.

American Institute of Architects. *Journal of the American Institute of Architects,* Vols. I–XV, 1912–1927.

———. *Proceedings of the Annual Convention.* 1869–1927.

American Monthly Magazine, see National Society of the Daughters of American Revolution.

American Scenic and Historic Preservation Society. *Annual Report.* New York, The Society, 1896–1925. (From 1895–1898 called Trustees of Scenic and Historic Places and Objects in the State of New York; from 1898–1901 called Society for the Preservation of Scenic and Historic Objects.)

———. *Scenic and Historic America,* Vols. I–IV, 1929–1940.

American Society of Architectural Historians, see Society of Architectural Historians.

Anderson, Clinton P. "The Adobe Palace." *New Mexico Historical Review*, XIX, April, 1944, pp. 98–118.

Anthony, Walter C. "Washington's Headquarters, Newburgh, New York." Historical Society of Newburgh Bay and the Highlands. *Publication XXI*. 1928. 67 pp.

Appleton, William Sumner. "Destruction and Preservation of Old Buildings in New England." *Art and Archaeology*, VIII, May, 1919, pp. 131–184.

Architectural Record, Vols. XXXVIII–LXVII, 1915–1930.

Association for the Preservation of Virginia Antiquities. *Yearbook of the Association for the Preservation of Virginia Antiquities*. Richmond, Virginia, The Association, 1896–1926/7.

"Balch House." *Historic Preservation*, XII, 1960, p. 113.

Bather, F. A. "The Triumph of Hazelius." *Museums Journal*, XVI, December, 1916, pp. 132–136.

Blanford, B. W. "Commodore Uriah P. Levy, Adventures and Experiences Including Hitherto Unpublished Reminiscences by His Widow—Former Chatelaine of Monticello." *American Hebrew*, CXVI, 1925, pp. 694, 739, 743, 770, 784, 786, 807, 822.

Boston *Post*. Clippings of 1910–1911. Files of the Society for the Preservation of New England Antiquities, Boston.

Boston *Transcript*. Clippings of 1910–1911. Files of the S.P.N.E.A., Boston.

Bostonian Society. *Proceedings*. Boston, The Society, 1882–1926.

Bowen, Archie L. "A. Lincoln: His House." *Lincoln Centennial Association Papers*. Springfield, Illinois, The Association, 1925, pp. 17–73, 103–125.

Brooke, Arthur. "A Colonial Mansion of Virginia." *Architectural Review*, VI (n.s.), July, 1899, pp. 91–94.

Brooklyn Institute of Arts and Sciences. *Museums of the Brooklyn Institute of Arts and Sciences, Report*. Brooklyn, The Institute, 1914–1929.

——. *Brooklyn Museum Quarterly*, Vols. X–XVIII, 1923–1931.

Browne, Margaret Fitzhugh. "A Twin of Lincoln's Birthplace Ten Miles from Boston's State House." Boston *Evening Transcript*, March 12, 1924, III, p. 4.

Bulletin of the S.P.N.E.A., see Society for the Preservation of New England Antiquities.

Chase, Enoch Aquila. "The Arlington Case." *Virginia Law Review*, XV, January, 1929, pp. 207–233.

Christian Science Monitor (Boston), 1914–1922.

Collier's, Vols. XXXVI–LVII, 1905–1916.

Commissioners of Fairmount Park. *Annual Report of the Commissioners of Fairmount Park*. Philadelphia, The Commissioners, 1869–1878. (Four reports.)

Committee on Plans and Improvements. *Report of the Committee on Plans and Improvements of the Commissioners of Fairmount Park upon the Extension of the Park*. Philadelphia, King and Baird, 1868. 31 pp.

Country Life in America, Vols. XXVI–XXX, 1914–1916.

Cummings, Amos J. "A National Humiliation." New York *Sun*, August 24, 1902.

Cunningham, Ann Pamela. "To the Ladies of the South." Charleston *Mer-*

cury, December 2, 1853. ER I, p. 1. Archives of the M.V.L.A., Mount Vernon, Virginia.

————. "To the Ladies of the South." Washington *Union,* April 20, 1854. ER I, p. 2. Archives of the M.V.L.A., Mount Vernon, Virginia.

Curl, Mervin J. "New York Art Centre Buys Historic New Hampshire House." Boston *Herald,* March 2, 1919.

Curtis, Natalie. "An Historic House on the Hudson: The Silent Witness of the Growth of American Freedom." *Craftsman,* XVII, October, 1909, pp. 3–11.

Danvers Historical Society. *Historical Collections of the Danvers Historical Society.* Danvers, Massachusetts, The Society, 1913–1924. Vols. I and II.

D.A.R. Magazine, see National Society of the Daughters of the American Revolution.

Deyo, Robert Emmet. "The Unsuccessful Attempt of the Trustees of the Village of Newburgh to Make an Improvement Which Involved the Destruction of Washington's Headquarters." Historical Society of Newburgh Bay and the Highlands. *Publication XVII,* Newburgh, New York, The Society, 1916, pp. 17–22.

Dill, Alonzo Thomas. "Tryon's Palace, a Neglected Niche of North Carolina History." *North Carolina Historical Review,* XIX, April, 1942, pp. 119–167.

Dix, Dorothy. "Monticello—Shrine or Bachelor's Hall?" *Good Housekeeping,* LVIII, April, 1914, pp. 538–541.

Dow, George Francis. "The Work of the Society for the Preservation of New England Antiquities." *House Beautiful,* LVIII, November, 1925, pp. 556–562.

Driver, Josephine P. "Ben: Perley Poore of Indian Hill." *Essex Institute Historical Collections,* LXXXIX, January, 1953, pp. 1–18.

"Editor's Easy Chair." *Harper's New Monthly Magazine,* LVI, December, 1877, p. 141.

Elson, Ruth Miller. "American Schoolbooks and 'Culture' in the Nineteenth Century." *Mississippi Valley Historical Review,* XLVI, December, 1959, pp. 411–434.

Essex Institute. *Annual Report of the Essex Institute.* Salem, Massachusetts, The Institute, 1898–1927.

Fairbanks Family in America, Inc. *Ye Fayerbanke Historial,* I, November, 1903, June, 1904, and November, 1904.

"Final Report of the Committee on the Authenticity of the Tradition of the First Church—Built in 1634." *Essex Institute Historical Collections,* VII, 1865, pp. 116-118.

Fort Ticonderoga Museum. *The Bulletin of the Fort Ticonderoga Museum,* X, No. 2, 1958.

Frank Leslie's Illustrated Newspaper (New York), February 8, 1862, p. 182.

Geiger, Maynard, O. F. M. "Preservation and Restoration of the California Missions." *Historic Preservation,* XIV, 1962, pp. 105-107.

Gleason's Pictorial (Boston), V, October 29, 1853.

Gleason's Weekly Line-of-Battleship (Boston), I, 1859.

Hatch, Charles E., Jr. "The Moore House: A National Shrine." *William and Mary College Quarterly Historical Magazine,* XXI, Second Series, October, 1941, pp. 293-317.

Hays, Roy. "Is the Lincoln Birthplace Cabin Authentic?" *Abraham Lincoln Quarterly,* V, September, 1948, pp. 127-163.

Hodgdon, Charles. "Dorchester Historical Society." *The Dorchester Book,* Boston, Branch Alliance of Christ Church (Unitarian), 1899, pp. 57, 58.

Hoffmann, Henry B. "President Washington's Cherry Street Residence." *New York Historical Society Quarterly Bulletin,* XXIII, July, 1939, pp. 90-102.

Hooper, John H. "The Royall House and Farm." *Medford Historical Register,* III, October, 1900, pp. 133-153.

House of Seven Gables Settlement Association. *Fourth Annual Report of the House of Seven Gables Settlement Association.* Salem, Massachusetts, The Association, 1913-1914.

Ipswich Historical Society. *Publications,* I–XXVIII, 1887–1934.

"The Isaac Royall House or the 'Plantation,' Medford, Mass." *American Architect and Building News,* XXIV, October 13, 1888, pp. 171, 172.

Kanof, Abram. "Uriah Phillips Levy: The Story of a Pugnacious Commodore." *Publications of the American Jewish Historical Society,* XXXIX, September, 1949, pp. 1-66.

Kentucky Pioneer Memorial Association. "Replica of Fort Harrod, Harrodsburg, 1923–1928." *The Historical Quarterly* (Filson Club and University of Louisville), III, October, 1928, pp. 19-22.

Kimball, Fiske. "Philadelphia's 'Colonial Chain.' " *Art and Archaeology,* XXI, April, 1926, pp. 198-203.

Krauss, Sidney Frank, and Mancill, Frank H. *Philadelphia Forum Magazine.* Date unknown. Archives of the M.V.L.A., Mount Vernon, Virginia.

Kuper, Theodore Fred. "Collecting Monticello." *Manuscripts,* VII, Summer, 1955, pp. 216-223.

Lexington Historical Society. *Proceedings of the Lexington Historical Society, 1886–1910, and Papers Relating to the History of the Town Presented at Its Meetings.* Lexington, Massachusetts, The Society, 1910. 4 v.

Lossing, Benson J. "Monticello." *Harpers New Monthly Magazine,* VII, July, 1853, pp. 145-160.

Magazine of American History, Vols. II–XXI, 1879–1889.

Mason, George C. "Colonial Architecture." *American Architect and Building News,* X, August 13, 1881, p. 72.

Massachusetts Society of Colonial Dames of America. *Report of the Historian,* 1903/4, 1908/9.

McDowell, William O. Letter inviting women to join the Daughters of the American Revolution. Washington *Post,* July 21, 1890. D.A.R. Library, Washington, D. C.

Metropolitan Museum of Art. *Bulletin of the Metropolitan Museum of Art,* Vols. XIV–XXI, 1919–1926.

Miller, Amelia F. "The Indian House." *Deerfield Alumni Journal,* XVII, Autumn, 1960, pp. 3-12.

Monticello Association. *Annual Report of the Monticello Association, 1924.* Washington, D. C., National Capital Press, 1924. 16 pp.

Mount Vernon Ladies' Association of the Union. *Mount Vernon Record* (Philadelphia), July, 1858–July, 1860. 2 v.

————. *Reports of the Mount Vernon Ladies' Association of the Union, 1858–1895.* Baltimore, Maryland, Friedenwald Company, 1896. (Each report paginated separately.)

National Society of the Colonial Dames in the State of New York. *Report of the National Society of Colonial Dames in the State of New York.* New York, The Society, 1896–1923.

National Society of Colonial Dames of America. *Historian's Report to the National Council of the National Society of Colonial Dames of America,* 1900–1927. (From 1900–1910 referred to as *Historian's Address.*)

National Society of the Daughters of the American Revolution. *D.A.R. Magazine,* Vols. I–XCIV, 1892–1960. (From 1892–July, 1913, referred to as *American Monthly Magazine.*)

——. *Report of the National Society of the Daughters of the American Revolution.* Washington, Government Printing Office, 1897–1927.

"Neglected Mount Vernon." Boston *Herald,* November (?), 1883. Archives of the M.V.L.A., Mount Vernon, Virginia.

Nelson, G. E. "The Genesis of Restored New Salem." *Journal of the Illinois State Historical Society,* XXXVI, December, 1943, pp. 368-377.

New Haven Colony Historical Society. *Reports Presented at the Annual Meetings.* New Haven, Connecticut, The Society, 1918–1926.

New London County Historical Society. *Records and Papers of the New London County Historical Society, 1890–1912.* New London, Connecticut, The Society, 1912. 3 v.

"The New Old City Hall." Hartford *Courant,* September 14, 1916.

Newport Historical Society. *First and Second Annual Reports.* Newport, Rhode Island, The Society, 1886 and 1887.

New York Times, 1896–1926.

New York *Tribune,* June 15, 1900, June 27, 1900, and February 15, 1902.

New York *World,* February 1, 1925.

"News of Members." *Historic Preservation,* XI, 1959, p. 145.

Newspaper clippings on the American Wing. Library of the Metropolitan Museum of Art, New York.

Newspaper clippings on the Fruitlands Museum. Scrapbooks at the Museum, Harvard, Massachusetts.

Newspaper clippings on the Washington Association of New Jersey. Files of the Morristown National Historical Park, Morristown, New Jersey.

Newton, Mary Mann Page. "The Association for the Preservation of Virginia Antiquities." *American Historical Register,* I, September, 1894, pp. 11-21.

Old Constitution House Association. *Old Constitution House Association Bulletin* (Windsor, Vermont), Nos. 1 and 2, April, 1912 and April, 1914.

Old-Time New England, see Society for the Preservation of New England Antiquities.

[Peabody, R. S.]. "Georgian Houses of New England." *American Architect and Building News,* II, October 20, 1877, pp. 338, 339.

Pennsylvania Museum. *Pennsylvania Museum Bulletin,* XXII, September, 1926–June, 1927.

Perry, William Graves. "Restoration of Williamsburg, Notes on the Architecture." *Architectural Record,* LXXVIII, December, 1935, pp. 363-381.

Philadelphia. Bureau of City Property. Two Scrapbooks, numbered 2 and 3, containing newspaper clippings dealing with the work of the Bureau. Now in the possession of Independence National Historical Park, Philadelphia, Pennsylvania.

Philadelphia *Public Ledger,* July 3, 1908, July 5, 1908, and November 30, 1913.

Pocumtuck Valley Memorial Association. *Historical Scrapbook I,* containing newspaper clippings dealing with the early history of the Association. Archives of the Pocumtuck Valley Memorial Association, Memorial Hall, Deerfield, Massachusetts.

————. *History and Proceedings of the Pocumtuck Valley Memorial Association, 1870–1920.* Deerfield, Massachusetts, The Association, 1920. 6 v.

"Preserve the Landmarks" (Editorial). Philadelphia *Record,* March 9, 1919.

Pressy, Park. "Preserving the Landmarks." *House Beautiful,* XXXVI, September, 1914, pp. 97-100.

Prosch, Thomas. "Effort to save the Historic McLoughlin House." *Washington Historical Quarterly,* I, January, 1907, pp. 36-42.

Pryor, Mrs. Roger A. "The Mount Vernon Association." *American Historical Register,* I, January, 1895, pp. 407-420.

Randall, James G. "When Jefferson's Home Was Bequeathed to the United States." *South Atlantic Quarterly,* XXIII, January, 1924, pp. 34–39.

"The Restoration of Congress Hall." *Old Penn,* November 1, 1913, p. 204.

Reynolds, Marcus T. "The Colonial Buildings of Rensselaerwyck." *Architectural Record,* IV, June, 1895, pp. 415-438.

Roosevelt House Bulletin, see Woman's Roosevelt Memorial Association.

Roosevelt Memorial Association. *Annual Report.* New York, The Association, 1919–1926.

San Francisco *Examiner,* November and December, 1915.

Scenic and Historic America, see American Scenic and Historic Preservation Society.

Site and Relic Society of Germantown. *Germantown History,* II, 1914.

Society for the Preservation of New England Antiquities. *Old-Time New England,* Vols. I–L, 1910–1960. (From May, 1910–January, 1920, called *Bulletin of the Society for the Preservation of New England Antiquities.*)

Society for the Protection of Ancient Buildings. *Annual Report.* London, The Society, 1878–1927.

Society of Architectural Historians. *Journal of the Society of Architectural Historians,* Vols. I–XIX, 1941–1960. (Until 1946 called *Journal of the American Society of Architectural Historians.*)

Society of the Descendants of Pilgrim John Howland. *Howland Homestead,* I, July and October, 1911.

Stockton, Frank R. "The Later Years of Monticello." *Century Magazine,* XXXIV, September, 1887, pp. 653-658.

Tatum, George B. "The Origins of Fairmount Park." *Antiques,* LXXXII (November, 1962), pp. 502-507.

Thomas, David Y. "Report upon the Historic Buildings, Monuments, and Local Archives of St. Augustine, Florida." *Annual Report of the American Historical Association for the Year 1905.* Washington, Government Printing Office, 1906, I, pp. 339-352.

Thomas Jefferson Memorial Foundation. *Report of the President, February 1, 1941.* New York, The Foundation, 1941. 8 pp.

Tilley, Edith May. "The Newport Historical Society in Its Earlier Days." *Bulletin of the Newport Historical Society,* No. 12, April, 1914, pp. 1-16.

Topsfield Historical Society. *Historical Collections of the Topsfield Historical Society,* XIX, 1914. Topsfield, Massachusetts, The Society, 1914. 120 pp.

True Democratic Banner (Morristown, New Jersey), 1873. Files of Morristown National Historical Park, Morristown, New Jersey.

"Unbalanced Patriotism," and "The Mount Vernon Papers" (Editorials) *Saturday Evening Post,* January 1, 1859.

Wallis, Frank E. "What and Why Is Colonial Architecture?" *House and Garden,* XVI, December, 1909, pp. 189-192, vi, vii.

Walpole Society. *Walpole Society Notebooks.* Boston, The Society, 1926–1948.

Washington *Post,* December 15, 1907, and August 7, 1921.

White Pine Bureau. *White Pine Series of Architectural Monographs.* Vols. I–XII, 1915–1926. (After 1925 published by Russell Whitehead, New York.)

Woman's Roosevelt Memorial Association. *Roosevelt House Bulletin,* Vols. I–II, 1919–1926. (From December, 1919–February, 1921 called *Woman's Roosevelt Memorial Bulletin.*)

Ye Fayerbanke Historial, see Fairbanks Family In America, Inc.

LEAFLETS AND PAMPHLETS

Alden, Edward S. *Alden Homestead, Duxbury, Mass., Shrine of Millions of Descendants of John Alden and His Wife, Priscilla Mullens.* Holyoke, Massachusetts, Alden Press, 1932. 64 pp.

Alden Kindred of America, Inc. *Alden Kindred of America, Inc. Reunion, Duxbury, 1926.* Holyoke, Massachusetts, Alden Press, 1926. 48 pp.

[Appleton, William Sumner]. *The Colonial Homes of New England, Shall They Be Preserved?* Boston, Society for the Preservation of New England Antiquities, 1913. 15 pp.

Associate Committee of Women of the Pennsylvania Museum of Art. *The Chain of Colonial Houses.* Philadelphia, The Committee, 1932. 23 pp.

Association for the Preservation of Lindenwald. *Lindenwald, Home of Martin Van Buren, Why It Should Be Made a Public Historic Reservation.* N. p., The Association, 1937. 16 pp.

The Augustus Saint-Gaudens Memorial. Cornish, New Hampshire, Augustus Saint-Gaudens Memorial, 1926. 16 pp.

Bagg, Winthrop. *The Old Day House.* West Springfield, Massachusetts, Ramapogue Historical Society, 1905. 16 pp.

Bangs, Ella M. *An Historic Mansion: The Wadsworth-Longfellow House.* Portland, Maine, Lamson Studio, 1902. 23 pp.

Bear, James A., Jr. *Old Pictures of Monticello.* Charlottesville, Virginia, University of Virginia Press, 1957. 31 pp.

Beekman, Katharine M., and Isham, Norman. *The Story of Van Cortlandt.* New York, National Society of Colonial Dames in the State of New York, 1917. 30 pp.

Bush, Celeste E. *The Old Lee House, East Lyme, Connecticut.* East Lyme, Connecticut, East Lyme Historical Society, 1917. 15 pp.

Caldwell, Richard. *A True History of the Acquisition of Washington's Headquarters at Newburgh by the State of New York.* Salisbury Mills, New York, Stivers, Slauson and Boyd, 1887. 46 pp.

Codman, John. *Preservation of Historic Districts by Architectural Control.* Chicago, American Society of Planning Officials, 1956. 35 pp.

Coleman, Emma L. *Frary House, Deerfield, 1685.* Deerfield, Massachusetts, Pocumtuck Valley Memorial Association, 1940. 24 pp.

Coles, Elizabeth. *Historical Sketch of the Washington Headquarters, Prepared under the Auspices of the White Plains Chapter, Daughters of the*

American Revolution. White Plains, New York, White Plains Chapter, Daughters of the American Revolution, 1917. 53 pp.

Committee for the Preservation of Park Street Church. *The Preservation of Park Street Church, Boston*. Boston, The Committee, 1903. 75 pp.

Committee on Standards and Surveys. *Criteria for Evaluating Historic Sites and Buildings*. Washington, D. C., National Trust for Historic Preservation, 1956. 7 pp.

Corning, A. Elwood. *The Story of the Hasbrouck House, Washington's Headquarters, Newburgh, New York*. N. p., Board of Trustees, State of New York of Washington's Headquarters, 1950. 68 pp.

Darneille, Frank. *History of the Lincoln Homestead*. Springfield, Illinois, The Author, 1938. 31 pp.

Directors of the Old South Work. *Freedom and the Old South Meeting-House*. (*Old South Leaflet*, No. 202.) Boston, Directors of the Old South Work, n. d. 34 pp.

———. *The Old South Meeting-House*. (*Old South Leaflets*, No. 183.) Boston, Directors of the Old South Work, n. d. 16 pp.

Documents Relating to the Proposed Purchase of Mount Vernon by the Citizens of the United States, in Order that They May at All Times Have a Legal and Indisputable Right to Visit the Grounds, Mansion and Tomb of Washington. Washington, T. Barnard, 1846. 2 pp. Archives of the M.V.L.A., Mount Vernon, Virginia.

Dyson, Arthur Thomas. *An Appeal for the Preservation of the Edgar Allan Poe Cottage, in Fordham, New York City, by Arthur Thomas Dyson, with Some Comment by "Pendennis" in the New York Times*. New York, n.n., 1915. 3 pp. (Reprints from *New York Times* of August 12 and 20, 1905.)

Elliott, Mrs. R. Sherman. *The Seventh Day Baptist Meeting House, Newport, Rhode Island*. (Read before the Newport Historical Society, November 18, 1929.) Newport, Rhode Island, Newport Historical Society, n. d. 11 pp.

Etting, Frank M. *Memorials of 1776*. (Originally written for *Penn Monthly*.) Philadelphia, W. W. Bates, 1873. 14 pp.

Everett, Edward. *Oration on the Character of Washington*. Boston (?), Little, Brown and Company, 1913. 29 pp.

Ferris, Mrs. Morris Patterson. *Van Cortlandt Mansion Erected 1748, Now in the Custody of the Colonial Dames of the State of New York*. New York, National Society of Colonial Dames in the State of New York, 1897. 23 pp.

Fewhagen, Mary F. Pringle (Compiler). *A History of the Maryland Society of the Colonial Dames of America, 1891–1951*. N. p., n. n., 1951. 48 pp.

Fuller, W. O. *An Old Town by the Sea*. Portsmouth, New Hampshire, Thomas Bailey Aldrich Memorial, 1910. 14 pp.

Goold, Nathan. *The Wadsworth-Longfellow House, Longfellow's Old Home, Portland, Maine, Its History and Its Occupants*. Portland, Maine, Maine Historical Society, 1905. 28 pp.

Gottlieb, Theodore D. *The Origin and Evolution of the Betsy Ross Flag Legend or Tradition*. Newark, New Jersey, The Author, 1938. 8 pp.

Hancock House. N. p., New York State Historical Association, 1925. Unpaged.

History of St. Augustine under Four Flags. St. Augustine, Florida, W. J. Harris Company, Inc., 1936. 26 pp.

The Hyland House, Guilford, Connecticut. N. p., n. n., n. d. Leaflet.

Jillson, Willard Rouse. *The "Old Kentucky Home."* (Reprint from *Register of the Kentucky State Historical Society,* May, 1921, Vol. 19, No. 56.) N. p., n. n., n. d. 11 pp.

Keyes, John S. *Story of an Old House.* (Read before the Concord Antiquarian Society.) Concord, Massachusetts, Concord Antiquarian Society, 1902. 17 pp.

Keyser, Charles, and Cochran, Thomas. *Lemon Hill and Fairmount Park, Papers Relative to a Public Park for Philadelphia.* Philadelphia, Horace J. Smith, 1886. 54 pp.

Kuper, Theodore Fred. *Thomas Jefferson the Giant.* (*Monticello Papers,* No. 7.) New York, Thomas Jefferson Memorial Foundation, 1926. 32 pp.

Lawson, Edward W. *The Saint Augustine Historical Society and Its "Oldest House," a Documented Study of Fabricated History.* Nashville, Tennessee, Collom and Ghertner Company, 1957. 73 pp.

Lincoln Farm Association. *Second Annual Meeting of the Board of Directors of the Lincoln Farm Association, Report of the Executive Committee, Secretary, Treasurer and General Manager, February 26, 1908.* New York, The Association, 1908. 38 pp.

Littleton, Maud. *Monticello.* New York, n. n., 1912. 52 pp.

Longyear Foundation. *Certificate of Incorporation of the Longyear Foundation, Dated December 12, 1934.* Photostat of original document in Files of the Longyear Foundation, Brookline, Massachusetts. (Text identical with Mrs. Longyear's Assignment and Declaration as amended.) 3 pp.

————. *Longyear Foundation, Created Under an Assignment and Declaration of Trust, Dated 5th April, 1926. Assignment and Declaration of Trust (Endowment Trust), Dated 5th April, 1926. Amendments to Longyear Foundation, Dated 17th August, 1927. Amendments to Longyear Foundation, Dated 11th December, 1928. Amendments to Endowment Trust, Dated 17th August, 1927. Amendments to Endowment Trust, Dated 12th December, 1928.* Printed copy in Files of the Longyear Foundation, Brookline, Massachusetts. 55 pp.

————. *Longyear Foundation, Its Purpose and Unfoldment.* Boston, Trustees of Longyear Foundation, 1946. 31 pp.

————. *Will of Mary Beecher Longyear, Dated December 7, 1928 and Compromise Agreement Dated April 26, 1932.* Printed copy in Files of the Longyear Foundation, Brookline, Massachusetts. (Each document paginated separately.)

Maryland Society of Colonial Dames of America. *"Mount Clare" Carroll Park, Baltimore, and Historical Sketch.* Baltimore (?), Maryland, The Society, 1926. Unpaged.

Memorial Association of the District of Columbia. *Words from Many Sources Commendatory of its Work; and Especially of the Plan to Purchase the House in Which President Lincoln Died.* Washington, D. C., The Association, ca. 1893. 63 pp.

Merrill, Walter M. *New England Treasury of American Beginnings.* New York, Newcomen Society in North America, 1957. 28 pp.

Moore, George H. *Prytaneum Bostoniense, Examination of Mr. William H. Whitmore's Old State House Memorial and Reply to His Appendix N.* (Includes complete text of Whitmore's *Old State House Defended* with footnote answers, and text of what Whitmore deleted from *Prytaneum* in the Rededication volume; also includes a list of all the publications on the State House.) Boston, Cupples, Upham & Co., 1887. 40 pp.

Moore, George H. *Prytaneum Bostoniense, Notes on the History of the Old State House.* (Read before the Bostonian Society, May 12, 1885.) Boston, Cupples, Upham & Co., 1885. 31 pp.

———. *Prytaneum Bostoniense, Notes on the History of the Old State House.* (Second paper read before the Bostonian Society, February 9, 1886.) Boston, Cupples, Upham & Co., 1886. 80 pp.

Mount Vernon Ladies' Association of the Union. *Catalogue of the Centennial Exhibition Commemorating the Founding of the Mount Vernon Ladies' Association of the Union, 1853–1953.* Mount Vernon, Virginia, The Association, 1953. 84 pp.

Municipal Art Society of Hartford, Connecticut. *Bulletin No. 5: Preservation and Restoration of City Hall.* Hartford, The Society, 1906. 16 pp.

———. *Bulletin No. 15: The Old State House, Hartford, Why It Should Be Preserved.* Hartford, The Society, 1911. 20 pp.

Murray, Martha Lucy. *Ye Olde Burnham House, in Ipswich, Massachusetts, Built in 1640, Quaintest Place in All New England.* Ipswich, Massachusetts, The Author, (193?). 19 pp.

National Society of Colonial Dames of America. *The Story of Sulgrave Manor and a Few Reasons Why Americans Should Create This Endowment.* N. p., n. n., ca. 1923. Unpaged.

National Trust for Historic Preservation. *Primer for Preservation: A Handbook for Historic-House Keeping.* (Historic-House Keeping Series No. 1.) Washington, D. C., National Trust for Historic Preservation and New York State Historical Association, 1955. 23 pp.

Naulty, Edwin Fairfax. *Historic Harewood, of Pleasant Memory and Patriotic Association.* Philadelphia, Washington Manor Association for the Purchase and Preservation of Historic Harewood, 1901. 31 pp.

Nilson, Axel, and Keyland, Nils. *Guide to Skansen I, the Historical and Ethnological Department of Skansen.* Tr. by Nils Keyland and Edward Adams Ray, 5th Edition. Stockholm, Northern Museum, 1923. 162 pp.

Nordiska Museet. *Skansen, a Short Guide to the Visitor.* Stockholm, Nordiska Museet, 1930. 30 pp.

[Nutting, Wallace]. *The Wallace Nutting Colonial Chain of Picture Houses.* N. p., n. n., 1915. Unpaged.

Old South Meeting-House; Report of a Meeting of the Inhabitants of Cambridge, in Memorial Hall, Harvard College, January 18, 1877. Boston, George H. Ellis, 1877. 29 pp.

Otis, Harrison Gray. *An Address to the Members of the City Council, On the Removal of the Municipal Government to the Old State House.* Boston, John H. Eastburn, 1830. 15 pp.

Parry, Oliver. *Betsy Ross and the United States Flag.* Paper read before the Bucks County Historical Society, at Doylestown, Pennsylvania, January 19, 1909, N. p., n. n., n. d. 34 pp.

Paul Revere Memorial Association. *Handbook of the Paul Revere Memorial Association.* Boston, The Association, 1956, 25 pp.

Peck, Mamie Downard. *Thomas Jefferson and His Home, Monticello.* Corsicana, Texas, Marr Publishing Company, 1928. 7 pp.

Pell, Stephen H. P. *Fort Ticonderoga, a Short History.* Ticonderoga, New York, Fort Ticonderoga Museum, 1961. 118 pp.

Pennsylvania Museum of Art. *Mount Pleasant, Fairmount Park, Philadelphia.* Philadelphia, The Museum, 1931. 32 pp.

Perry, B. F. *Reminiscences of Mrs. Louisa Cunningham.* Greenville, South Carolina, J. C. Bailey's Book and Job Press, 1874. 8 pp.

Pickering, John. *The Pickering House, 1651.* Salem, Massachusetts, The Author, ca. 1950. 11 pp.

Pilgrim John Howland Society. *The Pilgrim John Howland House, 1667.* N. p., The Society, n. d. Unpaged.

Poe Cottage Committee. *The Poe Cottage.* New York, Bronx Society of Arts and Sciences, 1915. 2 pp.

The Popular History of St. Augustine, an Authentic Guide to the Many Attractions of the Ancient City. St. Augustine, Florida, n. n., 1890. 46 pp.

[Powers, L. M.]. *The Story of an Interesting and Historic Old House in Gloucester, Massachusetts.* Boston, Murray Press, ca. 1916. 15 pp.

Rawle, William Brooke. *Laurel Hill, and Some Colonial Dames Who Once Lived There* (reprinted from *Pennsylvania Magazine of History and Biography,* October, 1911). Philadelphia, J. B. Lippincott Company, 1911. 30 pp.

Reynolds, Charles B. *"The Oldest House in the United States," St. Augustine, Florida, an Examination of the St. Augustine Historical Society's Claim That Its House on St. Francis Street Was Built in 1565 by the Franciscan Monks.* New York, Foster and Reynolds Company, 1921. 31 pp.

Roof, Katharine Metcalf. *The Story of the Abigail Adams Smith Mansion and the Mount Vernon Estate.* New York, Colonial Dames of America, 1949. 12 pp.

Scales, John (Editor). *Catalog of Articles in Ye William Dam Garrison at Woodman Institute, Dover, N. H.* Dover, New Hampshire, Woodman Institute, 1917. 55 pp.

Sears, Clara E. *Revised Catalog of "Fruitlands" at Harvard, Mass.* Harvard, Massachusetts, The Author, ca. 1915. 23 pp.

Shakespeare Society of New York. *The Poe Cottage: Poe Park: And the New York Shakespeare Society.* (Containing two reprints from *New York Times.*) New York, The Society, 1905. 8 pp.

Sheldon, George, and Sheldon, J. M. Arms. *The Rev. John Williams House.* Deerfield, Massachusetts, Pocumtuck Valley Memorial Association, 1918. 32 pp.

Sketch of Fairmount, Lemon Hill, and the Adjoining Grounds, as a Public Park. Philadelphia, n. n., 1855. 29 pp.

Smith, Emma A. F. *Historical Sketch of Washington's Headquarters.* New York, Washington Headquarters Association, 1908. 18 pp.

Stanard, Mary Newton. *John Marshall and His Home.* Richmond, Virginia, William Ellis and Sons, Inc., 1913. 39 pp.

Stark, James H. *History of the Old Blake House and a Brief Sketch of the Dorchester Historical Society.* Dorchester, Massachusetts, Dorchester Historical Society, January, 1907. 13 pp.

Stevens, Maud Lyman. *The Vernon House, Newport, Rhode Island, 1758–1915.* Newport, Rhode Island, Charity Organization Society of Newport, 1915. 56 pp.

Thayer, M. Russell. *The Real Founder of Fairmount Park, a Unilateral Correspondence.* Philadelphia, Dunlap Printing Company, 1903. 10 pp.

Thomas Jefferson Memorial Foundation. *The Story of the Thomas Jefferson*

Memorial Foundation. (No. 4B of "Monticello Papers.") N. p., The Foundation, ca. 1925. Unpaged.

Tower, Elizabeth A. *The John Hancock House.* Ticonderoga, New York, New York State Historical Association, 1926. 16 pp.

Trustees of Scenic and Historic Places and Objects. *Memorial to the Legislature of the State of New York,* January, 1895; and *Act of Incorporation and By-laws,* March 26, 1895. N. p., n. n., n. d., 16 pp.

Trustees of the Henry Whitfield House. *Historical Papers Relating to the Henry Whitfield House, Guilford, Connecticut.* Guilford, Connecticut, Tuttle, Moorehouse, and Taylor Press, 1914. 59 pp.

————. *Proceedings at the Formal Opening of the State Historical Museum, Henry Whitfield House.* Guilford, Connecticut, The Trustees, 1904. 43 pp.

Tuesday Club. *The Story of the Loring-Greenough House.* Jamaica Plain, Massachusetts, Tuesday Club, ca. 1939. 16 pp.

Tutt, Hannah. *The Lee Mansion, What It Was and What It Is.* Marblehead, Massachusetts, Marblehead Historical Society, 1911. 17 pp.

Vollbrecht, John L. *St. Augustine's Historical Heritage as Seen today: With Historical Notes on the Oldest House.* St. Augustine, Florida, The Record Press, 1952. Unpaged.

Washington, Bushrod. Printed notice, signed and dated July 4, 1822. Archives of the M.V.L.A., Mount Vernon, Virginia.

Weaver, Addie Guthrie. *The Story of Our Flag, Colonial and National, with Historical Sketch of the Quakeress Betsy Ross.* Chicago, The Author, 1898. 94 pp.

Webster Birthplace. N. p., n. n., ca. 1910. Leaflet.

Whitmore, William H. *The Old State-House Defended From Unfounded Attacks upon Its Integrity, Being a Reply to Dr. G. H. Moore's Second Paper, Read before the Bostonian Society, February 9, 1886.* Boston, Rockwell and Churchill, 1886. 8 pp.

Whittier Home Association. *The Amesbury Home of Whittier.* Amesbury, Massachusetts, The Association, n. d. 30 pp.

Wilkes, Marion R. *Rosemont and Its Famous Daughter.* Washington, D. C., The Author, 1947. 36 pp.

Winthrop, Benjamin Robert. *The Washington Chair, Presented to the New York Historical Society.* New York, Charles B. Richardson, 1857. 10 pp.

BOOKS

Alden, Augustus E. *Pilgrim Alden, the Story of the Life of the First John Alden in America.* Boston, James H. Earle and Company, 1902. 232 pp.

Alexander, Frederick Warren. *Stratford Hall and the Lees Connected with Its History.* Oak Grove, Virginia, The Author, 1912. 332 pp.

Ashbee, C. R. *A Report by Mr. C. R. Ashbee to the Council of the National Trust for Places of Historic Interest and Natural Beauty, on His Visit to the United States on the Council's Behalf, October, MDCCCC, to February, MDCCCCI.* London, Essex House Press, 1901. 24 pp.

Barrington, Lewis. *Historic Restorations of the Daughters of the American Revolution.* New York, Richard R. Smith, 1941. 210 plates.

Benham, William Burton. *Life of Osborn H. Oldroyd.* Washington, D. C. Beresford Press, 1927. 31 pp.

Benjamin, Marcus (Editor). *Washington during War Time, a Series of Papers Showing the Military Phases during 1861 to 1865; Official Souvenir of the Thirty-Sixth Annual Encampment of the Grand Army of the Republic.* Washington, D. C., Byron Adams, 1902. 215 pp.

Bloomfield, Max. *Bloomfield's Illustrated Historical Guide, Embracing an Account of the Antiquities of St. Augustine, Florida.* St. Augustine, Florida, The Author, 1882. 184 pp.

Brown, Glenn. *1860–1930 Memories, a Winning Crusade to Revive George Washington's Vision of a Capital City.* Washington, D. C., The Author, 1931. 585 pp.

Brown, Gregory Baldwin. *The Care of Ancient Monuments.* Cambridge, England, Cambridge University Press, 1905. 260 pp.

Burdett, Everett W. *History of the Old South Meeting-House in Boston.* Boston, B. B. Russell, 1877. 106 pp.

Chandler, Joseph Everett. *The Colonial House.* New York, Robert H. McBride and Company, 1924. 222 pp.

Civic Services Committee. *This Is Charleston.* Charleston, South Carolina, Carolina Art Association, 1944. 141 pp.

Clark, William H. *The History of Winthrop, Massachusetts.* Winthrop, Massachusetts, Winthrop Centennial Committee, 1952. 313 pp.

Coleman, Laurence Vail. *Historic House Museums.* Washington, D. C. American Association of Museums, 1933. 187 pp.

Colonial Dames of America. *Patriotic and Historical Record of the Colonial Dames of America, 1890–1926.* New York, Colonial Dames of America, 1926. 28 pp.

Committee on Handbook of the Conference of Historical Societies. *Handbook of American Historical Societies.* Madison, Wisconsin, Cantwell Printing Company, 1926. 81 pp.

Confederate Memorial Literary Society. *In Memoriam Sempiternam.* Richmond, Virginia, The Society, 1896. 98 pp.

Curti, Merle. *The Roots of American Loyalty.* New York, Columbia University Press, 1946. 267 pp.

Davies, Wallace Evan. *Patriotism on Parade, the Story of Veteran's and Hereditary Organizations in America, 1783–1900* (Vol. LXVI of *Harvard Historical Studies*). Cambridge, Massachusetts, Harvard University Press, 1955. 385 pp.

Donaldson, Thomas. *The House in Which Thomas Jefferson Wrote the Declaration of Independence.* Philadelphia, The Author, 1898. 119 pp.

Dorris, Mary C. *Preservation of the Hermitage, 1889–1915.* Nashville, Tennessee, Ladies' Hermitage Association, 1915. 221 pp.

Emmerton, Caroline O. *The Chronicles of Three Old Houses.* Boston, Thomas Todd Company, 1935. 58 pp.

Ernst, George. *New England Miniature, A History of York, Maine.* Freeport, Maine, Bond Wheelwright Company, 1961. 284 pp.

Everett, Edward. *The Mount Vernon Papers.* New York, D. Appleton and Company, 1860. 491 pp.

Federal Writer's Project of the Works Progress Administration of the State of Massachusetts. *Massachusetts, a Guide to Its Places and People (American Guide Series).* Boston, Houghton Mifflin Company, 1937. 675 pp.

Frothingham, Paul Revere. *Edward Everett, Orator and Statesman.* Boston, Houghton Mifflin Company, 1925. 495 pp.

Goodwin, Rutherfoord. *A Brief and True Report Concerning Williamsburg in Virginia.* Richmond, Virginia, Colonial Williamsburg, Inc., 1940. 406 pp.

Goodwin, The Reverend William Archer Rutherfoord. *Historical Sketch of Bruton Church.* Petersburg, Virginia, Franklin Press, 1903. 183 pp.

———. *The Record of Bruton Parish Church.* (Edited, with revisions and additions, by Mary Frances Goodwin.) Richmond, Virginia, Dietz Press, 1941. 203 pp.

Gutstein, Morris A. *The Story of the Jews of Newport.* New York, Bloch Publishing Company, 1936. 393 pp.

Halsey, Edmund D. *History of the Washington Association of New Jersey.* Morristown, New Jersey, The Author, 1891. 39 pp.

Hill, Hamilton Andrews. *History of Old South Church (Third Church) Boston, 1669–1884.* Boston, Houghton, Mifflin Company, 1890. 2 v.

Historic Philadelphia. (Issued as Volume 43, Part 1, of *Transactions of the American Philosophical Society.*) Philadelphia, The Society, 1953. 331 pp.

Historical Sketch of Boston Containing a Brief Account of Its Settlement, Rise and Progress, with a Glance at Its Present Prospective and Prosperity. Boston, Edward L. Mitchell, 1861. 96 pp.

Homes of American Statesmen: With Anecdotal, Personal, and Descriptive Sketches, by Various Writers. New York, G. P. Putnam and Company; London, S. Low, Son and Company, 1854. 469 pp.

Horn, Stanley F. *The Hermitage, Home of Old Hickory.* Richmond, Virginia, Garrett and Massie, 1938. 225 pp.

Howe, Winifred E. *A History of the Metropolitan Museum of Art.* New York, Metropolitan Museum of Art, 1946. Vol. II (1905–1941), 269 pp.

Hudson, Charles. *History of the Town of Lexington, Middlesex County, Massachusetts, from Its First Settlement to 1868, Revised and Continued to 1912.* Boston, Houghton, Mifflin Company, 1913. Vol. I (History), 583 pp.

Isham, Norman. *In Praise of Antiquaries.* N. p., Walpole Society, 1931. 22 pp.

Isham, Norman, and Brown, Albert F. *Early Rhode Island Houses.* Providence, Rhode Island, Preston and Rounds, 1895. 100 pp.

Jacobus, Donald L. (Editor). *The Pardee Genealogy.* New Haven, Connecticut, New Haven Colony Historical Society, 1927. 693 pp.

Jefferson Club of St. Louis. *The Pilgrimage to Monticello, the Home and Tomb of Thomas Jefferson, by the Jefferson Club of St. Louis, Mo., October 10 to 14, 1901.* St. Louis, Con. P. Curran Printing Company, 1902. 78 pp.

Jones, Alvin Lincoln. *Under New England Roofs.* Boston, C. B. Webster, 1894. 237 pp.

Keith, Eliza D. *Report of the Historical Landmarks Committee of the Native Daughters of the Golden West.* San Francisco, The Author, 1902. 71 pp.

Kelly, J. Frederick. *The Henry Whitfield House, 1639, the Journal of the Restoration of the Old Stone House, Guilford.* Guilford, Connecticut, Henry Whitfield State Historical Museum, 1939. 60 pp.

Keyser, Charles Shearer. *Fairmount Park, Sketches of Its Scenery, Waters, and History.* Philadelphia, Claxton, Remsen, and Haffelfinger, 1871. 159 pp.

Kimball, Frances P. *Albany, Birthplace of the Union.* Albany, New York, National Savings Bank of the City of Albany, 1940. 66 pp.

Knowland, Joseph R. *California, a Landmark History, Story of the Preserva-*

tion and Marking of Early Day Shrines. Oakland, California, Tribune Press, 1941. 245 pp.

Lamar, Mrs. Joseph Rucker. *A History of the National Society of Colonial Dames of America from 1891 to 1933.* Atlanta, Georgia, Walter W. Brown Publishing Company, 1934. 272 pp.

[Lamar, Mrs. Joseph Rucker]. *The National Society of Colonial Dames of America. Its Beginnings, Its Purpose and a Record of Its Work, 1891–1913.* N. p., Gilliss Press, 1913. 141 pp.

Levy, Uriah P. *Defence of Uriah P. Levy before the Court of Inquiry Held at Washington City, November and December, 1857, Prepared and Read by His Senior Counsel, B. F. Butler, of New York.* New York, C. Bryant and Company, 1858. 169 pp.

Little, Arthur. *Early New England Interiors, Sketched in Salem, Marblehead, Portsmouth and Kittery.* Boston, A. Williams and Company, 1878. Unpaged.

Longyear, Mary Beecher. *The History of a House, Its Founder, Family and Guests.* Boston, Longyear Foundation, 1925. 70 pp.

Lowrie, Sarah Dickson. *Strawberry Mansion, First Known as Somerton, the House of Many Masters.* New York, Committee of 1926 of Pennsylvania, 1941. 224 pp.

Mayo, Bernard. *Myths and Men.* Athens, Georgia, University of Georgia Press, 1959. 71 pp.

McPherson, Grace Finlay. *A History of the First Fifty Years of the New Jersey Society of the Colonial Dames of America, 1892–1942.* Somerville, New Jersey, Somerset Press, 1942. 68 pp.

Metropolitan Museum of Art. *Addresses at the Opening of the American Wing.* New York, The Museum, 1925. 34 pp.

Moore, Charles. *Daniel H. Burnham, Architect, Planner of Cities.* Boston and New York, Houghton Mifflin Company, 1921, 2 v.

Morrison, Hugh. *Early American Architecture.* New York, Oxford University Press, 1952. 619 pp.

Morrison, Jacob. *Historic Preservation Law.* New Orleans, Louisiana, Pelican Publishing Company, 1957. 113 pp.

Morse, John T., Jr. *Life and Letters of Oliver Wendell Holmes.* Boston, Houghton Mifflin Company, 1896, 2 v.

Mount Vernon Ladies' Association of the Union. *Historical Sketch of Ann Pamela Cunningham, "A Southern Matron," Founder of the "Mount Vernon Ladies' Association."* Jamaica, New York, Marion Press, 1903. 49 pp.

Muir, Dorothy Troth. *Presence of a Lady, Mount Vernon, 1861–1868.* Washington, D. C., Mount Vernon Publishing Company, 1946. 90 pp.

National League of American Pen Women, Inc. *Historic Homes of Alabama and Their Traditions.* Birmingham, Alabama, Birmingham Publishing Company, 1935. 314 pp.

Nevins, Allan, and Hill, Frank Ernest. *Ford: Expansion and Challenge, 1915–1933.* New York, Charles Scribner's Sons, 1957. 714 pp.

Newcomb, Rexford. *The Old Mission Churches and Historic Houses of California.* Philadelphia, J. B. Lippincott Company, 1925. 379 pp.

Northend, Mary. *Remodeled Farmhouses.* Boston, Little, Brown and Company, 1915. 264 pp.

Nutting, Wallace. *Wallace Nutting's Biography*. Framingham, Massachusetts, Old America Company, 1936. 295 pp.

Patton, John S., and Doswell, Sallie J. *Monticello and Its Master*. Charlottesville, Virginia, Mitchie Company, 1925. 78 pp.

Peterson, Merrill D. *The Jefferson Image in the American Mind*. New York, Oxford University Press, 1960. 548 pp.

Pratt, Dorothy and Richard. *A Guide to Early American Homes, North*. New York, McGraw-Hill Book Company, Inc., 1956. 251 pp.

Proceedings on the Occasion of the Centennial Celebration of the Occupation of Valley Forge by the Continental Army under George Washington, June 19, 1878 and also Dedication of Headquarters, June 19, 1879. Philadelphia, J. B. Lippincott, 1879. 138 pp.

Quaife, Milo M.; Weig, Melvin J.; and Appleman, Roy E. *The History of the United States Flag*. New York, Harper and Brothers, 1961. 182 pp.

Reep, Thomas P. *Lincoln at New Salem*. Petersburg, Illinois, Old Salem Lincoln League, 1927. 147 pp.

Rhodes, Thomas L., as told to Frank B. Lord. *The Story of Monticello*. Washington, D. C., American Publishing Company, 1928. 94 pp.

Roos, Frank John. *Writings on Early American Architecture*. Columbus, Ohio, Ohio State University Press, 1943. 271 pp.

Ruskin, John. *The Seven Lamps of Architecture* (Everyman's Library). London, J. M. Dent and Sons, Ltd.; New York, E. P. Dutton and Company, 1907. 228 pp.

Scharf, J. Thomas, and Westcott, Thompson. *History of Philadelphia*. Philadelphia, L. H. Everst Company, 1884. 3 v.

Schuyler, Georgina. *The Schuyler Mansion at Albany*. New York, De Vinne Press, 1911. 43 pp.

Seymour, George Dudley. *Documentary Life of Nathan Hale*. New Haven, Connecticut, The Author, 1941. 627 pp.

Spencer, Richard H. *Carlyle Family and Descendants of John and Sarah (Fairfax) Carlyle: The Carlyle House and Its Associations*. Richmond, Virginia, Whittit and Shepperson, 1910. 58 pp.

Stevens, Walter B. *The Forest City, Comprising the Official Photographic Views of the Universal Exposition Held in Saint Louis, 1904*. St. Louis, Missouri, N. D. Thompson Publishing Company, 1904. Unpaged.

Stokes, Isaac Newton Phelps. *The Iconography of Manhattan Island, 1498-1909*. New York, R. H. Dodd, 1915–1928. 6 v.

Tolman, George. *Catalog of a Portion of the Concord Antiquarian Society*. Boston, Thomas Todd Company, 1911. Unpaged.

Townsend, George Alfred. *Monticello and Its Preservation since Jefferson's Death 1826–1902, Correspondence of George Alfred Townsend, "Gath."* Washington, D. C., Jefferson M. Levy, 1902. 56 pp.

Trowbridge, Bertha Chadwick (Editor). *Old Houses of Connecticut*. New Haven, Connecticut, Yale University Press, 1923. 519 pp.

Viollet-le-Duc, Eugene Emmanuel. *On Restoration, and a Notice in Connection with Historical Monuments of France*. Tr. by Benjamin Bucknall. London, Sampson, Low, Marston, Low, and Searle, 1875. 110 pp.

Walpole Society. *The Twenty-Fifth Anniversary Meeting of the Walpole Society*. Boston, The Society, 1935. 55 pp.

Ware, William Rotch (Editor). *The Georgian Period*. Boston, American Architect and Building News Company, 1901. 3 v.

Waterman, Thomas Tileston. *The Mansions of Virginia, 1706–1776.* Chapel Hill, North Carolina, University of North Carolina Press, 1945. 456 pp.

Waterman, Thomas Tileston, and Barrows, John A. *Domestic Colonial Architecture of Tidewater Virginia.* New York, Charles Scribner's Sons, 1932. 191 pp.

Whitefield, Edwin. *Homes of Our Forefathers in Massachusetts.* (New Edition.) Boston, The Author, 1892. 40 plates.

Whitehill, Walter Muir. *Boston, a Topographic History.* Cambridge, Massachusetts, Belknap Press of Harvard University, 1959. 244 pp.

———. *Independent Historical Societies.* Boston, Boston Athenaeum, 1962. 593 pp.

Wilcox, David F. (Editor). *Quincy and Adams County History and Representative Men.* Chicago, Lewis Publishing Company, 1919. 2 v.

Index

373